D1268476

The Book of Music

The Book of Music

Macdonald

Opposite title page
St Cecilia at the organ. A stained-glass window by Burne-Jones at Christchurch, Oxford (1874).

Concept, design and illustration
by QED, 4 Kingly Street, London W1
Alastair Campbell
Edward Kinsey
John Stevenson
Artists Sally Launder, Laura Rogers and David Worth

Editor
Gill Rowley
Managing editor
Chester Fisher
Production
Philip Hughes
Editorial co-ordinator
Susan Ward
Picture research
Jenny de Gex

Contributing authors
Neil Ardley
Dave Arthur
Hugh Chapman and John Perry
Mary Clarke and Clement Crisp
Robert Cruden
Dave Gelly
Lionel Grigson
Susan Sturrock

Consultants
Professor Denis Arnold
Michael Burnett
Anna Pollak

Research and editorial assistance
David Briers, David Jones, Anthony Laude, Robert Royston, Robert Scott, David Sharp

Contributing artists and photographers
Peter Niczewski, Walter Rawlings, Rodney Shackell, Nigel Soper, Negs Photographic

© Macdonald Educational Ltd. and QED Ltd. 1977
First published 1977
Second impression 1978
Macdonald Educational Ltd.
Holywell House
Worship Street
London EC2A 2EN

Made and printed by Hazell Watson & Viney Ltd., Aylesbury, Bucks.
Filmsetting by Oliver Burridge Filmsetting Ltd., Crawley, Sussex.
Origination by Fotomecanica Iberico, Madrid.

ISBN 0 356 05579 5

Contents

III
Music-Makers

IV
Listening to Music

V
A Chronology of Music

VI
The Glossaries

Editor's Preface

The Book of Music is planned in six main sections, each divided into short chapters. The sections, and indeed the chapters themselves, may be read in whatever order the reader pleases, but it is hoped that the material contained in each section will complement and illuminate the information contained elsewhere in the book.

To read, for example, the chapter on nationalistic music together with that on folk music – perhaps glancing at the same time at the pages dealing with ethnic instruments ("Instruments around the world") – will provide a wider view of the nationalist movement in music than merely reading "Nationalism" in isolation. Similarly, the significance of J. S. Bach's *Well-tempered Clavier* will be better understood if the reader has looked at our brief section on musical theory at the beginning of the book (in particular, page 13).

The "Chronology" (pages 144–59) relates musical developments and composers' lives and works to major events in history. The three glossaries, of composers, musical terms and instruments, form a reference section of both general interest and particular relevance to the preceding text.

Music being one of the few fields in which the Englishman's innate distrust of foreign languages is not overwhelmingly apparent, it has been thought best to let the rough logic of common practice prevail. Names of foreign works, therefore, appear in the form most generally accepted and most commonly used in English-speaking countries. For example, we refer to *Madam Butterfly* rather than *Madama Butterfly*, but English titles have not been insisted upon in the case of works which are far better known by their vernacular names: Verdi's *Woman Gone Astray* remains, therefore, *La Traviata*, and *The Bat* appears as *Die Fledermaus*.

G.R.

Foreword

As the first fully-illustrated guide to music in its broadest sense, *The Book of Music* fills a long-felt need. Its careful balance of authoritative text and outstanding illustrations has produced a book which is a delight to browse through and at the same time an invaluable work of reference. All music-lovers, from record-collectors and concert-goers to practising musicians, will find their appreciation of music widened by the book's range of information and original presentation.

The Book of Music explores both the traditional centre of musical interest – that is, the development of Western "classical" music – and important related topics such as dance, jazz, popular and folk music, recording and broadcasting, concert halls and musical education. The large instrumental section features award-winning illustrations which portray each instrument's physical qualities, as well as beauty of form and craftsmanship.

Not intended for the musical elitist or the narrow-minded listener, *The Book of Music* is designed to inspire readers not only to enquire further but to broaden their listening horizons and, it is hoped, reform a few prejudices. It has been produced by experts with widely differing backgrounds who share in common one lifelong passion – music.

1

From Nature to Music

Sound is an ordinary natural phenomenon: music, on the other hand, is the result of man's conscious development of sound into an art and a science. The basic principles on which all music is based are rhythm, tonality, dynamics and timbre. Some degree of familiarity with these elements and how they are organized will provide anyone who listens to music with a valuable insight into how music "works".

A pebble dropped in water causes outward-moving concentric waves. Sound travels from its source in a similar way, but in three dimensions.

Music and Sound

The word "sound" is used in two senses. In its precise meaning, it is the *sensation* caused in the brain by vibrations. The ear receives these and converts them into electrical nerve impulses. In this sense, sound is something apart from its external cause. Sound sensations can be stimulated by inserting an electrode in the appropriate part of the brain, without the ear being involved.

More generally, "sound" means any kind of *vibration* which can be detected by the ear. The vibration is carried to it from a source through air or some other homogeneous medium, such as water, wood or one's own skull.

A sound source is a vibrating system of some sort, such as the vocal cords in a bird's larynx, a stretched string or a column of air enclosed in a pipe. Vibrating systems are set in motion by some kind of mechanical energy. Sound vibrations are a particular case of the general natural phenomenon of periodic motion, which manifests itself in many other ways, from the movements of subatomic particles to the motions of tides, seasons, planets and pendulums.

The process by which sound vibrations are carried through air or another medium is called *sound propagation*. Air molecules are bunched together in tiny particles. Each "swing" of a vibrating object, such as a string, knocks the neighbouring air particles out of position.

As the string swings back, the displaced air particles return to their original position – but not before they knock their neighbours out of position, and so on.

Therefore, sound travels away from its source by a series of tiny pendulum-like movements of air particles. There is no over-all movement of the medium, but a series of temporary thickenings and thinnings occurs as adjacent particles swing into and then away from each other.

At the end of the line, the vibrating air particles set the ear-drum in motion. Inside the ear, the ear-drum's vibration is converted first into hydraulic movement and then into electrical impulses which are carried to the brain by the aural nerve. The electrical conversion is done by the organ of Corti in the snail-like cochlea, which lies in the ear's "innermost sanctum".

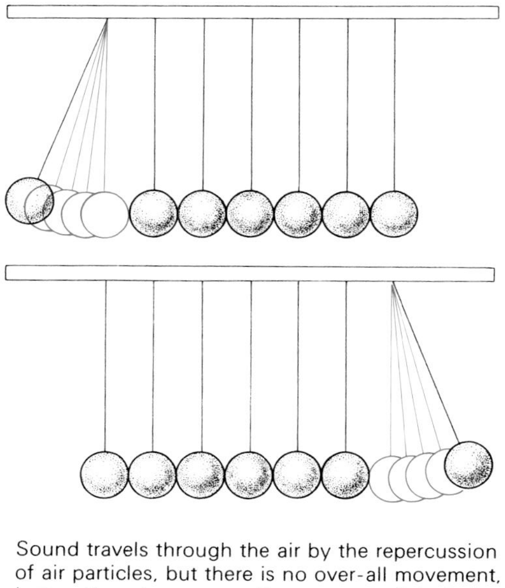

Sound travels through the air by the repercussion of air particles, but there is no over-all movement, just as there is no over-all movement of the balls in a Newton's cradle.

Noise and music: when is a note a note?
A subjective definition of "noise" is any unwelcome sound. This can obviously include music, if the hearer is not in the mood for it, so for musical sound an objective definition is necessary. This definition exists in the difference between vibrations of irregular and regular *frequency* (see diagram opposite).

Noise consists of a jumble of irregular frequencies, but a musical sound, or *note*, has a regular, constant frequency. (Even this definition is not hard and fast, however.)

Pitch: high and low, fast and slow
The particular frequency of a note determines its *pitch*. Conventionally, a note is described as "high" or "low" when what is meant is that its frequency is fast or slow. Other things being equal, the length of a vibrating string is inversely proportional to the frequency of its note. In other words, the longer the string, the lower the note, and vice versa.

Frequency is measured in cycles per second, or Hertz (Hz). The lowest note audible to the human ear has a frequency

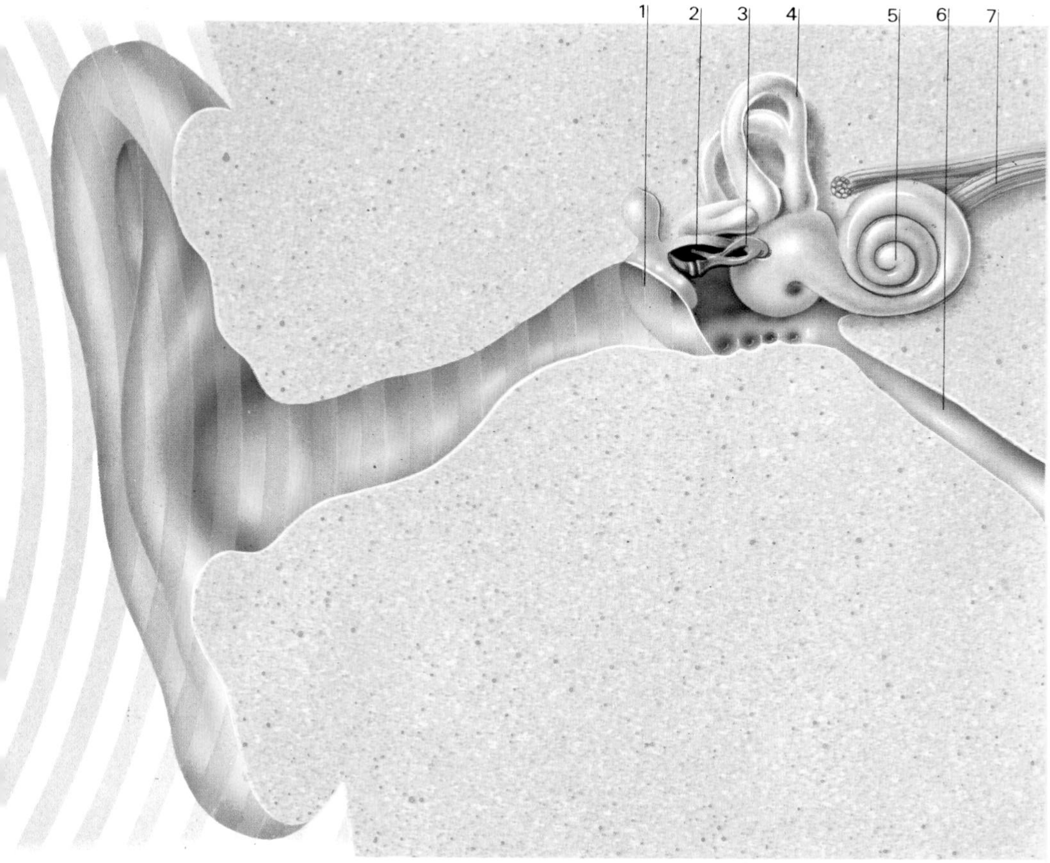

Sound spreads outwards from its source as air particles, set in motion by the source's vibration, swing backwards and forwards into each other. This causes momentary thickenings and thinnings of the air – like the crests and troughs of ripples caused by dropping a pebble in water, but in three dimensions. The ear-drum picks up these vibrations and the inner ear turns them into nerve impulses which the brain registers as sound.

1 Ear drum
2 Tensor tympani
3 Three-bone lever
4 Semicircular canals
5 Cochlea
6 Eustachian tube
7 Auditory nerve

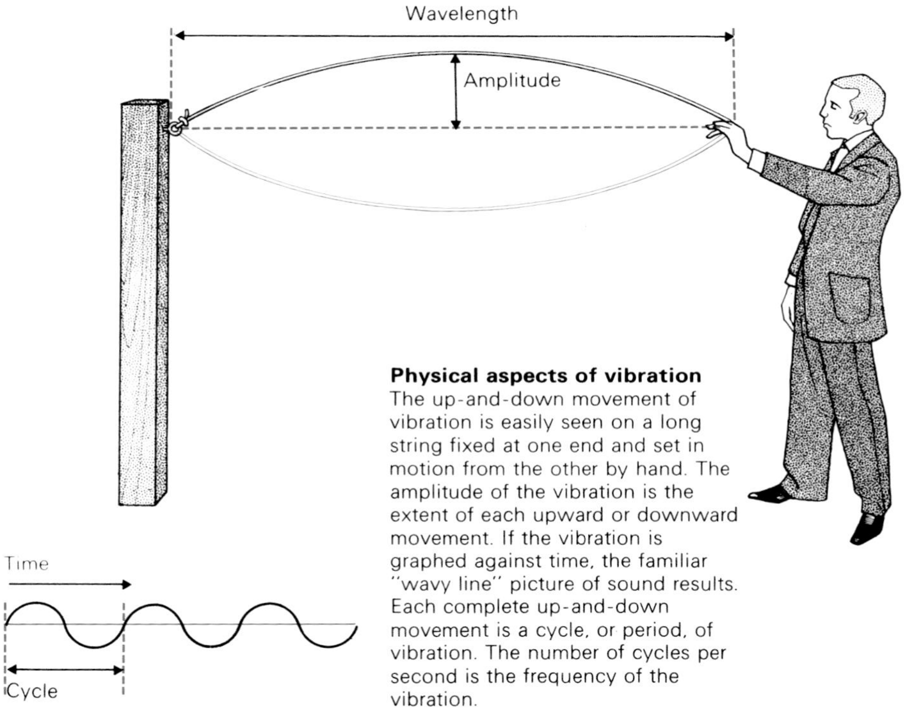

Physical aspects of vibration
The up-and-down movement of vibration is easily seen on a long string fixed at one end and set in motion from the other by hand. The amplitude of the vibration is the extent of each upward or downward movement. If the vibration is graphed against time, the familiar "wavy line" picture of sound results. Each complete up-and-down movement is a cycle, or period, of vibration. The number of cycles per second is the frequency of the vibration.

of about 16 to 20 Hz, and the upper limit is about 25,000 Hz. Bats and dogs, for example, can hear much higher frequencies, and whales can hear lower ones.

Volume: loud and soft
The volume of a sound or a musical note depends on the *amplitude* of its vibration (see diagram). The greater the force applied to start a sound source vibrating, the greater is its amplitude and the louder the sound, and vice versa.

There is an important difference between frequency and amplitude. Other things being equal, the frequency of, say, a vibrating string stays constant until its movement is finally *damped* by resistance from its fixed ends and from the surrounding air. But its amplitude constantly decreases until the sound dies away (unless the string is kept in *forced* vibration, as by a violin bow).

The raw materials
The frequency and amplitude of musical notes give us two of the essential ingredients of music: *pitch relationships*, the organization of which is known as *tonality*, and *dynamics*, or loudness and softness.

The two other essential ingredients are *rhythm*, the position and length of musical notes in time; and *timbre*, or tone colour, by which we can recognize the sounds of particular instruments.

Tying music together
These principles of rhythm, tonality, dynamics and timbre are parts of the seamless whole of music. They have no separate existence, though in different kinds of music one aspect may be emphasized more than another.

In musical theory, however, the different aspects of music are described separately, using different terms and concepts. Non-specialist music-lovers are often confused by the variety, and sometimes the apparent inconsistency, of musical terms. It can be helpful, therefore, to look at music simply as relationships of movement.

In this way, for instance, the separate notions of pitch and rhythm can be equated. As has been stated, the pitch of a note results from the frequency of a regular movement (e.g. vibration of a string). Rhythm – music in time – also depends on movement. The beat of a drummer is carried by the fast frequencies of the sound of his drum. The speed, or tempo, of the drum beats, however, depends on the (slower) frequency of his hand or stick movement.

Music and Reason

Music and mathematics have always been closely related. They both involve responses of human reason – rationality – to surroundings. Mathematics was inspired by our recognition of natural regularities and patterns. In the same way, music is made possible because of our awareness (intuitive or rational) of regularity in the behaviour of sound. Because sound relationships are physical ones, they can be described mathematically. This is why the two subjects have always "informed" each other.

Melodies, intervals and scales

A *melody* is a series of notes of different pitches. Pitch differences between notes are called *intervals*. Melodic intervals can be large or small. The smallest can be called steps. If we take all the different notes of a melody, delete those which occur more than once and arrange those that remain in stepwise order, we have a *scale*. Therefore scales can be regarded as sets of notes from which melodies are selected. Of course, melodies came first, and scales were later rationalized from them. But once this happened, scales often served as starting points for melodies.

Divisions of the scale

Almost everyone can sing, whistle or at least recognize what has probably become the world's most used scale, the so-called "diatonic" scale of Western music (see diagram). Its seven separate notes carry the letter names A to G. The eighth, or finishing note, has the same letter name as the starting note, and is the starting note for continuing the scale an octave higher. The Roman numerals I to VII can also be used to designate the notes of the scale.

There is a fixed interval between each pair of notes in the scale. In other words,

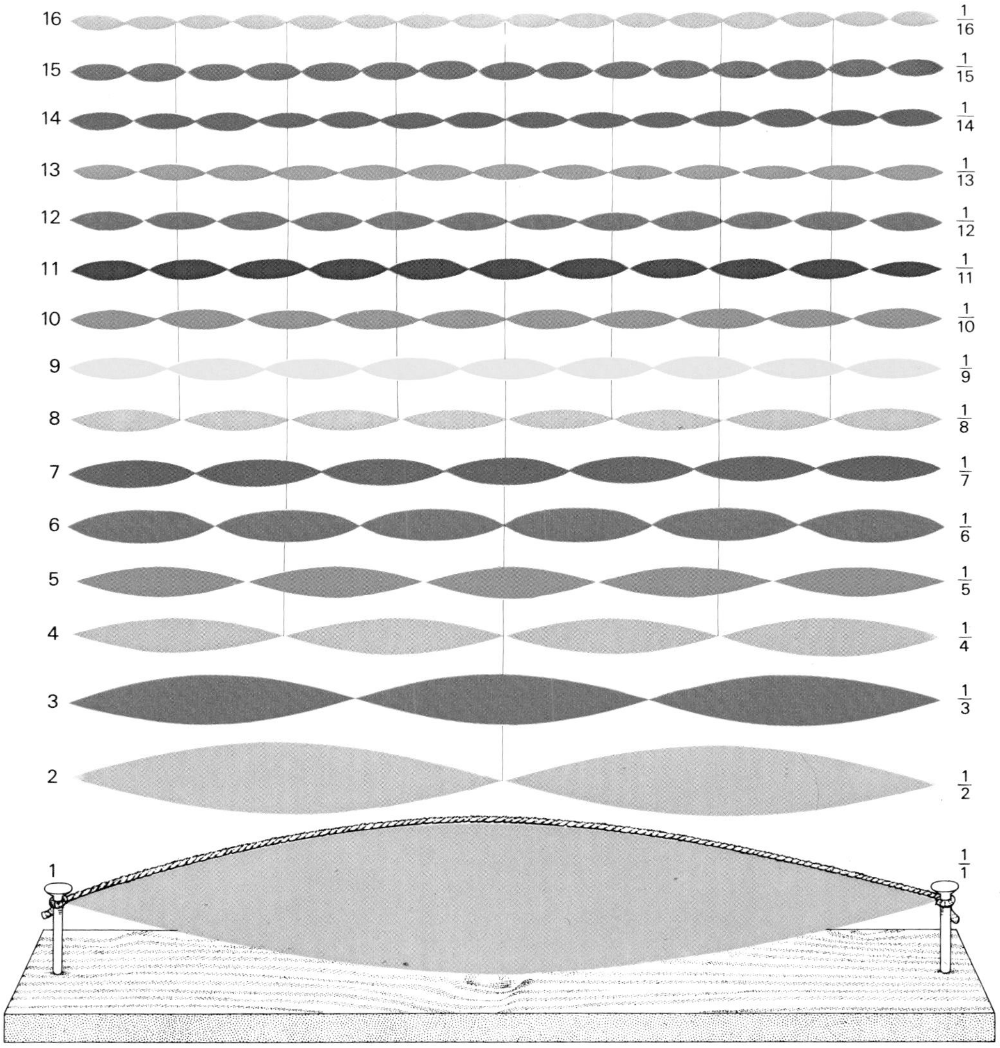

Above Harmonics are produced by the vibrations of a string in decreasing fractions, as this "exploded" view shows. As the fractions decrease, their frequencies increase, producing higher harmonics. **Below** The approximate position on the piano of the harmonic series of a low C. Notice that the harmonics get closer together the higher they are. Because of the way the piano is tuned, by the "equal temperament" system, only octave harmonics (2, 4, 8, 16, etc.) are exactly matched on the keyboard.

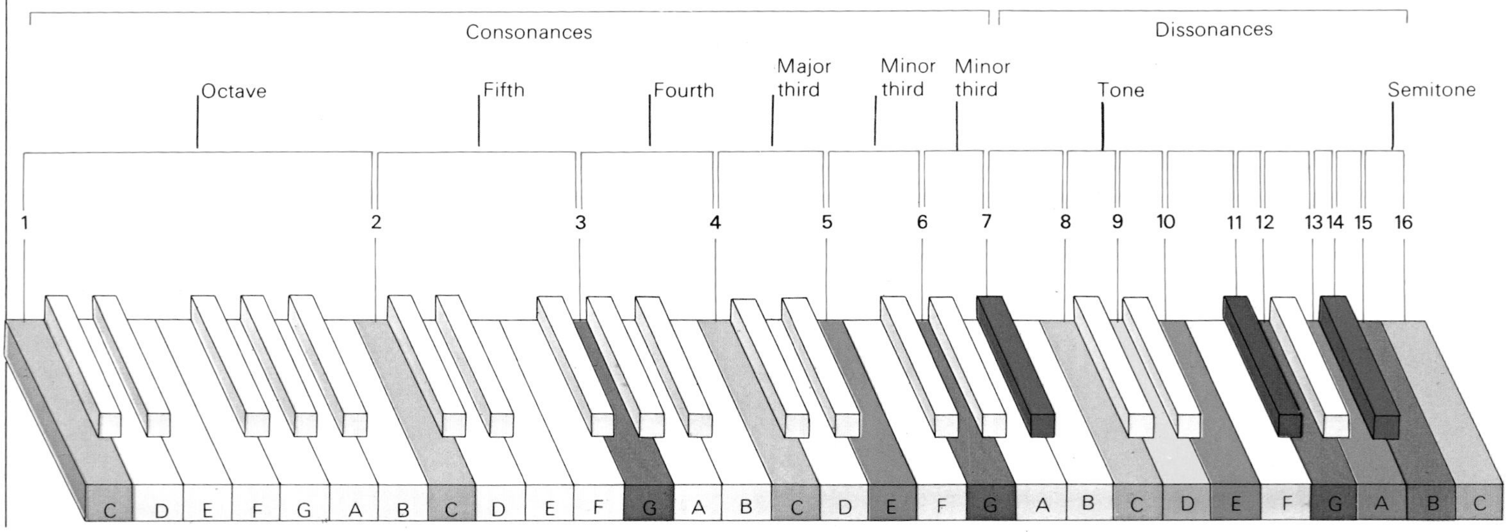

Below Starting with C, the note to the left of the two black notes, eight consecutive piano white notes give one octave of a diatonic scale (C major). The scale has seven different notes, each with a letter name. The eighth has the same name as the starting note, and is the starting point for the same scale an octave higher. As well as a letter name each note has a (numerical) degree name, which defines its relationship to the starting note, or tonic.

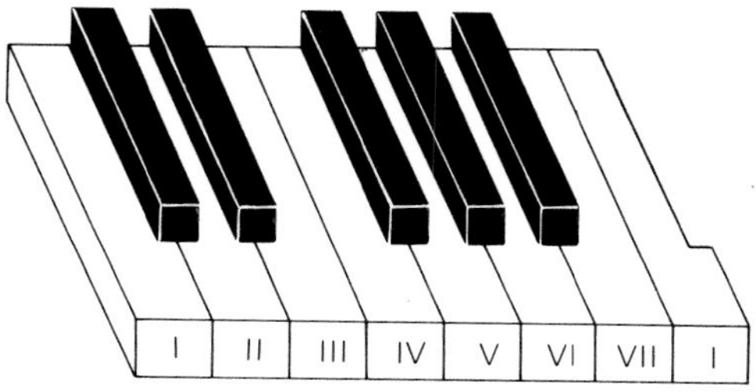
I
II
III
IV
V
VI
VII
I

I	Tonic	C
II	Supertonic	D
III	Mediant	E
IV	Subdominant	F
V	Dominant	G
VI	Submediant	A
VII	Leading note	B
I	Tonic	C

its notes are always tuned in the same relative pitches. This particular set of relationships is used because they are easy for the ear to distinguish and appreciate.

The harmonic series

Our ability to distinguish between different kinds of intervals stems from the fact that musical notes are actually composite sounds. They include not only a basic frequency (by which we identify a note) but multiples of that frequency. These multiples produce fainter, higher notes called harmonics, which result from the fact that a sounding object (such as a string) vibrates in decreasing fractions as well as along its whole length (see diagram). The frequency of each harmonic is in inverse proportion to the size of its fraction, so that equal halves produce double the frequency of the whole, equal thirds triple the frequency, and so on. The series of notes so produced is called the harmonic series.

Consonance and dissonance

When two notes sound together as an interval, we recognize the effect as *consonant* or *dissonant*. Consonances are usually considered sweet or smooth-sounding, whereas dissonances sound rough and harsh. Each of the two notes of an interval carries its own harmonics (frequency multiples). When two notes are in a simple frequency ratio, they have low common harmonics (common frequency multiples) and form a consonance. The ear relates the two notes in terms of the common harmonics because vibrations of the same frequency *reinforce* each other.

On the other hand, vibrations of slightly different frequencies *interfere* with each other, and the ear senses a regular swelling of sound, or "beating", as they go in and out of phase. This happens between the lower harmonics of dissonant intervals, such as the tone or major second.

"Perfect" consonances have the simplest frequency ratios, and are the unison (1:1, i.e. two of the same note), octave (1:2), fifth (2:3) and fourth (3:4). These intervals have the smoothest blend of harmonics.

Major and minor thirds (4:5, 5:6) and major and minor sixths (3:5, 5:8) are called "imperfect" consonances. They sound richer and sweeter than perfect consonances because there is some beating as well as agreement between their lower harmonics.

Apart from the tone or major second (8:9), dissonances include the semitone or minor second (15:16), the minor seventh (9:16) and the major seventh (8:15).

The natural scale and equal temperament

The table shows the "natural" or "true" scale which was used in European music until the seventeenth century. Its intervals were in "just intonation", i.e. tuned to simple ratios, which the ear could easily appreciate.

However, in the seventeenth century, when composers started to write music that modulated, or changed key, the "natural" scale started to cause problems on keyboard and some other instruments. To change key it was necessary to divide the octave into twelve equal semitones, and make the interval of a tone exactly equal to two semitones. In this way, the scale could start on any of the twelve semitones.

The "natural" semitone (15:16) did not divide a tone exactly, and was too large to be used to divide the octave into twelve parts.

For a time, a compromise tuning called "mean temperament" was used. By Bach's time this had begun to be replaced by the system of "equal temperament" tuning which is in general use today. This divides the octave into twelve equal semitones by giving the semitone the ratio of $1:\sqrt[12]{2}$, or about 84:89. On instruments tuned this way, such as pianos, every interval except

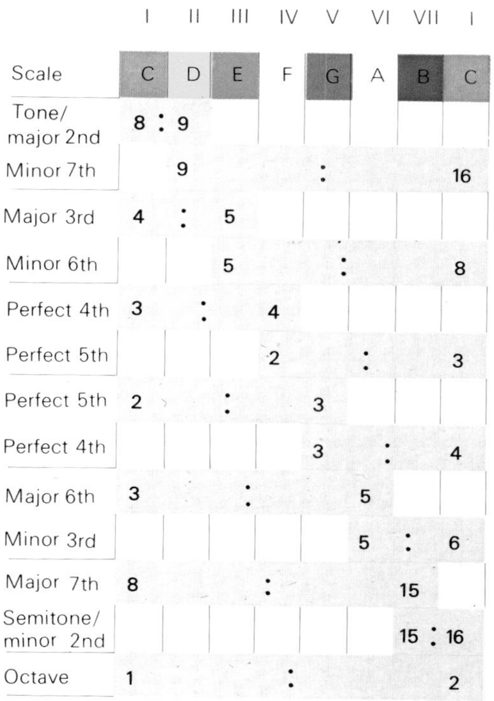
I II III IV V VI VII I
Scale C D E F G A B C
Tone/ major 2nd 8 : 9
Minor 7th 9 : 16
Major 3rd 4 : 5
Minor 6th 5 : 8
Perfect 4th 3 : 4
Perfect 5th 2 : 3
Perfect 5th 2 : 3
Perfect 4th 3 : 4
Major 6th 3 : 5
Minor 3rd 5 : 6
Major 7th 8 : 15
Semitone/ minor 2nd 15 : 16
Octave 1 : 2

Above The natural scale was tuned in intervals with simple frequency ratios. The diagram shows the names and ratios of the intervals between the tonic (first note) of this scale and its successive notes, together with the inversions of these intervals (formed by taking the lower note up an octave). In this scale, the second, third, fifth, seventh and eighth notes match harmonics of the tonic (colours cross-refer to diagrams on page 12). **Below** The tempered scale is based on dividing the octave (shown here as a circle) into twelve notes spaced by equal semitones. Seven of these notes make up the scale. All intervals except octaves are slightly out of tune compared with natural intervals.

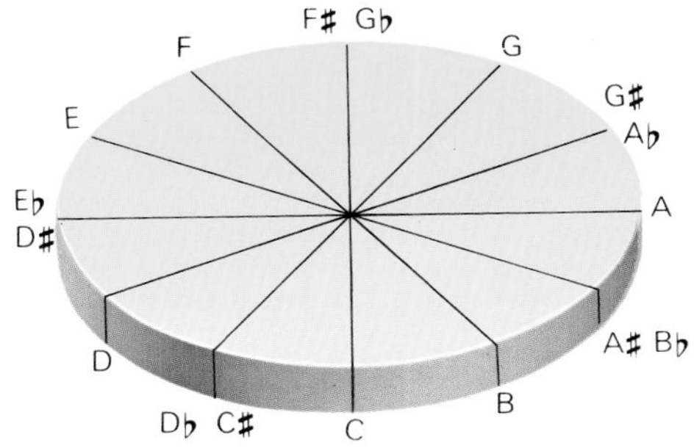

the octave is very slightly out of tune in comparison with the intervals of just intonation.

Harmonics and tone colour

Harmonics enable us to recognize the characteristic timbres of different instruments. The particular structure of an instrument affects the strength and weakness of its harmonics. Flute notes, for instance, lack odd-numbered harmonics, which is why they sound mellow and simple. Clarinet notes sound reedy because their higher harmonics are fairly strong.

Sound and Symbol

Only in the West has a comprehensive way of notating music been developed. This does not mean that Western music is better than that of other cultures. The Indians, Arabs, Chinese and other non-Western peoples elaborated musical theory together with astronomy and mathematics. But they were content to leave musical performance mainly to memory rather than to develop a detailed notation.

Up, down and along

Western notation is a way of graphing music, using the vertical axis for pitch ("up and down") and the horizontal axis for the movement of time (left to right). It is not a clear visual description of its subject, but a set of compressed instructions. It tells a performer what to play rather than what is actually happening. For this reason, beginners are well advised to concentrate on developing their *ear* as much as on learning to read notation.

Rhythm – music in time

Rhythm is the pattern made by music in time. It has two main aspects: *position* of notes in time, and their relative *durations* or lengths.

Pulse Rhythm is organized around a regular *pulse*, or succession of beats, which can be stated or implied. The pulse is what you tap your feet to (if so inclined). Its speed is called the *tempo*. In classical music, there is a range of names for different tempos (see glossary).

Metre When we hear an undifferentiated pulse we tend to *group* it in twos or threes. Such a regular grouping is called *metre* or measure. Groups of two or three pulses are not the only metres in music, but all other metres can be regarded as being "put together" from two or threes, or both.

Subdividing the pulse Pulse and metre are the foundation of rhythm rather than rhythm itself. This comes from *subdividing* the pulse into simple fractions of beats: basically halves or thirds. Rhythm patterns come from combining pulse subdivisions in various ways.

Time values and time signatures The table gives the note forms used to show time values and their equivalent *rests* (silences). Metre is shown by vertical *bar-lines*, and, at the beginning of a piece, by a *time signature* (which should not be confused with a fraction).

In *simple time*, where the division of the pulse is *binary* (into halves), the upper number of the time signature gives the number of beats in each measure or bar. The lower number tells you the type of note in which these beats are expressed – the value of the unit pulse. The time signature $\frac{3}{4}$ means that there are three beats to the bar and that the unit pulse is a crotchet or quarter-note, i.e. a quarter of a semi-breve or whole note.

In *compound time*, the pulse subdivision is *ternary* (into thirds). The lower number of the time signature gives the value of each *third* of a beat, and the upper number is the total number of thirds of a beat to the bar. So the time signature $\frac{6}{8}$ means that there are six thirds of a beat to the bar and that each third is the value of a quaver or eighth-note, i.e. an eighth of a semibreve. So, in compound time, the beat is regarded as "compounded" of $1\frac{1}{2}$ beats of simple time, and is shown as a simple time value followed by a dot, e.g. a dotted crotchet. (The dot adds half the value of the note to the note preceding it.)

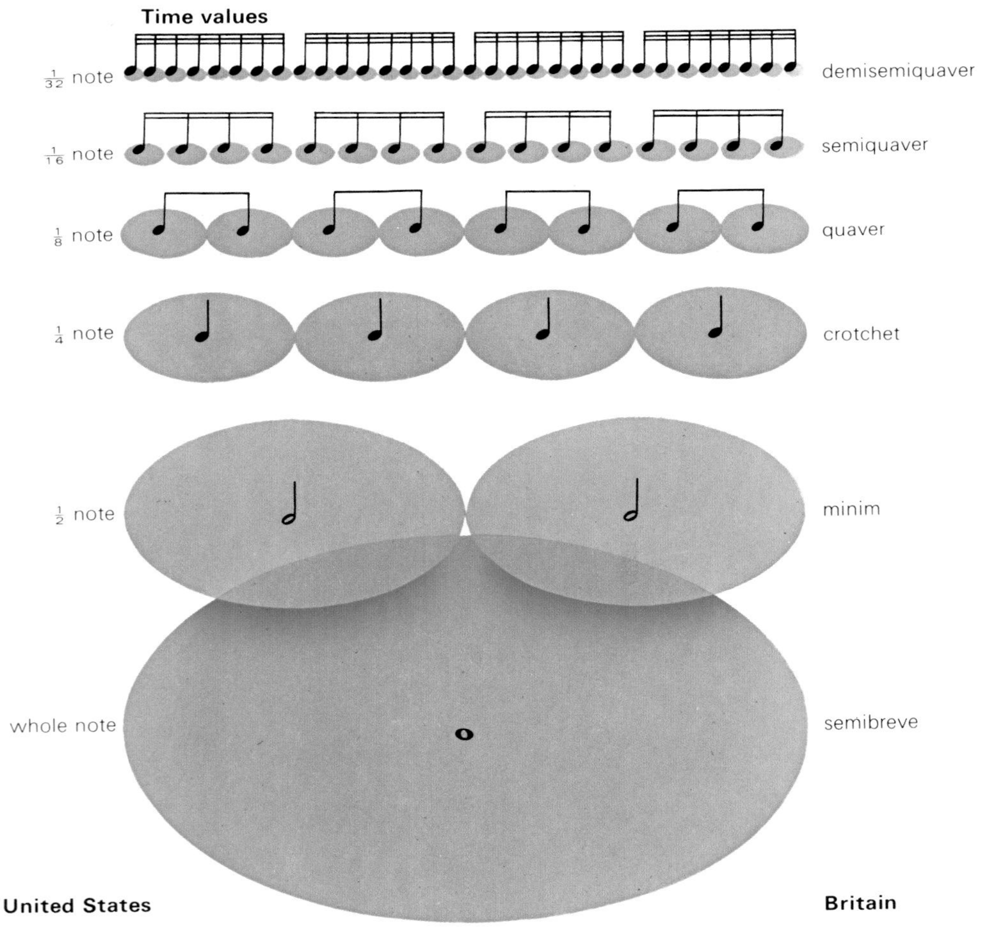

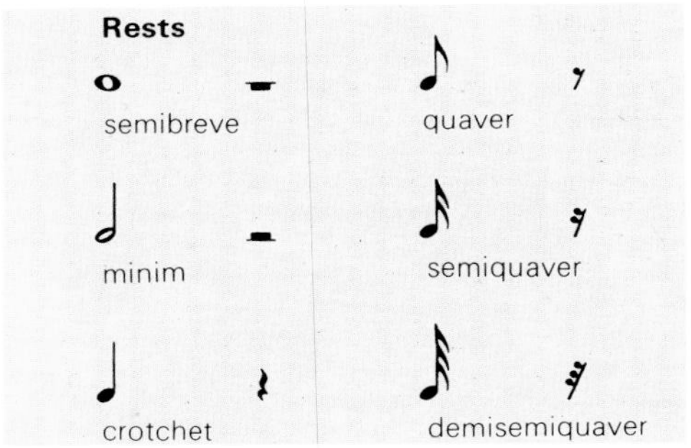

For each time value there is a sign for an equivalent rest. A dot after a rest increases its length by half, as it does after a note. (Note that quavers and shorter notes can be connected in groups, as on the left, or written separately, as above.)

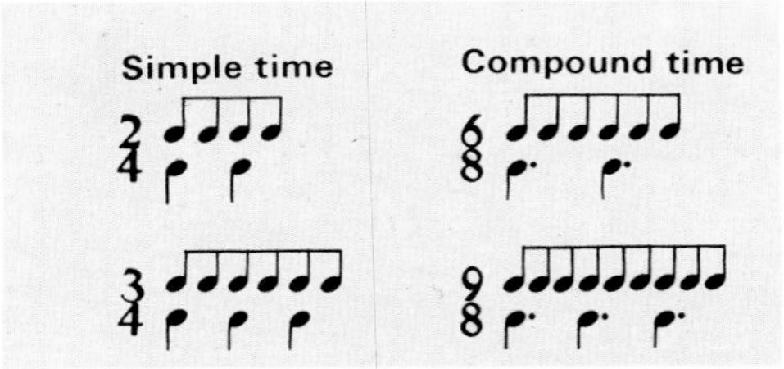

The basic metres (groupings of beats) are duple (two beats) and triple (three beats). If these metres are in simple time (beat divided into halves) they are shown by the time signatures $\frac{2}{4}$ and $\frac{3}{4}$. The same metres in compound time (beat divided into thirds) are written as $\frac{6}{8}$ and $\frac{9}{8}$, with the beat shown as a dotted crotchet (dotted quarter-note) worth three quavers (eighth-notes).

Pitch notation

The pitch of a note is shown by its position on a five-line *staff* or *stave*. The lines and spaces indicate positions of notes. To go above or below the stave's range, *ledger lines* are used.

A *clef* sign at the start of the stave indicates the range of notes: high, low or medium. The treble or G clef, for instance, curls round the second line of the stave, identifying that line as the G above middle C, and giving the stave the range of a treble voice or instrument.

Accidentals and key signatures An accidental is a sign placed in front of a note to temporarily alter its pitch. In the treble clef, the scale of C major is written starting on the first ledger line below the stave (middle C), without any accidentals. The steps of the major scale are tones (T) and semitones (S), in the order TTSTTTS. To write the same scale structure starting on another note, i.e. to change key, one or more accidentals must be used to achieve the correct order of intervals.

Accidentals listed immediately after the clef are called *key signatures*. The key of G, for example, is shown by a sharp sign on the F line of the stave. This raises every note on that line a semitone, to F sharp.

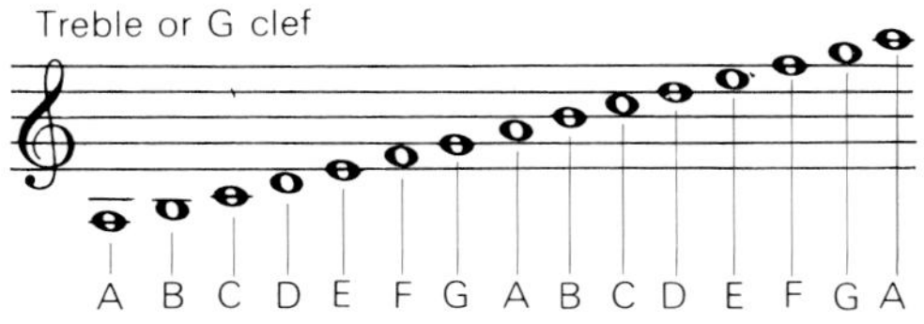

♯ **Sharp** raises a note by a semitone.
♭ **Flat** lowers a note by a semitone.
𝄪 **Double sharp** raises a note by a tone.
♭♭ **Double flat** lowers a note by a tone.
♮ **Natural** restores a note to its original pitch.

Major and minor intervals and scales

The terms *major* (= greater) and *minor* (= smaller) are used to distinguish between intervals that cover the same number of scale steps but which are of different sizes.

For example, in the key of C, the major third C–E covers three scale steps (C–D–E) and two tones (C–D and D–E). The minor third D–F also covers three scale steps (D–E–F) but only a tone and a semitone (D–E and E–F).

The major/minor terminology is also used to distinguish between the two main kinds of scale in Western music. The diatonic sçale discussed so far is called the *major scale* because the interval between its first and third notes is a major third.

The minor scale is so called because the interval between its first and third notes is a minor third (tone and semitone). This scale has two forms, *melodic* and *harmonic*. The melodic minor scale has different ascending and descending orders of tone (T) and semitone (S) intervals. Ascending, it is TSTTTTS; descending, it is TTSTTST. The harmonic minor, which is the same both ways, has one step of a tone and a semitone ($T\frac{1}{2}$), called an "augmented second". Its interval order is $TSTTST\frac{1}{2}S$.

Relative major and minor scales Any minor scale shares the same key signature as the major scale starting three semitones above, and so is called the *relative minor* of that major scale, which in turn is the *relative major* of the minor scale starting three semitones below.

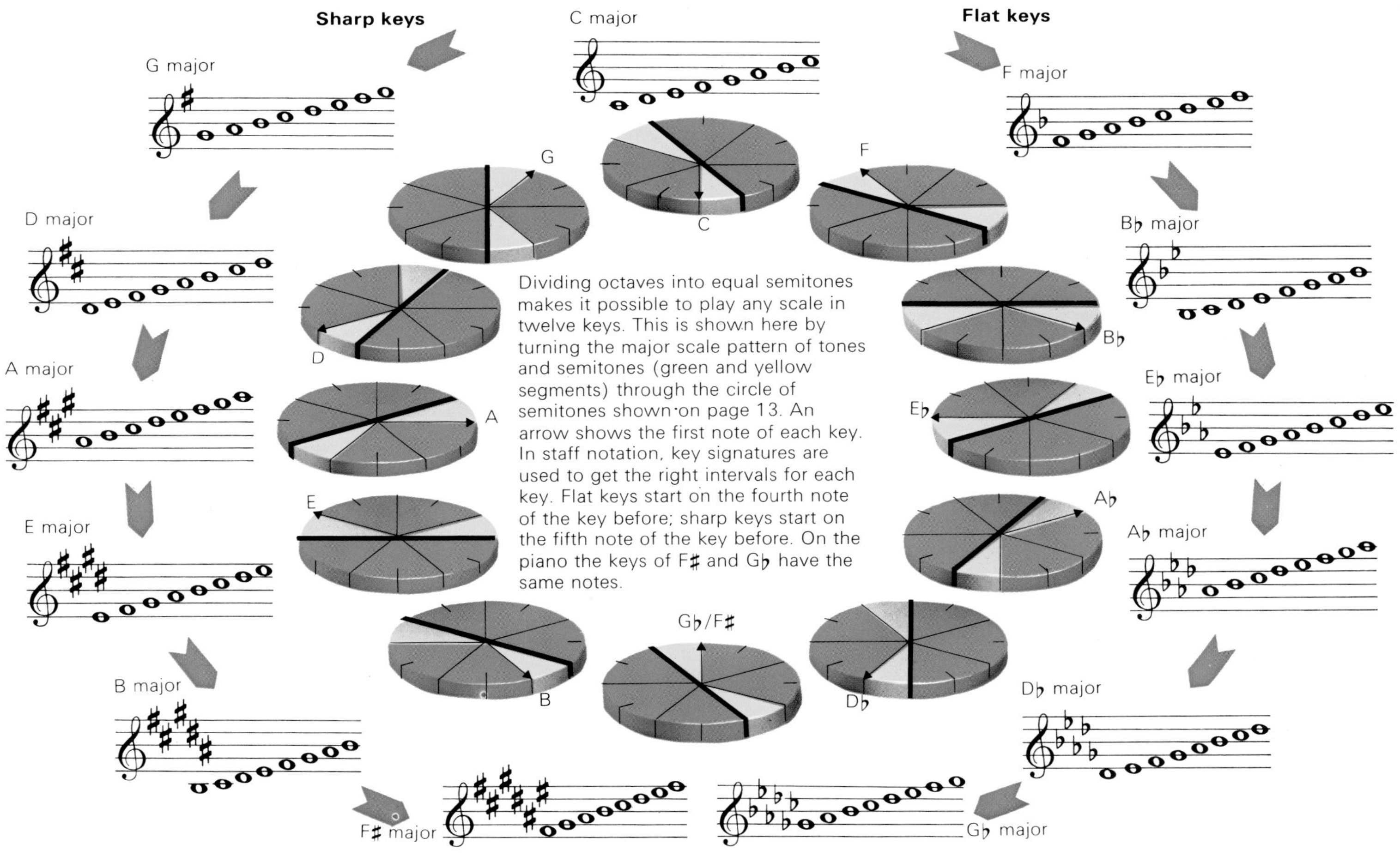

Dividing octaves into equal semitones makes it possible to play any scale in twelve keys. This is shown here by turning the major scale pattern of tones and semitones (green and yellow segments) through the circle of semitones shown on page 13. An arrow shows the first note of each key. In staff notation, key signatures are used to get the right intervals for each key. Flat keys start on the fourth note of the key before; sharp keys start on the fifth note of the key before. On the piano the keys of F♯ and G♭ have the same notes.

11
The Heritage of Music

The wealth of music to which we now have access, through live performance, broadcasting and recordings, is immense, and emphatically confirms what Constant Lambert once described as "the Appalling Popularity of Music". The weight of interest for most music-lovers, as the programmes of the world's great temples of music indicate, is still centred in European art music. However, there is hardly a period in history or a race of people on Earth which cannot boast some sort of musical tradition. The following section, it is hoped, will provide a starting-point for all those whose horizons have so far been confined to the concert music of the classical and romantic periods.

The heavenly orchestra sculpted on the choir vault above the high altar in Gloucester Cathedral (fourteenth century)

Primitive and Ancient Music

There is a tendency to see musical history as a process of continuous development culminating in the pinnacle of Western art music. The study of primitive music does not support such ethnocentric assumptions, and reminds us that a materially simple culture, such as that of the African pygmies, is no bar to the creation of complex, highly structured music.

There have been various ideas about the origins of music. Darwin thought that singing began with imitating animal cries, and Rousseau that the origin of song was in speaking with a raised voice. Others have thought that music originated with rhythm or work rhythms. Still others believed that music had the same origins as speech, both beginning with sound communication.

The earliest "scales" were probably groups of notes which evolved by "filling in" simple, easily recognizable intervals of fourths and fifths which occurred when people sang together. When such note groups were sung at different pitches, they overlapped to make five- or seven-note scales. Pentatonic (five-note) scales are found in Chinese, Celtic, Eskimo and African music, and may date back to Neolithic times.

In primitive choral singing, it is common for each singer to sing his or her own version of the tune, rather than sing exactly what everyone else is singing. This is called heterophony ("mixed voices") and it is the origin of polyphony (music woven from independent parts). Some primitive peoples, such as the African and Malaysian pygmies, have highly developed polyphony, featuring canon (following a line with the same line) and hocket (each person singing one note of a melody, as in bell-ringing). The call-and-response pattern (chorus answering soloist) also originates in primitive music.

The first instruments were often adaptations of existing implements which had other uses (e.g. musical bow from hunter's bow, pot-drum from clay pot, rattle from seed-drill). Rhythm instruments seem to have developed first, to accompany singing and dancing, and melody instruments came later. For a description of primitive instruments, see pages 120–1.

Ancient music

After the discovery of farming, some favoured areas became "cradles of civilization", where crop surpluses made it possible for a proportion of the people to live in cities. Ancient music (as opposed to primitive music) begins with this social transformation.

Western musical theory is usually assumed to date from the ancient Greeks, but there is no doubt that they, in turn, took their ideas about music from ancient Mesopotamia and Egypt. The ancient Chinese and Indians, as well as the Mesopotamians and Egyptians, knew the consonant intervals of octave, fifth and fourth, and made them the starting point of various scale systems, including ultimately our own. The ancients had no conception of relating pitch to frequency, but they worked out the relationship between notes of different pitches and the string (or pipe) lengths needed to produce them, which came to the same thing.

As civilization developed, earlier animist beliefs gave way to a more "scientific" view, in which music, mathematics, astronomy and religion were closely intertwined. The Mesopotamians came to worship the planets, and believed in a harmony between macrocosm (universe) and microcosm (man), which was mirrored in music and caused by number.

Mesopotamia and Egypt both contributed to Greek musical theory, particularly through Pythagoras, who studied in the temples of both countries in the 6th century BC. In both countries, the number 7 had great significance, and it is likely that both the Mesopotamians and the Egyptians possessed a seven-note scale which was borrowed by the Greeks.

Ancient Greece

The origins of Greek music are shrouded in the myths and legends of the Heroic Age beginning with the separation of mainland Greece from Minoan Crete, *c.*1400 BC. According to these, the small lyre (*chelys*), flute and reed-pipe (*aulos*) were invented by Hermes, Hyagnis and Marsyas, while Orpheus was the "father of songs" and Olympus introduced the traditional reed-pipe melodies or *nomoi*.

By the Epic Age (8th–7th centuries BC) there were three overlapping trends. Professional bards or minstrels sang epic poems about the gods and heroes, accompanied by the *kitharis* or large lyre. The first great work of Western literature, Homer's *Iliad* (*c.*850 BC) was based on such bardic songs. Then there was the music and dance of the countryside, associated with the pan-pipes or *syrinx*. Finally there was the communal music of citizen choruses, which sang at religious ceremonies, weddings, funerals and other public and festive occasions.

After the Epic Age, the bards widened their repertoires to include popular and topical themes. It is because such poems

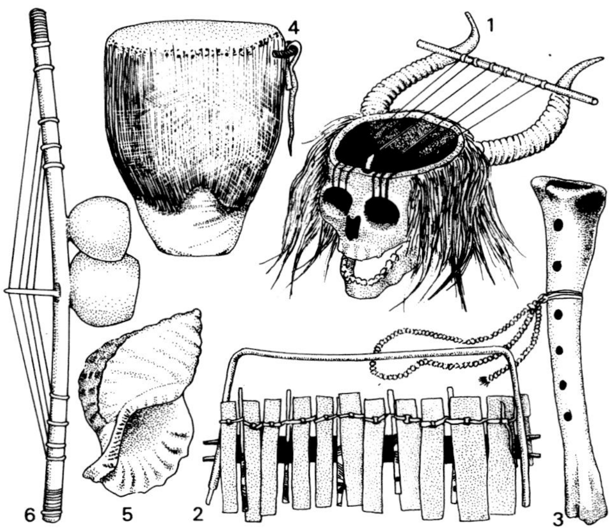

Above left Ancient Egyptian musicians playing an early flute, a lute and a harp, from a tomb painting. **Above right** Assyrian relief, 705–681 BC, showing musicians at the head of a religious procession at the Temple of Ashtar. From the Palace of Sennacherib, Nineveh. **Left** Cave painting of the Middle Magdalenian culture in the grotto of Trois-Frères, Ariège, France. It shows a man disguised as a bison playing a musical bow. **Right 1** African *kissar*, a type of lyre, made of animal horn and a skull. **2** A primitive predecessor of the marimba (Latin-American xylophone). **3** An early bone flute. **4** A wooden drum. **5** Conch-shell horn. **6** Kithara with gourd resonators.

were accompanied on the lyre that song-like poetry is still called "lyric" poetry.

In the Athens of the 6th and 5th centuries BC, the tradition of lyric poetry merged in the classical Greek drama, written by poet-musicians (dramatists) such as Aeschylus, Sophocles, Euripides and Aristophanes. The music was sung in unison by the chorus, either unaccompanied or sometimes with aulos or lyre, as a commentary on the principal action. The dance (*orchesis*) was performed by the chorus in a space, called the *orchestra*, in front of the stage. (The modern meaning of the word orchestra dates from early Italian opera, when musicians were seated in front of the stage.)

For the Greeks, and other ancient as well as primitive peoples, the modern concept of music as a self-contained activity had little meaning. "Music" (*mousike*) meant mental culture in general, as opposed to physical culture (*gymnopedia*), which together were the main branches of Greek education. Plato stressed the importance of music in education, believing that it revealed the principles (*noumena*) rather than the mere appearances (*phenomena*) of nature.

Greek scales were based on descending four-note groups called *tetrachords*, after the four strings of the early lyre. The top and bottom notes of these groups were fixed a perfect fourth apart while the tuning of the two "inside" notes was varied to give different *genera* or types of tetrachord. Seven-note scales, or *harmoniai*, were formed by linked tetrachords, e.g. G A B C D E F. Such scales were extended over two octaves (e.g. G A B C D E F G A B C D E F G), from which different octave scales, or modes, were selected. The mode from C to C, for example, corresponded to our modern major scale.

Pythagoras (*c.*585–*c.*479 BC), the founder of Greek musical theory, used a *monochord* (stretched string) to calculate the length ratios of every conceivable musical interval. Following his Mesopotamian and Egyptian teachers, he and his followers developed the correspondence of music and number into a cosmology which decisively affected Greek and later European thought.

The body of Greek musical theory was passed to medieval Europe by the later Roman writers, such as Boëthius, and to a great extent by the Arabs. Almost all the actual music played by the Greeks has, however, been lost. Notation was introduced only in the 4th century BC, after the decline of classical music, and less than twenty fragments of written music survive.

The Jews

The Jews became distinct from the other Semitic nomads of the Middle East under Abraham in *c.* 2000 BC. Jewish instruments of the nomadic period were the frame drum (*tabret* or *tof*), flute (*'ugab*) and small lyre (*kinnor*). Their cult instruments were the ram's-horn (*shofar*), blown in times of danger or repentence; the trumpet (*hazozra*), used for signalling; and jingles (*pa'amon*) worn by priests for magical reasons.

By 1050 BC the Jews had conquered Palestine and settled there as shepherds and farmers. Their culture drew on a varied background of Mesopotamian, Egyptian, Phoenician and Canaanite influences. In Solomon's temple (built *c.* 950 BC), ritual music was provided by the priests and Levites (men of the Levi tribe). Sung psalms were the basis of temple music, accompanied by the *kinnor* and large ten-stringed harp (*nevel*). Trumpets and *shofarim* were also sometimes used, and dance was important.

The earliest Christians were, of course, Jews, and as Christianity spread from the 1st century AD the influence of Hebrew temple music was carried over into the Christian church.

Following the Jewish dispersal from about AD 200, the synagogue became the characteristic place of worship. The rabbis discouraged secular music and the use of instruments, and only the shofar was allowed. Individual rather than choral music became the basis of worship, in the form of cantillation of the Bible and prayers.

Rome

The music of the ancient Romans combined Greek, Middle Eastern and native Etruscan influences. From the Etruscans came the *tuba*, a long straight trumpet of bronze or leather-covered wood; the *cornu*, a semicircular horn; and the *buccina*, an animal horn trumpet. In the Roman army the tuba sounded the attack or retreat, while the buccina sounded the watches. Other wind instruments included the Greek aulos or reed-pipe (called *tibia* by the Romans), the Middle Eastern bagpipe and, by Imperial times, the water-blown organ or *hydraulis*.

Stringed instruments included a larger version of the Greek *kithara*, with more strings; various-sized harps and the long-necked *pandore*. Percussion included the *scabellum*, a flapping hinged board, the *sistrum* (jingles based on the Egyptian *sehem*) and cymbals, tambourines and bells.

Music was an important feature of Roman social life at banquets and entertainments and on state occasions such as Imperial triumphs. Musicians had a well-defined status and virtuosi were highly valued. Street entertainers (*joculators*) combined music with juggling and acrobatics, and were the forerunners of the medieval *jongleurs*.

Left An Etruscan wall-painting in the Tomba dei Leopardi, Tarquinia (480–70 BC), showing a *tibia*-player. **Below** A carved relief of an aulos-playing courtesan found on the side of an altar in Greece. The aulos, an early shawm, was the Greek equivalent of the Roman *tibia*.

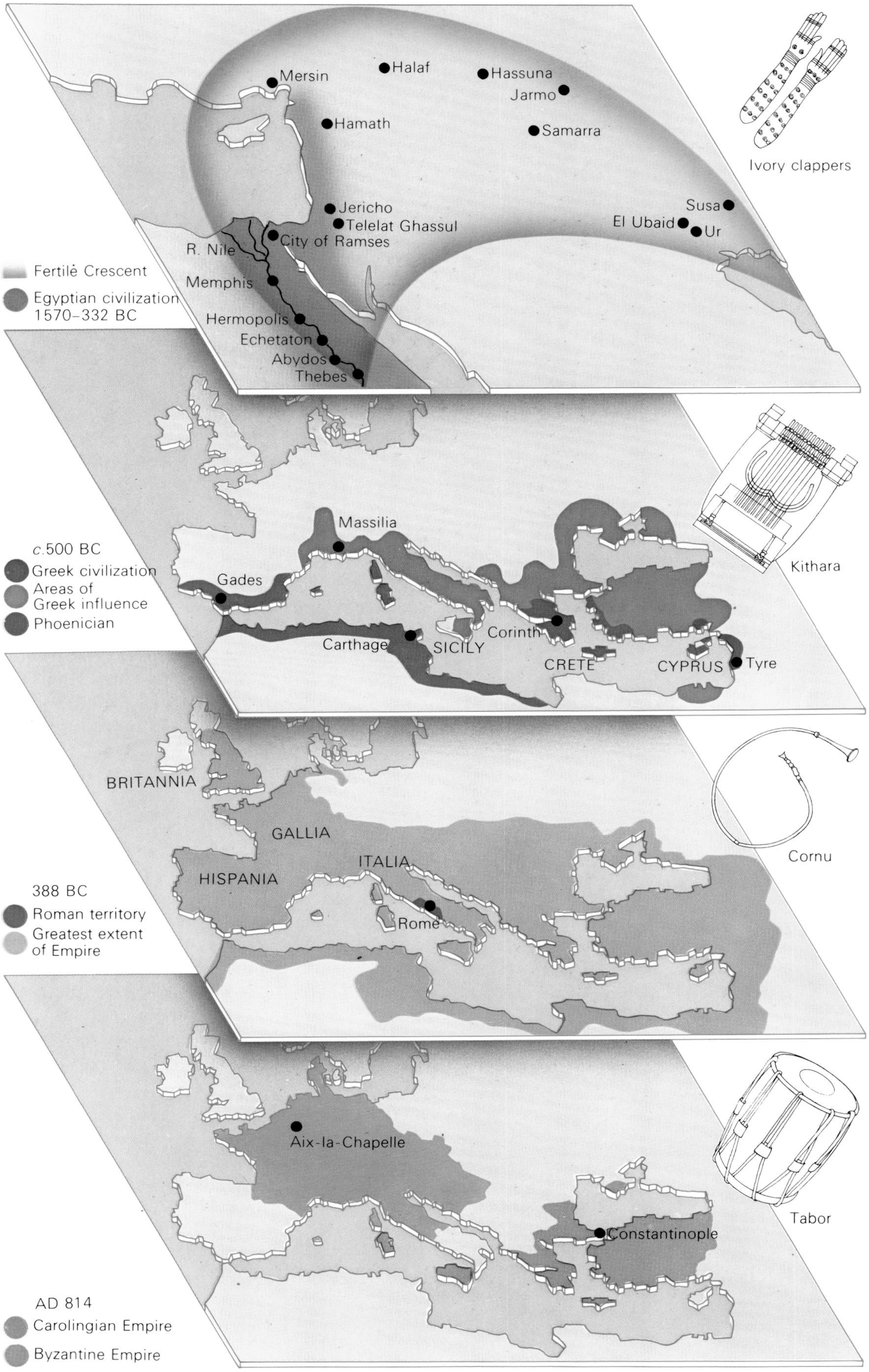

Ivory clappers

Left The map shows the extent of the (New Kingdom) Egyptian Empire and the "Fertile Crescent", a 3,200-km arc extending from Egypt, up the eastern Mediterranean and across to the Persian Gulf, where two of the world's earliest civilizations developed. Based upon the fertile lands of the Nile valley and delta, the Egyptian Empire was unified under the Early and Middle Kingdoms before 2000 BC and gave rise to a highly sophisticated culture. Music was important in both religious and court life. The land between the rivers Tigris and Euphrates supported the highly advanced Sumerian people. Their culture was absorbed by the Babylonians, reaching a peak under the great king Hammurabi in *c.*2200 BC.

Kithara

Left The map shows the extent of Greek civilization in the 5th century BC and the main areas of Phoenician settlement. The influence of the Greek peoples spread over much of Asia Minor, the Nile delta and much of the Italian peninsula. Greek culture, which was strongly musical, was therefore known far and wide. The sea-faring peoples of coastal Palestine created numerous settlements in the Mediterranean, of which Carthage, in what is now Tunisia, became the most famous.

Cornu

Left The map shows the Roman Empire at its greatest extent. From small beginnings, the Roman city-state grew to encompass the whole Mediterranean basin and extended as far as Britain, Germany and Mesopotamia. Roman civilization owed much to the Greeks, whom the Romans conquered, and also to the early peoples of Italy, such as the Etruscans. With the rise of the empire, the Romans became more cosmopolitan in their culture.

Tabor

Left The map shows the extent of the Carolingian and Byzantine empires in the Dark Ages. After the fall of the western Roman Empire, the most important kingdom to emerge was that of Charlemagne (AD 768–814). It maintained the Christianity of the later Roman Empire and helped to re-establish classical learning. In the East, the Byzantine Empire created a brilliant civilization which combined the best of Greek and Christian traditions.

The Middle Ages and Renaissance

The Middle Ages and Renaissance cover more than a thousand years of European history, from the collapse of the western Roman Empire to the beginning of the seventeenth century and the start of "modern times". The foundations of Western art music were laid in this long period, but the musical achievements of pre-1600 have their own lasting value and should not be seen just as a lengthy preparation for Mozart and Beethoven.

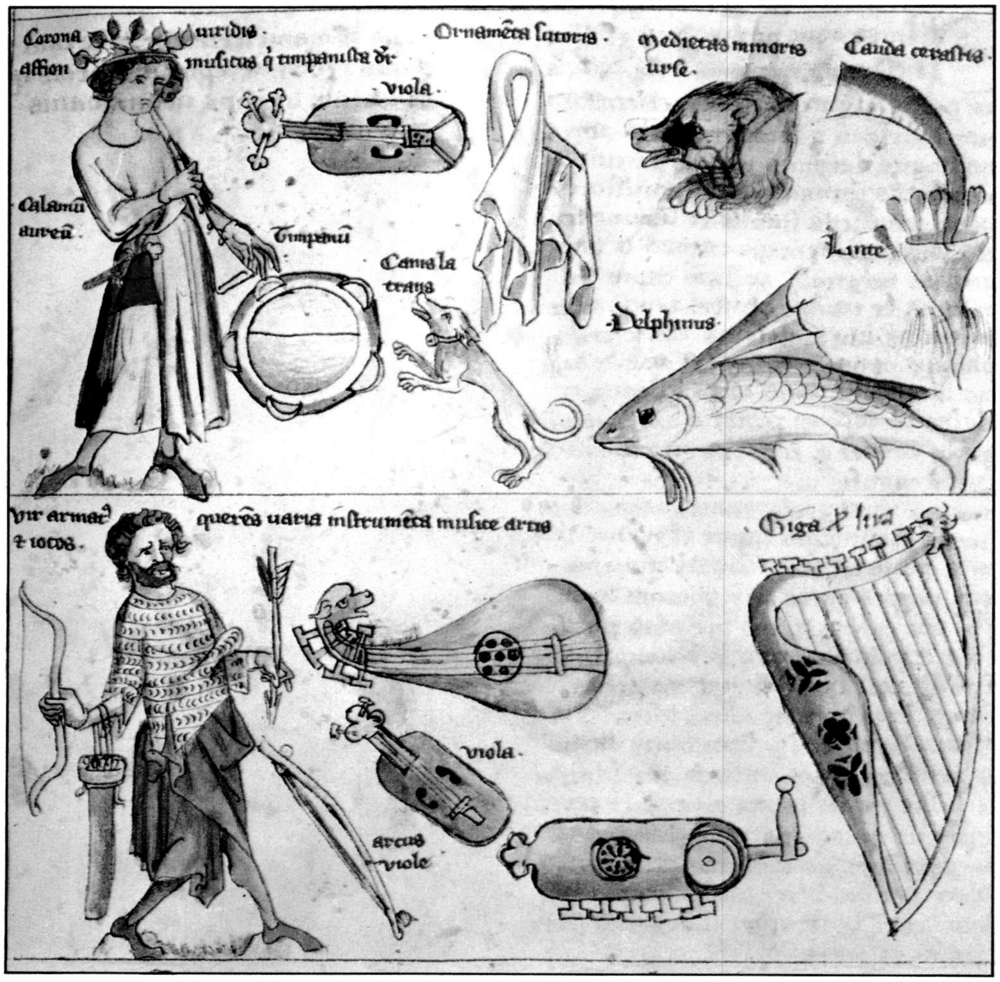

The rise of polyphony

The style which began to develop in the ninth century and which reached its height in the Renaissance is vocal polyphony – music for many voices. In polyphony, musical interest is shared equally between the parts, which move independently to produce an interwoven texture. The subtlety of polyphony can be easily missed by ears accustomed to the mainly homophonic music of later periods, in which a "top line" is supported by subordinate parts moving in chordal blocks. Polyphony was written not in fixed major or minor keys, but in different sections, or modes, of one diatonic scale.

The technique of polyphony is counterpoint. The word came from the earliest way of writing music in two parts, in which the two parts were fitted together note-against-note ("point counter point").

The starting point for the development of polyphony was the church plainsong, or plainchant, of the early Middle Ages. This was unaccompanied, single-line music, sung in unison, which stemmed from Greek and Jewish sources. Gregorian chant, the body of plainsong codified by Pope Gregory in the 6th century AD, is still the standard chant of the Catholic Church. It perfectly expresses the Latin words of the liturgy.

The first elaboration of plainsong, by the ninth century or before, was to parallel the plainsong melody in bare intervals of octaves, fifths and fourths. This was called *organum*, perhaps because early organs also played in these parallel intervals. The next step, taken by about the tenth century, was to enrich the spare harmony of organum with parallel thirds and sixths. This device came from secular music, where it was called *fauxbourdon*. Then a free-moving, sometimes improvised part called the *discantus* (descant) was added above the melody (*cantus*).

Polyphonic composition

With polyphony came the beginnings of composition as a specialized activity. Early polyphony reached a peak in the twelfth and early thirteenth centuries with the "Notre Dame School", i.e. the musicians associated with the church of Notre Dame in Paris. The greatest of these were Léonin (twelfth century) and Pérotin (flourished *c.*1183–1236).

The *motet* and *conductus* were the main polyphonic forms of the earlier Middle Ages. The motet, based on a plainchant melody, or *cantus firmus*, was sung in long notes by the tenor voice, and other faster-moving parts were added. The form developed from *tropes* or insertions to the plainsong mass. The conductus was in simpler rhythm and its cantus firmus was a secular or original melody rather than a piece of plainsong.

Notation

The rise of polyphonic composition depended on the development of adequate ways of describing and notating musical sounds. The Greeks had used letter names for the notes of the scale, and this system was passed on to medieval Europe by Boëthius (*c.* AD 470–525). From about the seventh century, the system of *neumes* began to be used as an approximate notation for plainsong. The neumes were signs for notes or groups of notes, which reminded the singer when to go up or down but did not indicate exact intervals.

In the eleventh century the Benedictine monk Guido d'Arezzo invented syllable names for the notes of the scale as an aid to sight-singing. This principle has remained useful ever since and is the basis of the modern tonic sol-fa system.

Meanwhile, to enable composers to set out their music in score, and to solve the problem of showing pitch, staff notation gradually evolved, together with a system of proportional notation for time values.

Old and new arts

The later medieval polyphony of the fourteenth century was known as the *Ars Nova* ("new art") to distinguish it from the organum-based polyphony of the twelfth and thirteenth centuries – the *Ars Antiqua* ("old art"). Among the leading composers of the often cerebral counterpoint of the *Ars Nova* were the Frenchmen Philippe de Vitry (1291–1361) and Guillaume de

Left Upper panel shows a musician playing a shawm and a frame drum with jingles which also has a snare for altering the tension. A four-stringed oval fiddle ("viola") is also shown. Lower panel shows an armed man together with a three-stringed oval fiddle and bow, a five-stringed citole and a harp. **Right** Venus playing a psaltery with fifteen strings. On her left is a three-stringed fiddle and bow, on her right a mandora. Both pictures are from a Dutch astrological treatise of the early fourteenth century. **Below** The music of Western Europe was influenced by the Crusaders' contact with Turkish martial music. On their return from the Middle East, they brought with them two different types of drum, the nakers and the tabor, which became standard instruments in medieval European music.

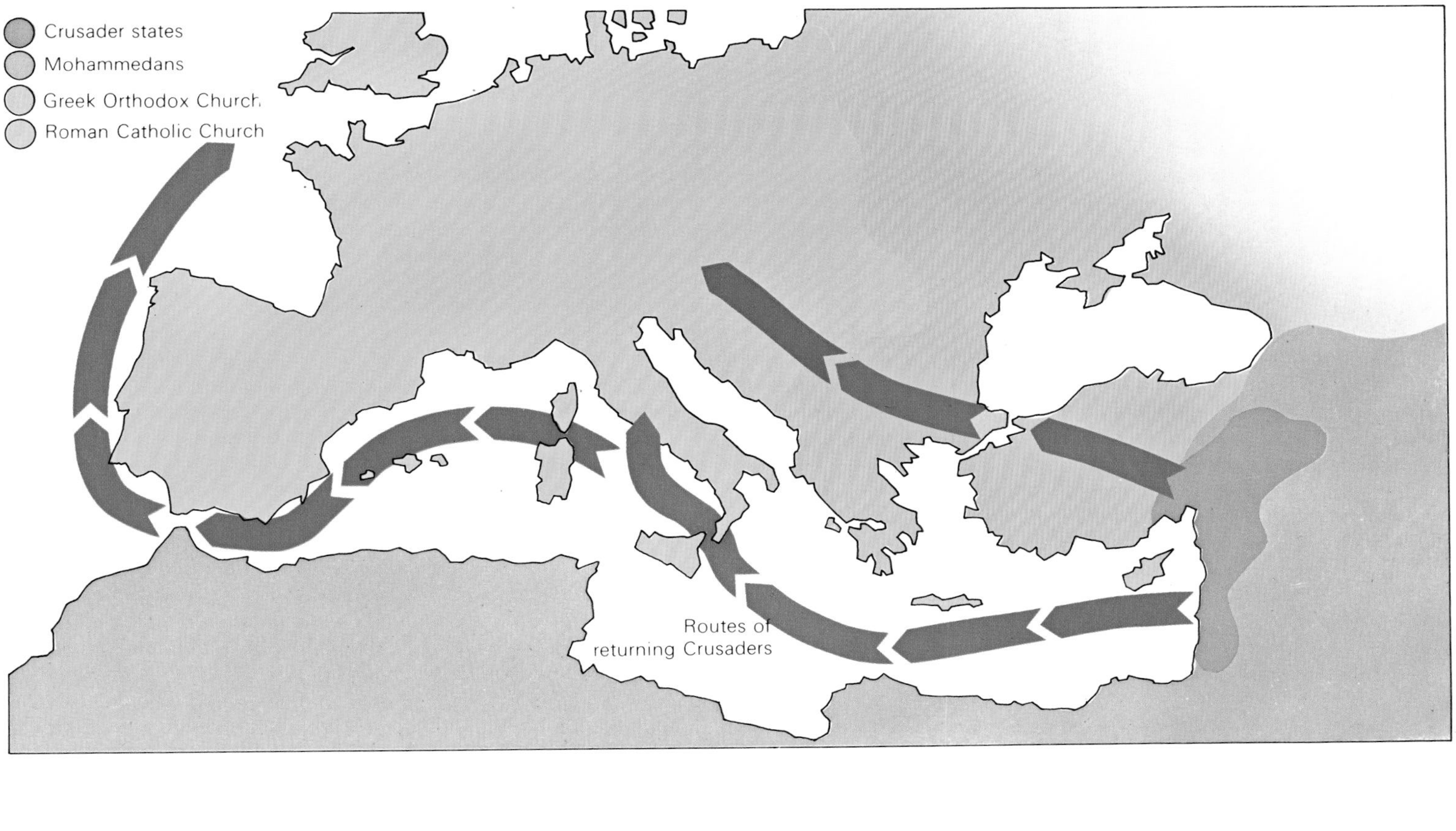

Machaut (1300–77) and the Italian Francesco Landini (1325–97).

In general, the *Ars Nova* represented a freeing of style from the parallelism of organum, with greater variety of rhythm and more independently moving parts.

Medieval secular music

Outside the Church, everyday musicianship in the early Middle Ages was part of the stock-in-trade of the wandering *jongleurs*, who amused the peasants, nobles and townspeople with singing, dancing, acrobatics and the like. Superior jongleurs, known as *jongleurs de geste*, specialized in singing epic narrative songs called *chansons de geste*.

At the upper end of the social scale were the knightly poet-composers whose influence spread from France in the eleventh, twelfth and thirteenth centuries, and who represented the "Age of Chivalry". Depending on whether they were from southern or northern France, they were known as *troubadours* or *trouvères* (the Provençal and French words for "finders" or "inventors" of poetry and music). Their highly developed poetry dealt with courtly love, chivalry and heroism, and greatly influenced the rise of European vernacular literature. Thousands of their verses and many of their songs survive (usually in neume notation). Two of the best-known poet-composers were Adam de la Halle (trouvère, *c.*1240–87), who left many compositions including three-part motets, and Bernard de Ventadour (*c.*1130–95).

The word minstrel or *menéstrel* was first applied to jongleurs who "ministered" to the troubadours with musical backing. By the fourteenth century, it had become a general term for a professional musician.

Minnesänger and Meistersinger

The *Minnesänger* ("love-singers") were the German equivalents of the French poet-composers, who combined German folk and French troubador influences.

In the later thirteenth century the noble *Minnesänger* declined and their art was taken up by the traders and craftsmen of Germany's towns and cities, who became known as *Meistersinger* ("mastersingers"). From the early fourteenth century they formed guilds with rigid rules for composing and performing songs. These guilds lasted three hundred years and were later depicted by Wagner in his opera *The Mastersingers of Nuremberg* (1868).

Medieval instruments

The Church in medieval Europe regarded the instruments of music as pagan, and approved of none except the organ. Medieval organs ranged from small portatives carried in processions to huge instruments such as that built at Winchester Abbey in the tenth century, with 400 pipes. It needed two players and seventy blowers.

Medieval music, whether in or out of church, was mainly vocal, and there was little conception of purely instrumental music. In secular music, however, a wide range of wind, string and percussion instruments was used.

Some of these, such as the bagpipe and simple flute, were European folk instruments of ancient origin. Others, like the harp and the natural trumpet (as well as the organ) were inherited from antiquity via the Romans. Many medieval instruments were borrowed from the Arabs and/or Turks via Moorish Spain, the Crusades and Byzantium. These included the lute, psaltery (zither) and the small kettledrums or "nakers". Various bowed stringed instruments, such as the three-stringed lira, were collectively known as "fiddles". Their prototype was the Arab *rebab*.

Medieval instruments were classified by the amount of sound they made rather than the method of sound production. "Haut", or loud, instruments included trumpets, drums, bagpipes, shawms (double-reed wind instruments) and hunting horns, and were mostly played outdoors. "Bas", or soft, instruments, for indoor use and accompanying voices, included bowed and fretted strings, flutes and harps.

Left The Angel of the Apocalypse as the South Wind, with trumpets. Twelfth-century painting in the church of St Martin Zillis, Switzerland. **Right** The famous *Minnesänger* Heinrich von Meissen, or Frauenlob ("praiser of women"). He is playing a fiddle, while his fellow-musicians hold bagpipes, a psaltery and, behind, a shawm.

As a historical term, "Renaissance" describes the period between the end of the Middle Ages and the beginning of "modern history". Beginning in fourteenth-century Italy with the reawakening of interest in the principles of classical (Greek and Roman) culture, the art, literature and attitudes of the Renaissance spread over Europe in the next two centuries.

The Renaissance in music began roughly in the mid-fifteenth century, later than the Renaissance in art and literature, and the transition from the late-medieval *Ars Nova* was gradual rather than abrupt.

From the late fourteenth century there was a steady increase in the number of singers employed in the better-off cathedrals and chapels. This led to the most important development in early Renaissance music: the rise of choral polyphony – that is, music with several voices to each part, rather than the one-voice-per-part polyphony of the Middle Ages. The earlier motets had been sung by small groups of contrasting voices. With choral polyphony, the chief aim was to achieve a blend of voices. This led to a greater concern with harmony. Renaissance composers "tamed" the dissonances which had been freely used in medieval music by "preparing" and "resolving" them – that is, by preceding and following dissonances with consonant harmonies. This development paved the way for the harmonically based music of the later periods.

Early and late Renaissance

In the seventeenth and early eighteenth centuries, Italy was to be at the centre of musical development, influencing the music of other countries. In the early Renaissance, northern composers such as the Englishman John Dunstable (?–1453) and the Flemings Guillaume Dufay (pre-1400–74), Johannes Ockeghem (*c.*1430–*c.*1495) and Josquin Després (*c.*1450–1521) were dominant. Many of them migrated to Italy, where their polyphonic expertise stimulated the local product.

Josquin Després linked the music of the earlier and later Renaissance as Beethoven later spanned the classical and romantic periods. His contribution to sacred and secular music was to result in the culmination of polyphony in the musical High Renaissance, whose greatest figures were Roland de Lassus (*c.*1530–1594), Giovanni Pierluigi da Palestrina (*c.* 1525–1594), Tomás Luis de Victoria (*c.* 1549–1611) and William Byrd (1543–1623).

Renaissance forms

With the rise of choral polyphony came the first large-scale form – the polyphonic mass. Composers were able to develop the musical mass (consisting of choral settings of passages from the Ordinary of High Mass) as an extended form with thematically linked sections – whereas the earlier motets had been self-contained insertions to the mass. Masses continued to be built around a cantus firmus until about 1550, but this no longer had to be a plainsong melody. That of Dufay's famous mass *Se la face ay pale* ("If my face is pale"), for example, was his own song of the same name, which was also widely popular as a chanson.

The most important secular form of the sixteenth century was the *madrigal*, a

polyphonic part-song with one voice per part. This grew from the Italian part-song or *frottola*, under the influence of emigré northerners, and its prime characteristic was its matching of words and music in a very detailed way. It was re-exported, to reach a high peak in England in the hands of composers such as Thomas Weelkes and John Wilbye. Later Italian madrigalists, such as Carlo Gesualdo (*c.*1560–1613) and Claudio Monteverdi (1576–1643) made the madrigal a vehicle for daring experiments in chromaticism – heralding the breakdown of the old modal system.

Renaissance instruments

In the fifteenth and sixteenth centuries vocal music remained dominant. But the Renaissance saw the beginnings of a rationalized approach to instrumental design and a greater concern with balanced instrumental groupings. As in choral music the idea of definite voice ranges (soprano, alto, tenor and bass) became established, so there developed "families" of different sizes of the same instrument,

Left Singing children, from a marble relief by Lucca della Robbia (1400–1482) in the cathedral at Florence. **Below** Painting by Hans Memlinc, *c.*1480, showing an orchestra of angels playing (left to right) psaltery, tromba marina, lute, folded trumpet, tenor shawm, (this page) straight slide trumpet, folded slide trumpet, portative organ, harp and fiddle.

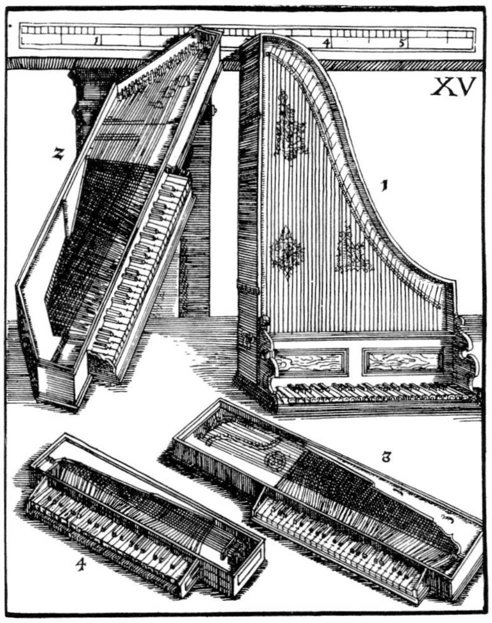

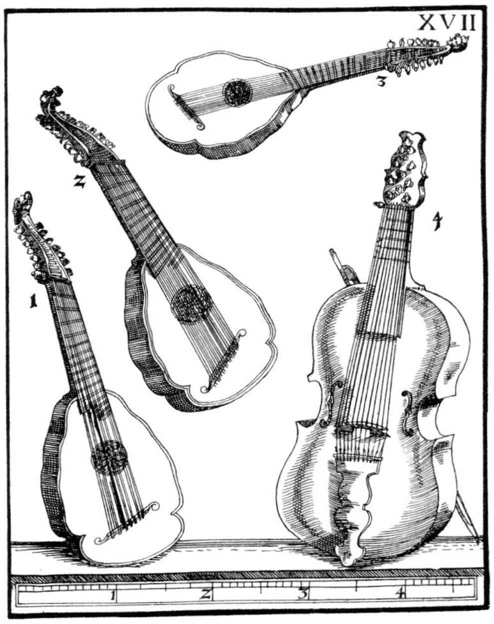

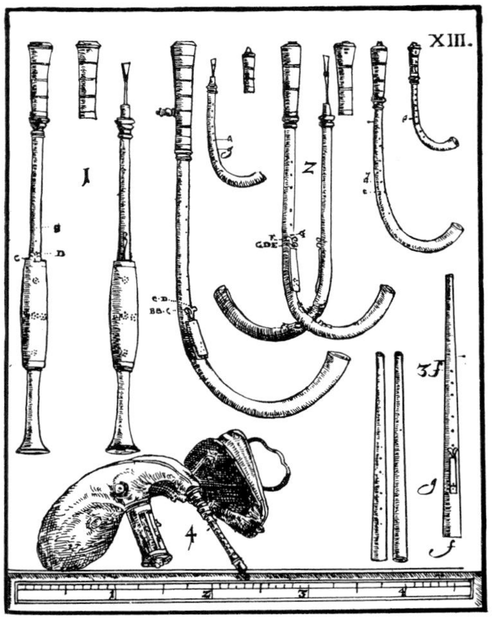

each size roughly corresponding to a voice range.

The most important was the consort of viols – soft-toned, fretted stringed instruments, played with a bow, which blended admirably with voices. Another family was the "chest" (boxed set) of recorders.

An innovation of the greatest importance for future music was the appearance of the keyed strings. These instruments were the result of marrying the idea of the zither or psaltery (i.e. strings over a flat sound-box) with an organ-type keyboard to actuate a mechanism for plucking or striking the strings. The early keyed strings included the harpsichord, virginals and clavichord.

As the splendour of their courts increased, Renaissance kings and princes hired more instrumentalists as well as singers. This gave composers the scope to experiment with varied instrumental and vocal groupings. Voices and instruments could be contrasted or combined with each other, as could consorts and "broken" consorts (homogeneous or mixed groups of instruments).

Music and the Renaissance mind

The Renaissance was perhaps the last period in which music held a central, even commanding, position in culture. Every educated person, whether artist, scholar or diplomat, was expected to know both the theory and practice of music. This was emphasized by Castiglione in his *Book of the Courtier* (1528) in these words: ". . . I am not pleased with the Courtier if he be not also a musician, and besides his understanding and cunning upon the book, have skill in like manner on sundry instruments."

In other words, music was of general as well as particular significance. The ancient association of music, number and cosmology was retained in the Renaissance *quadrivium* of the "liberal arts", which included music, astronomy, arithmetic and geometry. The key to understanding music was a knowledge of the proportions of simple intervals as shown on a divided string (monochord). The perfection of these intervals was thought to depend on their simple number ratios, and was taken as a proof of God's existence. For these reasons, Renaissance artists applied musical proportions in many fields, particularly architecture. Alberti and Palladio, for example, deliberately made the dimensions of their buildings conform to musical proportions.

Reformation and Counter-reformation

The sixteenth-century schism in which the Protestant churches of northern Europe hived themselves off from the Catholic Church shattered the religious unity of western Europe, and had important side-effects in music. In northern Germany, a tradition of Protestant hymn-tunes or chorales grew up. These uniquely expressed the religious fervour and seriousness of Lutheranism, and were to be an important influence on the music of J. S. Bach.

Meanwhile, in southern Europe, the Catholic Church went on the offensive and launched the Counter-reformation. At the Council of Trent (1545–63), it was decreed that "music in which anything impious or lascivious finds a part" should be excluded from the Church. There were even demands that harmonized music should be banned. That Catholic church music escaped this fate was largely due to a group of High Renaissance composers, led by Palestrina, who showed that harmony was not incompatible with purity of line and clarity of text.

Left A page from John Dowland's *First Booke of Songs* (1613). Each singer's part is printed in a different direction, allowing the performers to sit round a table and share the music.

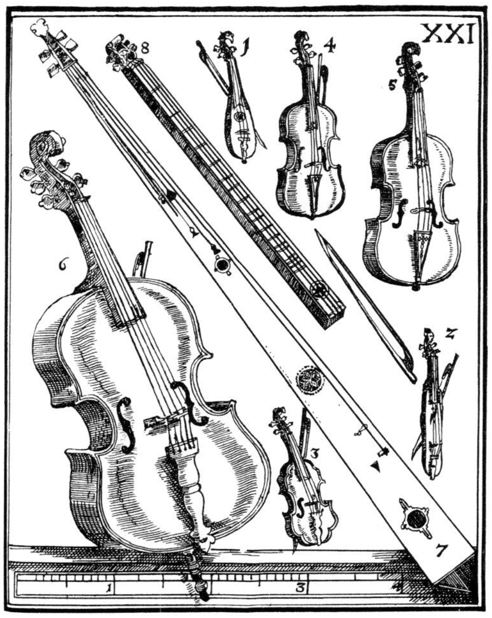

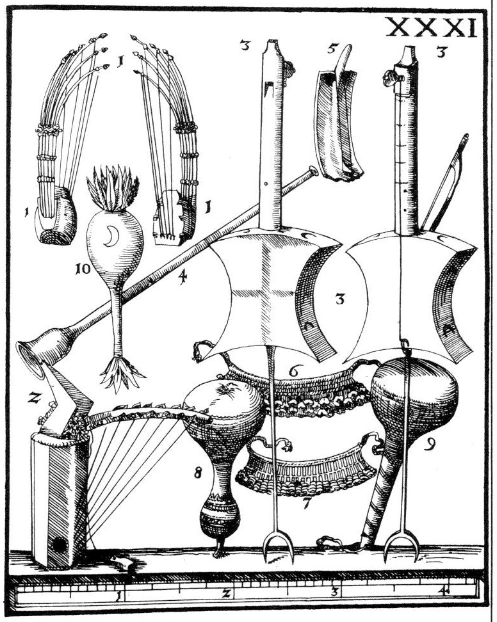

Above Illustrations taken from an appendix to *Syntagma Musicum* by Michael Praetorius, published in Germany in 1618. Much of this important work is devoted to descriptions and illustrations, which have proved invaluable in the study of the history of musical instruments. The instruments depicted here are (**XV**) harpsichords and clavichords, (**XVII**) citterns and a viol, (**XIII**) shawms, crumhorns, cornetts and bagpipes, (**XXI**) members of the string family (the largest instrument is a tromba marina), (**XXIII**) drums and (**XXXI**) a selection of instruments from the East. **Below** A map indicating the main centres of musical activity in Europe during the Renaissance.

The Baroque Era

Though in architecture the word "baroque" denotes the highly decorated, twisting and curving style prevalent in seventeenth- and eighteenth-century Germany, such a definition has very limited validity in music. The baroque period in music is conventionally considered to run from 1600 to 1750, dates which are in fact significant musical landmarks: the first extant opera dates from 1600, and in 1750 J. S. Bach died. Despite an underlying continuity of development from the Renaissance to the Baroque, there was a rapid and dramatic change of style towards the end of the sixteenth century. A late mass of Palestrina's, such as the *Missa Aeterna Christi Munera* (1590), and a work of Monteverdi's maturity, such as his opera *Orfeo* (1607), might have come from different worlds, let alone different centuries. Fundamental to this change of style were the teachings of humanism.

The impact of humanism on music

For the sixteenth-century composer of vocal music, the humanist doctrine of individuality implied domination of the music by the text. Hitherto, music had taken precedence. By the turn of the century the text was so important that musicians were asserting that music should be the faithful servant of the words. No longer were words merely a convenient support on which to erect an intricate musical edifice: as the personal utterance of an individual, they were crystallizations of emotions, such as tenderness, fear or anger. Composers were therefore expected to set the words in such a way that they would be clearly audible, and to write music that would heighten their effect. To satisfy the first condition, the early baroque composers used a new style consisting of a single melodic line with a harmonic accompaniment: homophony. The task of portraying drama and emotion was achieved in various ways.

Patronage

In the seventeenth and eighteenth cen-

"Entry of the lute-players", from the *Ballet des fées des forêts de Saint-Germain*, a court ballet danced at the Louvre on 11 February 1625. Water colour by Daniel Rabel.

turies, as previously, composers were employed by patrons of the arts, and would write music only for the purposes of their profession. Patrons included royalty, ruling aristocrats of European states and the Church. The occasions for which composers were expected to provide music were many and various: Monteverdi's *Orfeo* was commissioned for the carnival festivities at Mantua; Lully wrote ballets and operas to entertain Louis XIV and his court; Bach wrote cantatas at Leipzig for the principal Sunday service at St Thomas's, where he was *Kapellmeister*. Composers rarely wrote merely from inspiration or because they wished to give vent to their emotions.

The system of patronage was in itself neither good nor bad: a patron was just as likely to be a connoisseur of cultivated taste as he was a philistine concerned merely to impress. Nor did the practice of composing to order necessarily preclude the creation of a masterpiece: Bach's *St Matthew Passion* alone is a monumental vindication of this fact.

Baroque style, forms and technique

The basic principle of baroque music was a notational device known as *basso continuo* or thorough-bass. It was a type of bass line, usually for keyboard, with figures underneath to indicate the required harmonies. *Basso continuo* was used for recitative and aria in early opera.

The opening of the first public, commercially run opera-house at Venice in 1637 had two results: the domination of opera by the *aria*, which, having a measured rhythm and greater melodic interest, had much more appeal for a musically uneducated audience than the unmelodic vocal lines and free rhythms of *recitative*; and the cult of the soloist, which is still with us today. Singers enjoyed displaying the agility and range of their voices in virtuoso arias, and audiences loved to marvel at the soloists' technical prowess. The two principles of *bel canto* ("beautiful singing") and virtuosity may be traced from Monteverdi to Handel.

Below This detail of a mural (artist unknown) commissioned by Sir Henry Unton, an ambassador to France at the time of Elizabeth I, depicts musical entertainment at a wedding feast and shows a typical instrumental ensemble of the period. The next hundred years were to see the development of large-scale secular forms, such as the opera and the opera-ballet, while instrumental music was to attain an importance it had never known before.

Virtuosity spread from opera to instrumental music, such as Vivaldi's many solo violin concertos. Such a transference of idiom is characteristic of baroque music, and is usually from opera to another genre. Similarly, the type of overture (or *sinfonia*) found in the operas of Alessandro Scarlatti lent its fast-slow-fast pattern, as well as certain stylistic features, to the *concerto grosso*. The structure of the *ritornello* aria, in which the vocal passages are broken up by brief orchestral statements, was also adopted in instrumental works.

Another important principle in baroque music was the *stile concertato*, in which the sounds of several solo instruments or groups of instruments are contrasted with those of the orchestra. This technique was well-known in the sixteenth century since the composers at St Mark's, Venice, had utilized the two opposing galleries there for such a purpose. (Among them was Giovanni Gabrieli, in his canzonas.) Baroque composers used the idea for concertos, sacred music (mass, motet, oratorio and Passion) and opera.

Baroque composers were the first to distinguish between vocal and instru-

Below Four buildings which were centres of music in the baroque period: Westminster Abbey, where Henry Purcell succeeded John Blow as organist in 1679; the palace of Versailles, France, where Louis XIV kept a large retinue of musicians and staged sumptuous entertainments; St Thomas's, Leipzig, where J. S. Bach was *Kapellmeister* from 1723 until his death; St Mark's, Venice, where musical personnel included Adriaan Willaert, Andrea and Giovanni Gabrieli and Monteverdi. The building's design was ideal for antiphonal singing, which became a feature of Venetian vocal music.

mental idioms and, moreover, between different instrumental styles: violin parts, for example, became different from those for flute. They also started to exploit both the expressive and the purely technical capabilities of each instrument, developing skill in both "emotional" and virtuoso composition. The harpsichord music of Domenico Scarlatti (1685–1757) illustrates admirably this new-found awareness.

In the early seventeenth century the desire to make the words clearly audible in vocal music made homophony predominant in both church and secular forms of vocal music. Polyphony was to enter a new phase: in the baroque era, the art of instrumental counterpoint reached its peak in J. S. Bach's fugues.

Underlying the various techniques and styles is the emergence during the seventeenth century of modern tonality, or key sense. By a process of gradual simplification the eight church modes of the Renaissance had slowly disappeared. By 1700 the modern Western system of tonality with only two modes, major and minor, was firmly established.

One of the two major instrumental forms to emerge in the baroque period was the *suite*. It was the custom in ballrooms to alternate dances of different tempi and different measures; the suite was a selection of dances, similarly contrasted, and usually in the same key. Each dance would be in simple binary form, that is, in two parts; the first modulated into a related key, the second returned to the home key. Each half would be repeated.

A standard format for the suite was gradually established: allemande, courante, sarabande and gigue. However, the numbers and types of dances varied widely from suite to suite.

The *sonata*, derived from the (vocal) chanson, was at first little differentiated from the suite, but consisted simply of one or more movements in binary or ternary form. There were two types: the chamber sonata (*sonata da camera*) based on dance movements, and the church sonata (*sonata da chiesa*) of a more serious nature. Domenico Scarlatti wrote a great many one-movement sonatas for harpsichord.

Major baroque composers

Claudio Monteverdi (1567–1643), born in Cremona, Northern Italy, became director of music at St Mark's, Venice, in 1613. Until he was forty, he concentrated upon madrigals. In 1607 he produced *Orfeo*, a landmark in operatic development which gave the medium greater dramatic power and more vivid orchestration. Besides opera, he is well-known for the oratorio *Il combattimento di Tancredi e Clorinda* (1624) and the *Vespers* (1610).

Georg Philipp Telemann (1681–1767) worked at Eisenach, Frankfurt and St Thomas's, Leipzig, where he was succeeded by J. S. Bach as cantor. Admired by Bach, a friend of Handel and composer of instrumental works, forty operas and forty-six oratorios, he held a major church post in Hamburg for forty-six years.

Antonio Vivaldi (*c*.1685–1741) was a priest who spent much of his life as the violin teacher of an orphanage-conservatory for girls in Venice. Noted as both a violinist and a composer, he wrote nearly 250 string concertos and forty operas. His best-known work is the programmatic *Four Seasons* (1725).

Johann Sebastian Bach (1685–1750) was born at Eisenach into a musical family. While studying at Lüneburg in Saxony he came into contact with the church music of Hamburg and the French court music of Hanover. He was court organist and director of music at Weimar (1708–17) and director of chamber music at Cöthen (1717–23). In 1723 he settled in Leipzig as cantor or musical director at St Thomas's church and school and later became director of music to the university.

Few of Bach's works were published in his own lifetime. Many remained unknown until the nineteenth century. Bach was not a pioneer of musical expression, but built upon the form and technique developed by other composers and perfected such forms as the fugue, chorale cantata, chorale prelude, Passion, mass, suite, *concerto grosso* and toccata. His music encompasses the rich variety of the baroque period: it has the force, intricacy and ultimate symmetry of German baroque style, yet makes skilful use of French and Italian ideas.

His choral works include the five Passions, over three hundred sacred and secular cantatas, the Mass in B minor and several oratorios. His vast instrumental output includes concertos, suites and chamber works, best-known among which are the *Brandenburg Concertos* (1719). Amongst numerous solo works are *The Art of Fugue* (organ), *The Well-tempered Clavier* (or *Forty-eight Preludes and Fugues*) and the six cello suites.

George Frideric Handel (1685–1759) was born in Saxony and became organist at Halle when only twelve. As a young man he visited Italy and was deeply influenced by its music. In 1712 he gave up his post as *Kapellmeister* to the Elector of Hanover for a position at the English court. When the Elector became George I of England in 1714, Handel concentrated on staging Italian-style operas in London. Of the forty-six he wrote himself, *Ottone* (1723), *Julius Caesar* (1724), *Rodelinda* (1725) and *Xerxes* (1738), with its famous "Largo" (in fact marked *larghetto*), are best-known. On the financial failure of his opera company he turned to the composition of oratorios, including *Saul* (1738), *Samson* (1741) and the *Messiah* (1741). The latter restored Handel's fortunes when he was ill and near bankruptcy. *The Water Music* (1715) and *Music for the Royal Fireworks* (1749) are among his many orchestral works.

The Age of Classicism

As a musical style, classicism is usually associated with the eighteenth century. In musical terms, it may be defined as the attempt to create music which is formal, strict in proportion and moderate in expression. Classicism tends to avoid emotionalism, whereas romanticism is closely identified with the expression of emotion, fired by the inspiration of the individual.

The classicists, shunning subjectivity, sought to create a perfect, disciplined order based on pure beauty, reason and structure, whereas the romantics sought to revolt against established rules and traditions and to express their own creative identities.

First impulses of classicism

After the Peace of Westphalia in 1648 the various states of Germany, freed from Habsburg domination, began to develop their own styles of literary and musical culture. An economic revival took place, resulting in the creation of a number of courts, cities and corporate bodies which were prepared to patronize music and the other arts. During the late sixteenth and early seventeenth centuries a division in musical expression had grown up, broadly speaking, between the Protestant North, whose greatest representative was J. S. Bach, and the Catholic South, where Italian and French influences were more readily absorbed.

Of the German states, Prussia, Saxony and Austria, politically dominant in the eighteenth century, came to provide in their capitals musical centres in which the two traditions gradually combined. It was in the South that the first impact of the French and Italian *style galant* ("courtly style") became apparent. This light, elegant mode of expression was used extensively by composers of harpsichord. It contrasted strongly with the serious and more restrained nature of northern counterpoint, and gave rise to the development of the great Viennese classical school led by Haydn and Mozart.

Just as in other arts, such as architecture, painting and poetry, rococo elegance had begun to soften the severity of the high baroque style, in music the new *style galant* was intended to achieve a simpler, more directly evocative form of expression while retaining baroque precision. The new style caused something of a sensation, despite the fact that initially its influence was confined to chamber music. Larger-scale works, such as masses and operas, had yet to be affected. One direct result of the *style galant* was that the form

Haydn directing his opera *L'incontro improvviso* (*"dramma giocoso"*, 1775) from the harpsichord in the Esterházy Theatre. The Esterházy family were Haydn's patrons for the best part of thirty years.

of the suite gradually gave way to the sonata, which became the most common basis of musical expression in the following periods.

Precursors of the Viennese school

Of the cosmopolitan influences that affected German music, none was more important than that of the Italians in Vienna, where a flowering of the arts was beginning to reflect the state's political and social ascendance. Austria had become a significant power, and its capital city a major European centre. Animated interest in the arts at every level, from the magnificent court down to the new bourgeoisie, and, as always, the patronage of the Church, raised the city's cultural stature. Italian composers such as Antonio Caldara (1670–1736) and Giovanni and Antonio Bononcini were making a profound impact on the city's musical life. The *Kapellmeister* to the court, Johann Joseph Fux (1660–1741), responded to Italian influence in his secular works and operas while retaining in his religious compositions the solemnity of a tradition unchallenged since Palestrina. Fux, well-known as the author of *Gradus ad Parnassum* (1725), an immensely influential treatise on counterpoint, had begun directly to reflect the dichotomy in musical expression in Germany, accepting to some extent the Italian and French influence while continuing to rely on traditional German sources.

A new musical vocabulary was taking shape, and though the Viennese influence slowly declined, it was in that city that the young Joseph Haydn received his formative training.

Parallel with Vienna, another musical centre was emerging at Mannheim, where the Elector Palatine had set up his court after moving from Heidelburg after the Thirty Years War. Mannheim's small chapel was to become one of the foremost musical centres in Europe, with an orchestra of unassailable renown. Two men dominated Mannheim's musical life: Johann Stamitz (1717–57) and Franz Xavier Richter (1709–89). Stamitz was appointed *Kapellmeister* to the court in 1745, at the age of twenty-four. Under the guidance of these two men orchestral technique was revolutionized, and the

Mannheim orchestra became the finest in Europe. Here, the contrasting small and large ensembles which characterized chamber and symphonic music became more obviously separated. Richter, Stamitz and the latter's Italian pupil Cannabich (1731–98) wrote numerous fine symphonic pieces which were to influence both Haydn and Mozart.

When the Elector succeeded to the Bavarian throne in 1778, musical life moved to Munich, although Mannheim remained important. Most of Mozart's operas were later performed there, in the National Theatre. One important figure associated with the musical life of both cities was the Abbé Vogler (1749–1814). He founded a conservatory at Mannheim and then moved to Munich with the court. A brilliant organist, he played in London and Paris and helped found conservatories in Stockholm, Prague and Darmstadt. In the 1790s, he toured Ottoman Greece, Morocco and Algeria, hoping to find the origins of polyphony. His two most famous pupils were Weber and Meyerbeer.

In the Protestant court of Berlin musical life still followed pre-classical traditions. Musical development was given little encouragement during Frederick William's reign in the first half of the eighteenth century. His opposition to his son's love of music forced the young Frederick to leave the city and found a musical centre at Rheinsburg, where C. P. E. Bach was to find employment.

Frederick ("the Great"), a composer and flautist himself, gathered around him musicians of talent and, in the case of Johann Quantz (1697–1773), astonishing fecundity. Apart from writing an influential treatise on the flute, Quantz composed some three hundred flute concertos for his employer. Carl Heinrich Graun (1704–59), Frederick's *Kapellmeister*, supervised the Berlin Opera, which was opened in 1742, and the Bohemian Georg Benda (1722–95) gained fame through his melodramas, a form of entertainment in which words were spoken against a background of musical accompaniment. Mozart was an admirer of the declamatory style of utterance used in Benda's melodramas, and it probably influenced his own recitative style.

The most important figure in Frederick's circle was C. P. E. Bach (1714–88). A brilliant keyboard composer, he worked for Frederick for thirty years before succeeding Telemann at Hamburg. He wrote two hundred keyboard pieces and fifty keyboard concertos; many of his pianoforte sonatas were among the first major contributions to the repertoire of this new keyboard instrument. C. P. E. Bach influenced both Haydn and Beethoven, and indeed received far greater recognition in his lifetime than his father had.

The musical importance of Berlin continued after Frederick's death in 1786. Frederick Fasch founded the *Singakademie* and his pupil Carl Zelter helped to revive interest in J. S. Bach. It was Mendelssohn, Zelter's pupil-prodigy, who introduced Bach's *St Matthew Passion* to Berlin society in 1829.

While musical life in the south prospered, in the north, at Hamburg, a centre had begun to flourish. Hamburg's important musical figure in the eighteenth century was Telemann (1681–1767).

In Saxony, too, musical life had found impetus, dating from about the time of Frederick Augustus's accession. Whilst Bach had been developing his musical ideas at Leipzig, the Italian influence of Veracini and Lotti and, more impressively, that of the Saxon Johann Hasse (1699–1783) had led to a climax of creative activity in Dresden, the capital. Hasse, who studied under Porpora and A. Scarlatti in Naples, became one of the foremost operatic composers of the day. He travelled widely during his brilliant career.

The apotheosis of classicism

As music moved towards what was to become known as classicism, in France after the 1770s the neo-classical school of painting evolved a distinct visual style. Inspired by the recent excavations at Pompeii and the works of the German antiquarian J. J. Winckelmann, this new classical style evoked the simplicity and order of ancient Rome. Jacques David, who was much influenced by the Greek and Roman past, was a major exponent of classicism in art.

The composers of the classical period were to establish the symphony, the sonata and the string quartet as the major forms of musical expression. Yet in England and Germany new ideas had already emerged which were to shake the stability of classicism and lead to the phenomenon of romanticism in nineteenth-century European culture.

Vienna, already a significant musical centre, grew even more important. Numerous composers, among them Wagenseil, Hummel, Czerny and Albrechtsberger, expanded its musical development. The rising bourgeoisie and the nobility cultivated an intense interest in concerts of every kind, and gradually French and Italian influences became absorbed into a truly Germanic identity.

By the middle of the eighteenth century, the *sonata* had assumed its characteristic shape: typically, it had a first movement in sonata form, a second in ternary form, a minuet and trio for the third movement and a rondo for the finale.

Sonata form was an essential element of many compositions, notably first movements of instrumental works. It is essentially a system of thematic and key relationships. The first section, the exposition, introduces the main thematic material; it has two contrasting "subjects", the first in the tonic, or main, key of the whole piece, the second in a different but related key. The second section is the development, in which the stated ideas are developed in various ways. The last is a recapitulation of the exposition, but with the second subject in the tonic key.

The *symphony*, in which sonata form was a major structural element, was brought to its full stature by the immensely prolific Haydn. In its format, it was similar to the sonata, though composers were just as likely to vary the typical structure of the symphony as they were that of the sonata. The *concerto*, which comprised three movements, as opposed to the symphony's four, emerged in the late eighteenth century as the major vehicle for the solo instrument, especially the new pianoforte and the violin. The arrangement of movements again corresponds to that of the sonata, but there is no minuet and trio.

Chamber works, particularly the quartet, quintet and trio, acquired great importance during the classical period.

The masters of classicism

The first great figure of Viennese musical life was a wheelwright's son, Franz Joseph Haydn (1732–1809), born in Rohrau, Lower Austria. His musical talent was apparent early in his life. He was a choirboy at Vienna Cathedral and later acted as accompanist at the musical academy of the great singing teacher Porpora. In 1776 he was appointed *Kapellmeister* to the Esterházy household, a title he held for some thirty years. During this time he wrote some of his finest masses and oratorios. In 1791 and 1794 he made two memorable visits to London, where he was a great musical and social success. He died in Vienna as Napoleon invaded it.

Though to call Haydn "the father of the symphony" may be to exaggerate the case, there is no doubt that his works were of major importance in fashioning

Left William Hogarth's "A Chorus of Singers", from the series "Four Groups of Heads", portraying a rehearsal for the oratorio *Judith* by the Belgian composer William Defesch (1697–1758), who lived in London from 1731. **Below** A music party. The radiant young woman is seated at a spinet.

the new symphonic style. In instrumental music his string quartets are hardly less important. His ideas were so brilliantly imaginative and so concisely and gracefully expressed, his structures so logical and moods so varied that he increased the status of every genre in his output.

Haydn's daring modulations, impressive codas, peasant-dance movements and deeply serious adagios prompted Mozart to name him an unequalled master of form. Mozart also dedicated some of his own quartets to him. The two men learnt much from each other, without trace of rivalry.

"I declare," said Haydn to Mozart's father, "that I consider your son the greatest composer I know, either personally or by name."

Mozart and Beethoven both studied with Haydn for a while. Each admired him, though Beethoven was not happy with Haydn as a teacher.

In his symphonies, Haydn successfully resolved the difficulties of containing a unified idea within a large musical structure. His most famous are the twelve *Salomon* (or *London*) symphonies (nos. 93–104), named after the impresario who brought Haydn to England. They abound with striking effects – strong syncopation, sudden crescendos, dramatic contrasts and modulations – which mark Haydn out as the spiritual mentor of Beethoven.

Haydn's church music includes fourteen masses and two popular oratorios based on English poems. *The Creation*, based on Milton's *Paradise Lost*, was completed in 1798 after he returned to Vienna from England, where he had heard some of Handel's oratorios. *The Seasons*, Haydn's last major work, completed when he was seventy, was based on James Thomson's nature poem. Both works were well received and still enjoy great popularity.

Wolfgang Amadeus Mozart (1756–91) was born in Salzburg, the son of Leopold, a well-known composer-violinist at the Archbishop's court. Mozart started composing at the age of five, and at seven was taken on tour by his father. They visited London, Paris and Munich and young Mozart astonished all who heard him play. By the time he was thirteen, he had written music in almost every form, and

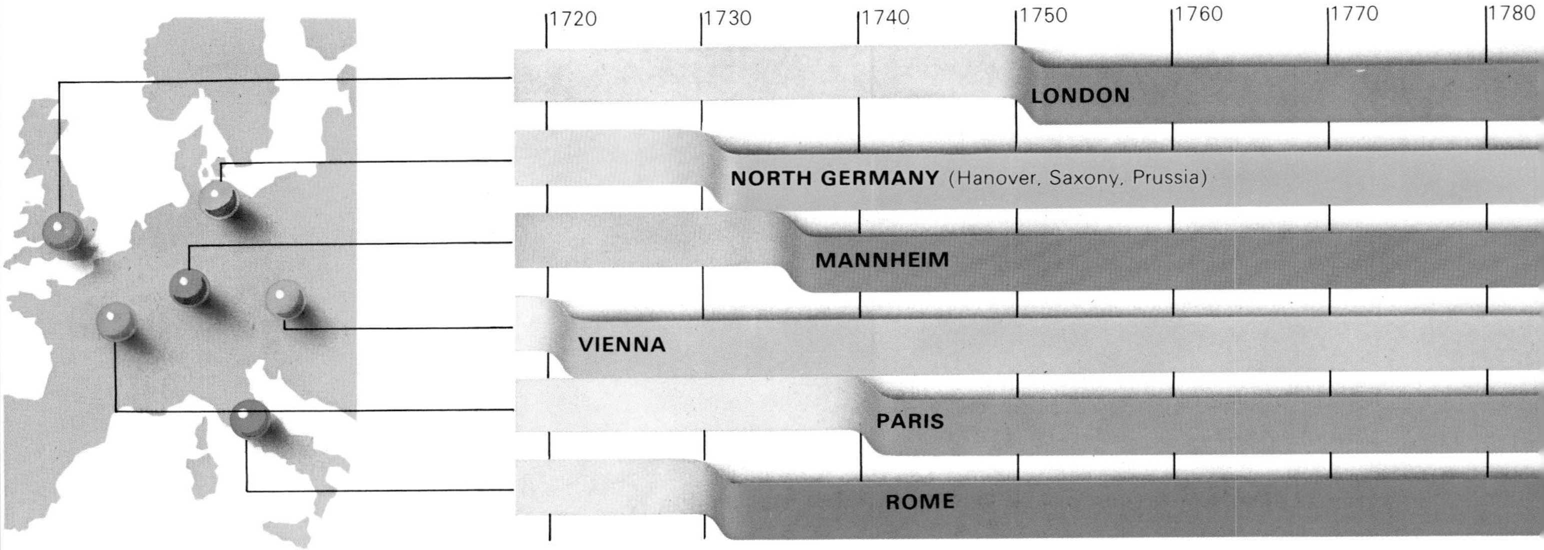

Above The major centres of musical activity during the classical period, at its height in the second half of the eighteenth century. Though the period is primarily associated with composers of German extraction, several of whom became well-known figures in London society, musical life was also flourishing in France and Italy. The first public concerts (known as *concerts spirituels* owing to the high proportion of religious music included) had begun in France in 1725 under Louis XV's patronage, and Paris audiences flocked to see the comic operas of the Belgian composer André Grétry, who settled in France in 1767. Gluck had his first operatic success in Rome in 1760. Italy produced three important composers during this period: Luigi Boccherini (1743–1805), a brilliant cellist, highly regarded for his ensemble compositions; Muzio Clementi (1752–1832), piano virtuoso, prolific sonata-writer, admired by Beethoven; and Luigi Cherubini (1760–1842), whose operas strongly influenced Beethoven. Resident in Paris from 1788, Cherubini was eventually to become director of the Conservatoire. **Right** Europe's political boundaries at the end of the eighteenth century and the main centres of German classicism. **1** Berlin: Quantz, Graun, Benda, C. P. E. Bach; **2** Hamburg: Telemann, C. P. E. Bach; **3** Mannheim: Stamitz, Richter, Vogler; **4** Vienna: Haydn, Mozart, Fux, Gluck; **5** Saxony: Veracini, Lotti, Hasse; **6** Leipzig: J. S. Bach; **7** Eisenstadt: Haydn.

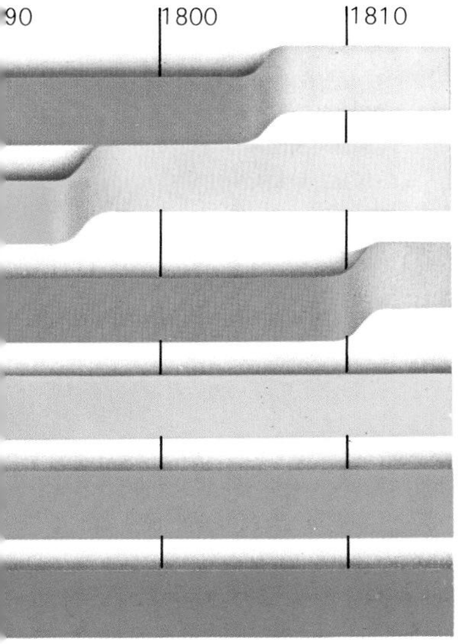

Mozart with his wife Constanza (1763–1842), a soprano singer whom he married in 1782, and his two sons Karl Thomas, later to be known as a gifted pianist, and Franz Xaver Wolfgang, who was to become a pianist, composer and orchestral conductor, based mainly in Lemberg and Vienna. The family lived in poverty even after 1787, the year of Mozart's appointment as royal chamber composer to the Emperor Joseph II of Austria.

he entered manhood with an enviable mastery of his art. He found employment at the Archbishop's court restricting so, after quarrelling with his patron, he left for Vienna. He was to live only ten more years.

In the capital he struggled to make a living, but was ill-served by the Emperor Joseph II who rewarded him too little or too late. In 1782 he married Constanza Weber, to whom he was devoted, but in doing so broke with his parents, who disapproved of the marriage. Much of his adult life was a constant struggle to secure an adequate income, and psychologically to recapture the vanished serenity of his childhood. It was not until his opera *The Marriage of Figaro* (1786) that he acquired some measure of popular success. The opera took Vienna by storm and its arias became popular dance tunes. Mozart was delighted: "They talked about nothing but *Figaro*, nothing, nothing but *Figaro*!"

Yet when, again with Da Ponte as his librettist, he produced *Don Giovanni* the following year, the public was baffled. His music had reached a degree of intensity and profundity which demanded greater attention than opera-goers were wont to give.

His final years were bleak, lacking in both musical success and financial reward. The last year of his life saw the performance of *The Magic Flute*, a fantastic opera in the *Singspiel* tradition, and *La clemenza di Tito*, an *opera seria*. After the failure of the latter, written for the coronation of the king of Bohemia, he returned to Vienna. Here, tired and in a spirit of defeat, he attempted to finish his Requiem, which he composed with feverish intensity, convinced that it would not be ready for his own funeral. He was right. He died with the work unfinished, just before his thirty-sixth birthday. He was committed to a pauper's grave, and the Requiem was completed by his pupil Franz Süssmayr.

Mozart's music perfectly reflected the European culture of his age, embodying the melodic line of the Italians, the elegance and lucidity of the French and Germanic orchestration and cohesiveness. It was music which, like Haydn's and Beethoven's, overrode national frontiers. Although his forms appear simple, his textures limpid and translucent, Mozart's music is, on examination, abundantly sophisticated.

He wrote some twenty operas, seventeen masses, twenty-seven piano concertos, numerous wind concertos, twenty-seven string quartets and forty-one symphonies. It was a prolific output, yet he had occasion to claim, "People make a mistake who think that my art comes easily to me."

Of his string quartets, the last ten (six of which are dedicated to Haydn) are masterpieces of the medium. Mozart was a remarkable pianist and though less experimental than Haydn, he did develop one form, the concerto for piano and orchestra. In his symphonies he tended towards richness of orchestration, diversity and sweetness of sonorities and great depth of emotion. He used wind instruments more effectively than Haydn, being especially fond of the tonal range and colour of the new clarinet. His last six symphonies contain profound philosophical statements.

His fine religious music includes the Mass in C minor and the Requiem in D minor, in both of which Mozart used symphonic language to convey the meaning of the liturgical text.

It was in his operas that Mozart fully exploited all sides of his complicated musical personality. He solved the problems of pitting voice against orchestra, of recitative and aria, of dramatic action and musical expression and created melodic lines which perfectly suited the natural range of the human voice.

It may seem strange that Mozart should have used the *Singspiel* tradition for two major operatic works. The *Singspiel*, a popular entertainment in late eighteenth-century Germany, was essentially a play with songs. As such, it was written in the vernacular, and to the young Mozart the very idea of opera in German was anathema. However, *The Abduction from the Seraglio* and *The Magic Flute*, both in German and both with speech instead of recitative, proved that the *Singspiel* could be an important art form. Mozart of course made the music central to the drama, unlike other creators of *Singspiele*. It is likely that his successful adaptation of the *Singspiel* format strongly influenced later composers such as Weber, Wagner and Richard Strauss.

It was, however, for his *opera buffa* that Mozart won widest acclaim. There is no doubt that in Lorenzo da Ponte, whose adaptation of Beaumarchais' play *The Marriage of Figaro* perfectly suits the fresh, witty quality of Mozart's music, he had found a librettist of genius. The two also collaborated on *Don Giovanni* and *Così fan tutte*. Both are among Mozart's most frequently staged works, though the former is a stronger dramatic vehicle.

Mozart's greatest achievement in his operas was to convey convincingly in musical terms the psychological tensions of his characters and to create, in a few bars, a mood perfectly reflecting a specific dramatic situation.

The Romantic Movement

After Haydn and Mozart had established classical form, composers inevitably began to seek ways of extending the boundaries that any developed form imposes. The romantic composers sought to express emotion through music in a more direct way than had been thought desirable before. This development in music was mirrored by similar changes in painting and literature, and was also a reflection of the upheavals taking place in European thought and politics at the end of the eighteenth and the beginning of the nineteenth centuries. The "Age of Revolutions", between 1789 and 1848, was closely identified with the active involvement of artists and intellectuals. In France, writers, painters and musicians – among them George Sand, Baudelaire, Flaubert, Hugo, Rimbaud, Delacroix and Berlioz, and the great impressionist painters of the latter half of the century – sought to shock contemporary society out of its complacency and materialism.

In the mood that pervaded Europe at this time, men found themselves in a social climate that led their nations out of the autocratic rule of the princely courts into the democratic participation of the new middle class. Everyone was imbued with the desire for participation, for liberation and for the brotherhood of man.

The creative consciousness of the romantic artist was inspired by many external forces: by the quest for national and personal liberty, by nature, poetry, the primitive, the childlike, and by oppressed peoples and their destinies. The new self-awareness was however coloured by a corresponding disillusion. Revolutionary idealism had proved abortive and equality had not banished oppression. When Napoleon, who had declared himself the enemy of oppression and had led the struggle for liberty, equality and fraternity, went on to declare himself emperor, Beethoven tore up the title-page dedication (to "General Bonaparte") of his *Eroica* symphony, and substituted the words "To the memory of a great man".

Failed idealism triggered off another strong element of romantic art: escapism. The novels of Scott and Dumas *fils*, the music of Berlioz and Mendelssohn, the paintings of Turner and Delacroix and the poetry of Tennyson, Baudelaire and Rimbaud all share a longing for the exotic, for faraway lands and for experiences outside the tedium of everyday life. The past, particularly the Dark and Middle Ages, exerted a strong attraction for romantic artists. So did the strange, the macabre and the distorted, as the writings of Dostoevsky, Poe and Baudelaire show.

During Beethoven's lifetime and after, the orchestra was enlarged to accommodate the new forms of expression. The number of instruments in the woodwind section was increased, and many technical improvements were made, especially to the key action, which improved both intonation and technique. Trombones were added to the brass section, and by Wagner's time trumpets and horns with valves were beginning to be used. The percussion section was also enlarged.

The emergence of the middle class after the French Revolution provided a large new audience for public concerts. Lengthy programmes were arranged. Two or three symphonies, movements from other works, concertos and overtures were often included in a single concert. With the rise of the large symphony orchestra, and the increasing complexity of the music, conductors became essential. This period saw the direction of the orchestra transferred from the leader to the conductor. Spohr, Weber and Mendelssohn instigated a tradition of discipline in rehearsals which made the orchestra a more competent exponent of the massive and difficult compositions then being written. Berlioz, Liszt and Wagner were all celebrated conductors in their time.

Beethoven: herald of the romantic age

The man who, more than any other, typifies the romantic movement is Ludwig van Beethoven (1770–1827). Born in Bonn of Flemish ancestry, he came to Vienna at a time when the search for liberty, equality and fraternity was at its height. Such idealism was then thought capable of achievement, for man was to bring about his own redemption by the strength of his humanity. The desire to live fully and nobly and to achieve redemption through experience is evident in the poetry and drama of Goethe and Schiller, the great German writers of the early romantic movement. To this ideal, Beethoven was irresistibly drawn. Here is a perfect example of the moment bringing forth the man. The idealism of the early romantic movement and Beethoven's musical idealism came together to produce works of such tremendous power that they seemed to embody the very spirit of the times.

Beethoven's attitude toward his patrons and his audience was never that of a servant – the sense of which role had remained with Haydn and had at times been forced upon Mozart – but that of an equal commanding a vigorous and rebellious authority. At one recital, when someone in the audience persisted in talking, Beethoven stormed out shouting, "I do not play for such pigs!" He wrote to Prince Lichnowsky, "Prince, what you are, you are by accident of birth; what I am, I am through my own efforts. There have been many princes, but there is only one Beethoven!"

The question of whether Beethoven was a classic or a romantic composer continues to be discussed. It is generally accepted that he stood with a foot in both centuries, and belongs to both. There is no doubt that many elements of Beethoven's work may be traced to the later romantics, or that Beethoven was attracted to the spiritual ideals of the romantic movement. But Beethoven was a product of the eighteenth century: his achievement lay in taking the elements of classicism and resynthesizing them – not abandoning them. The classical style was the result of bringing into balance the opposing forces of form and material; the romantic style came when the material overflowed the form. Shapes of melodies became vaguer and less defined, and harmony lost its structural foundation and took on colour and variety instead. Beethoven was drawn to these new ways, but his nature was such that he needed to mould the raw material of his composition to achieve the tension that comes from bringing strength under control. He never faltered in his belief that it was the duty of the creative artist to organize his material; his sketchbooks give ample evidence of his struggle to do this. It was in such organization that the form of his compositions lay. This discipline and strength of purpose gives his work its singular authority.

Beethoven's powerful and uncompromising personality rose from the spirit of the struggle for freedom. When he knew that he was going deaf – perhaps the most

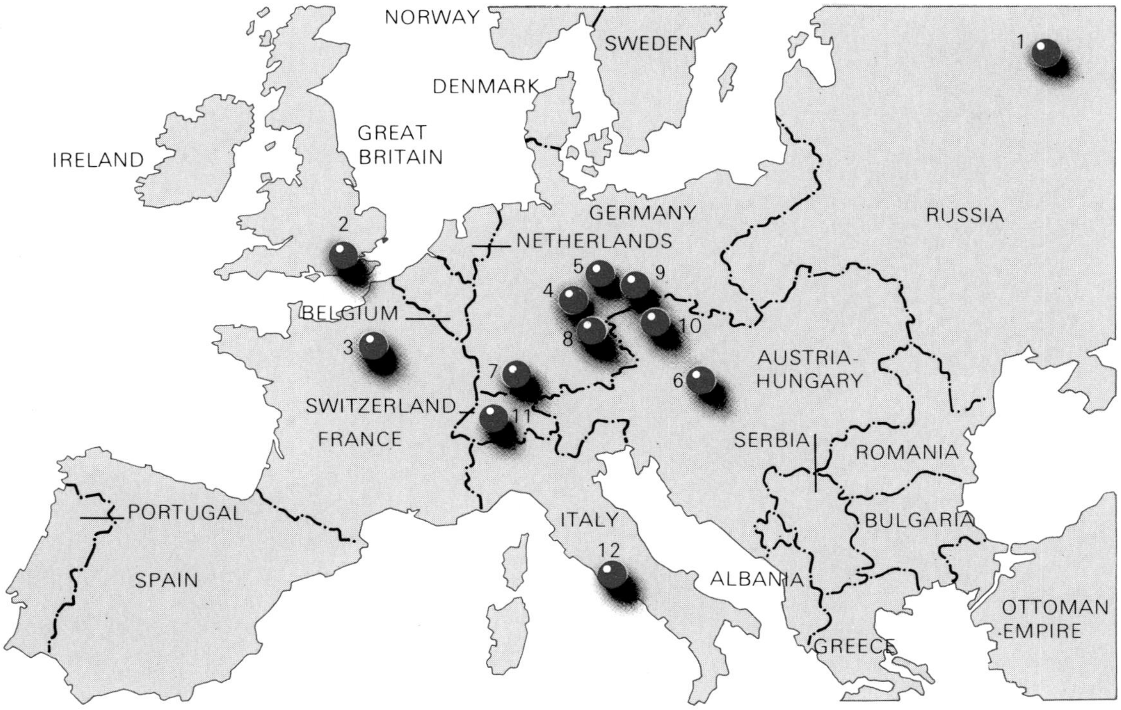

Europe's political boundaries at the end of the nineteenth century, by which time Germany had become a nation state. The main centres of musical activity for the foremost romantic composers were: **1** Moscow: Tchaikovsky; **2** London: Mendelssohn, Weber, Chopin; **3** Paris: Meyerbeer, Berlioz, Chopin, Liszt; **4** Weimar: Liszt; **5** Leipzig: Mendelssohn, Schumann; **6** Vienna: Schubert, Beethoven, Brahms; **7** Würtemberg: Weber; **8** Bayreuth; Wagner; **9** Dresden: Wagner; **10** Prague: Weber; **11** Switzerland: Wagner; **12** Rome; Liszt, Berlioz.

dreadful fate for a musician – he prayed for strength "to conquer myself".

To Beethoven the association of words and music – the great obsession of the nineteenth-century romantics – was not of much importance. He wrote one opera, *Fidelio*, which is not one of his greatest compositions. Indeed, where words are used in his other large-scale works, such as the *Choral* symphony, the music is in no way enriched by the addition. Music was the expression of Beethoven's creativity and his thoughts could not adequately be expressed in words. It is true that the *Choral* symphony was the progenitor of several other choral symphonies by composers ranging from Spohr to Mahler, but the entry of the voices in the final movement cannot be regarded as a setting of Schiller's "Ode to Joy", for the music does not arise out of the words. Only a few of Schiller's verses are used, arranged in a completely arbitrary manner; indeed, the words sung at the first baritone entry are Beethoven's own. Nothing could be further from the union of poetry and music so dear to the romantics. The architecture of the *Choral* symphony is entirely unaffected by the voices or the poem.

The central formal conception of all Beethoven's compositions is symphonic; this can be heard as much in his sonatas, chamber music and concertos as in his symphonies, since all are dominated by sonata form – the great invention of the classical age. Beethoven's personality found its most adequate expression in the dramatic contrasts of classical sonata form. Although he was capable of writing the most lyrical melodies, lyricism nevertheless took second place in his musical language. Lyricism was the quality most desired by the romantics and it was this characteristic that led to the break-up of form in the romantic symphony, to a lesser emphasis on the sonata and to the success of the smaller types of work.

Beethoven's life can be divided into three periods of composition. The first, up to about 1800, is dominated by Beethoven the virtuoso pianist – a composer who brought his own music before the public by performing it himself. This is the period that produced the first eleven piano sonatas, the six early quartets and the Septet in E-flat, the first piano concerto and the first symphony. These early works reveal a strong affinity with Haydn, particularly in the first piano sonata. This work is dedicated to Haydn and could easily be taken to be Haydn's own.

By about 1801, Beethoven had realized that he was going deaf, and from this time, the career of concert pianist changes to that of composer. The second symphony (1802) heralds this second period of composition. Nobody could mistake this work for one of Haydn's. To this second period belong the works that are best known today, and that most greatly influenced his followers. This includes the symphonies nos. 2–8, the opera *Fidelio* together with the three "Leonora" overtures, all the piano concertos, the violin concerto and all the other piano sonatas except the final four.

Far left Caricature after Grandville, 1846, of Hector Berlioz. The baton was then an innovation, becoming standard conductor's equipment only towards the end of the nineteenth century. **Left** The piano was for over a century a central element of family entertainment. A little pianistic ability was essential for all young ladies claiming to be in any way "accomplished". A great many four-handed and even six-handed works were written and arranged for amateur pianists.

In this middle period, Beethoven expanded the central (development) section of sonata form. This is where the various themes that have been introduced in the first section (exposition) are developed, expanded, taken through new keys and subjected to a variety of technical musical devices before returning to the home key for the restatement (recapitulation) which ends the movement. It was Beethoven's innovative development sections, a feature of all his works in sonata form – symphonies, chamber music, concertos and sonatas – that were to become so important to later composers who took Beethoven as their authority for departing from the classical model.

The sixth symphony (the *Pastoral*) is of historical importance for another reason. Beethoven gave each of its movements a descriptive title: "Cheerful feelings aroused on arrival in the countryside"; "By the brook"; "Peasants' dance"; "Storm"; "Shepherd's song – thanksgiving after the storm". In spite of these subtitles, the construction is entirely symphonic and is governed by musical considerations only. Had it been a programmatic work, Beethoven's primary task would have been to portray the non-musical ideas present in its conception. However, it later came to be regarded as a tone poem, or symphonic poem, and Beethoven's successors used it to justify their own departure from abstract symphonic music. As in the case of the *Choral* symphony, it was the attitude of succeeding generations that established the idea that the work was revolutionary.

The middle period was rounded off with the *Hammerklavier* sonata. It is possible to view this powerful work as a sort of symbol of Beethoven's inner struggle during these years to come to terms with the knowledge that he would soon be totally deaf. It was when this struggle was resolved that Beethoven entered his third period of composition. From this point, he began to look back to the older forms – back to Haydn and Bach. His creative energy was now occupied with the manipulation of the raw material of music in the most concise and pregnant forms. The works that display this ascetic, compressed style of expression are the last five quartets and the *Grosse Fuge*, an alternative finale to one of the quartets which proved too vast to be performed as such. The quartets depart from the usual four-movement pattern, and have other formal differences within movements, too.

To the last period also belong the last piano works – three sonatas, opp. 109, 110 and 111, and the bagatelles. The sonatas, like the quartets, do not conform to what we might expect from his earlier work. Here Beethoven moves into the realm of pure music, with no regard for the limitations of either the instrument or the performer. On paper and to the inner ear the work is totally satisfactory, and this was Beethoven's concern. In these last compositions, he finally broke out of classical form.

Weber

Carl Maria von Weber (1786–1826) could with justification be called the first purely romantic composer. He studied with Abbé Vogler and later became director of the Dresden Opera. He wrote some three hundred works in his short musical career, and his music reflected the new nationalistic German spirit; he used the *Singspiel* style for several operas and in 1810 was the first to apply the term "romantic opera" to a work – in this case to *Silvana* which, with *Der Freischütz*, based on German folk legend, was acclaimed as a patriotic composition. In the latter, Weber's use of folk melodies foreshadows the development of the *Lied*,

Left Beethoven's birthplace in Bonn, where many of the composer's personal belongings, including his ear trumpets and his piano, may be seen. **Right** "I shall hear in Heaven." Beethoven began to suffer deafness in about 1800. The condition worsened until in about 1820 he was totally deaf. The "Heiligenstädter Testament", a letter which Beethoven wrote to his brothers in 1802, describes the emotional anguish which he felt when he first realized the seriousness of the disease causing the trouble. Shown here are some of the ear-trumpets he used. **Below** Part of the manuscript of Beethoven's Sonata op.53 (*"Appassionata"*), second movement.

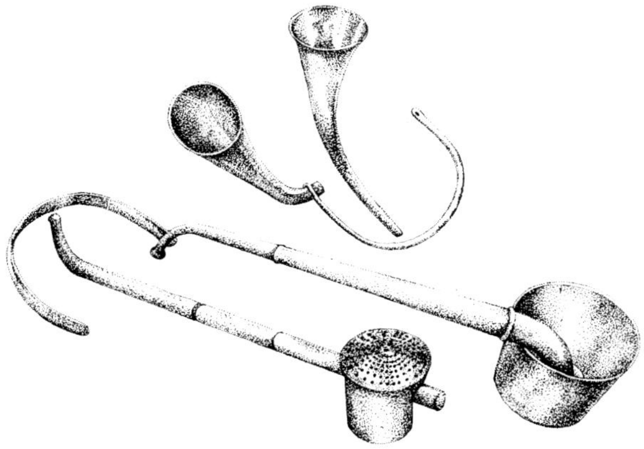

and is certainly a major factor in the work's enduring popularity.

Schubert

Beethoven's contemporary Franz Schubert (1797–1828) built on classical form in quite a different way. His great gift was that of melody. He could produce a well-turned phrase quite effortlessly. This gift is most apparent in his many small-scale works. In his songs, piano music and chamber music he excels, his lyrical gift being especially suited to the miniature forms.

He was not so happy with large-scale works. His operas are largely forgotten, and it is only the last two symphonies, the *Unfinished* (B minor) and the *Great* C *major*, that successfully use the form. His earlier symphonies were comparatively modest works in the manner of Mozart.

His most successful unified works are the song-cycles *Die Schöne Müllerin* (1823) and *Die Winterreise* (1827), the quartets and the quintets. Schubert's chamber works were the gateway to new forms, for in them the melody assumed such great importance that the old formal key relationships, the basis of classical style, had to take second place to lyricism.

Chopin, Schumann, Mendelssohn and Brahms

After Beethoven, there was a move away from the larger forms of composition. The instrument that was perhaps most influential in bringing about this change was the piano. From the time of Beethoven, the piano was steadily being developed and improved. The most significant change was probably the strengthening of the frame by means of metal bars and plates, a development which by the 1850s had resulted in the metal frame. The strength of the new frame allowed for greater stress, therefore more strings could be added and the compass of the piano could be increased.

To take full advantage of this new capability, composers tended to abandon the piano sonata in favour of what can only be called the "piece". Among the leading keyboard composer-performers of the century was Fryderyk (or Frédéric) Chopin (1810–49), born in Warsaw of Polish-French parentage. His song-like piano pieces had strong melodies of great beauty supported by accompaniments of remarkable harmonic subtlety.

Chopin's virtuosity as a performer, and as a writer for performers of similar ability, was remarkable. His touch, tone and use of *rubato* were probably unrivalled in his day. The irridescent colour and long, sustained *legato* lines of Chopin's music marked a new development in keyboard composition which was to influence piano-writing well into the twentieth century. He combined a Slavic melancholy with an essentially French elegance. His style was influenced by the Irishman John Field (1782–1837), inventor of the nocturne, and by Johann Nepomuk Hummel (1778–1837), whose use of decorative filigree passages became in Chopin more inherently functional. Chopin's nocturnes, poetic mood-pictures, are tender and melancholy. His twenty-four preludes composed from 1826 to 1839 are concise lyrical statements which were much admired by Schumann. The *études* (studies) are powerful concert works, not just vehicles for the development of technique. The ballades are large-scale pieces, dramatic and strongly Polish in inspiration. They reveal a range of melodic, rhythmic, harmonic and dynamic invention that makes them one of the high points of Chopin's creative achievement. The mazurkas, and the grander militaristic polonaises, are vigorous reflections of dances traditionally performed by Polish nobility.

Robert Schumann (1810–56) was born in Zwickau, Saxony, into a literary family. While a law student, his absorption with music led him to take lessons with Friedrich Wieck, a famous teacher and the father of Clara, the woman Schumann eventually married. Concurrent with his musical interests, he founded a journal, the *New Magazine for Music* (*Neue Zeitschrift für Musik*), which became very influential. In this magazine, he criticized middle-class taste, which tended to be conservative, and tried to popularize the new romanticism. Whilst giving due credit to the musical traditions of the past, he inveighed against the philistinism of those who refused to consider new ideas just because they were new. As a music critic, he was astute and far-sighted, introducing Chopin to German audiences and encouraging the young Brahms, whom he called "the eaglet descended from Hamburg". Towards the end of his life, he suffered from psychological disorder. He ended his days in an asylum in Bonn.

Schumann turned to composition as a young man, having failed as a concert pianist after damaging his left hand whilst developing a technique for stretching the hand to reach larger intervals. It is in his piano music that Schumann's romantic genius is most strikingly apparent. His themes tend to be short and contrasting in mood. For many works, he abandoned classical forms and composed in his own fragmented but concise style. Between 1828 and 1839, in *Papillons*, *Carnaval* and the *Davidsbündlertänze*, a number of characters appear under fictional names. The most prominent of these are Eusebio and Florestan, who represent the two sides of his own nature, and they also appear in his music magazine. Other characters were Clara and Mendelssohn (under the name Dr Meritus) and in *Carnaval* these are joined by Chopin, Paganini and Schumann's musical ancestors Bach, Beethoven and Weber. Together they formed the "League of David" (*Davidsbünd*) who were to march forth against the Philistines – those composers who wrote empty virtuoso pieces or, as Schumann liked to put it, "music by the yard".

The later piano pieces such as *Fantasiestücke* and *Scenes from Childhood* are character studies and atmospheric portraits. By 1840, Schumann had again turned to song-writing (he had written some songs between 1827 and 1828) but it was his engagement to Clara that inspired him to a great new lyrical outpouring, and in 1840 he composed 140 songs, over half of his total output. He also wrote four major song-cycles – *Liederkreis* of 1839 and 1840, *Frauenliebe und Leben* and *Dichterliebe*.

Schubert's amusing violin "piece" in which cats play havoc on every stave.

His compositions also include four symphonies which, provided they are not measured by the yardstick of classical form but judged for what they set out to be, are most successful. Schumann suffers from being judged as a classicist, when all the evidence shows that he was not.

Born into a wealthy Christian-Jewish family, Felix Mendelssohn (1809–47), like Schumann, is often criticized for what he was not rather than praised for what he was. Living when he did, he might be expected to have written in the same style as Schumann, Chopin and the other romantics, but Mendelssohn required even his most lyrical music to be subject to stricter rules of form than the romantics felt necessary. His *Songs without Words* often suffer from an over-emotional interpretation, stemming from the belief that he was using a romantic idiom, and probably their popularity has led to his six preludes and fugues for piano being entirely overlooked. The preludes of this set are treated in the form of *études*, while the fugues bring the contrapuntal devices of Bach's music into the middle of the romantic era. It is thanks to Mendelssohn that the revival of interest in Bach's music took place in the nineteenth century, and he did a great deal towards getting Bach's Passions performed again.

Mendelssohn himself wrote two oratorios, *Elijah* and *St Paul*, both based on biblical texts. Here again one cannot but think that Bach was his model.

In his *Italian* and *Scotch* symphonies (1837 and 1842 respectively), written after visits to the countries in question, Mendelssohn moved towards programme music. This tendency is even more evident in his *Hebrides* overture. Perhaps his greatest innovation was his use of the orchestral woodwind instruments, as in the incidental music to *A Midsummer Night's Dream*: in the scherzo, the woodwind instruments are made to dance as never before.

Johannes Brahms (1833–97) was born in Hamburg, the son of a double-bass player. He studied first with his father, then with Marxsen. In 1853 he accompanied the violinist Reményi on a concert tour.

Brahms' introduction to Joachim, the celebrated violinist of whom he became a life-long friend, occurred at Göttingen after a performance of Beethoven's *Kreutzer* sonata with Reményi. Brahms, finding the piano pitched a semitone too low, transposed the entire piece flawlessly throughout, and so excited the admiration of Joachim that he introduced himself to the young composer. It was Joachim who brought Brahms into the circle of Liszt and Schumann. Brahms became Schumann's protégé and friend, and was described by him as "the eaglet descended from Hamburg". As a composer, he was of a very different temperament, being diffident and conservative. In his symphonies, he uses a smaller orchestra than his contemporaries, preferring a size more akin to that of Beethoven's time.

Brahms's themes are emotionally powerful, but the emotion is always contained within a disciplined musical structure. His early piano works are orchestral in texture, avoiding ornamentation and obviously virtuoso elements. Brahms tends to favour strong rhythms, sometimes strikingly syncopated, and solid chordal textures. The first piano works are his three sonatas. After this, he turned his attention to smaller forms – with the exception of his six sets of variations. In his chamber works he preserved classical form. The works are untypical of the romantic period in that they avoid bravura, but they are richly inventive, often meditative in mood, and sometimes – as in the sonata for cello and piano, the two sonatas for clarinet and piano and the celebrated clarinet quintet – tinged with sublime melancholy.

The four symphonies were all written after Brahms was forty, the first in the years 1855–76, the second in 1877, the third in 1883 and the fourth in 1895. Though written mainly on traditional lines, they are strongly individual and full of melodic invention, earning Brahms the reputation of the greatest symphonist after Beethoven. The two piano concertos, violin concerto and double concerto for violin and cello are all masterpieces which stress the serious symphonic potential of the genre rather than its role as a vehicle for virtuosity.

Brahms wrote much fine music for voice. His two song-cycles *Romanzen aus Magelone* (1862) and *Vier ernste Gesänge* ("Four Serious Songs", 1896), embody a wealth of rhythmic and melodic invention. The *German Requiem* (1857–68) is based on texts from the Lutheran Bible. The music, stylistically free, is dominated by the choir, while the soprano and baritone soloists are used sparingly.

Berlioz, Liszt and programme music

In terms of symphonic music, one might be forgiven for thinking that Berlioz was the only French romantic composer of the early nineteenth century, later followed by César Franck, but this is not quite true. Most of the French composers were writing opera, which had become a specialized occupation.

Hector Berlioz (1803–69) was perhaps the first who tried to express through music the inner feelings of the artist, and more especially the inner suffering. In his *Symphonie fantastique*, Berlioz prepared a set of programme notes so that the audience should be able to follow what the music was intended to convey. The work, subtitled "Episodes in the Life of an Artist", describes how a young musician who has taken opium (not enough to kill him) sees his beloved continually coming to haunt him. The beloved is represented in the music by a "motto theme" (*idée fixe*) that recurs in different situations.

This use of a motto theme to identify certain situations and feelings was Berlioz's innovation in symphonic writing. He had a keen literary taste, being a journalist and music critic as well as a composer, and much of his music has a literary framework. His overtures are really tone poems, based on currently popular literature – works by Shakespeare, Goethe, Scott and Byron. Byron's "Childe Harold" was the inspiration for *Harold in Italy*, which Berlioz composed for Paganini. In this work Berlioz combined the form of the concerto with powerful symphonic writing.

Mendelssohn at work, by Aubrey Beardsley. Mendelssohn enjoyed one of the most successful – and remunerative – careers of any composer, renowned in his lifetime not only for his compositions but for his performances as a concert pianist and his work as a conductor. His status fell after his death, some critics being of the opinion that his works lacked profundity, but today he is recognized as one of the major figures of romantic composition.

He wrote three religious works: the *Grande Messe des morts* (1837), a requiem mass scored for military bands as well as orchestra, chorus and soloists; a *Te Deum* for organ, orchestra, choruses and soloists; and, by contrast, *L'Enfance du Christ*, a tender and lyrical oratorio. Other large-scale works include his two operas *Les Troyens* and *Béatrice et Bénédict*, which are so lengthy and so difficult to stage that they are not often performed.

In his *Treatise on Orchestration* of 1844, Berlioz provided a valuable survey of orchestral and symphonic techniques of the time. He increased the size of the orchestra to create stupendous volumes of sound and stirring instrumental contrasts.

Ferencz (or Franz) Liszt (1811–86) was born in Hungary. As a young man, his talent earned him a bursary to study music in Paris, where he met the great figures of his day – George Sand, Delacroix, Victor Hugo and Berlioz. Liszt's wide reading and literary interests were to inspire many compositions. As a keyboard virtuoso, he was unrivalled. He had learnt from Paganini what effect a little showmanship could have, but he was nevertheless a serious and innovative composer. He was also an advocate of the works of Schumann, Berlioz and Wagner. Some of these he conducted in the 1850s at Weimar, where he also composed his *Dante* and *Faust* symphonies.

As a keyboard composer, Liszt explored the full range of the instrument, reaching new heights of virtuosity, and inventing new kinds of expression. The one-movement Sonata in B minor of 1853, a thirty-minute work built on four themes, combines in its structure fugue, recitative, fantasia and variation. It occupies a unique place in the keyboard repertoire. He also wrote two piano concertos, the *Hungarian Rhapsodies*, the four *Mephisto* waltzes and *Années de pèlerinage*.

Of his symphonic works, the two symphonies were eclipsed by the thirteen symphonic poems, which carry individual descriptive titles. Written between 1840 and 1860, they gave a new name and a new form to orchestral music. The *symphonic poem* was important for two reasons. First, it developed the idea of running together all the movements of a work in what was now to be called *cyclic form*. Secondly, it exhibits Liszt's idea of the "transformation of themes" technique, in which themes are subjected to a number of changes – in rhythm, harmony, tempo and dynamics – while giving to the whole work a unity which had previously been provided by sonata form. It was this second idea which led naturally and inevitably to the *Leitmotiv* of Wagner. The definition of programme music also comes from Liszt. He defined the "programme" in this application as "any preface in intelligible language added to a piece of instrumental music, by which the composer intends to guard the listener against a wrong poetical interpretation, and to direct his attention to the poetical idea of the whole or to a particular part of it".

Tchaikovsky and the late-romantics

Romanticism was essentially a German movement, but its influence spread throughout the whole of Europe. In different ways, it influenced the various major operatic composers of the nineteenth century and afterwards, notably Verdi and Wagner. At the same time, nationalist feeling was beginning to be seen and many composers were consciously trying to develop music which

was typical of their own country. Nowhere is this more apparent than in Russia. The last Russian to write in the German tradition was Tchaikovsky, who was nevertheless a contemporary of the first Russian nationalist composers.

Peter Ilyich Tchaikovsky (1840–93) was born in Votkinsk. He abandoned a legal career to become a student at the St Petersburg Conservatory, and was eventually made a professor at the Moscow Conservatory. Profoundly Russian by temperament, he generally preferred classical forms and was influenced more by Western music than by the music of Russia. It is probably because of this that his first three operas, *Voyevoda*, *Oprichnik* and *Vakula the Smith*, were failures. Had it not been for Hans von Bülow, his first piano concerto, in B-flat minor, might have suffered the same fate. Anton Rubinstein had condemned it as unplayable, but after Bülow's success in performing the work he agreed to play it.

Tchaikovsky wrote six symphonies. Using folk-song-like material, he found it difficult to develop themes as Brahms did, and his larger symphonic movements therefore tend to be sectional. Instead, like Berlioz and Liszt, he would often use a motto theme which suggests a programme, although not as detailed a programme as those of Berlioz. His obsession with the ravages of fate and with death infects his last three symphonies, most particularly the sixth, or *Pathétique*. This work ends with a tragic slow movement in place of the usually brilliant finale. In

Liszt at the keyboard. His eight arms suggest his astonishing technical ability and the halo his religious affiliations – in the 1860s he took minor orders in the Franciscans and became known as the Abbé Liszt.

Left A Schubert evening at Josef von Spaun's, with the composer seated at the piano. The host, von Spaun, was one of Schubert's closest friends. Oil sketch by Moritz von Schwind. **Right** Brahms conducting in the latter part of his life, from pencil sketches by Willy von Beckerath.

contrast with this, his ballet scores *Swan Lake*, *Sleeping Beauty* and *The Nutcracker* are lively, vivid and full of charm. Tchaikovsky's most frequently performed operas are *Eugene Onegin* and *The Queen of Spades*.

In Germany, the symphonic tradition was being continued in the works of Bruckner and Mahler, and later in the tone poems of Richard Strauss.

Anton Bruckner (1824–96) is known chiefly for his eleven symphonies (nos. 1–9 and two unnumbered ones). He stands in the line of development that runs from Beethoven's *Choral* symphony, and was an admirer of Wagner's writing, but he had little interest in the works of Berlioz, Schumann or Liszt. He was trained as a church organist, and wrote a considerable amount of church music, including masses. It is perhaps because of this training that he tends to use the departments of the orchestra as an organist would use the departments of the organ – changing from woodwind tone to string tone in his symphonies as an organist might change from one manual to another. Although Bruckner is an interesting and typical late-romantic composer, his influence on those that followed was slight. His sole successor was Mahler, but despite the opulent orchestration and large-scale forms favoured by both, the two have little in common.

Gustav Mahler (1860–1911) composed in two genres only – song and symphony. His efforts to create symphonic song, a kind of concerto for voice and orchestra, came to fruition in *Das Lied von der Erde* ("Song of the Earth") the most massive of song-cycles. The chief precursors of his symphonic works were Beethoven's *Eroica* and *Choral* symphonies and the symphonies of Berlioz and Liszt. Not surprisingly, he strove to expand the symphonic form. To do this he used massive orchestral forces, including quadruple woodwind (that is, four of each of the woodwind instruments), eight horns and a large chorus of brass and percussion. His works are also massive in terms of the time needed to perform them: the eighth symphony (*Symphony of a Thousand*), for example, has been described as "an evening's worth of oratorio".

In the romantic movement, we can observe two trends, persisting side by side. One is the expansion of form, seen in the huge symphonies of Bruckner and Mahler, and the other is the striving towards a more concise form of expression. This is most evident in some of the piano pieces – particularly in the later piano works of Brahms. An increased interest in orchestral colour, and in textures of sound for their own sake, arose from the romantic preference for lyrical melodies, which tended to break down the old sonata-like structures. This new interest was to be fully exploited later in the work of the French "impressionist" composers. Impressionism lies at the end of a journey which began with the union of poetry and music (exemplified in the *Lied*), passed through the union of literature and music (exemplified in the symphonic poem) and culminated in the union of poetry, painting and music. This final fusion exploits to the full the romantic ideals of unity and brotherhood.

Nationalism

The expression of love and pride in one's country and its customs and character became a marked feature of the romantic era. The development of patriotic ideals in music resulted in the emergence of several nationalist schools of music from the mid-1800s until about the turn of the century. Of course, each country already had its own tradition of music and made music in its own particular way. In many cases, this tradition was so strong that the course of music continued unaffected by nationalist aspirations. Such was the case in Germany and Italy, and in non-European countries where music was highly ethnic in character.

But away from the centre of Europe and in America, nationalism took hold. Composers began to use elements of the ethnic music of their countries, usually folk tunes and dance rhythms, as a basis for their works. Chopin, though he spent little time in his native Poland, was one of the first composers to use dance forms peculiar to his birthplace, such as the mazurka and polonaise. Liszt wrote a number of rhapsodies based on Hungarian gypsy music. Many nationalist composers made important studies of the folk music of their homelands. Some incorporated these ethnic elements into works in classical forms, such as symphonies and concertos, whereas others produced programme music based on legends or historical events.

The production of nationalist music was fired not only by the composers' patriotic ideals. The use of ethnic elements could give an exotic flavour to their music and also enable them to react positively against the academic musical education that they had received, often in Germany.

Russia

The nationalist movement began in Russia with the work of Mikhail Glinka (1804–57). After studying opera in Italy and Germany in the 1830s, he returned home and wrote the operas *A Life for the Tsar* or *Ivan Sussanin* and *Russlan and Ludmilla*. With *Kamarinskaya*, a fantasia for orchestra based on Russian folk-song, Glinka extended nationalism to instrumental music. These works so successfully utilized Russian folk elements that Glinka founded a new school of Russian music and he is now regarded as the father of Russian music.

The Russian school brought to fruition the nationalist ideal in music. Its principal members were a group of composers (Balakirev, Borodin, Rimsky-Korsakov, Mussorgsky and Cui) known as "The Five" or "The Mighty Handful", such was their regard in Russia. The colour and vitality gained by developing its Russian qualities have given their music wide appeal far from home.

Mily Balakirev (1837–1910) was the leading activist of the group. The first composer to write nationalist music in symphonic form, one of his best-known works is the piano composition *Islamey*, which uses themes from Asiatic Russia.

Alexander Borodin (1833–87), a professor of chemistry, had a superb gift for melody and exciting rhythms. His major compositions include the unfinished opera *Prince Igor*, which contains the well-known "Polovtsian Dances", and the symphonic poem *In the Steppes of Central Asia*.

The rich and colourful music of Nikolai Rimsky-Korsakov (1844–1908) is exemplified by *Scheherezade* and the *Spanish Caprice*, which is based on Spanish themes, and by his lesser-known full-length operas based on Russian fairy tales, such as *The Golden Cockerel* and *The Snow-maiden*. Modest Mussorgsky (1839–81) reflected Russian speech inflections in a rugged style well illustrated in the opera *Boris Godunov*. Although César Cui (1853–1918) was the chief champion and propagandist for The Five, his own works are not strongly Russian in character and are of little interest.

The music of Peter Tchaikovsky (1840–93) is often Russian in flavour but does not have the patriotic overtones of The Five. It is regarded as essentially romantic rather than nationalist.

Other Russian composers continued to write nationalist-inspired music into the 1900s. The early work of Igor Stravinsky (1882–1971) contains elements of folk music – Rimsky-Korsakov was his teacher – often used as motifs for the construction of the music. Aram Khatchaturian (1903–), continuing in the Russian school, has used the folk music of his native Armenia. His works include a piano concerto in which instruments imitate Armenian folk instruments, and the ballets *Spartacus* and *Gayaneh*, which includes the famous "Sabre Dance".

Eastern Europe

As nationalism emerged in Russia, parallel movements were developing elsewhere in Europe, notably in Bohemia (now part of Czechoslovakia). Following the unsuccessful Czech revolt in 1848, Bedřich Smetana (1824–84), one of the participants, began in a ferment of patriotism to develop a Czech national style of concert music. He produced a peasant comedy opera *The Bartered Bride*, historical operas

(often pointing contemporary analogies) such as *Dalibor* and *Libussa*, and the cycle of six symphonic poems *Má Vlast* (*My Homeland*).

Smetana's compatriot, Antonín Dvořák (1841–1904), was the son of a village butcher. He came under the influence of Smetana and the first works he composed in the Czech nationalist style included two sets of *Slavonic Dances* (written for piano duet and later orchestrated). Dvořák also wrote a series of overtures and symphonic poems based on Czech legends and ten Czech operas. His abstract works, including the symphonies and chamber music, reflect the invigorating rhythms and melodies of Czech folk music. Nevertheless, they also reflect Dvořák's admiration for Brahms and, of all the nationalist writers of symphonies, his are the best constructed. Towards the end of his life, Dvořák toured widely. In New York he wrote his ninth (sometimes numbered fifth) symphony, *From the New World*, erroneously supposed to be based on American Indian melodies. In fact, its themes are Dvořák's own, though they reflect his interest in the pentatonic scales of folk music.

Leoš Janáček (1854–1928) had a strong interest in Moravian folk-song and speech patterns (Moravia is also now part of Czechoslovakia). His works are astonishing for their economy of expression and vigorously independent style, permeated with the subtle inflections of Moravian

Folk music inspired a great deal of "nationalist" music. Here, a group of Russian folk-musicians play instruments of art music in folk manner: the violins are not held under the chin, the cellos have no spikes and therefore cannot rest on the floor, and the cellists' bow-grips are unusual.

folk-song. They include the *Sinfonietta*, the orchestral rhapsody *Taras Bulba*, and the *Glagolitic Mass* (using an ancient Slav form of the text of the mass).

Hungary was the birthplace of two important nationalist composers, Béla Bartók (1881–1945) and Zoltán Kodály (1882–1967). Both men spent much time collecting folk-songs in the Balkans and subsequently used it in their work. Kodály's music is lyrical and often sensuous, well in the nationalist tradition that had grown up around him. His works include *Psalmus Hungaricus*, a choral work based on a Hungarian translation of a psalm with nationalist associations, and an opera about a folk hero, *Háry János*, which contains folk tunes.

Bartók's music, while developing from nationalist convictions, is very original. Bartók was very concerned with the structure of his music, and often used folk-music elements as motifs or note cells that functioned rather as the bricks in the construction of a building. The resulting music had little regard for conventional harmony or melody and is formally complex – often built in symmetrical patterns – but also, because of its ethnic origins, full of life and character. The use of complex rhythms, which are characteristic of Balkan folk music, often produces immense vitality in Bartók's work. In his best-known piece, *Concerto for Orchestra*, Bartók's qualities are readily accessible. Other great works of his include the six string quartets, *Music for Strings, Percussion and Celesta* and the opera *The Miraculous Mandarin*.

Northern Europe

While dominated by the German tradition, Scandinavia nevertheless gave rise to two great nationalist composers – Edvard Grieg (1843–1907) in Norway and Jean Sibelius (1865–1957) in Finland.

Grieg wrote relatively few large-scale works, but in his transcriptions of folk-song and dance he managed to create intimate pictures of Norwegian life. His style varies from that of the romantic Piano Concerto in A minor and the popular *Peer Gynt* suites to that of his late *Norwegian Peasant Dances* for piano, an economical and harmonically uncompromising work.

Sibelius developed a personal style by writing music based on ancient Finnish legends – allegorical protests against the Russian domination of Finland. Though nationalist in conviction, his works do not always use folk music. They include *Karelia* and *Finlandia*.

Britain

Britain was largely unaffected by the rise of nationalism during the 1800s. However, at the turn of the century, Edward Elgar (1857–1934) produced the *Enigma Variations* and, with its strong lyricism, established a national school of British music. Elgar in fact made little use of British folk-song, but his music is imbued with its melodic flow. Ralph Vaughan Williams (1872–1958) collected British folk music and was also interested in early English music. These influences may be heard in his *Fantasia on a Theme of Tallis*. The music of the British school is popular, at least in Britain, for its pastoral quality, which may also be heard in the music of Gustav Holst (1874–1934) and Frederick Delius (1862–1934).

Spain and France

The ethnic music of Spain, with its Eastern influences, is particularly individual. It is not surprising that it shaped Spanish composers, even though Spain was separated from the main nationalist movements. The principal Spanish composers are Isaac Albéniz (1860–1909), whose set of piano pieces *Iberia* is very Spanish in idiom, and Manuel de Falla (1876–1946). The character of his well-known piano work *Nights in the Gardens of Spain* is evident from its title.

France had a strong musical tradition and its own ethnic music did not succeed in influencing its composers. They found Spanish music much more attractive, and so the Spanish nationalists include some eminent French composers – notably Debussy with his own *Iberia* and Ravel with *Rapsodie espagnole*.

America

In America, nationalism in music came later than in Europe, but there was a wealth of ethnic material to be explored: the folk music developed by white settlers, Latin-American dance rhythms, blues and jazz originated by the black people, and indigenous Indian music. Charles Ives (1874–1954), who is often considered America's greatest composer, made use of folk elements in some of his music but he was so completely individual in style that he could not be said to have founded a nationalist school. An American counterpart of European nationalism is to be found in the work of Aaron Copland (1900–). His ballet *Rodeo* includes traditional American songs and dances, and *El Salón México* utilizes Latin-American music. However, the most important Latin-American composer is the Brazilian composer Heitor Villa-Lobos (1887–1959). In his *Bachianas brasileiras*, he evokes the spirit of Bach in a Brazilian context.

The significance of nationalism

As a reaction to academic music, the spirit of life and vitality that the use of ethnic qualities can bring to concert music is very refreshing. In the best pieces, these may be allied to the formal qualities of composed music to create a new and valid form of music. However, not all nationalists succeed in transferring ethnic qualities to their music, nor are they always the best composers, and the result may seem synthetic and second-hand compared to the best ethnic and composed music. In addition, approaching ethnic music too closely may bring dangers. Its subtle inflections – the often haunting slides of pitch and infectious rhythmic spring, for example – are usually beyond the experience and grasp of concerto performers and they may be unable to approach the true heart of the music.

The Twentieth Century

By the end of the 1800s, concert music was showing signs of strain. The intense expression of romantic music, especially in the work of Wagner and Liszt, had been achieved by increasing chromaticism – using intervals outside the usual diatonic scale to create greater harmonic flexibility. This process had been set in motion by Bach some two centuries before and involves increasing departure from a home key. It could go no further without destroying the tonal system (the system of conventional major and minor chords) and replacing it with new systems of harmony.

Wagner's influence extended well beyond Germany, but the problems that his music posed were grappled with in different countries in different ways. They did not of course extend to all music. Nationalist trends continued well into the twentieth century and are still with us. Opera continued in its established format too, especially with Puccini in Italy, but both were sooner or later to be faced with the need to develop and progress. Outside Europe, countries continued their ethnic traditions unaware of the torments facing many European composers. In Europe and America, ethnic music declined as popular music, aided by technology, began its inexorable rise to public favour. As composers coped with the problems of progress, so their audiences began to desert them. To a great extent, they have not returned, the public preferring traditional and popular music. This does not invalidate the concert music of the twentieth century. In fact, its diverse strands help to make our epoch perhaps the most exciting in the history of music and, because a common direction has by no means been found, that excitement is still current.

A new view of harmony

In Germany, opera rather than instrumental music bore the brunt of the onslaught on harmony. Richard Strauss (1864–1949; no relation, musically or otherwise, to the Strauss family of Vienna) continued along the path of Wagner's operas, though not at such length. In *Salome* (1905) and *Elektra* (1909), the music surges and the vocal line is impassioned, constantly stretching harmony to the point of dissonance or discord. This is no mere whim on the composer's part; such means were necessary to express adequately the torments of his tragic heroines. But after these operas, Strauss felt that he could not progress further on this course and stepped back, as many other twentieth-century composers were to do. His next work, the opera *Der Rosenkavalier* (1911), is altogether calmer and more relaxed, as was much of his subsequent music, remaining late-romantic in its harmonic schemes. The complex textures of Schoenberg's *Verklärte Nacht* (1899) for strings strained tonality to its limits. By 1909, in *Erwartung*, Schoenberg had left tonality behind him.

At the same time, progress was being made in Russia, principally with the work of Stravinsky, who is discussed later, and Alexander Scriabin (1872–1915). The latter was something of a mystic. In 1911 he produced the symphonic poem *Prometheus*, which is based on his "Mystic Chord" made up of the notes C, F♯, B♭, E, A, D. This chord has a mysterious sound that permeates the work. In addition, Scriabin wished the work to be performed with a display of coloured lights related to the music – foreshadowing today's rock concerts, perhaps – and, like the extended harmony, similarly intensifying the effect of the music.

In France came a reaction to this extreme romanticism. French composers found a solution to the problem of extending harmony that was in keeping with the delicate and restrained nature of French art. Much French music had retained the use of modes – scales that go back to medieval church music and beyond to ancient Greece. Modal music, rather static in quality, offered an alternative way forward to the increasing restlessness of chromaticism. It was first heard in the music of Erik Satie (1866–1925), especially in his piano pieces *Gymnopédies*.

Claude Debussy (1862–1918) went further and created a music in which comparatively simple chords were placed together in unusual ways. He also often used the whole-tone scale, which expanded the possibilities of tonal composition. These techniques were used to paint sound pictures such as *Prélude à l'après-midi d'un faune* ("Afternoon of a Faun", 1894) and *La Mer* ("The Sea", 1905), his best-known orchestral pieces. This music is called *impressionistic*, from the way its use of sound parallels the use of colour in impressionist painting. The music of Maurice Ravel (1875–1937) was often impressionistic, but his music made no use of the whole-tone scale, though it was often modal. A master of orchestral writing, Ravel also incorporated exotic elements in his music, spicing it with flavours of Spanish, Eastern and American music. A concern with tone colour and the use of "foreign" devices are both features of modern music.

The renaissance of rhythm

Any audience of this century listening to the concert music of the previous two centuries may well have believed that it was hearing the most complete of all music to be produced by mankind. But in one important respect, concert music until 1900 was deficient. This was in the use of rhythm. The music was invariably composed in simple metres containing a basic two, three or four beats to the bar, and the rhythms imposed on this basic structure were, like the metres themselves, simple and regular.

The reason for this was not a lack of rhythmic feeling in the composers, for one can find instances where composers sometimes managed to override simple and regular metres with complex rhythmic patterns. It was the necessity for simple and regular harmonic movement of cadences that shackled rhythm in simple set patterns. But by the beginning of this century, harmony was becoming either unpredictable or static – either way, rhythm could be freed from its previous constraints.

In 1893, Tchaikovsky wrote a whole movement of his last symphony in a five-beat metre; Ravel did likewise with the final section of his ballet *Daphnis and Chloe* in 1912. Such a metre is familiar in the folk music of Eastern Europe, but it was difficult at the time for concert audiences to follow; even Ravel's dancers had to chant the name of their impresario – *Ser-ge Dia-ghi-lev* – over and over again to themselves to keep time! But more was to come. Béla Bartók (1881–1945) in Hungary and Igor Stravinsky (1882–1971) in Russia were independently stirred by the complex rhythms of their folk music. They not only employed unusual metres, but placed bars of different metres next to one another and imposed complex rhythms across bars so that accents fell in unpredictable places. The effect, once mastered, is one of great vitality and energy, making much earlier music sound leaden by comparison. It can

Picasso's "Violin and Grapes". Just as artists in the late nineteenth and early twentieth centuries were finding new visual means of expression, composers such as Schoenberg, Richard Strauss, Bartók and Stravinsky were trying various new approaches to the presentation of musical sound. As in the field of fine art, the changes followed quickly upon each other, and the audiences lost in this turbulent period have never been fully recovered.

be heard throughout both composers' musical output, beginning with Bartók's early piano works – even those for children – and in two ballets that Stravinsky composed for Diaghilev: *Petrushka* (1911) and *The Rite of Spring* (1913).

Melody, usually being related to both harmonic and rhythmic movement, invariably had to change as well. Unused intervals could be included in a theme as well as skips in the rhythm. Freed of simple cadences, it could wander in any direction it liked. The result could be disconcerting or, to the ear that delights in surprise, as beautiful as any elegant classical theme or grand romantic tune.

Simultaneous events

New freedoms in harmony and rhythm enabled composers to put musical events together in unusual combinations, and several soon tried to get two or more harmonies or rhythms going at the same time. This development was mirrored in painting, where artists combined different views of the same object. In harmony, new sounds were achieved by having separate parts of the music sounding in different keys. For example, Bartók wrote piano pieces in which the hands play in different keys. The individual sound of Stravinsky's *Petrushka* is largely due to a harmony made by simultaneously sounding chords of C major and F-sharp major. This choice was not arbitrary; the two keys, totally unrelated, are combined to represent the half-human and half-puppet nature of Petrushka.

This combining of different keys is called *polytonality*. Composers also sought to combine rhythms, producing *polyrhythms*. These rhythms, like the separate keys in polytonality, may be heard independently or they may be heard together so that one influences the other. A good example may be heard in Stravinsky's *The Soldier's Tale* (1918), where regular march-like rhythms are combined with melodic lines in irregular skipping rhythms.

Both polytonality and polyrhythms were hard for audiences to accept. They provoked arguments as well as catcalls. The première of Stravinsky's *The Rite of Spring* (Paris, 29 May 1913) caused a riot, but the work was soon acknowledged to be a masterpiece. Another masterpiece of the time received no such treatment, simply because it was not performed until many years later. In 1908, the American composer Charles Ives (1874–1954) wrote *The Unanswered Question*. In it, a trumpet repeatedly plays a phrase answered by the woodwind in ever-increasing agitation; beneath the strings independently sound soft slow-moving chords. The piece is of great beauty and anticipates European ideas of simultaneous events in music. Ives went on to write more music in which he first demonstrated most of the discoveries later made in Europe. But he lived in isolation and heard little of his music played – people could not or would not perform it. Only now is his music being discovered.

New forms and styles

As the concepts that had sustained concert music for so long collapsed, composers had to think of new ways in which to pick up the pieces and build afresh. How were new ideas of harmony, melody and rhythm to be organized into coherent pieces of music? One solution, which was to prove very influential, came from Vienna, Austria, where Arnold Schoenberg (1874–1951) wrote atonal music. *Atonality* produces unusual harmony, often dissonant, and consciously avoids a sense of key. Schoenberg's *Pierrot Lunaire* (1912), a chamber work for voice and five instruments, is atonal music. In 1923 Schoenberg launched a system of composition in which all the notes of the chromatic scale are treated as being exactly equal and none is singled out for "favourable" treatment, thereby removing the feeling of tonality or key present in classical music but retaining a strong form. He did this by basing his composition on a theme or series of twelve notes, all of them different, which made up the notes of the chromatic scale placed in a certain order. This theme, or *note-row*, was subjected to various treatments in the music: it could be played upside-down and/or backwards, for example. The resulting music, which is called *twelve-note* or *dodecaphonic music*, was revolutionary in concept and in sound; its method was

Top left The Austrian-born composer Arnold Schoenberg, who worked in Germany until Nazi harassment drove him to leave, in 1933, for the United States. His style ranged from post-romantic to atonal, from which point he developed his twelve-note system of composition. The pictures on the wall are self-portraits.
Above left Jean Cocteau, French poet, novelist and writer, Señora Picasso and Erik Satie by Picasso (1919). **Bottom left** Cover illustration by Picasso for Stravinsky's *Ragtime* (1918).

totally unlike anything that had come before. It is difficult to perceive the rows of notes flowing past, but there is no doubt that Schoenberg's concept thrust composers into areas of music that they would otherwise never have approached, enabling them to conceive music of great power and beauty.

Schoenberg had two great pupils and followers, both fellow Austrians. Alban Berg (1885–1935) created works of great expression using both atonal and twelve-note methods. In his unfinished opera *Lulu* (first produced in 1937), different note-rows are used for the main characters, making an immediate impact on the listener. The pieces of Anton Webern (1883–1945) are above all concise, like exquisite crystals in the perfection of their form.

Other composers endeavoured to create a new approach to music by seeking inspiration in the past. They returned to classical forms but used modern devices – unusual harmonic patterns, vital rhythms and strange sonorities. Early examples of *neoclassicism* in music include the *Classical* symphony (1918) by the Russian composer Serge Prokofiev (1891–1953), which is rather like a Haydn symphony wrenched into the twentieth century. The neoclassical movement was spearheaded by Stravinsky with *Pulcinella* (1920), a ballet suite based on the music of the Italian composer Giovanni Pergolesi (1710–36). The best neoclassical music shows how old forms can be effectively reworked in new ways. Two examples are Stravinsky's *Octet* (1923) and his *Symphony of Psalms* (1930), the second movement of which contains an extraordinary double fugue. Stravinsky did not remain a neoclassicist but, in his seventies, took up his own particular interpretation of twelve-note music, as in *Requiem Canticles* (1966).

Many composers preferred not to enter the battle that ensued between the schools of twelve-note and neoclassical music. Some, such as the group of French composers known as "The Six" (Auric, Durey, Honegger, Milhaud, Poulenc and Tailleferre) deliberately made use of popular music following the example of Satie, much of whose music used popular idioms for parody and ironic humour (one of his ballets was called *Relâche*, meaning "closed", so as to confuse members of the audience arriving at the theatre). The German composer Kurt Weill (1900–1950) worked with the dramatist Bertholt Brecht to produce works for the theatre that use popular dance rhythms with simple but unusual harmonic patterns and angular but very singable tunes. The result, as in *The Threepenny Opera* (1928), is among the most individual music of the twentieth century.

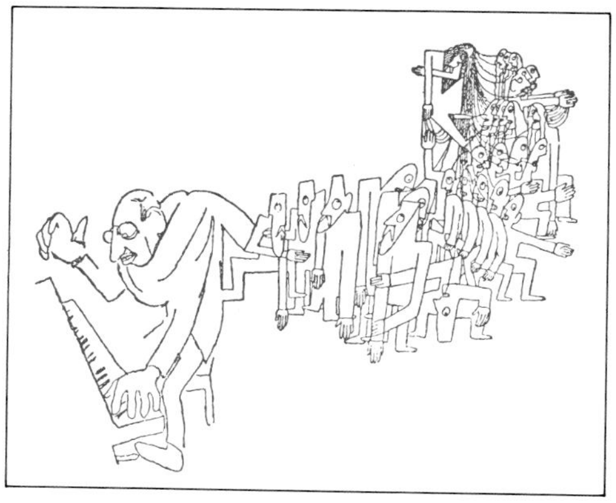

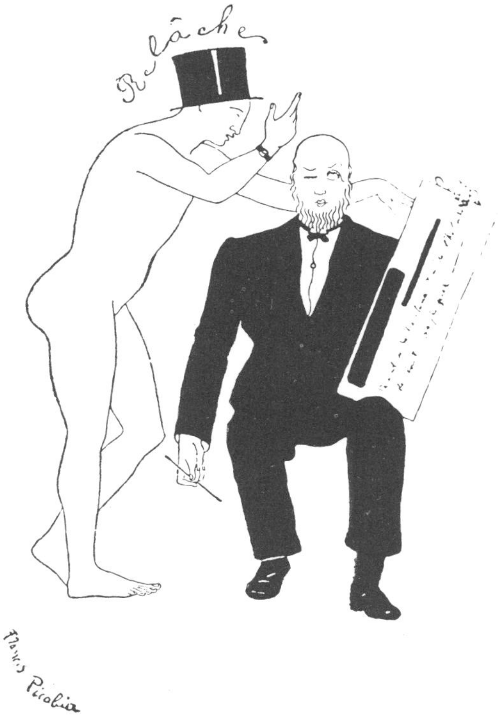

Schoenberg condemned the use of popular idioms as unworthy of concert music, but he did allow that much good tonal music remained to be written. Many composers have taken this path and have created music that is not violently different from that which has come before but still has an individual quality. Among the most highly regarded composers and their representative works are the German Paul Hindemith (1895–1963) and his opera *Mathis der Mahler* ("Mathis the Painter", 1938), from which he derived a symphony; the Russians Dmitri Shostakovich (1906–75) and his fifth symphony (1937) and Serge Prokofiev (1891–1953) and his ballet *Romeo and Juliet* (1935); and the Britons William Walton (1902–) – first symphony (1937), Michael Tippett (1905–) – *Concerto for Double String Orchestra* (1939), and Benjamin Britten (1913–76) – *War Requiem* (1961) and many operas. Tonal composers such as these were often experimental in their youth, though in the case of Shostakovich and Prokofiev, a return to more traditional methods was required of them by the government of the Soviet Union.

Sounds and sonorities

However it is achieved, new music must produce a new sound. Composers of the twentieth century have been fascinated with sound in itself as well as its organization. The new harmonies that arose as the tonal system disintegrated at the turn of the century were new sounds in themselves. Beginning with Debussy, clusters of notes played close together, for example, became common. In writing music for the orchestra, composers sought new sounds

Top left Cocteau's impression of Stravinsky rehearsing *Rite of Spring*. **Above left** Drawing by Francis Picabia to accompany the music of Satie's ballet *Relâche* (meaning "closed": Satie, a noted *farceur*, aimed to disconcert ticket-holders arriving at the theatre). **Bottom left** Bartók at the grand piano, caricatured by Aline Fruhauf. He might well have been in the throes of his famous early piano piece *Allegro barbaro* which, with its harsh discords (sheer cacophony for contemporary listeners), was calculated to shock. However, the music would be unlikely to upset present-day audiences by requiring instruments sometimes to play in the extremes of their ranges – the eerie opening of *The Rite of Spring* is created by a bassoon being played as high as possible. Instruments were combined in new ways to give new sounds even to simple harmonies, as in much neoclassical music. The human voice also came in for scrutiny and Schoenberg in *Pierrot Lunaire* originated *speech-song* (*Sprechstimme*), a way of using the voice that involves both speaking and singing.

Composers also became interested in the use of noise (sounds without any definite pitch), and enlarged the percussion sections of symphony orchestras. The French-American composer Edgar Varèse (1885–1965) produced *Ionization* (1931), in which six players handle thirty-seven percussion instruments between them. Another Frenchman, Olivier Messiaen (1908–) continued the practice of previous French composers in finding inspiration in exotic sounds, but he went much further, basing much of his work on bird-song and, in *Turangalîla* (1947), Indian music. Both Varèse and Messiaen produced music that is highly individual.

Developments in technology also opened up new areas of sound for musicians. Electronic instruments called the theremin and the ondes-martenot (Martenot waves) were invented in the late 1920s. They produced their sounds by creating electric signals that powered loudspeakers, and were played in concerts. The synthesizer, though it works on different electronic principles, is used today in much the same way. But it was not until the development of the tape-recorder in about 1950 that electronic music could get under way. With tape, sounds could be recorded and treated in all kinds of ways to produce sound structures totally unlike anything achieved before. Two schools arose. The use of natural sounds in this way had begun in France and was called *musique concrète* (concrete music); the use of sounds that are electronic in origin began in post-war Germany. However, tape techniques soon came to utilize both kinds of sounds together. A pioneer in this field is the German composer Karlheinz Stockhausen (1928–) and one of his greatest electronic works is *Hymnen* (1967). The Italian composer Luciano Berio (1925–) treated the voice electronically in *Homage to James Joyce* (1958).

Composers also sought different ways of playing conventional instruments to find new sonorities. In the 1940s, the American composer John Cage (1912–) obtained new sounds from a piano by inserting objects in the strings, making it sound both percussive and gong-like. This "prepared" piano may be heard in Cage's *The Perilous Night* (1942). Another American, Harry Partch (1901–74) has constructed his own instruments, which may be heard in the recording of his *Delusion of the Fury* (1963–69). Several composers ask players in conventional orchestras to obtain various sound effects from their instruments rather than to play actual notes; the score of such a piece of music consists more of diagrams than usual musical notation. An example is *Threnody* (1961), a work for string orchestra by the Polish composer Krzystof Penderecki (1933–).

Control and chance

Following the example of twelve-note music, some composers of the 1950s sought to produce *serial music*, in which every aspect – rhythm and volume as well as pitch – was worked out according to a predetermined series of values. The methods used were mathematical and the music that resulted was virtually impossible to understand. However, they could produce some attractive pieces, such as *Le Marteau sans maître* ("The Hammer without a Master", 1955) by the French composer Pierre Boulez (1925–). Mathematical procedures were also used by the Greek composer Iannis Xenakis (1922–), not to obtain total control over what was to be played but to subject it to degrees of probability. This thinking is demonstrated in his *Metastasis* (1955). Composition has also been relegated to the computer, though the result must always be the product of its programmer.

As a reaction to such procedures, many composers have produced music that leaves much to chance. John Cage, who once said that his purpose was to eliminate purpose, has written music by marking in the imperfections in a piece of music paper. Others have drawn a musical staff on a fish tank and played the notes produced as the fish inside swam past. Many have written pieces of music in sections whose order could be decided by the performer. Often, performances have been staged theatrically, the actions of equal importance to the music.

The most popular of these innovations has been a school known as *process music*. In such works, short phrases are repeated over and over again in accordance with a set of instructions (the process) so that they interact in continually varying ways. Hypnotic in effect, the music easily but unpredictably produces complexities of rhythm that could not be achieved by conventional means. Examples are *In C* (1964) by the American composer Terry Riley (1935–), and *Drumming* (1971) by another American, Steve Reich (1936–).

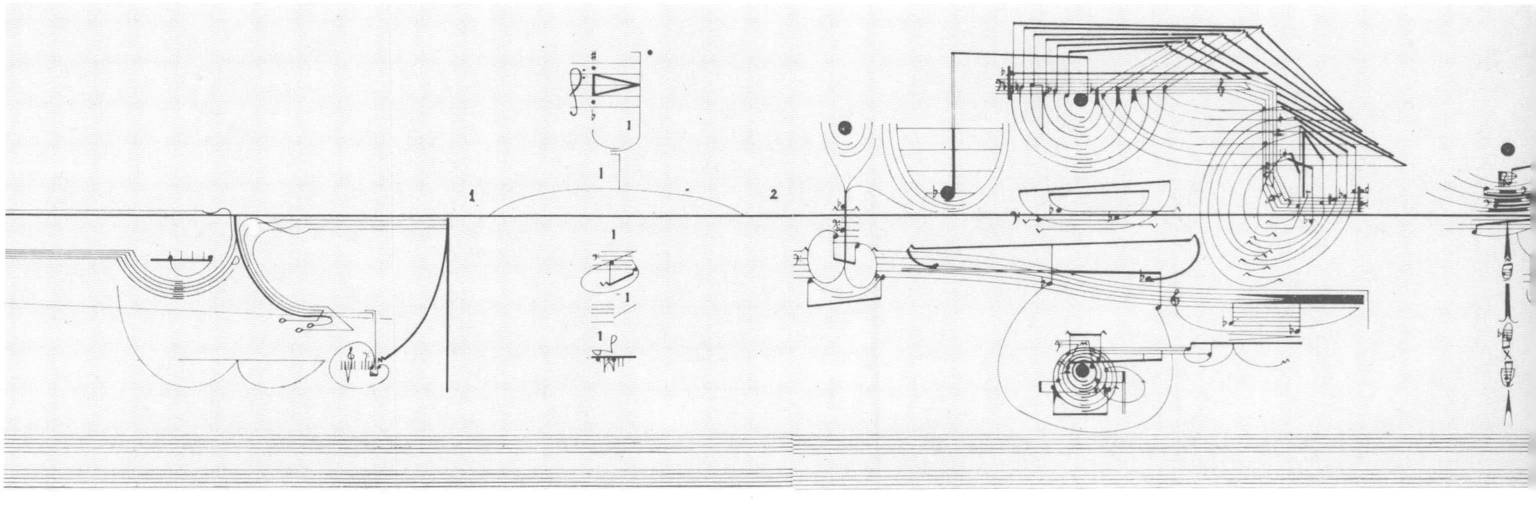

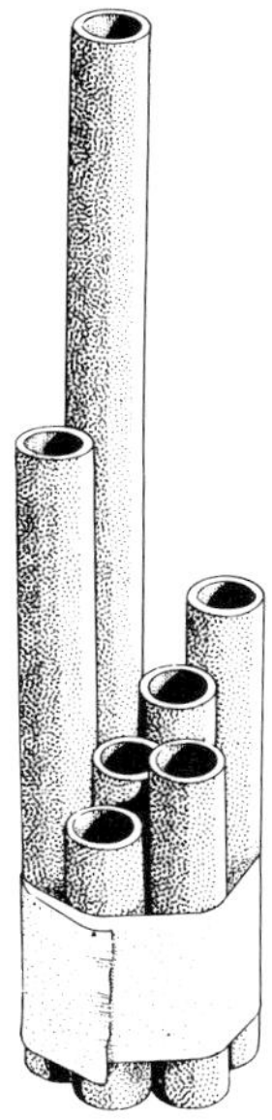

1

2

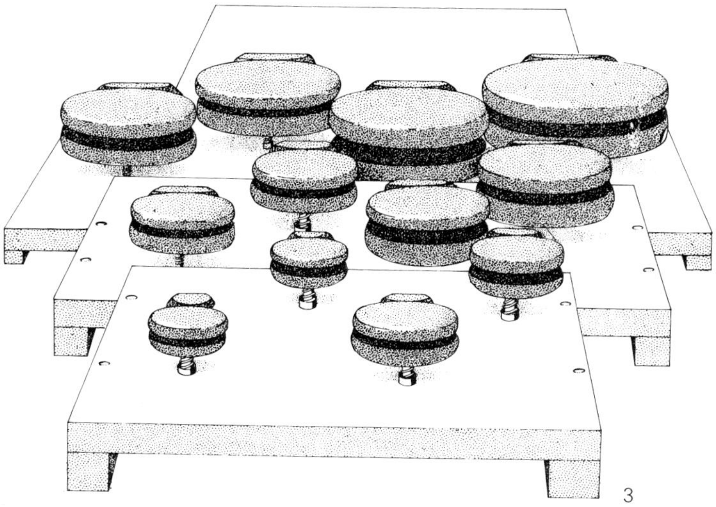

3

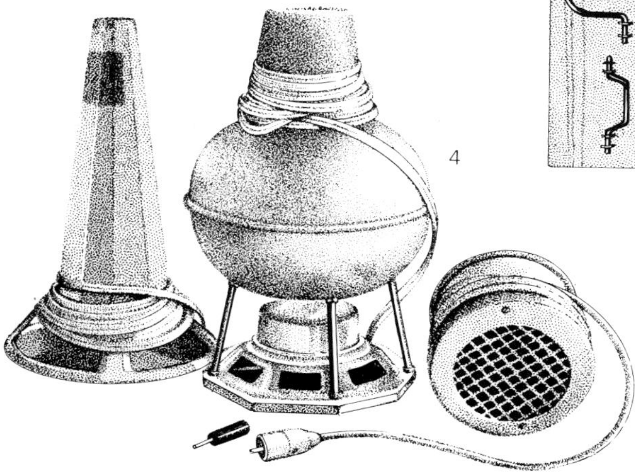

4

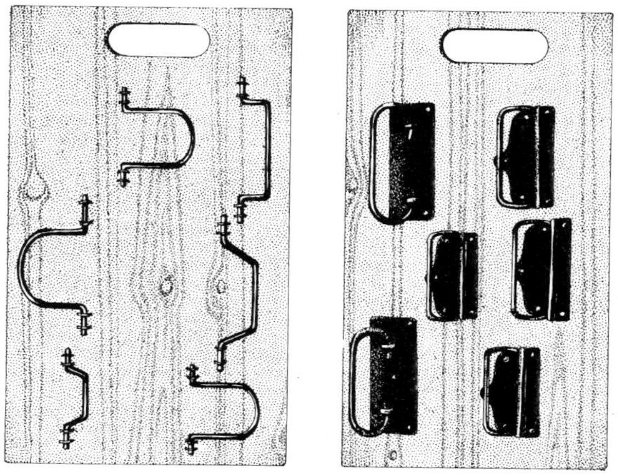

5

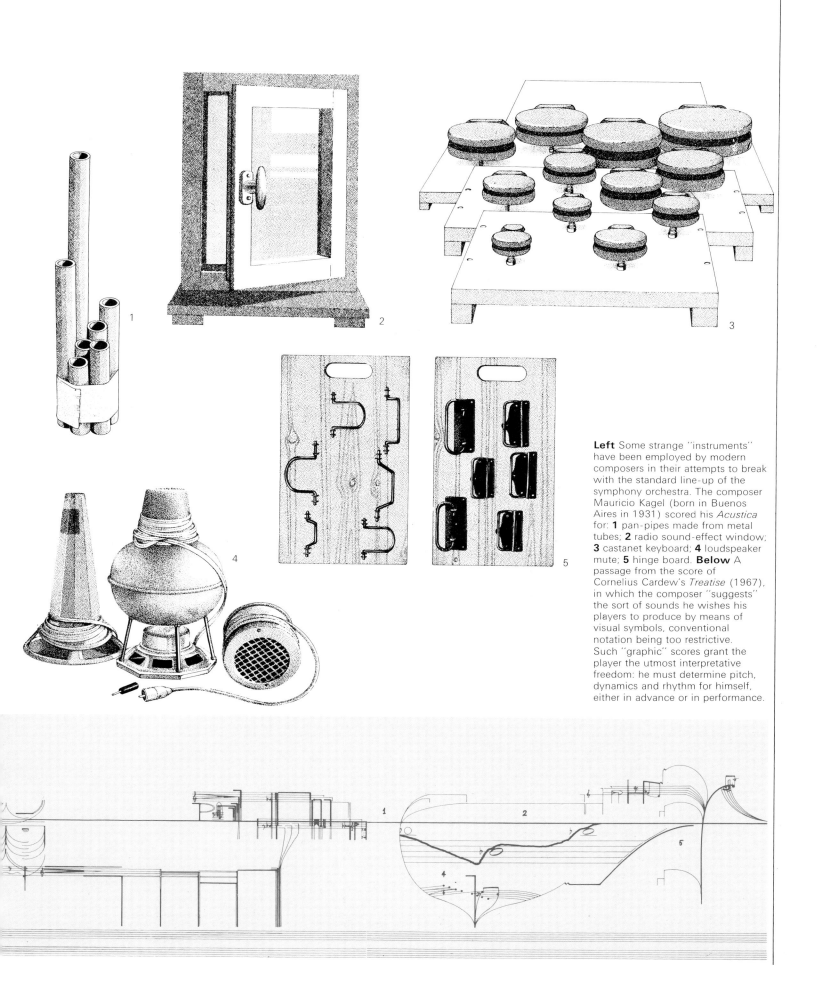

Left Some strange "instruments" have been employed by modern composers in their attempts to break with the standard line-up of the symphony orchestra. The composer Mauricio Kagel (born in Buenos Aires in 1931) scored his *Acustica* for: **1** pan-pipes made from metal tubes; **2** radio sound-effect window; **3** castanet keyboard; **4** loudspeaker mute; **5** hinge board. **Below** A passage from the score of Cornelius Cardew's *Treatise* (1967), in which the composer "suggests" the sort of sounds he wishes his players to produce by means of visual symbols, conventional notation being too restrictive. Such "graphic" scores grant the player the utmost interpretative freedom: he must determine pitch, dynamics and rhythm for himself, either in advance or in performance.

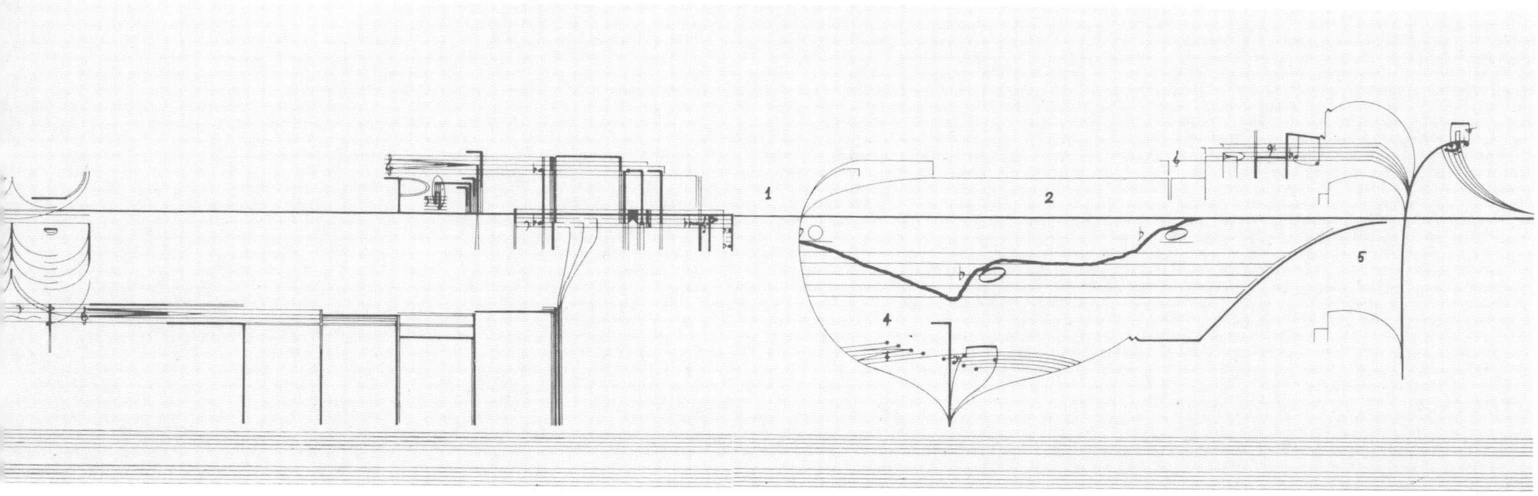

Song and Choral Music

Music for voices has its origins in religious rites. It was recognized from the earliest times that an enhanced form of speech could add a magical quality to the human voice. In ancient Greece, various devices were used to make the human voice both "magical" and more audible in a sacred context. The prophesies of the oracle were produced by means of a rock formation which acted as a megaphone, and the actors of Greek drama – primarily a religious activity – used masks to magnify and alter their voices. Jewish priests and cantors used chant, a stylized speech form, for the words of their scriptures. The initiation rites of many early societies included chant. The Christian Church adopted many of the Jewish chants, and added some of its own. These unaccompanied melodies of the Roman Church, codified by Pope Gregory I at the end of the sixth century, are now called plainsong. It is the only music of which we have certain knowledge up until the appearance of the troubadours and trouvères in the eleventh century.

Popular, or secular, music at this time was not written down, and none has therefore come down to us. Part-writing dates from about the ninth century, beginning with simple elaboration of church plainsong. From this time onwards, there were two main vocal traditions – solo song and choral music.

Solo song

The first kind of solo song of which we have any record is in the music of the troubadours and trouvères, the poet-musicians of eleventh- and twelfth-century France. Their songs were the art of an aristocratic class which, when not involved in wars or civil strife, would turn to courtly leisure pursuits. The songs were written in a great variety of forms on a great variety of subjects, and were accompanied by musical instruments. However, the form of notation used is still the subject of research, and it is not known for certain how the music would have sounded.

Three of the song forms – *ballade*, *rondeau* and *virelai* – became models for the French *chansons* of the fourteenth and fifteenth centuries. Though these began as solo songs, they frequently developed into part-songs. The best-known composers of French chansons were Guillaume de Machaut, Guillaume Dufay and Johannes Ockeghem. These last two were musicians of the Burgundian or Franco-Flemish school which flourished in the fourteenth century. Many musicians travelled from

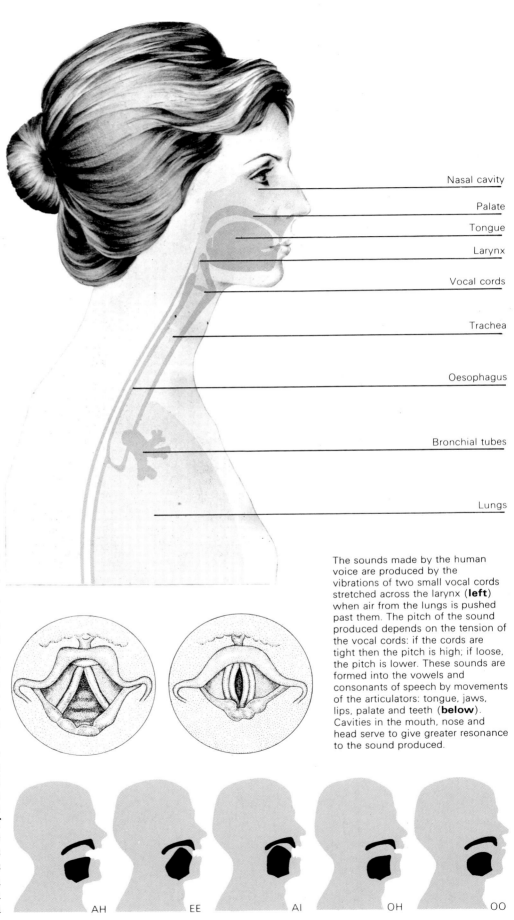

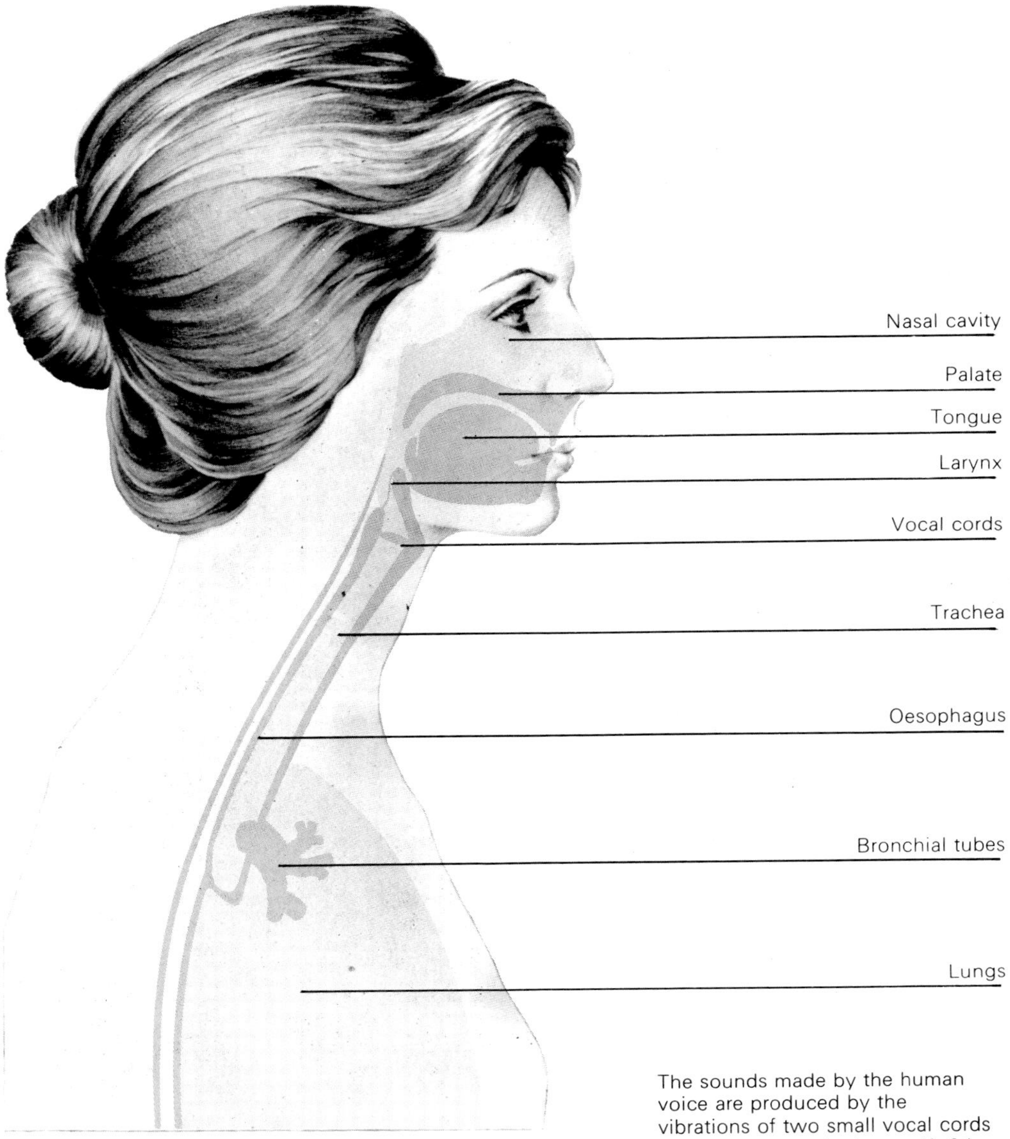

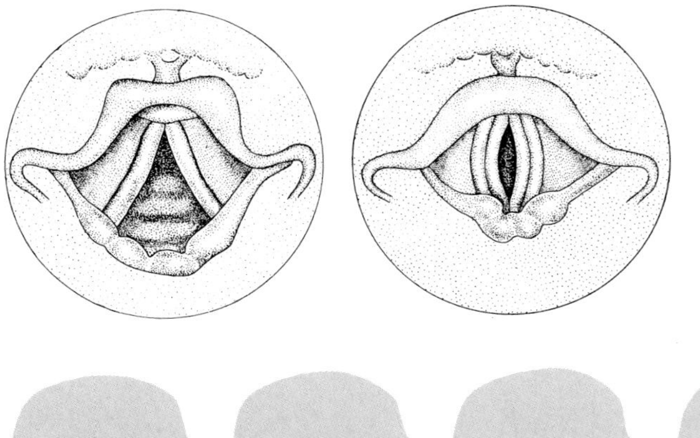

The sounds made by the human voice are produced by the vibrations of two small vocal cords stretched across the larynx (**left**) when air from the lungs is pushed past them. The pitch of the sound produced depends on the tension of the vocal cords: if the cords are tight then the pitch is high; if loose, the pitch is lower. These sounds are formed into the vowels and consonants of speech by movements of the articulators: tongue, jaws, lips, palate and teeth (**below**). Cavities in the mouth, nose and head serve to give greater resonance to the sound produced.

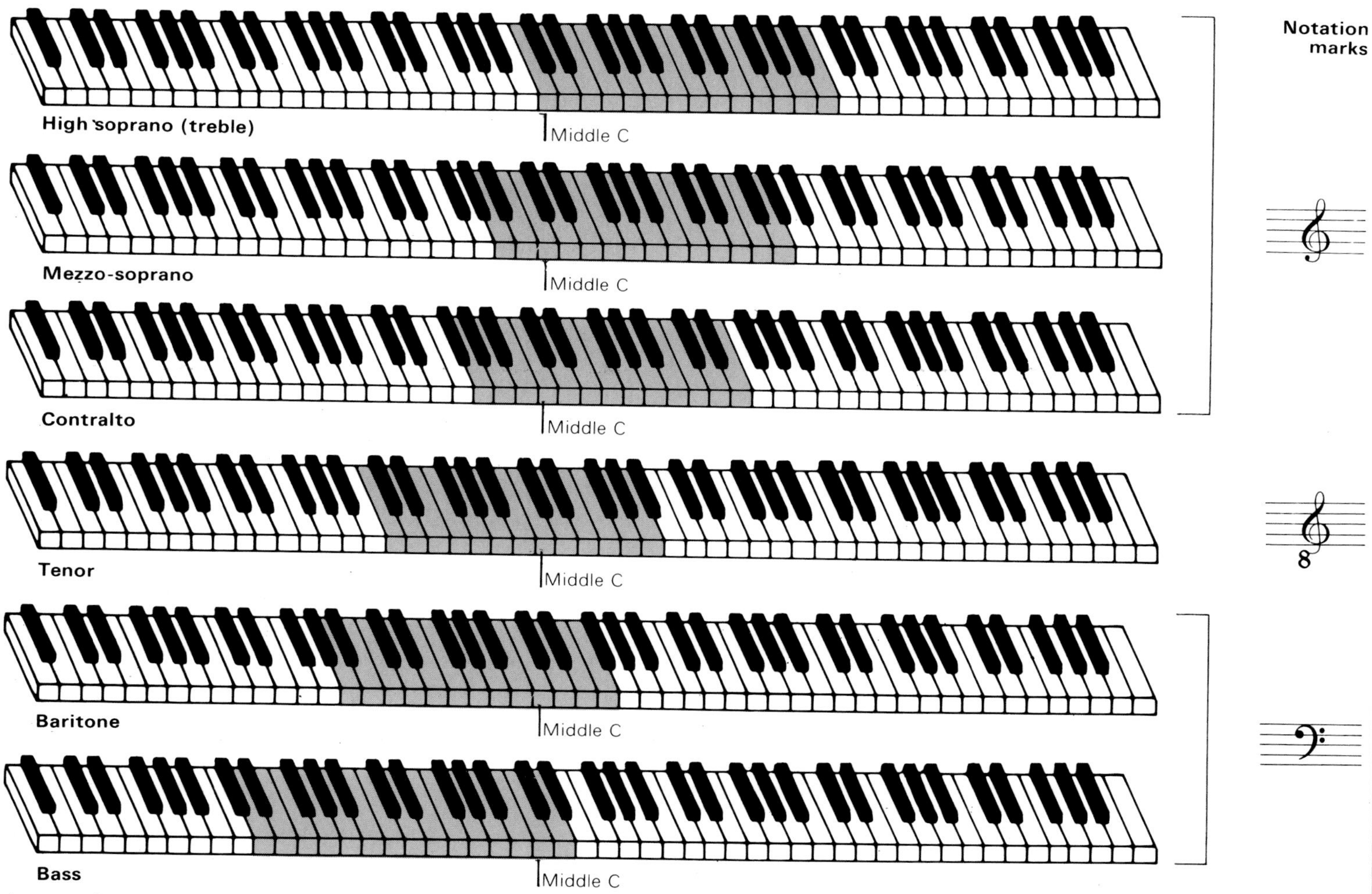

The human voice in its higher registers can be divided into three areas: soprano, reaching two octaves above middle C; mezzo-soprano, overlapping soprano and contralto; and contralto, extending to G below middle C. All these ranges apply to women's voices. Counter-tenor (alto) is an unusually high adult male voice, employing falsetto. Other men's voices are tenor, in the higher range, baritone, overlapping tenor and bass, and bass, the lower range. Boys' voices, which have a clear, flute-like tone with little vibrato, are called treble.

this northern centre to Italy, taking the art of the chanson with them. There it combined with the native secular solo song, the *frottola*, to produce the Italian *madrigal*. The Italian madrigal was choral, not solo, song, and will be discussed under "Choral music".

From the time of the Renaissance, interest in solo song was eclipsed when two new forms were introduced: opera in the Catholic South and cantata in the Protestant North. Only with the advent of Schubert was the art song to come dramatically to the fore.

Though the form of the *Lied* had evolved from works by earlier composers, Schubert (1797–1828) established a new character for German solo song which was to remain unchanged throughout the nineteenth century. From his time, the word *Lied* acquired a particular meaning in the English-speaking world, and should therefore be applied only to the type of German art song established by Schubert. He made song a major genre, giving it a prestige that none of his predecessors, not even Bach, Handel, Haydn, Mozart or Beethoven, had given it. Schubert's genius as a song-writer was evident from an early age: he wrote "Gretchen at the Spinning-wheel" when he was only seventeen. The accompaniment suggests not only the spinning-wheel but the endless turning of the young girl's thoughts as she spins and the dull regularity of her daily life. The poignant vocal line is in sharp contrast, telling of the girl's longing for the return of her lost lover, who brought such magic into her world.

Though none of Schubert's successors – Schumann, Brahms and Wolf – were innovators, they continued and developed the form. Schubert's natural successor was Schumann (1810–56). He stands historically between Schubert and Wolf and is the link between the natural spontaneity of the one and the polished sophistication of the other. Schumann, essentially a pianist, evoked the mood of the poems he set in his piano accompaniment. In many of his songs, the piano part incorporates the vocal line. Often the words are interpreted in piano interludes. In the songs of Brahms (1833–97), the music takes precedence over the words. His settings are more a response to the general mood of the poem than an attempt at word-painting. The emphasis is on expressing the thoughts aroused in the composer by the poem, as opposed to reflecting the words of the poet.

Hugo Wolf (1860–1903) is one of the few composers known mainly for his songs. In Wolf is found the perfect synthesis of music and poetry, and his settings of the poems of Mörike are among the most perfect songs ever written. Extreme clarity, economy of expression and delicate use of original harmonies are married in Wolf's songs to subtle poetry: the whole forms an artistic entity that is more than the sum of its parts. The use of dissonance and chromatic harmonies and the fragmentation of rhythmic patterns derive from Wolf's admiration of Wagner and prepare the way for Schoenberg.

Since Wolf, no song composer of like stature has emerged. Songs continued to be written, of course, but most composers wrote them as a sideline while concentrating on larger works. Richard Strauss wrote some 150 songs, many of them specifically for his wife, a professional singer. Mahler wrote *Kindertotenlieder*, *Rückertlieder* and *Das Lied von der Erde* – a large symphonic song-cycle.

Arnold Schoenberg (1874–1951), whose revolutionary ideas changed the shape of music in the twentieth century, also changed the history of song. Schoenberg was more concerned with the timbre of the voice as an instrument than with the words being sung, an attitude typical of his whole approach to tonality.

The heyday of the domestic performer was declining by the time of the First World War. Amateur music-making became increasingly the province of choirs, operatic clubs and small orchestras, and came to be considered as much a social as a musical activity. Since then, composers have tended more and more to write for professional singers and to exploit technique. The future development of song is likely to be towards the exploration of sounds for their own sake, rather than the musical expression of words. Composers will no doubt continue to write in the *Lied* tradition, but it is hardly likely that this form can be developed further than the point reached by Hugo Wolf. New directions must be sought.

The composers of nineteenth-century France took their starting point in song-writing from Schumann. Gabriel Fauré (1845–1924) was the first master of the *mélodie*, the French equivalent of the *Lied*, and his settings of the poems of Verlaine were among his finest work. Fauré regarded the art of song as the joining of two melodic forces – voice and piano – and not as voice with piano accompaniment. Such an attitude served to widen the range of expression.

The later French song-writers, Debussy and Ravel, built on these foundations. These two composers used the voice in the way foreshadowed by Schoenberg. Beauty of singing was not a necessity for Debussy, because the piano part contains the emotion and the musical interest. The voice provides just another melodic strand, and the over-all sound is more important than the sense of the words. Piano and voice combine in Debussy's songs to produce the same kind of sensuous languor and shifting colour as was sought by the impressionist painters.

Ravel, Debussy's contemporary, was a musical craftsman who delighted in the manipulation of the materials and techniques of music. Though his interest in song-writing decreased after 1912, he has left us some beautifully constructed songs. His *Histoires naturelles* is a remarkable song-cycle, revealing a biting irony and wit. These qualities were developed in his operas, and were used by later composers: a notable example is William Walton, in his *Façade* (1923), an "entertainment" for verse speaker and six instrumentalists.

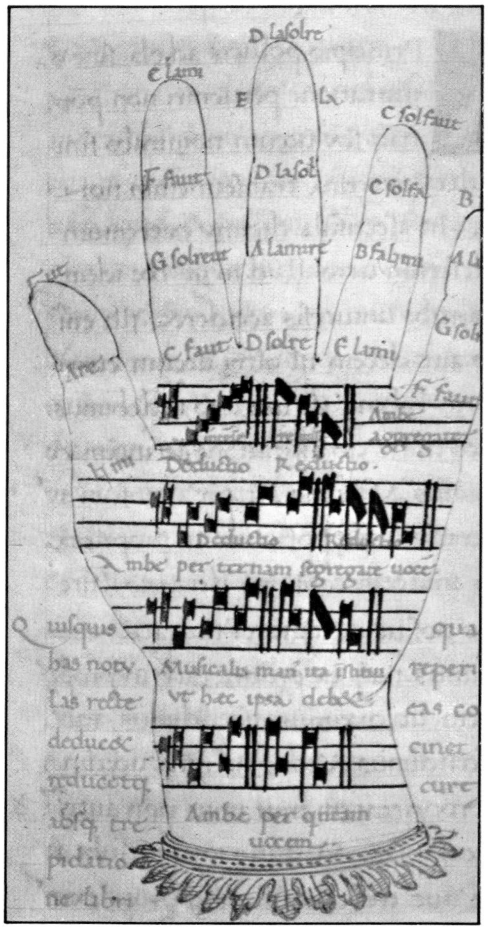

The Guidonian hand, an invention of Guido d'Arezzo, the eleventh-century monk, was an *aide-mémoire* for singers in which the tips and joints of the fingers each corresponded to a different note.

In the early years of this century, Ralph Vaughan Williams went to study in Paris with Ravel in order to refine and improve his technique. The influence of his French master is evident in the song-cycle Vaughan Williams wrote on his return to England, *On Wenlock Edge*.

Perhaps the greatest modern British song-writer has been Benjamin Britten, whose frequently unconventional choice of poems and ability to marry them to evocative music is an inheritance from Wolf. His accompaniments show traces of French impressionistic technique. His partnership with Peter Pears was the inspiration for many fine songs and song-cycles. One of his most striking inventions is in "Canticle II", where the baritone and tenor voices sing in intervals of fourths and seconds to depict the supernatural voice of God. This marvellously effective device looks back to the earliest use of the enhanced human voice for religious purposes.

Choral music

After the Christian Church had established its forms of service, and plainsong had been devised specifically for them, musicians had little further scope for the exercise of the craft of inventing new melodies. Their attention turned instead to embellishment, and when the plainsong melodies had been made more ornate, they began to add extra parts to the original melodies. This was the start of choral music. The rise of humanism in the twelfth and thirteenth centuries and the decline in the authority of the Church over music had gradually led to the relaxing of the more rigid requirements of the liturgy. So began a tradition of choral music which was not dependent on plainsong for the foundation of its composition. This new freedom allowed later generations to introduce melodic and rhythmic complexity, producing music that could satisfy the mind and ear of the listener as well as serving the Church.

In the middle of the twelfth century, in Paris, arose the Notre Dame School of composers, who were to take a significant step forward in choral composition. Among the first of them were Léonin and Pérotin, followed later by Guillaume de Machaut (1300–77). The developments they achieved depended on a more precise form of musical notation than had been available hitherto. Musical technique was now beginning to develop in its own right, without the philosophic and theological justifications that had been required earlier. This period has been termed *Ars Nova*, after the title of a treatise on music by Phillipe de Vitry (1291–1361).

Ars Nova was the harbinger of the Renaissance in music. From Machaut there is a steady development, through England's John Dunstable (?–1453) to Dufay (pre-1400–1474) and Binchois (1400–1467) in Burgundy, who represent the high point of the first Burgundian School. The next generation of Burgundian composers included Ockeghem (*c*.1430–*c*. 1495) and Josquin Després (*c*.1450–1521). It was this generation of composers that took the Franco-Flemish polyphony to Italy, where it was to influence the works of Palestrina (*c*.1525–1594).

Palestrina represents the pinnacle of unaccompanied polyphonic church music. He stands at the end of a line: while he was writing his masses and motets, his contemporaries were exploring the possibilities of the madrigal, the result of a fusion between the old Franco-Flemish polyphony and the native Italian secular song. Palestrina himself wrote spiritual madrigals – songs in madrigal style on a devotional subject – but the true madrigal was a *secular* part-song, for two or more voices, sometimes accompanied and sometimes not.

The madrigal enjoyed great popularity all over Europe and many collections were published. *Musica transalpina*, a collection of Italian madrigals with texts translated into English, was printed in England in 1588. It was quickly followed by other collections, including *The Triumphs of Oriana*, a set of twenty-nine madrigals in praise of Elizabeth I composed by twenty-six English composers including Morley, Weelkes, Byrd, Gibbons and Wilbye.

The Reformation did more to influence the shape of music than any other single event. In Germany, Luther's desire that everyone should be trained to take part in chorale-singing laid the foundations of the *oratorio* and *cantata* traditions.

The religious cantata began with Heinrich Schütz (1585–1672). In his time, this was a work based on a continuous narrative text in several movements that was lyrical, dramatic or religious. It was the development of the religious cantata based on the Lutheran chorales that initiated a style that came to full flowering in the vocal works of J. S. Bach.

By Bach's time, the form and style of the various movements of the cantatas had been strongly influenced by the operatic forms of aria and recitative. Opera was to influence all choral music for the next hundred years and more. Accordingly, the masses of Mozart and Schubert are much more operatic than liturgical in character. Beethoven's *Missa Solemnis* established the mass as a concert form.

When Handel turned from opera to oratorio, he was to shape the choral tradition for the next 150 years. So successful was the *Messiah* that it became the yardstick by which all other oratorios – basically, extended settings of religious texts in generally dramatic form – were measured.

Even Mendelssohn's *Elijah* and *St Paul* were compared with the *Messiah*. The rise of the choral societies in the nineteenth century preserved this tradition. The enduring reverence for the *Messiah* made any development away from this model almost impossible. Change came eventually in works such as Elgar's *Dream of Gerontius* and Walton's *Belshazzar's Feast*, but these works were accepted only after great difficulty. Perhaps the most important choral work of the twentieth century is Britten's *War Requiem* (1961), written for the consecration of the new Coventry Cathedral. It brings together the sacred – the Catholic mass for the dead – and the secular – the poems of Wilfred Owen – to make a powerful appeal to audiences all over the world.

Berlioz conducting choristers at a concert of the Société Philharmonique in the Jardins d'Hiver, Paris. Caricature by Gustave Doré, engraved by Dumont. The Société was founded in 1850 by Berlioz, but lasted only two years.

Opera

The beginnings of opera may be traced back to medieval plays and court entertainments such as the masquerade (a development of the carnival song), to the Renaissance revival of classical plays and to the pastoral drama, such as Tasso's *Aminta*, which enjoyed great popularity during the sixteenth century. By then, music had become an important factor in the drama, albeit as a "fringe benefit" in the form of choruses, dances and solo songs for the entr'actes: nonetheless, these musical interludes were beginning to emerge as an art form in their own right. The impetus for opera – that is, for complete dramatic entertainments presented in terms of vocal and instrumental music – was largely the result of the activities of a group of Florentine intellectuals known as the *camerata*. This group of poets and musicians, formed in 1576, hoped to rediscover the aesthetic ideals of the ancient Greek theatre and, in particular, to recreate the lost art of musical declamation. To write accompanied solo song in which the words could be clearly heard necessarily precluded the use of counterpoint; the *camerata*'s solution was recitative – free solo expression of ordinary speech, usually accompanied by a harpsichord or other continuo instrument. Recitative made it possible to perform whole dramas without the spoken word.

Early experiments in opera include *La Dafne* (produced 1597) by Peri, of which the score is now lost, and two versions of *Euridice* based on the same libretto (Peri's produced in 1600, Caccini's in 1602, both in Florence). In 1600 Emilio de' Cavalieri established opera in Rome with *La rappresentazione dell' anima e del corpore*, a sort of morality play set to music. These early operas were somewhat dry and academic. With Monteverdi's *Orfeo* (performed in Mantua in 1607), the true possibilities of the new art form were revealed.

Monteverdi achieved greater dramatic impact in his works by placing less emphasis on the declamatory style of monody which predominates in the earlier works, and interspersing recitatives with arias and *arioso* passages, choruses and dances. He used instrumental timbre to dramatic effect – sombre trombones for the shades of the underworld, and the nasal sound of the reed-organ to accompany Charon, guardian of the Styx.

Monteverdi was the foremost interpreter of the ideals of *Le nuove musiche* ("the new music"), described by Caccini in 1601 in his preface to this famous collection of vocal pieces. As such, Monteverdi's intention was to heighten the meaning of the words and portray emotion through his music. This he achieved memorably in "*Lasciatemi morire*", all that has come down to us from *Arianna* (1608), and his later operas *Il ritorno d'Ulisse in patria* (1641) and *L'incoronazione di Poppaea* (1642). The latter in particular, moving from mythology to history (Rome in the time of Nero), expresses human character and emotions vividly and movingly.

During the seventeenth century, Italian opera became the province of the public, as opposed to the court. Accordingly, orchestras became smaller (for *Ulisse* and *Poppaea*, only strings and continuo were used), for reasons of economy; choruses – for the same reason – were used less and less, and arias became the dominant feature of operatic works. A regularly-patterned song with some element of repetition was easier for the untutored audience to follow and remember than a free vocal line with little melodic interest; moreover, the cult of *bel canto*, or "beautiful singing", was establishing itself, and for this style the aria was the ideal vehicle.

In Venice, the major operatic centre of the seventeenth century, *castrati* became the vogue. Theatre audiences revelled in the purity, versatility and strength of the male soprano voice, generally heard in the role of the hero. For over a hundred years, beginning with *Poppaea* (first performed in Venice), few Italian operas were written without a major role for a *castrato*. These singers became so influential that they would have the music changed to allow them more opportunity for vocal display.

During the seventeenth century, opera became so popular in Venice that ten opera-houses were built there. Money and ingenuity were lavished on magnificent scenery and breathtaking stage effects (including manifestations of the immortals and transformation scenes) made possible by machinery. The major Venetian operatic composers were Cavalli and Cesti.

In France, the Italian-born Jean-

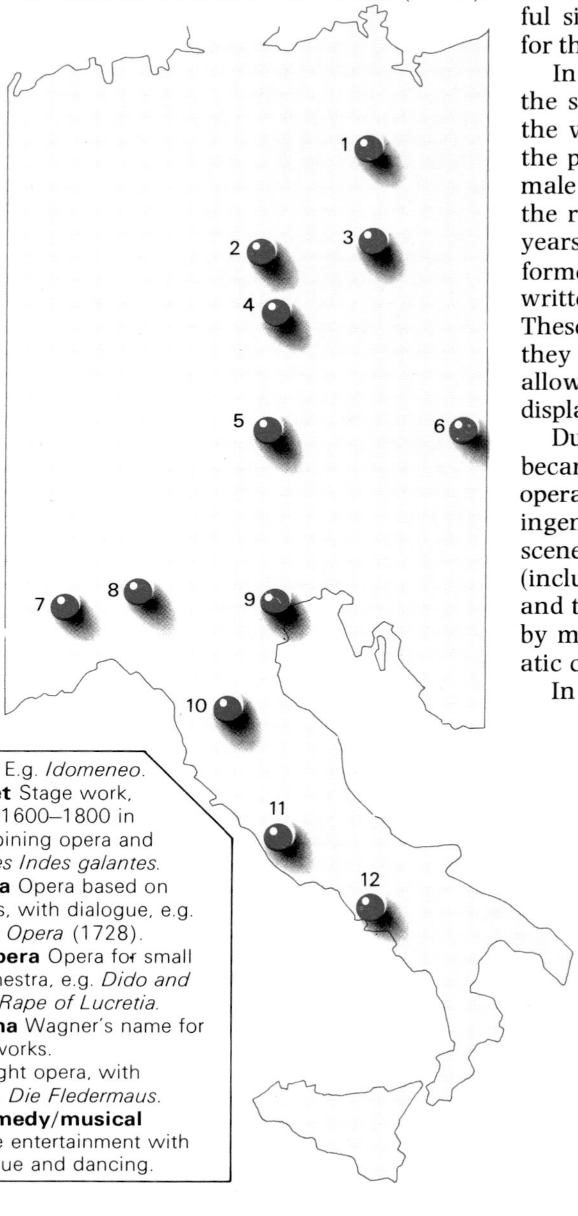

TYPES OF OPERA

Grand opera Large-scale opera, heroic in theme, grand in design, setting and costume, e.g. *Norma*.

Opera buffa (It.) Light-hearted, contemporary opera, e.g. *La serva padrona*. *Opéra bouffe* (Fr.) is similar, not identical, in meaning.

Opéra comique (Fr.) In eighteenth century, French comic opera; in nineteenth, any opera substituting speech for recitative (e.g. original *Carmen*).

Opera seria (It.) Serious opera of eighteenth century, heroic or mythological in theme, with Italian libretto. Consists of arias (especially *da capo* type) linked by recitative. E.g. *Idomeneo*.

Opera-ballet Stage work, especially of 1600–1800 in France, combining opera and ballet, e.g. *Les Indes galantes*.

Ballad opera Opera based on popular tunes, with dialogue, e.g. *The Beggar's Opera* (1728).

Chamber opera Opera for small cast and orchestra, e.g. *Dido and Aeneas*, *The Rape of Lucretia*.

Music-drama Wagner's name for his operatic works.

Operetta Light opera, with dialogue, e.g. *Die Fledermaus*.

Musical comedy/musical Popular stage entertainment with music, dialogue and dancing.

Left Italian and Central European opera centres: **1** Berlin: Weber, Berg; **2** Weimar: Wagner; **3** Dresden: Wagner, R. Strauss; **4** Bayreuth: Wagner; **5** Munich: Mozart, Wagner; **6** Vienna: Gluck, Mozart, Beethoven; **7** Turin: Puccini; **8** Milan: Bellini, Verdi, Leoncavallo, Puccini; **9** Venice: Monteverdi, Verdi; **10** Florence: Peri, Caccini; **11** Rome: Cavalieri, Rossini, Mascagni, Puccini, Verdi; **12** Naples: A. Scarlatti, Pergolesi, Donizetti.

1
2
3
4

Some famous opera-singers: **1** the celebrated Russian bass, Feodor Chaliapin (1873–1938); **2** Kirsten Flagstad (1895–1962), a Norwegian soprano famous for her Wagnerian roles; **3** the Italian tenor Enrico Caruso (1873–1921), an early recording star; **4** Rosa Ponselle (1897–   ), an American soprano who was discovered by Caruso.

Baptiste Lully (1632–87) was managing to glorify the reigning monarch, Louis XIV, in every work. Spectacle was an essential ingredient of French opera, whether for court or public performance. However, French opera differed from Italian in that the orchestra's role was more prominent and the librettos were generally more "literary", tending to avoid the violence and passion beloved of the Italian public. Lully's operas began with an overture of rich and complex contrapuntal texture (contrasting with the simpler Italian overture, or *sinfonia*), and usually included a ballet.

In the late seventeenth century, Naples became the main operatic centre. Voice-training was of paramount importance here, with the result that the singer began to rival the composer in musical importance. It was not long before the whole fabric of opera was threatened by the whims of the singers, who not only altered arias to suit themselves but indulged in excessive spontaneous embellishment to the detriment of the drama as a whole. Opera became a means of displaying vocal virtuosity only. Had it not been for *opera buffa*, Neapolitan opera might have disintegrated.

However, despite this problem, Naples was to become, with Alessandro Scarlatti (1660–1725), the birthplace of modern Italian opera. The form of his operas was adopted all over Europe, and served as a model for Handel and Mozart. His style influenced not only opera, but also oratorio and cantata. One of Scarlatti's inventions was the "ensemble of perplexity", a song divided among three or four soloists who each declare that they do not know what to do.

In England, Purcell (1659–95) was writing the small-scale *Dido and Aeneas* (*c.* 1689), incorporating both French and Italian elements. It had only one major English predecessor, John Blow's *Venus and Adonis* (*c.*1685). Opera in English was never really successful, especially after Handel, a pupil of Scarlatti, had arrived in London with an Italian company for whom he composed magnificent operas in a totally Italian style. Nonetheless, the great majority of the English public preferred a lighter form of entertainment, such as John Gay's satirical *Beggar's Opera* (1728), which achieved the same kind of popularity as the operas of Gilbert and Sullivan did with later generations. It was Handel's inability to obtain a wider audience for his operas that made him turn his talents to the oratorio as a more profitable outlet for his operatic style.

German opera also suffered from Italian domination at first. Neither Schütz nor Christoph Gluck (1714–87) can be said to have founded a German operatic tradition. The latter, though German-born, studied in Italy and wrote all his operas to either French or Italian librettos. Gluck's achievement was to reform opera. In the hands of librettists such as Zeno and Metastasio, whose innumerable texts were the staple diet of the operatic composers of the day, opera had become over-dominated by its music, while the plots were largely stereotyped. Gluck attempted to go back to the original ideals of opera, aiming to show real people in credible situations: hence, the stories became simpler, and music was used to reveal character and create atmosphere, rather than to exploit vocal agility. Classical subjects tend to predominate in Gluck's works, which include *Orfeo* and *Alceste* (1762 and 1767). With these two operas, the balance between music and drama was restored.

In France, Rameau (1683–1764) had followed Lully, achieving great success with works such as *Les Indes galantes* (1735). The rich and complex idiom, high seriousness and essentially unrealistic plots of his works contrasted strongly with those of the Italians, who were now producing *opera buffa*. Paris witnessed a two-year quarrel, *la guerre des bouffons*, between the supporters of French opera and those of *opera buffa*. Pergolesi's *La serva padrona* (Naples, 1733) was a fine example of the latter, with flesh-and-blood characters, contemporary settings and uncomplicated music devoid of vocal embellishments. French opera had mythological characters, was musically very formal and often had leading roles for *castrati*.

Mozart embraced both the high seriousness of French opera and the lighter approach of *opera buffa*. *The Abduction from the Seraglio* (1781) and *The Magic Flute* (1791) – a masterly blend of spectacle, comedy, fairy tale and morality play – gave German opera a firm foundation at last. *The Marriage of Figaro* (1787), *Don Giovanni* (1788) and *Così fan tutte* (1790) are all Italian comic operas, the sparkling results of Mozart's collaboration with the gifted librettist Lorenzo da Ponte. *La clemenza di Tito* (1791) derives from an older, more formal tradition.

Mozart's brilliant orchestral writing, sublime vocal lines, comic flair and outstanding theatrical sense make him one of opera's greatest geniuses.

Beethoven's one operatic venture, *Fidelio* (1805, 1806 and 1814), has fine music but is less compelling as drama. Weber's deservedly popular *Der Freischütz* (1821) has humour, simple rustic melodies of immediate appeal and a thrilling catalogue of "terrors" in the spectacular Wolf's Glen scene. *Euryanthe* (1823) and *Oberon* (1826), despite their musical merit, are now rarely performed.

Italian opera's obsession with *bel canto* was celebrated in the nineteenth century by Gioacchino Rossini (1792–1868), Gaetano Donizetti (1797–1848) and Vincenzo Bellini (1801–35). Their best works, including Rossini's *The Barber of Seville* (1816), Donizetti's *Lucia di Lammermoor* (1835), *Don Pasquale* (1834) and *L'elisir d'amore* (1832) and Bellini's *Norma* (1831), stand out from the welter of florid, trivial music written for the opera stars of the time as masterpieces of the genre of virtuoso singing. All three composers were adept at exploiting dramatic situations.

It was at this point that comic opera went "underground" and the age of grand opera was born. Rossini's *William Tell* (1829), Meyerbeer's *Les Huguenots* (1836) and Halévy's *La Juive* (1835) were among the earliest examples. Grand opera demanded heroic themes, elaborate historical costumes, large choruses and scenes of magnificence and splendour, usually in a five-act framework.

These requirements inevitably led to a certain sterility, and when Giuseppe Verdi (1813–1901) began his career, Italian opera was at a low ebb. From undistinguished beginnings, his works gained real dramatic stature – and outstanding popular acclaim: choruses from *Nabucco* (1842) and *I Lombardi* (1843) were adopted by the Italian patriots in their struggle against Habsburg domination. His talent as a melodist was unrivalled. Dramatic genius is increasingly revealed in *Rigoletto* (1851), *Il trovatore* (1853) and *La traviata* (1853). *Aïda* (1871) is also noted for the grandeur of its spectacle and its superb music. Two other late works of Verdi's, *Otello* (1887) and *Falstaff* (1893 – his début, aged eighty, as a writer of comic opera) show how his style had changed since *Macbeth* (1847), a less happy Shakespearian vehicle. Before, there had been ample opportunity for the audience to applaud the various "numbers" and the singers to bow; now, there was a continuity to the music which prohibited such intrusion into the drama.

Verdi and Wagner tend to overshadow the achievements of other nineteenth-century opera-writers. Berlioz (1803–69) had little success with, for example, *Benvenuto Cellini* (1838), *Béatrice et Bénédict* (1862) and the bipartite *Les Troyens* (of which half was performed in 1863). However, audiences found Gounod's *Faust* (1859) irresistibly attractive.

Bizet's *Carmen* (1875) was disastrously received at first, but survived to become one of the most popular works ever written. It heralded a new approach to opera, later termed *verismo* (realism), in that it deals with "ordinary" people in contemporary situations. In fact, this usually meant violence and passion among the lower echelons of society (the tragically seductive Carmen is herself a gipsy who works in a tobacco factory). The inseparable *Cavalleria rusticana* (1890) by Mascagni and *I pagliacci* (1892) by Leoncavallo are prime examples of *verismo*, as were some of Puccini's works, notably *Il tabarro* (1919), also in one act. For contrast, there was the picturesque sentimentality of Massenet's *Manon* (1884) and *Werther* (1886).

The earliest works of Richard Wagner (1813–83) were largely traditional and derivative: *Rienzi* (1842), for example, is reminiscent of the grand opera style of Meyerbeer. In *The Flying Dutchman* (1843), *Tannhäuser* (1845) and *Lohengrin* (1850) Wagner turned to German legend, and thus began the realization of his ideas of "music drama". To approach opera from a purely dramatic standpoint was an innovation: most composers began with the premise that the libretto must be made to conform to the established operatic format of solos, duets, ensembles and choruses. Wagner wanted continuous drama, a concept inherently at odds with the tradition of set-pieces. His music was constructed in one long, richly orchestrated whole, broken only at the ends of acts.

Wagner's ideas, which he would probably not have been able to implement had he not possessed the literary skill to write his own librettos, demanded that audiences re-educate themselves. No longer could people wander into the auditorium to hear a favourite aria or watch a particularly exciting scene, nor could they applaud until the end of each act. Everything was subjugated to the workings of the drama, right down to such details as scene-shifting, which had to be as precisely orchestrated as the music, and turning off the auditorium lights – another innovation.

The consummation of Wagner's ideas is seen in the *Ring* cycle, the creation of which occupied over twenty years. During this time Wagner also produced two other masterpieces: *Tristan and Isolde* (1865) and

Costume design (early 1920s) for Tosca, Puccini's tragic heroine, by the French designer Erté.
One of the most famous partnerships in *Tosca* is that of Maria Callas, as the operatic *prima donna* of the title, and Tito Gobbi, as the wicked Scarpia, who tells Tosca that if she wishes him to spare her lover's life, she must give herself to him, Scarpia. The great aria *"Vissi d'arte"* is Tosca's reply.

The Mastersingers of Nuremburg (1868). To accommodate the *Ring* cycle – *The Rhinegold* (1869), *The Valkyrie* (1870), *Siegfried* and *The Twilight of the Gods* (both 1876) – based on Nordic and Teutonic mythology, Wagner built a new theatre, the *Festspielhaus*, in the village of Bayreuth. It was his wish (unfulfilled) that *Parsifal* (1882), his last work, should be performed only at Bayreuth, so sacred did he consider its content.

Wagner's "music drama" moved away from what had been the accepted aria-and-recitative operatic content and developed the fully accompanied recitative to its uttermost. He strove to achieve total fusion of the arts of music and drama, while earlier composers had aimed for a balance between the two.

Wagner used fragments of themes to identify various characters. This device, known as the *Leitmotiv* (leading motive), derived from symphonic music.

The nineteenth-century repertoire was also enriched by the Russian school, whose most famous operas include Glinka's *Russlan and Ludmilla* (1842), Mussorgsky's *Boris Godunov* (1874) and Tchaikovsky's *Eugene Onegin* (1879). Puccini's *La Bohème* (1896), *Tosca* (1900) and *Madam Butterfly* (1904) are developments from Verdi and *verismo*, while Wagner's closest successor is Richard Strauss. His finest works are *Salome* (1905), based on Oscar Wilde's play, *Elektra* (1909) and *Der Rosenkavalier* (1911), both with librettos by his habitual collaborator Hofmannsthal. Debussy's psychological drama *Pelléas et Mélisande* (1902) was his sole contribution to the operatic genre.

Other standard works in the repertoire of the twentieth century include Berg's *Wozzeck* (1925) and the unfinished *Lulu*, Schoenberg's unfinished *Moses and Aaron*, Hindemith's *Mathis der Maler* (1930), Stravinsky's *The Rake's Progress* (1951) and, by Benjamin Britten (1913–76), the most distinguished operatic composer England has ever produced, *Peter Grimes* (1945), *Billy Budd* (1951), *A Midsummer Night's Dream* (1960) and *Death in Venice* (1974).

The Dance

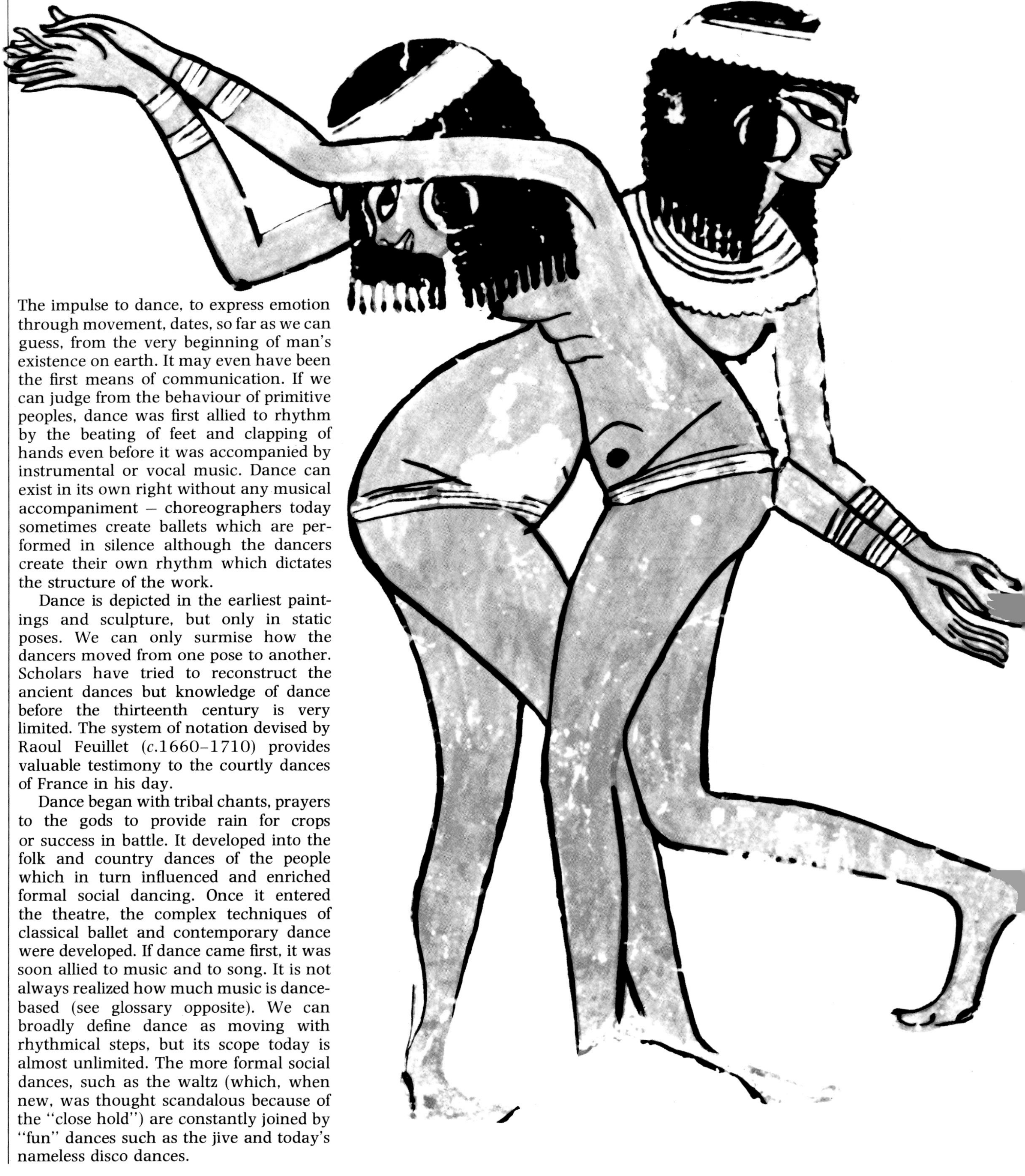

The impulse to dance, to express emotion through movement, dates, so far as we can guess, from the very beginning of man's existence on earth. It may even have been the first means of communication. If we can judge from the behaviour of primitive peoples, dance was first allied to rhythm by the beating of feet and clapping of hands even before it was accompanied by instrumental or vocal music. Dance can exist in its own right without any musical accompaniment – choreographers today sometimes create ballets which are performed in silence although the dancers create their own rhythm which dictates the structure of the work.

Dance is depicted in the earliest paintings and sculpture, but only in static poses. We can only surmise how the dancers moved from one pose to another. Scholars have tried to reconstruct the ancient dances but knowledge of dance before the thirteenth century is very limited. The system of notation devised by Raoul Feuillet (*c.*1660–1710) provides valuable testimony to the courtly dances of France in his day.

Dance began with tribal chants, prayers to the gods to provide rain for crops or success in battle. It developed into the folk and country dances of the people which in turn influenced and enriched formal social dancing. Once it entered the theatre, the complex techniques of classical ballet and contemporary dance were developed. If dance came first, it was soon allied to music and to song. It is not always realized how much music is dance-based (see glossary opposite). We can broadly define dance as moving with rhythmical steps, but its scope today is almost unlimited. The more formal social dances, such as the waltz (which, when new, was thought scandalous because of the "close hold") are constantly joined by "fun" dances such as the jive and today's nameless disco dances.

Left Women dancing at a banquet, from an Egyptian wall-painting, *c.*1500 BC. From the tomb of Nebamun, Thebes. **Right** By the eighteenth century, a number of dances had become standardized for use at court and in the ballroom. One of the most popular was the waltz, established by about 1800; the waltzers in the picture date from that period. **Below** The rise of music hall and vaudeville led to a number of spectacular dances becoming fashionable. The "can-can", at the height of its popularity in the "naughty nineties", was considered shocking and was never brought into use in the ballroom. **Far right** By the end of the Great War, dancing had become one of the most important forms of mass entertainment. Dance halls and dance bands flourished, whilst shows, records and films spread new dance fashions to millions of people. Here, Joan Crawford and Lester Vail dance the tango in MGM's *Dance, Fools, Dance*.

Brief glossary of dance

Allemande Moderate-paced dance of German origin in $\frac{4}{4}$ time.
Barn dance Lively American country dance.
Bolero Spanish dance in $\frac{3}{4}$ time. Usually has vocal or castanet accompaniment.
Bourrée Lively dance of French origin. Similar to the gavotte, it is in $\frac{4}{4}$ time with a $\frac{2}{2}$ pulse.
Branle ("brawl") Old country dance of French origin in which dancers hold hands in a circle.
Can-can Quick dance in $\frac{2}{4}$ time for stage dancers. Originated in Paris and made famous through Offenbach's *Orpheus in the Underworld.*
Chaconne Slow dance in $\frac{3}{4}$ time constructed over a ground bass.
Courante, coranto Quick Italian dance in $\frac{3}{4}$ time. Also, slower old French dance in $\frac{3}{2}$ time.
Csárdás National dance of Hungary with alternating slow and quick sections.
Ecossaise Dance in $\frac{2}{4}$ time, popular in the nineteenth century, possibly of French ballroom origin.
Fandango Lively Spanish dance in $\frac{3}{4}$ time, with breaks for song.
Farandole Dance from Provence in which a line of dancers hold hands. Usually has pipe and tabor accompaniment.
Galliard Lively dance usually in $\frac{3}{2}$ time.
Galop Lively dance in duple time.
Gavotte Graceful dance of French origin in $\frac{4}{4}$ time with $\frac{2}{2}$ pulse. Begins on weaker half of bar.
Gigue or **jig** Lively dance of Italian origin.
Gopak Lively Russian folk-dance for men in $\frac{2}{4}$ time.
Jota Spanish folk-dance in fast triple time.
Mazurka Traditional Polish dance in $\frac{3}{4}$ time in which weaker beats of bar are accentuated.
Minuet Originally a French rustic dance in $\frac{3}{4}$ time, adopted by the court.
Pavan, pavane Stately dance in duple time. May have originated in Padua.
Polka Popular dance of Bohemian origin in $\frac{2}{4}$ time which had become a craze in ballrooms and in ballets by the 1840s.
Polonaise Stately Polish dance in $\frac{3}{4}$ time.
Quadrille Popular nineteenth-century square dance of French origin.
Rumba First Latin-American dance, originally erotic, to become a ballroom standard.
Reel Quick dance for couples, popular in UK, Scandinavia and North America.
Saraband, sarabande Slow court dance in $\frac{3}{4}$ time.
Sardana National dance of Catalonia, with pipe and drum accompaniment.
Seguidilla Lively Spanish dance in triple time.
Square dance American dance with rectangular ground-plan.
Tango Argentinian dance which became popular in ballrooms around time of First World War.
Tap dance Dancing with repeated taps on floor from toes and heels. Formerly called "step-dancing", it is of folk origin, but is now generally associated with vaudeville and film musicals.
Tarantella Rapid Italian dance in $\frac{6}{8}$ time, reputedly originated by victims of tarantula spider.
Trepak Quick Russian dance in $\frac{2}{4}$ time.
Waltz Popular nineteenth- and twentieth-century dance in $\frac{3}{4}$ time.

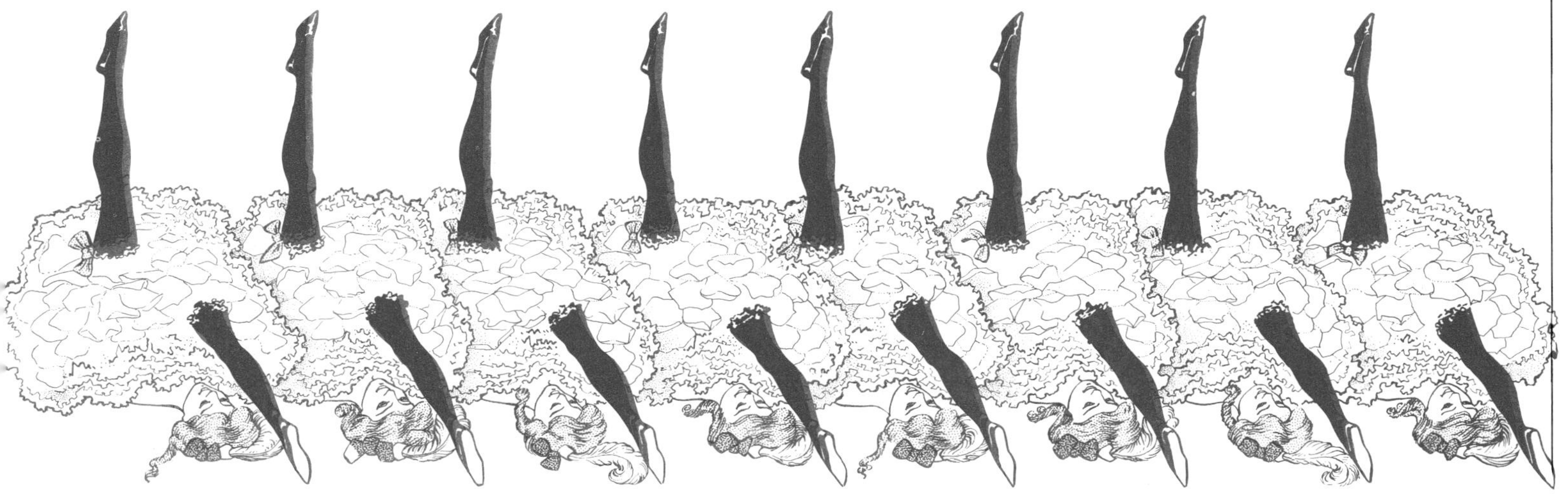

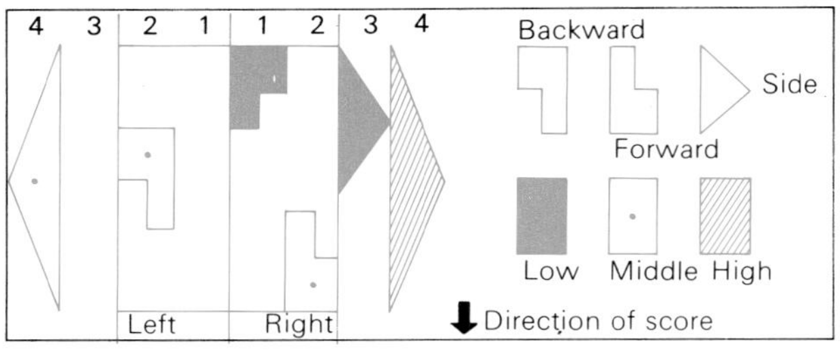

Dance notation, showing **1** step, **2** leg gesture, **3** body position, **4** arm position. In this system, Labanotation, which is read from the bottom up, each symbol's location on the staff shows the part of the body to be used. The shape of a symbol indicates direction, its shading shows level, and its length controls the time value of the dance movement.

The origins of ballet are to be found in the court spectacles of the Renaissance. From its very beginnings ballet has been associated with the world of the aristocracy and the fact that those of noble birth were expected to dance well is one of the guiding rules of ballet's development in the sixteenth and seventeenth centuries.

The first manuals of dancing were produced by itinerant Italian dancing masters who travelled round the courts of Italy instructing the nobility and acting as propagandists for new dances and new steps. Among the earliest manuals was that of Domenico of Piacenza which dates from the early years of the fifteenth century. By the end of that century a tradition had been established of elaborate court spectacles devised to celebrate some important event – a dynastic marriage, a treaty, a successful battle. An interesting manifestation was the "dinner ballet" such as that staged at Tortona in 1489 by Bergonzio di Botta for the marriage of Galeazzo, Duke of Milan to Isabella of Aragon. Each course in these banquets would be introduced by dancers impersonating the mythological beings associated with the dish: Neptune and sea sprites heralded the fish.

The tradition of court spectacles spread through Europe, becoming increasingly complex and opulent. Catherine de Medici made use of dance divertissements to make political statements as well as to entertain the court. *Le Ballet comique de la Reine* (1581) is a famous example.

In his younger days Louis XIV appeared in many *ballets de cour* (he earned his title of *Le Roi Soleil* from the role he took in *Le Ballet royale de la nuit* of 1653) but by the end of the 1660s he ceased dancing and it was at this moment that ballet became the province of the theatre. Louis had initiated academies for the development of the arts. In 1671 Jean-Baptiste Lully became the director of musical entertainments at the Académie which is now the Paris Opéra. The opera-ballets staged at this theatre set the style for over half a century. At the same time professional dancers were replacing the noble amateurs and developing a proper technique. Pierre Beauchamps, dancing teacher to Louis XIV and Lully's partner in directing the Paris Opéra, is generally credited with codifying the five positions of the feet upon which all ballet training is based.

The eighteenth century saw the steady development of technique. The first professional female dancers had appeared by 1681, but despite the eminence of such later performers as La Camargo (1710–70) and Marie Sallé (1707–56) the male dancer remained pre-eminent. This fact is explained by the costuming (which for women was too heavy and bulky to permit much agility) and the social attitude towards women in the theatre. Hence it is the example of Gaetano Vestris (1729–1808) and his son Auguste (1760–1842) that demonstrates the developing brilliance of technique in the period prior to the French Revolution.

Like technique, ballet itself was changing. The opera-ballets rigidly conformed to a prescribed formula of mythological themes, despite the musical excellence of the scores by Lully, Rameau and Campra. A movement developed in the mid-eighteenth century seeking greater dramatic and emotional truth in production. Its aims were embodied in Jean Georges Noverre's *Letters on Dancing and Ballet* (1760), the effect of which was to push back the expressive horizons of ballet.

The political and social convulsions that attended the birth of the nineteenth century were to influence the romantic movement – and romanticism affected ballet as it did every other art. In ballet, it brought an element of fantasy as well as the triumph of the female dancer. The appearance of Marie Taglioni (1804–84) in *La Sylphide* at the Paris Opéra in 1832 marked the triumph of romanticism in ballet, which Taglioni seemed to embody. Her performance was also remarkable for its intelligent use of *pointe* work to suggest the flight of the sylph. Taglioni's ethereal grace was but one aspect of dance romanticism. Its other, warmer and more earthly side was found in the dancing of Fanny Elssler (1810–84). Other divinities of the time were Fanny Cerrito and Carlotta Grisi, who was the original Giselle (1841). Musically, *Giselle* was the most distinguished ballet of the period. Its score by Adolphe Adam is notable not only for charm and dramatic expression but also for its early use of *Leitmotiv*.

Although the romantic movement had to some extent lost its impetus in Western Europe by about the 1850s, its effect in Russia in the second half of the century was to make ballet flourish as never before, in St Petersburg.

Three French ballet masters, Jules Perrot (1810–92), Arthur Saint-Léon (1821–70) and Marius Pétipa (1818–1910), had created an excellent repertory and a superb training system.

The latter years of the Imperial Ballet in Petersburg were dominated by Marius Pétipa's reign of nearly half a century, and by such achievements as *Swan Lake*, *The Sleeping Beauty*, *The Nutcracker* and *Raymonda*, with outstanding scores by Tchaikovsky and Glazunov (*Raymonda*).

The inevitable reaction against the mas-

sively complicated, evening-long spectaculars – accepted fare for the court – came in the early 1900s. It was instigated by the choreographer Mikhail Fokine (1880–1942) and the impresario Serge Diaghilev (1872–1929). Ironically, their work achieved its effect outside Russia. In 1909 Diaghilev organized a season of Russian ballet in Paris featuring the ballets of Fokine and the stellar dancing of Anna Pavlova, Tamara Karsavina, Vaslav Nijinsky and Adolph Bolm. From this developed the Ballets Russes which, under Diaghilev's absolute guidance, knew twenty glorious years of creativity. He commissioned scores from Stravinsky, Ravel, Debussy, Richard Strauss, Prokofiev, Satie, Poulenc and many more. It is from the Diaghilev enterprise of 1909–29 that our awareness of ballet as a vivid theatrical art has sprung. Through the work of former members of his company, such as George Balanchine, Ninette de Valois, Marie Rambert and Serge Lifar, ballet became securely established in Britain, France and the USA.

The work of De Valois and Rambert led to the creation of British ballet. Balanchine's work in America culminated in the creation of the New York City Ballet. Lifar's years at the Paris Opéra revived a moribund art in France.

These enterprises have subsequently influenced most of later worldwide development in ballet.

In Soviet Russia, the ballet has been cherished; the excellence of its training is unrivalled though its choreography has suffered from ideological restrictions.

The influence of "modern dance" has been remarkable in recent years. It sprang from a rebellion – above all by the American Isadora Duncan (1878–1927) – against the artificialities of classical ballet. It owes most of its eminence to the work of Martha Graham (1893–), whose dancing and teaching have been responsible for the real expansion and acceptance of modern dance. Most of its practitioners, Graham's heirs, are to be found in America.

Left and right A selection of ballet positions: **1–5** The five basic positions of the feet, from which all classical steps begin and in which they end. These are performed either with the feet flat, as illustrated, or, by women, on point (on the toes). The arm positions have never been firmly standardized, although there are generally accepted rules. **6** First *arabesque*, on point. **7** Arabesque *penché*, on point. **8** Attitude *croisée*, on point. **9** Attitude *allongée*, on point. **10, 11** Two positions of the *fouetté en tournant*: the whip and the turn. The typical ninety-degree "turn-out" of the legs from the hip socket, developed in St Petersburg in the nineteenth century, is essential for a good "line" in ballet. **Above** Margot Fonteyn and Rudolf Nureyev, one of the greatest partnerships in classical ballet, in the *grand pas de deux* in Act III of *The Sleeping Beauty*, in which the Princess Aurora celebrates her marriage to Prince Florimund.

Folk Music

The term "folk-song" has been current for about a hundred years, but there is still a good deal of disagreement as to what it actually is. Examples have ranged from Scots-Gaelic milking-songs to the Beatles' "Yellow Submarine". The definition provided by the International Folk Music Council, while not perfect, is the best so far. It states that folk music is the music of the common people which is passed on from person to person by being listened to rather than learnt from the printed page. Playground rhymes and football songs are examples of this aural process today. Three more factors help give folk-song its final shape. They are continuity (many performances over a number of years); variation (changes in words and melodies either through artistic interpretation or failure of memory); and selection (the acceptance of a song or tune by the community in which it evolves).

When songs have been subjected to these processes their origin is usually impossible to trace. For instance, if a farm labourer makes up a song and sings it and a couple of his friends like it and memorize it, it might happen that when *they* come to sing it one of them forgets some of the words and makes up new ones to fill the gap. The other man, who is perhaps more artistic, might add a few decorative touches to the tune and improve a couple of lines of text. If this happens a few times there will be many different versions. The song's original composer will be forgotten and the song will become common property. It is this constant re-shaping and re-creation which is the essence of folk music. This is why modern pop songs and other published music, even though widely sung by ordinary people, are not considered folk music. The music and words have been set by a printed or recorded source, limiting scope for further artistic creation. The songs' origins cannot be disguised and therefore they belong primarily to the composer and not to a community.

The ideal situation for the creation of folk music is a non-literate rural community, having no contact with, for example, city culture. In such a community folk-songs and dances have a special purpose at every stage in a person's life, from childhood to death. Epic tales of heroic deeds, seasonal songs relating to calendar events and occupational songs are also likely to be sung. The occupational songs provide a work rhythm. The "waulking" songs of the west of Scotland are good examples of this. "Waulking" is a tweed-shrinking process involving the wetting and beating of cloth; the songs provided a

Different types of instruments and highly individual styles of music and dancing make the folk tradition of Europe rich and diverse.

rhythm which helped to keep the work going at a steady pace – just as the rhythm of *sea-shanties* enables sailors to haul a rope or turn a capstan in unison. The functional and seasonal songs represent the earliest type of folk-song.

The sort of community in which folk culture flourishes has virtually disappeared in Europe. There are a few places where traces of the old-style folk community can still be seen, but, as happened in the Appalachian Mountains of North America earlier in this century, the flow of city culture spread by the mass media will eventually infiltrate even the most isolated areas. This, of course, is not a new phenomenon. In the Middle Ages the wandering troubadours sang their songs all over Europe. On their travels they picked up tales, legends and ideas and spread them around, thus mixing up folk ideas with more sophisticated courtly themes. The invention of the printing press and the development of trade further helped the spread of information. Into this cultural melting-pot went the old ceremonial and task songs, with their primitive one-line tunes and fragmented texts, to emerge with rounded melodies and regular verse forms alongside the (now familiar) carols, narrative ballads and lyric folk-songs.

Carols were originally dance songs – a "carole" being a dance – which during the Middle Ages became associated with the Christian celebration of Christmas and lost their dance connections. The subject matter of the folk carols was frequently taken from the legends of Christ in the Apocryphal Gospels. Some, such as "The Holly and the Ivy", display pagan origins, which in pre-Christian times were male and female fertility symbols. Other carols with a foot in the pagan past are the May Day and New Year carols.

Ballads such as "Chevy Chase" and "Sir Patrick Spens" are called *narrative* ballads because they tell a story. Some tell of heroes, such as Robin Hood, or of warfare, such as the border raids of Scottish clans. The majority, however, deal with romantic situations which end tragically. They tell their dramatic stories in a swift stylized way. The language is full of stock descriptions such as "milk-white steeds", "gay gold rings", and "snow-white breasts", partly as an aid to the singer's memory.

Although the ballads are probably the work of medieval clerics and minstrels, they were soon adopted by the ordinary people and therefore underwent the "folk process". The largest class of songs is that of the shorter lyric folk-songs where

Right The folk-songs and dances of the Americas are accompanied by instruments which have their origins either in the New World or were brought by settlers from overseas: **1** a Yaqui Indian of Arizona playing a pipe and drum; **2** a barn dance; **3** a guitar and harmonica being played simultaneously; **4** a banjo-player of the Appalachian Mountains; **5** a Mexican violinist; **6** a violinist from the Cuzco region of Peru; **7** a Tucurina Indian of Brazil playing a musical bow; **8** a Gaucho cowboy guitarist of the Argentinian Pampas.
Far right Many different instruments are used in folk music around the world: fiddles, lutes, zithers, harps, guitars, flutes, whistles, pipes and drums of all shapes and sizes. Those illustrated are: **1** Russian balalaika; **2** Bohemian friction drum; **3** Spanish bagpipe; **4** fife; **5** Swedish zither; **6** Polish fiddle.

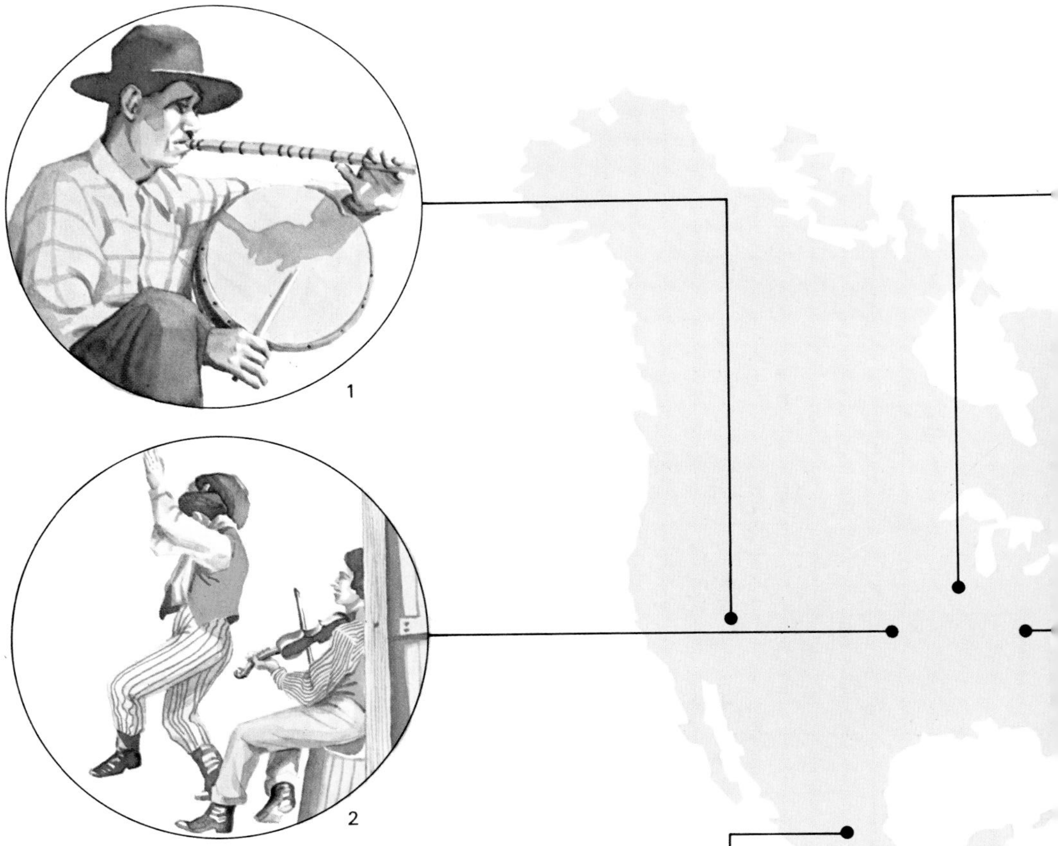

the predominant theme is love – either true, frustrated or false. There are also dialogue songs, songs descriptive of country life, and songs of sailors and the sea. In rural folk-songs there are, surprisingly, few complaints about a life which was at times very hard. However, in the songs that began to emerge from the cities in the course of the Industrial Revolution, the gentler lyric songs gave way to bitter complaints against social injustice and the harsh conditions of the mill towns.

When strict definitions of a folk-song are established, they provide only a framework within which collectors and scholars can work, and are not necessarily representing the most "typical" music of the "folk". In nineteenth-century England scholars realized for the first time that working people had a musical culture of their own. It included some old songs which were modal, as opposed to being in the major and minor keys which had long been standard in art music. These old songs were labelled "folk-songs", and some of the interested musicians began dashing round the country on bicycles noting them down. One of the most famous was Cecil Sharp (1859–1924), who collected, edited and performed English folk-songs and music for morris, sword and country dances. He published about three thousand of these tunes, but the collections gave the impression that country singers sang *only* old folk-songs, which was not the case. Folk-songs were only a part of the common repertoire. The average singer's repertory has been, for the last couple of hundred years at least, a rag-bag of songs and tunes, some of them anonymous folk-songs, but many of them songs learned from ballad operas, travelling shows and pleasure gardens, and from the printed song-sheets called *broadsides*. These, the equivalent of today's sensational popular newspapers, featured songs dealing with the latest murder, disaster or political event. Also, some of the old traditional folk-songs were reprinted in broadsides.

During the First World War Cecil Sharp spent a year in the Appalachian Mountains of North America where he found some 1600 tunes which had been taken to America by the first British settlers.

Many composers of art music have taken folk-songs as a basis for their compositions. Some of the masses of John Taverner (*c*.1495–1545) and Josquin Després (*c*.1450–1521) have folk-songs as a main theme or cantus firmus. The Elizabethan keyboard composers also made use of folk tunes. Haydn, Grieg, Dvořák and Smetana were among later

3

4

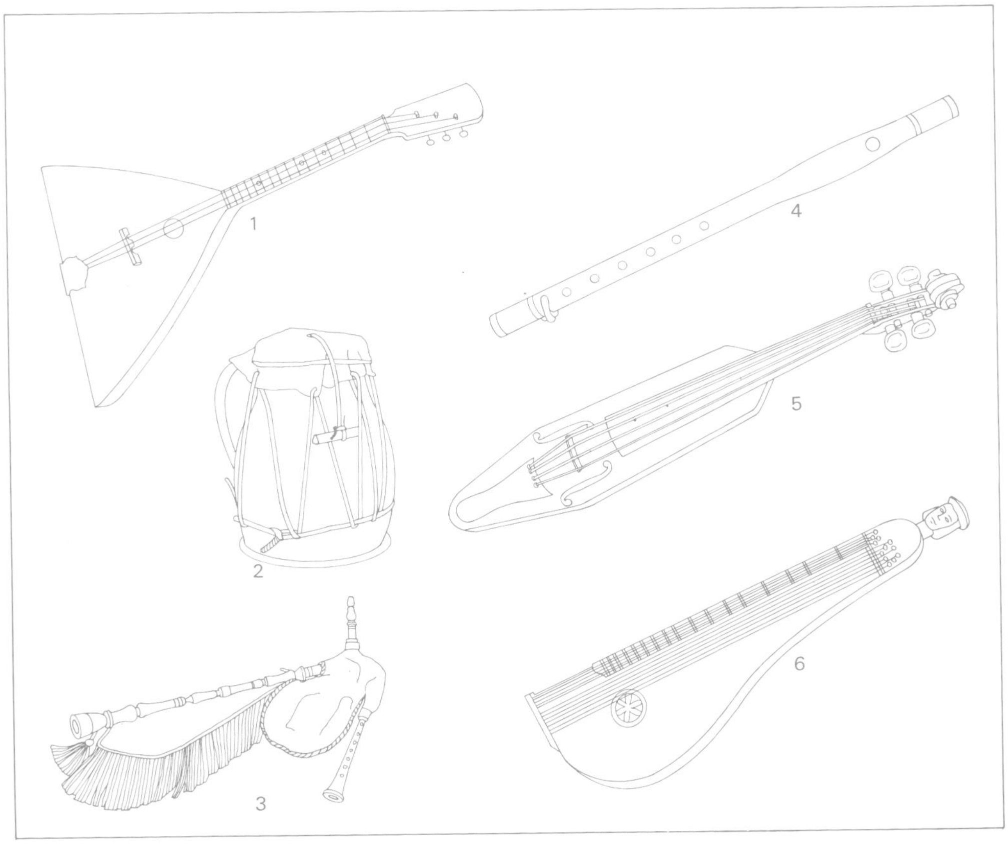

7

8

composers who used folk music in their works to reflect nationalist feeling.

The British and Anglo-American folk-song tradition is, in the main, an unaccompanied solo one. The use in America of banjos and guitars is a result of, among other things, Negro influence. It was the Negro who introduced the banjo to the poor Southern whites in the late nineteenth century, in the areas now famous for white bluegrass music and banjo-picking. In Europe, instrumental folk music was largely for dance accompaniment, either for ritual dances like the morris and sword dances, or the social country dances, certain of which were adopted by the upper classes for their formal balls.

Since the 1950s there has been a revival of interest in folk music in both Britain and the USA. It is probably being performed and heard by more people now than at any time in its history, thanks to the very elements which are helping to kill it off in its natural state: records, radio and television. Young people are taking up folk instruments such as fiddles, concertinas, flutes and bagpipes and developing into brilliant virtuoso musicians. The standard of their playing makes the old tunes exciting for modern audiences, and guarantees that the old songs will get a hearing for some time to come.

Jazz

Jazz is sometimes regarded as the United States' most important contribution to world music. Like other "Afro-American" styles – samba in Brazil, calypso in the West Indies – it represents a fusion between African and European music.

Jazz has become mainly – but not entirely – instrumental, but with a preference for vocalized tone and expressively varied intonation. While it can be composed, arranged and written down, jazz is essentially an improvised music. The rhythm is typically based on a regular, "swinging" beat, with frequent syncopation and cross-rhythms. Melodically, jazz gets its flavour from the *blues scale*, while seventh chords and their extensions are the typical harmonies.

Repertoire and ensembles

The jazz repertoire ranges from simple twelve-bar blues to thirty-two-bar "standards" (popular songs adapted to jazz use) and "originals" (custom-made jazz compositions) and usually includes improvised solos in performance.

Jazz groups usually include a rhythm section of piano and/or guitar; string, electric or brass bass; and drum kit, sometimes with additional percussion instruments; and a front line of one or more wind instruments, typically trumpet or saxophone. Groups range in size from trios (usually piano, bass and drums) to big bands (usually seven brass, five saxophones and four rhythm). In-between sizes include the traditional seven-piece ensemble of trumpet, trombone, clarinet and four rhythm, and the modern quintet of trumpet, saxophone and three rhythm.

History and development of jazz

Jazz was largely the creation of American blacks, who have continued to be its leading innovators. In the slavery period, they were strongly exposed to Protestant church music, which they adapted to their own purposes. Other European influences which were similarly transformed were marches, quadrilles and the like. From this combination of influences, various styles emerged which were to coalesce into jazz. Chief among these were the spirituals of the Negro churches, rural blues and work-songs, and the Negro marching bands of New Orleans.

The syncopated piano style of *ragtime* crystallized around the turn of the century. Ragtime was usually composed and written down, and was often published with some success. Important composers were Scott Joplin and later James P. Johnson.

The first jazz-bands appeared in New

The early days of jazz. In the 1920s jazz dance-bands sprang up throughout the USA. Good jazz is, however, very rarely suitable for dancing, owing to its rhythmic complexity and essentially improvisatory nature. For a time, much of what was loosely referred to as jazz was just syncopated dance music. Only once it had left the dance-halls could jazz continue to develop.

Orleans as scaled-down versions of the earlier marching bands. They featured a collective improvisation with trombone and clarinet weaving a counterpoint around the cornet or trumpet lead. The cornettist Buddy Bolden was a legendary figure of early New Orleans jazz. Others included the trumpeters Joe "King" Oliver, the young Louis Armstrong, Freddy Keppard and the clarinettist Sidney Bechet. In 1917, the white Original Dixieland Jazz Band made the first jazz recordings. In the same year, the closure of the New Orleans red-light district, an important source of musical employment, initiated a northward migration of New Orleans musicians to Kansas City and Chicago.

From the mid-1920s jazz changed to a virtuoso solo art when Louis Armstrong broke the bonds of the New Orleans ensemble with his historic "Hot Five" and "Hot Seven" recordings. His innovations were quickly matched by the tenor saxophonist Coleman Hawkins, the pianist Earl Hines and others.

The rise of the soloist was paralleled by the rise of big bands. The importance of the arranger-composer grew accordingly. The major big-band leaders of the 1920s were Fletcher Henderson and Duke Ellington, followed in the 1930s "swing era" by Count Basie and Benny Goodman.

Be-bop and modern jazz

In the early 1940s young black musicians developed *be-bop* (or just *bop*), a difficult, angular music, partly as a reaction to the now stereotyped swing music and partly to forestall the possibility of white exploitation. Basie's tenor saxophonist Lester Young, with his spare, laconic style, was the spiritual father of bop, but the alto saxophonist Charlie Parker was its direct instigator.

Hardly less important in this first phase of modern jazz were the trumpeters Dizzy Gillespie and Fats Navarro, the pianists Thelonious Monk and Bud Powell, and the drummers Kenny Clarke and Max Roach. Subsequent developments include the short-lived "cool movement" of the early 1950s, featuring white musicians such as Lee Konitz, Lennie Tristano and Gerry Mulligan, and the quasi-classical presentation of the Modern Jazz Quartet. During the 1950s trumpeter Miles Davies and saxophonists Sonny Rollins and John Coltrane extended the limits of bop in different directions, while the saxophonist Ornette Coleman and the pianist Cecil Taylor developed "free" jazz. Another leading figure was the bassist-composer Charles Mingus.

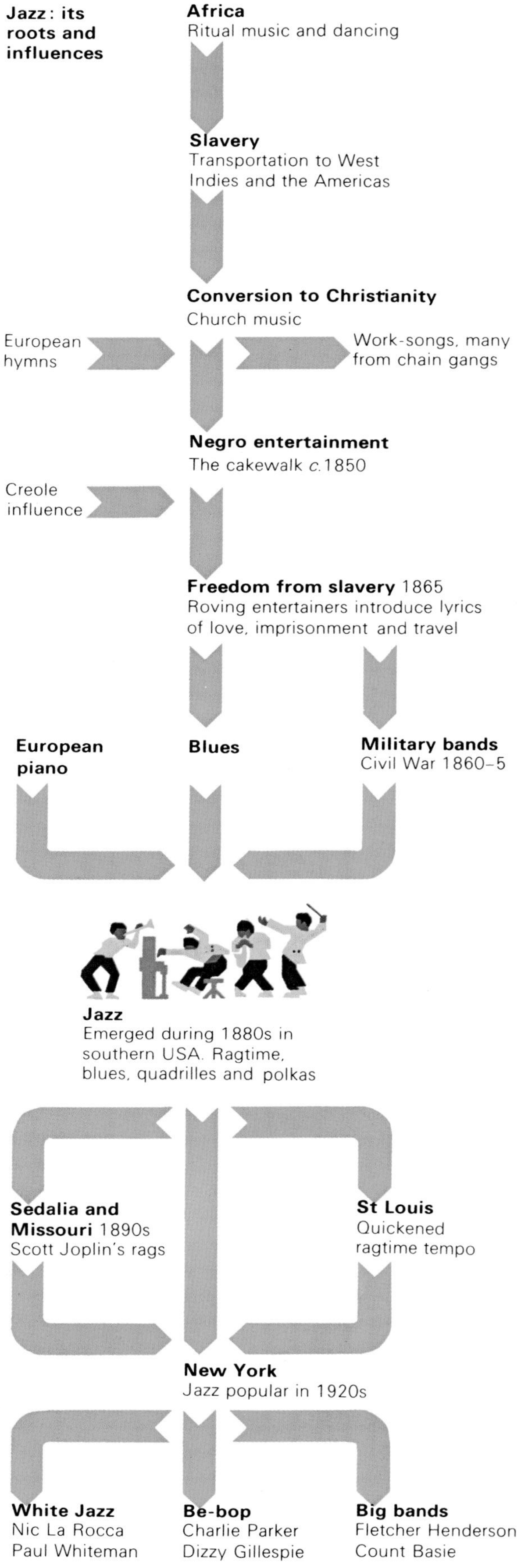

Joe "King" Oliver (1885–1938) Trumpeter King Oliver was one of the masters of traditional, New Orleans-style jazz, though his famous "Creole Jazz Band" recordings (with the young Louis Armstrong on second trumpet) were made in Chicago in the early 1920s.

Charlie Parker (1920–55) Alto saxophonist Charlie Parker, nicknamed "Bird", learned his craft as a teenager in Kansas City. In New York in the early 1940s he was the main founder of modern jazz. His style, combining harmonic and rhythmic innovation with emotional urgency, influenced a generation of musicians.

Bessie Smith (*c.*1898–1937) Born in Tennessee, Bessie Smith began her career as a singer with a minstrel group. Her recordings in the 1920s and early 1930s, backed by many fine jazz musicians, established her as the greatest blues singer of her time. Injured in a car accident, she died after being barred from a whites-only hospital.

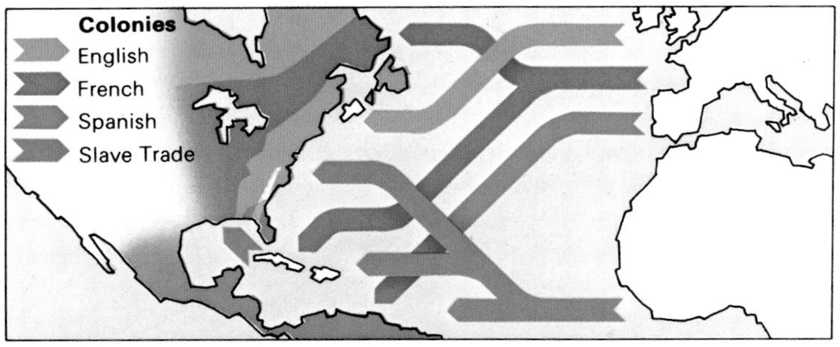

Left Colonization of America by the Europeans and the movement of slaves from West Africa. The southern states became a focal point for the intermingling of different cultures.
Below The idea that jazz "began" in New Orleans is no longer generally accepted. However, its use as riverboat entertainment was one aspect of its spread to the industrial north.

Scott Joplin (1868–1917) Joplin, the son of an ex-slave, became the best-known composer of ragtime, the syncopated piano music which was an important ingredient of early jazz. Joplin's music achieved a new vogue in the 1970s, and was featured in the popular movie *The Sting*.

Edward Kennedy "Duke" Ellington (1899–1974) As pianist, bandleader and composer Duke Ellington's many-faceted talent made him an outstanding figure in American music. The continuity of his band enabled him to achieve unique orchestral effects.

W. C. Handy (1873–1958) A southern pianist and bandleader, Handy became famous as the composer of the first published blues, "Memphis Blues" (1912) and "St Louis Blues" (1914). Though blind in later years, he was musically active until his late seventies.

Thelonious Monk (1920–) As house pianist at Minton's Club in New York, Monk helped pioneer the harmonic side of modern jazz in the early 1940s. His eccentric character and his unconventional style, with its off-centre harmonies and rhythms, gave him a certain mystique. His compositions are part of the jazz repertoire.

Louis Armstrong (1900–1971) Armstrong learned cornet in New Orleans, later switching to trumpet. After playing with King Oliver and Fletcher Henderson, he made his famous "Hot Five" and "Hot Seven" recordings (1925–8), with which jazz became a solo art. In the 1930s Armstrong fronted a big band, but reverted to small groups later.

"Jelly Roll" Morton (1885–1941) An upper-class New Orleans Creole (born Ferdinand la Menthe), Morton was one of the major early jazz composers and pianists. His tightly-organized "Red-hot Peppers" recordings, made in the 1920s, blended a "Latin tinge" with ragtime and jazz influences, reflecting his Creole background.

Popular Music

Usually contrasted with "serious" or "classical" music, and distinct from related forms such as jazz and folk, popular music typically consists of simple melodies, harmonies and words (ideally so simple that the songs can be largely remembered on one hearing). Produced specifically for a mass market, it is likely to be more ephemeral than most other types of music. Popular music was originally disseminated by means of sheet music, an important influence in the early days of its growth. It began to flourish in the late nineteenth and early twentieth centuries, mainly in the towns and cities that grew up in Europe and North America as a result of nineteenth-century industrialism. As cheap upright pianos and, later, phonograph records, became available, the sales of sheet music were greatly increased. Songs from popular operas, operettas, musical comedies and variety theatre began to find a ready audience.

Social dancing has always influenced and reflected the course of popular music. In the "Jazz Age" of 1920s America, white musicians adopted the styles of Negro jazz singers and musicians. Paul Whiteman, who ran a number of dance-bands in New York, became known as the "King of Jazz". One of his vocalists was the young Bing Crosby. Rudy Vallee was another popular singer of the inter-war years, which were also remarkable for the wealth of song-writers then active: George Gershwin, Cole Porter, Hoagy Carmichael and Jerome Kern were among them. The 'thirties and 'forties were the age of "swing", whose smooth, relaxed ambience was epitomized in the music of Glenn Miller. Any popular tune could be given the swing treatment, and while jazz was now considered old-fashioned, swing became the all-embracing style of popular music. After the war, a new breed of singers – Frank Sinatra, Johnny Ray, Guy Mitchell and Frankie Laine – who were younger than the dance-band leaders and appealed especially to young women, achieved worldwide fame.

The growth of affluence in post-war Europe and America gave rise to a distinctive youth culture. The generation of relatively high-wage-earning teenagers which grew up at this time provided a new market for music, clothes and other goods. "Rock 'n' roll", the fusion of (white) country 'n' western music and (black) rhythm 'n' blues, was specifically aimed at this new market, while singers such as Doris Day provided a quieter and less hectic type of music, still in essence swing. In 1954 Bill Haley's recording of "Rock

Sheet music was the first means by which popular music was disseminated. The songs of light opera, operettas and musical comedies were among the first to be published, then songs from music hall and vaudeville and patriotic songs. After the First World War, new music and dance fashions were spread rapidly through sheet-music sales.

around the Clock" was released. The first rock 'n' roll "hit", it established a new era in popular music – that of young people's music – with its own styles of dress, dancing (jiving) and socializing.

Haley's position at the top of the rock 'n' roll league was quickly taken by the younger, more attractive Elvis Presley, whose record "Heartbreak Hotel" (1956) sold eight million copies in six months. His extrovert performing style and his appearance were copied by other young performers and he was idolized by young people the world over. Other early figures on the rock 'n' roll front were Buddy Holly, Chuck Berry, Jerry Lee Lewis, Little Richard and Eddie Cochran. In Britain, following the success of Lonnie Donegan's "Rock Island Line" in late 1955, skiffle flourished briefly. Fast-tempo'd, strongly accented three-chord music characterized by hectic guitar-(and often washboard-) strumming, skiffle was one of the few purely British innovations of the 'fifties. Tommy Steele was Donegan's main British rival. He, like his successors Cliff Richard, Adam Faith and Billy Fury, was the British substitute for Presley, and their position was no doubt strengthened by the fact that the latter never appeared live in the UK.

By now pop music was an essential element of everyday life for young people. Juke boxes, together with portable (later transistor) radios and record-players, ensured that new record releases were constantly and ubiquitously heard. The best-sellers, jockeying for position in the hit-parade, were known to all young people.

Above all, pop records were for dancing to: the jive gave way to the "twist", promoted by Chubby Checker, in the early 1960s, then came the "shake", the "mod" dance.

A new wave in pop music began with the Beatles. After a rigorous apprenticeship in the rock clubs of Hamburg and Liverpool, they could produce a sound as authentically raw and exciting as any of their rhythm 'n' blues forebears. However, the distinction of their recordings most frequently lay in the original melodies, harmonies and lyrics of their own songs, composed in the main by John Lennon and Paul McCartney. The stark close-harmony style of their first British releases, "Love Me Do" and "Please Please Me" was one of the very few new sounds to have been heard in pop music since the birth of rock 'n' roll. By 1963 the Beatles had become the top pop stars in Britain. The following year they broke into the American market, their records achieving the unprecedented distinction of occupying the first five places in the hit-parade.

The Beatle phenomenon paved the way for many other British groups. Most notable among their rivals, though as performers rather than song-writers, were the Rolling Stones.

In a few years a clear division emerged between light and serious pop – or "rock", as it came to be called.

The change came from three directions, though they were by no means mutually exclusive. In California bands such as the Grateful Dead and Jefferson Airplane were growing out of the dawning youth revolu-

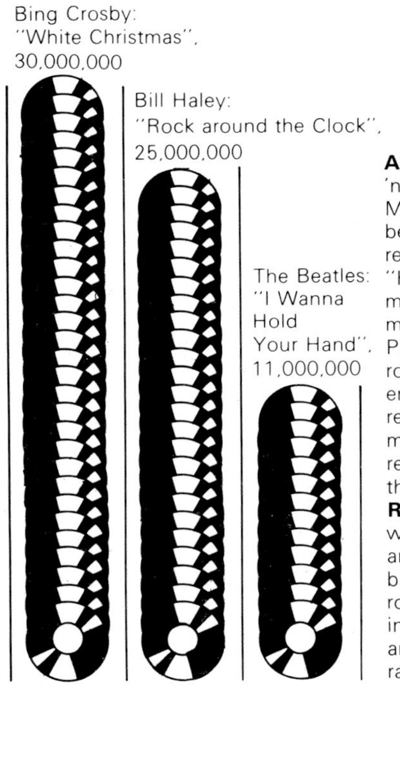

Above The first great star of rock 'n' roll was Elvis Presley. Born at Memphis, Tennessee, in 1935, he became the symbol of youthful rebellion. His records, starting with "Heartbreak Hotel", sold in millions during the 1950s. Ably managed by Colonel Tom Parker, Presley made the transition from rock 'n' roll to a mainstream entertainer. **Left** The best-selling records of all time (world sales), made in 1942, 1954 and 1963 respectively. The Beatles record is the top-selling British record. **Right 1** An early rock 'n' roll group with amplified acoustic instruments, an inheritance from jazz and the big-band era. **2** Modern pop, or rock, depends mainly on "electric" instruments, which allow for high amplification and a considerable range of special effects.

tion. They represented a radical freedom, not merely from authority but from the Establishment and all it stood for politically and economically, and also from planet Earth. The alternatives were mystical religion and psychedelic drugs.

The second root of the new music was embodied in Bob Dylan (né Zimmerman: he had changed his name out of admiration for the Welsh poet Dylan Thomas). Before the arrival of the Beatles, Dylan was rasping his Woody Guthrie-inspired songs in Greenwich Village. His guitar-playing was harsh and repetitive, punctuated by brief, wailing harmonica figures. "Bob Dylan", his first album, appeared in 1961. Later he was to create anthems for the civil rights movement, for the hippies and the far-left activists – indeed, for almost anyone who felt he was outside established society. He showed the Beatles that popular songs could be highly serious.

The Beatles demonstrated that real talent does not stand still. The strength of their early music was its ability to advance in terms of harmony, melody and lyrics while retaining its stylistic roots. This synthesis was shown in their album "Rubber Soul", but the 1966 album "Revolver" revealed startling development. "Eleanor Rigby", for example, presents a poignant and recognizable portrait, the haunting sadness of the music subtly assisted by the use of string-quartet accompaniment.

In 1967 "Sergeant Pepper's Lonely Hearts Club Band" introduced departures in popular music whose echoes are still heard today, blending fairground organ tunes, Indian *ragas*, ironic humour, melodic beauty and psychedelic flights. It is a song-cycle, compounded of surrealist imaginings and solid craftsmanship.

The pop industry has always been adept at providing new sounds and new artists for its novelty-loving clientele. The 'sixties, for example, saw the emergence of the "surfing sound", black soul music from the southern USA, and Tamla Motown's amazing stable of artists, while some of the early rock stars, notably Presley, continued to make successful records.

After once attempting to imitate the Beatles' mellower, more eclectic style (in the album "Their Satanic Majesties' Request"), the Rolling Stones reverted to producing aggressively sexual music.

The concert, perhaps more than the pop festival, typifies the experience of rock in the 'sixties. The music would erupt – so loud that its impact was almost physical.

Festivals which stand out as milestones of 'sixties "alternative culture" were Monterey in 1967, during the so-called

Left In 1960 George Harrison (lead guitar), Paul McÇartney (bass guitar), Ringo Starr (drums) and John Lennon (rhythm guitar) formed a band called the Beatles. By 1964 they were known all over the world. **Below** Bob Dylan faced his first audiences with guitar, harmonica and an extraordinary poetic gift. The Vietnam war and the race struggles in the southern USA provided ample material for protest, and Dylan's songs brought such issues to the notice of 'sixties youth. Poster by Milton Glazer.

"Summer of Love", Woodstock, and Altamont near San Francisco (1969), where a Hell's Angel killed a black man while Mick Jagger sang "Sympathy for the Devil".

On both sides of the Atlantic rock became richer and more varied as influences converged. The psychedelic tradition of the West Coast was developed in Britain by Cream, Pink Floyd and later Led Zeppelin, Jethro Tull and Yes. Pink Floyd built up a formidable armoury of sophisticated equipment. Electronic synthesizers provided limitless possibilities for controlled distortion and manipulation of sound. Floyd's music takes the listener through strange realms where clanking cash registers, screams and crazy laughter interrupt passages of psychedelic beauty.

The fusion of folk and rock was a fruitful one. While Dylan was rooted in tradition, he was not anxious to preserve that tradition unchanged – an attitude summed up in the line, "He who is not busy being born is busy dying". His album "Bringing It All Back Home" had shown the influence of the Beatles and Stones. "Highway 61 Revisited" (1965) continued the folk-rock synthesis, consolidated in 1966 by the album "Blonde on Blonde".

Dylan's platform as "one of the great warning voices of our time" (Ralph Gleason) was shared for a period by the singer Joan Baez, an equally committed campaigner for civil rights.

In Britain, Incredible String Band created their own legends and ballads – of Chinese emperors, witches, magic children and strange castles; Steeleye Span revived traditional ballads and "medieval" harmonies in their own style of electric folk.

Though born in a blaze of flowers and love, the new music soon claimed several casualties, including the virtuoso of the electric guitar and master of the creative use of feedback, Jimi Hendrix, and Janis Joplin, the blues-rock singer. She, like the Stones' Brian Jones, died of a drug overdose.

Some writers have lamented the "death" of serious pop. Their grief is unnecessary. David Bowie may not be today's answer to Mick Jagger, but certainly the superb Mike Oldfield ("Tubular Bells", "Ommadawn") has talent enough to make the musicians of the 'sixties, from John Lennon to Dylan, pay very serious attention. Rick Wakeman, Led Zeppelin, Bruce Springsteen and Patti Smith, Elton John and Joni Mitchell follow and develop the styles of the last decade in widely differing ways. Jagger, Dylan, McCartney, Pink Floyd, Grateful Dead and others still flourish, punk rock notwithstanding!

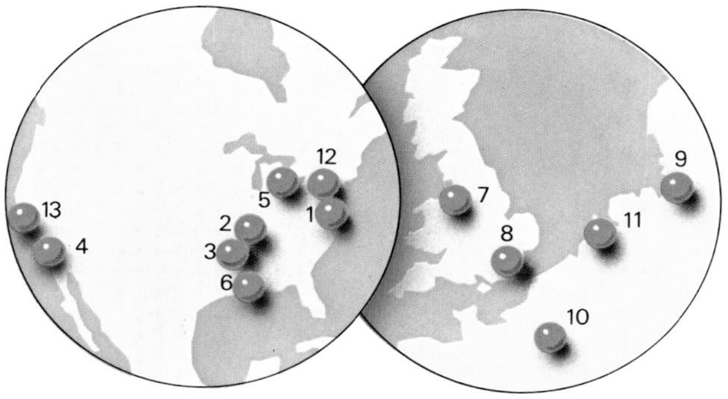

Left Pop music centres in the USA and Europe: **1** New York; **2** Nashville; **3** Memphis; **4** Haight Ashbury (San Francisco); **5** Detroit; **6** New Orleans; **7** Liverpool; **8** London; **9** Hamburg; **10** Paris; **11** Amsterdam; **12** Woodstock and **13** Monterey (pop festivals). **Below** Screaming Lord Sutch, a flamboyant exploiter of the spectacle typical of pop events. He made no hits but he did stand for Parliament, promising to introduce a bill to make the licensing of cats compulsory if he got into power. He didn't.

Islamic Music

Islamic music is essentially a vocal art, relying more on free expression and extemporization than on notation, though numerous celebrated theoreticians have tried to establish a more rigid system of notation, especially in seventeenth-century Turkey. Though conventions exist, a skilled artist is expected to elaborate and extemporize, suiting his song to the occasion.

The music usually contains a single melodic line, either simple and concentrated in form, or heavily decorated and improvisatory. Melodies are based on intervals of tones and semitones and on intervals slightly greater or smaller than either. Islamic music is rich in subtleties of tone and timbre, and exploits the human voice to the utmost. Like Indian music, the music of Islam is essentially modal and, as in the *ragas*, the modes have been given names to denote states of emotion, or associations with places or celebrated people. Whilst in India a preoccupation with the human voice relegated instrumental music to a secondary position, in Persia it still retains a sovereign influence.

Origins of Islamic music

The predominating sources of mature Islamic music emanate from the tribal kingdoms in the Arabian peninsula. The most basic Bedouin song, the *huda*, resembles in its rhythmic structure the peculiar gait of the camel. The *huda*, the *buka* (funeral lament) and the incantatory songs used in times of war were the foundations for the development of the art form. They were accompanied by the *mizraf*, or lyre, the *qussaba* or flute and the *duff* or tambourine. In settled communities, where leisure allowed for greater dexterity and accomplishment, the songs became more sophisticated. Instruments used for accompaniment included the harp (*jank*) and the shawm (Persian *surnay* or Turkish *zurna*).

Before AD 622, musical activity in south-western Asia encompassed many different instruments and styles of singing. An *Arabian Nights* story tells of a slave who presents his mistress with a lute from Damascus, a Persian harp, a Tartar pipe and an Egyptian dulcimer, all at once.

The poetry was, however, the important factor. Mohammed himself limited musical expression to the accompaniment of Koranic texts and to family celebrations. He did not encourage the use of music for secular purposes, for he assumed that its influence would debilitate religious sentiment and attitudes. Yet as the Moslem warriors came into contact with the cultures of the peoples they had conquered, Islamic music slowly lost its serious and primarily devotional nature. In time the virtuosity of the performers and the multiplicity of purposes for which the music was used led to the emergence of a wide variety of styles. Music became associated with pleasure and luxury, a tendency bitterly resisted by the traditionalists.

The first great period of Islamic music was between AD 661 and 750, when the solo lute song became enormously important. All theoretical expression was based on the *'ud*, or four- or five-stringed lute, the principal instrument of the period. In the ninth century, there was conflict between the traditionalists, who favoured a purely Arabic style, and the modernists, whose more eclectic expressive style was based on elaboration and virtuosity. Different styles flourished in different areas.

Islamic music was brought to Spain by a ninth-century musician called Ziryab, who fled Baghdad owing to the intransigence of his traditionalist master, Ishah al Mausili, over musical expression. Ziryab settled in Cordoba, founded an important music centre and had great influence in the development of new teaching methods.

The impact on European art of Moorish Spain was tremendous: in the Middle Ages, the lute and rebec, Western versions of the *'ud* and *rebab*, were soon adopted by European musicians and the intellectual qualities of Arab learning in various fields, including architecture, were quickly absorbed into European thinking.

Arab musical theory was much influenced by Greek thinkers, but the Arab masters far exceeded their European counterparts in the exploration of acoustics, rhythm, composition and instrumentation. Al Kindi, Avicenna and Safi al Din were eminent theoreticians whose studies of notation, musical intervals, concord and discord, the systematization of sound and rhythm and the development of the mode led to a great expansion in musical expression.

In Islamic music, as in all music which relies heavily on extemporization and free expression, rhythm was the unifying foundation of the art form. Rhythm was governed by regulations concerning time, percussion, symmetrical and assymmetrical rhythmic formulae and an essay on the seven rhythmic modes. In composition, melody corresponded closely to the Tagwid, or elaborate reading of the Koran. Each line, as in Arabic poetry, was complete in itself, and had its own distinctive melodic unity.

Islamic instruments

The *'ud* has always been, and remains, the most popular instrument. The modern *'ud* has no frets, unlike its early predecessor, and is played with a plectrum.

The *tunbur* is a long-stemmed instrument, originally from Baghdad, with two strings plucked by hand. The modern *tunbur* has eight strings, much like the *setar* of Iran. The *gunbri*, a lute-like instrument found in Morocco and Egypt, has two strings and a sound-box of shell or wood. The *qanum* is a form of zither with seventy-two strings grouped in threes and is played with a plectrum. The *santur*, a dulcimer with thirty-six strings, is played by being struck with two wand-like sticks.

Of bowed instruments, those of the *rebab* family, with one or two strings, are the most important.

Islamic music features a great variety of wind instruments, especially double-reed aerophones; the *zurna*'s equivalent in the Maghrib is the *gaita*.

Percussion instruments include the *zil*, small copper cymbals fastened between the finger and the thumb, and the *nuqayrat*, or kettle drums.

The influence of Islamic music

One European country which still reflects the immense influence of Arabic music is Spain. The Moorish occupation of Spain lasted from the eighth century, when the Moors were defeated at Tours, France, and were driven back to live in the already-conquered Spain, to 1492, when Granada was liberated from Arab domination by Ferdinand and Isabella.

In the seven hundred years of Arab occupation, the complicated rhythms, the microtonic scale (composed of intervals smaller than a semitone) and the various plucked and percussion instruments which the Moslem invaders used were all absorbed by the music of Spain.

The Moors were remarkably tolerant of Christianity during their occupation, and were eventually to be reconquered by Christian forces in the fourteenth and fifteenth centuries. The effect of the Moorish occupation on Christian music was to make traditional plainsong extremely florid and heavily ornamented, a style which persisted into the twentieth century. Another remnant of the Islamic past can be found in a chapel in the old cathedral at Toledo, where the old Mozarabic Rite is still permitted but has almost entirely lost its original Moorish nature.

As a result of Moorish cultural domination, plucked instruments such as the *vihuela* and the guitar have predominated in Spanish music.

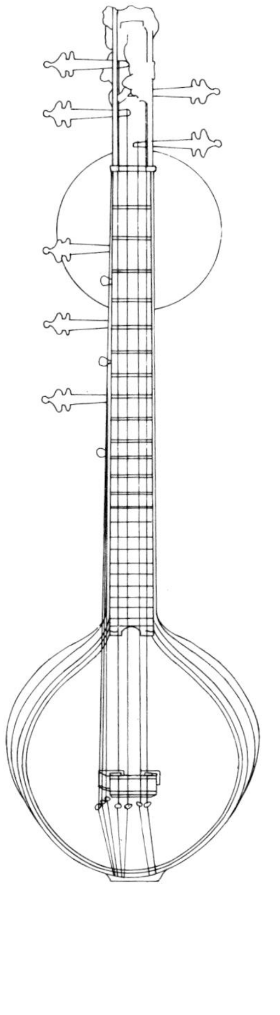

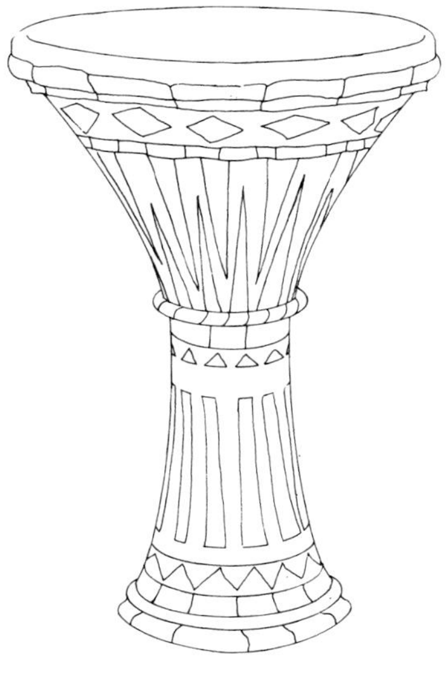

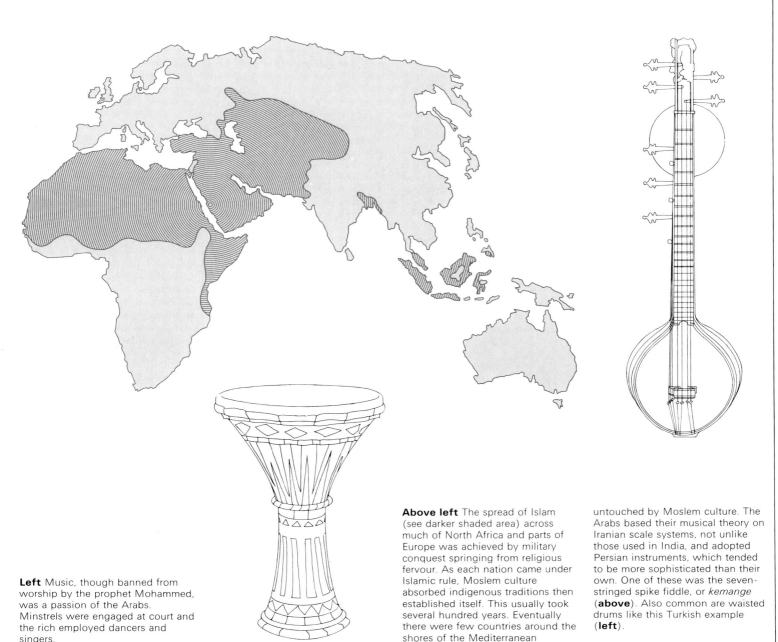

Left Music, though banned from worship by the prophet Mohammed, was a passion of the Arabs. Minstrels were engaged at court and the rich employed dancers and singers.

Above left The spread of Islam (see darker shaded area) across much of North Africa and parts of Europe was achieved by military conquest springing from religious fervour. As each nation came under Islamic rule, Moslem culture absorbed indigenous traditions then established itself. This usually took several hundred years. Eventually there were few countries around the shores of the Mediterranean untouched by Moslem culture. The Arabs based their musical theory on Iranian scale systems, not unlike those used in India, and adopted Persian instruments, which tended to be more sophisticated than their own. One of these was the seven-stringed spike fiddle, or *kemange* (**above**). Also common are waisted drums like this Turkish example (**left**).

African Music

In black Africa, as in few other parts of the world, music is essentially a communal activity. This gives an over-all unity to a diversity of forms, influences and instruments which is as rich as the continent is varied. African music exists for almost every kind of situation: religious rituals, the celebration of birth, adolescence, adulthood, marriage and death, and for regulating work, making war and dignifying chiefs and kings. It is so woven into the life of the community that in many African languages there exists no word for music as a self-contained activity.

Much of this functional quality is retained in Afro-American music – the general term for the idioms developed by the descendants of African slaves taken to Latin America (particularly Brazil), the Caribbean and the United States. These idioms include samba (Brazil), reggae and calypso (Caribbean) and gospel music, blues and jazz (United States). Blues, in particular, contributed greatly to modern rock and pop music, and it can therefore be said that much of today's "non-classical" music has its essential roots in Africa. Meanwhile, the feedback from these styles to Africa itself means that alongside traditional African music there is a growing area of modern African music, such as that of Hugh Masekela, Miriam Makeba and Fela Ransome-Kuti.

The communal values of traditional African music are epitomised in the way that simple figures are used in the building up of complex, driving rhythms, which depend for their effect on the willingness of individual musicians to play a regulated part in the ensemble. Whereas most Western rhythms are basically either in two (or four) or three beats to the bar, African rhythm is often in both at the same time (polyrhythm). This ties in closely with African dancing, in which feet, hips and shoulders move independently.

Despite the importance of drums and other instruments in African music, singing predominates, as in most other musical cultures. The call-and-response pattern, in which a choir swaps phrases with a soloist, is at the heart of African music. It can, with repetitions and improvisations, extend a musical performance for long periods – perhaps several hours.

Again in contrast to Western music, African singing tends to be rhythmically independent of instrumental backing, with the accents of the words falling between the accents of the instruments. *Melisma* (spinning a syllable out over several notes) is a pronounced feature of African song, as is the expressive contrast of "in-tune" notes and sounds of indefinite pitch.

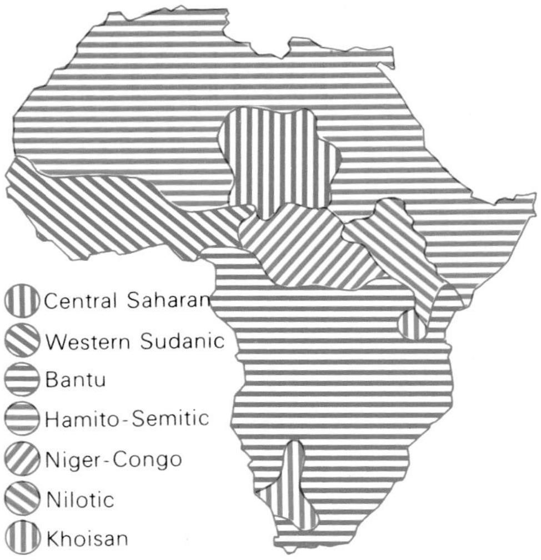

Map of Africa showing the continent's major linguistic groups.

Right Nigerian lute-players.
Below Traditional dancer of Luo, Kenya, playing a long drum.

African tunes are based on a variety of scales, ranging from four-note to seven-note types. Their tuning varies from region to region, and even from instrument to instrument. Scale intervals are usually closer to natural intervals than those of the Western tempered scale.

In African music harmony and polyphony are developed to a greater extent than in most other non-European music. Polyphony takes various forms, ranging from heterophony (individual variation of a melody) and organum (singing in parallel lines) to imitation (following a line with the same line) and hocket (dividing the notes of a melody between different voices or instruments). The pygmies of Zaïre's Ituri forest are great specialists in polyphonic singing and playing.

African musical instruments

Idiophones (anything that makes a noise, without having a skin, string or reed) are the commonest African instruments. Shaken idiophones include rattles of various kinds, either played by hand or worn on the body while dancing. Struck idiophones include clappers, iron and wooden bells, castanets and slit drums made from hollowed logs and played with sticks. Scrapers are also important.

The two main kinds of tuned idiophones are the *sansa* or *mbira* (thumb piano) and xylophone. *Sansas* have wooden or metal strips arranged over a sound-box, and are made in many sizes with from three to over forty notes. Xylophones also have different numbers of notes and pitch ranges. They are played both as solo instruments and in large ensembles.

Drums (membranophones) are made in many shapes and sizes, and may be single-headed or double-headed. They are played by hand or stick (or hand-and-stick), or sometimes by friction. The instruments of drum orchestras are graded in size (i.e. pitch) and tone.

The three main kinds of aerophones (wind instruments) are flutes, reed-pipes and trumpets or horns. Flutes are end-blown or side-blown and are usually bamboo, with varying numbers of finger-holes. Pan-pipes are sometimes found. Both single- and double-reed-pipes are used, the latter particularly in Arab-influenced areas. Side-blown trumpets made from elephant tusks or animal horns, or sometimes wood or metal, are common.

There is a wide variety of stringed instruments (chordophones), including many kinds of musical bows, and zithers, lutes, harps and lyres.

Indian Music

Two schools of music exist in India. In the south is the Carnatic school, which is heavily dependent on a rigid musical structure. In the north is the Hindustani school, which produces music in a freer form and style. The concept of *raga* is used in both systems; both schools use metre in poetry to determine musical time; and both strive for spiritual and intellectual illumination, for Indian music is closely linked with religion and philosophy.

The *raga*, a set of five, six or seven notes, is a sort of mode or ground-plan for all Indian music. It contains a tonic note (*shadja*) to which all notes must relate tonally. Among the composer-performers who contributed to the seminal form of the *raga* are Bade Gulam Ali Khan, Fayez Khan and Onkar Nath Thakur.

The performance of a *raga* is ascribed to certain times of the day, or to a specific season. Time association is instilled into pupils from the very start, and in Northern India *ragas* are sung only on the prescribed occasions.

Carnatic music

All music of the Carnatic school is based on the compositions of certain great composers who lived between the sixteenth and nineteenth centuries – Purandara Dasa, Dikshitar, Shyama Shastri, Swati Tirunal Tyagaraja and Subramanya Bharati. Teaching methods, which have changed little over the centuries, are based on a *raga*, the *mayamalawa gaula*, originally determined by the saint Purandara Dasa almost four hundred years ago. All compositions must be performed as far as possible as originally conceived, so memory, together with technical virtuosity, tempo and rhythm, is a prime concern of the Carnatic school. Original creation in performance, confined to a special section called *pallavi*, is considered less important than dexterity and interpretative skill.

Hindustani music

Hindustani music is far less rigidly defined. Each teacher makes his art entirely personal. He imparts the basic concept of *raga* to his pupil, together with a skeletal awareness of numerous compositions and teaching traditions. The student, whose listeners will expect a high standard of creativity in his extemporizations on the *raga*, must develop a personal and spontaneous approach. The few composers of the Hindustani school include Swami Hari Das, Tan Sen (Tansen), Kabir and Adarang, all poets. They provided a diffuse substructure on which talented performers could build. Great performances in the Hindustani tradition, in which reflective extemporization takes precedence over technical brilliance, will express the player's personality. Hindustani music has produced endless variations on each *raga*'s original form.

A girl, abandoned by her lover, plays to a wild animal. This subject is common in collections of Indian poetry. Painting from the Guler region, *c.*1790.

Underlying the creative aspects of the *raga* is the *tala*, or rhythm cycle, which consists of a fixed number of units of equal value. Today there are twenty *talas* in common use. Like the *raga*, each has its individual name and has to be learnt by heart. There may be six, eight, ten, twelve or sixteen *matras* (time sections) in each *tala*, grouped in bars. Throughout a performance, whatever contrapuntal/rhythmic exploration may occur, the various instruments must always coordinate on the first beat of the cycle, the *sam*.

Indian musical instruments

One of the commonest Indian musical instruments is the *tanpura* (or *tambura*). Used all over India, it is between one and two metres long, with a gourd bowl 30–45 centimetres wide. Its four metal strings, together with one of brass which gives a lower note, are plucked continuously to produce a drone. *Tanpuras* are often heavily decorated with leaf and tendril motifs and mystic symbols in gold and green.

The *veena*, which bears some resemblance to the lute, is traditionally associated with Saraswati, goddess of learning. It has two resonating chambers, the larger made from a gourd, the smaller from papier mâché. The upper end of the stem is often carved to resemble a serpent or dragon. There are seven strings, four passing over twenty-four frets (each marking a semitone), and three side strings for rhythmic accompaniment. The *veena* is held diagonally across the lap and is played with a wire plectrum fitted over the fingers. Its deep, resonant tone has greatly influenced Carnatic style.

The *sitar*, like the *tanpura*, has a bulbous gourd and a slender stem about a metre long, with twenty-two frets made of brass or silver. The rhythm and drone strings are called the *chikari*. Twelve sympathetic strings underlie the seven main strings and are tuned to the notes of the *raga* being performed. The right hand plucks the strings with a wire plectrum or *mizraf*. The left hand stops the sound. The *sitar* has a wide range of tonal colour.

The *sarod*, about a metre long, has six main strings, and twelve underlying strings tuned to the *raga* being played. Capable of great rhythmic complexity and haunting *pianissimo* effects, the *sarod* is often used to accompany the sitar.

The *tabla*, most popular of the northern percussion instruments, consists of two drums. The *tabla*-player governs the rhythm and may feature original coloratura passages in performance.

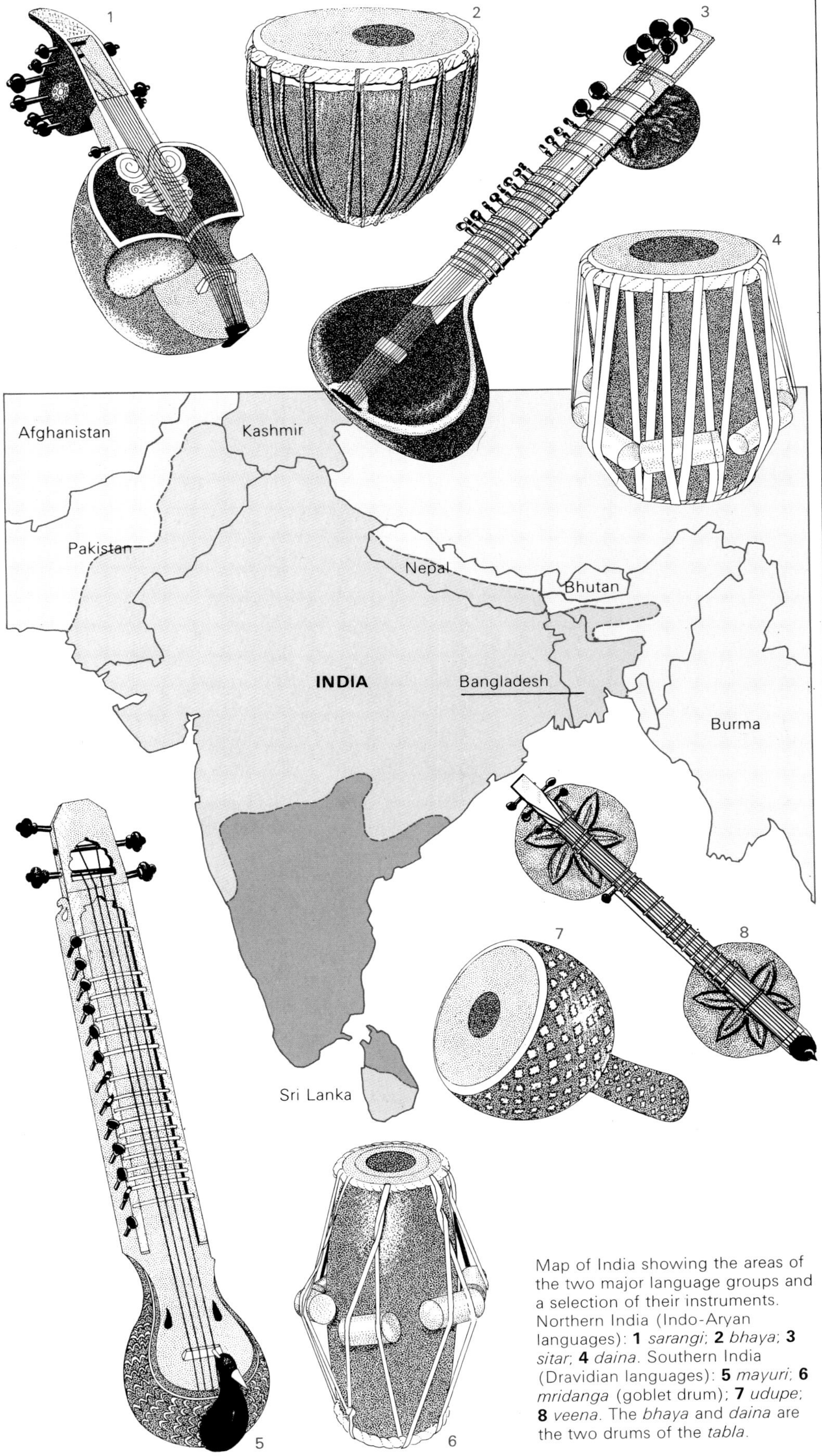

Map of India showing the areas of the two major language groups and a selection of their instruments. Northern India (Indo-Aryan languages): **1** *sarangi*; **2** *bhaya*; **3** *sitar*; **4** *daina*. Southern India (Dravidian languages): **5** *mayuri*; **6** *mridanga* (goblet drum); **7** *udupe*; **8** *veena*. The *bhaya* and *daina* are the two drums of the *tabla*.

Far-Eastern Music

The music of the Far East, which includes China, Japan, South-East Asia and Indonesia, has a common stock of features which distinguish it from European and African music. By and large, the music of the high oriental cultures has been the province of professional musicians, with a separate and distinctive "folk" music predominating within tribal cultures.

Far-Eastern music is noted for its stability and inertia: the major instruments of Chinese music have been known for about two thousand years, and its scales have been in use almost as long. The emphasis is very much on vocal, rather than instrumental music. As a result melody has reached a higher level of sophistication in the Far East than in the West.

Chinese music

Chinese musical instruments as old as the Shang dynasty (1766–1122 BC) have been found. They include musical stones, round flutes, bells and drums. The stone chime, the bell chime and the reed mouth-

organ were the most important instruments of the Chou dynasty (1122–249 BC), in which the first stringed zithers were also introduced.

The festivals of the agricultural year were celebrated in song and dance. Ballads and odes were sung in the imperial court from very early times, leading to the existence of a professional musical caste. Music was also a major element of the religious ceremonies of the early dynasties.

Musical theory became imbued with philosophical and mystical concepts during the time of Lao Tzu, the founder of Taoism, and Confucius in the 6th and 5th centuries BC. The five-note (pentatonic) scale – the basis of music in China and much of the Far East – was defined during this period. Like the *ragas* of Indian music, different scales were symbolically associated with different months and hours. Chant, accompanied by percussion instruments (bells, gongs, cymbals and blocks) was introduced in the 1st century AD, reflecting Buddhist influence. The zither (*ch'in*) was used to accompany meditation. By the 5th century AD dancing had become an established element of Confucian ceremonies. As the empire expanded, and especially during the Mongol invasions of the thirteenth and fourteenth centuries, Chinese music absorbed foreign influences.

Theatrical and operatic music was developed at court. The court dramas had secular themes; some were dramatized folk songs or epics. Some, such as *The History of Lute-Playing* (1513), are several hours long with as many as a hundred arias and sections of dialogue. The dramas were performed mostly by professionals, and until 1911 these performers belonged to separate male and female troupes.

Far left Japanese nobleman playing the flute while being attacked from behind by a bandit. From a pen drawing. **Left** Detail from a Chinese T'ang scroll showing ladies of the court playing musical instruments. **Below** Japanese short-necked lute, or "moon guitar".

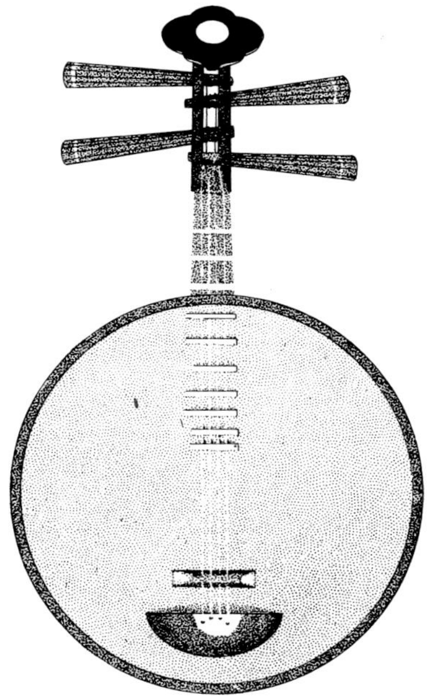

Japanese music

Japanese music, which probably began with the chants of Shinto temple ritual, took its main impetus from Chinese music in the 3rd century AD and was later influenced by Korean, Manchurian and Indian music.

Court music featured percussion instruments, such as drums and gongs, and a variety of wind instruments. The traditional, highly formalized *Noh* ("display of talent") plays, some dating from the fourteenth century, are musical dramas portraying scenes from everyday life but based on Buddhist themes. The plays are accompanied by drums, flutes, and solo and choral singing. The *Kabuki* theatre – a more popular dance-theatre – uses flute, drum and *samisen* (a long-necked lute).

The vertical bamboo pipe (*shakuhachi*), various stringed instruments and the zither (*koto*) came into use in the sixteenth century. The *koto*, used for both solo performance and accompaniment, is regarded as Japan's national instrument.

South-East Asian music

The music of South-East Asia, where the basic culture is Chinese, is again eclectic: India, Islam and more recently the West, together with the indigenous culture of native tribes, have all exerted influence. Indonesia shows heavier influence from Muslim and Indian culture.

A typical Balinese *gamelan* (orchestra) might consist of a drum, tuned chime instruments, a curved xylophone, bronze celestas, gong chimes, kettle-gongs and a bamboo rattle-chime, all fixed-pitch instruments. Larger orchestras would also have flutes and fiddles. *Gamelan* music is used to accompany dancing.

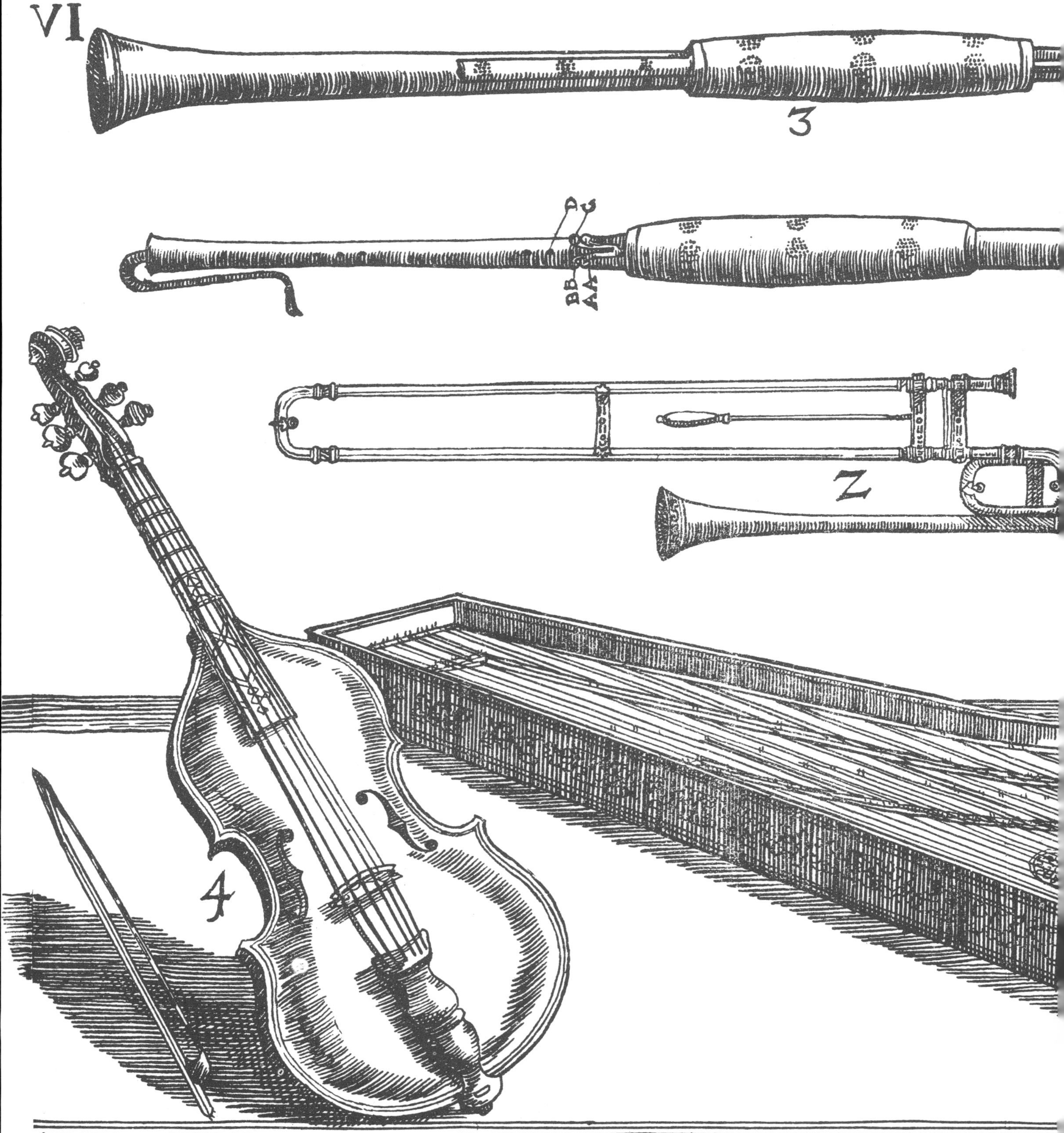
VI
3
D
C
BB
AA
Z
4
1
2
3
4
5
6
7

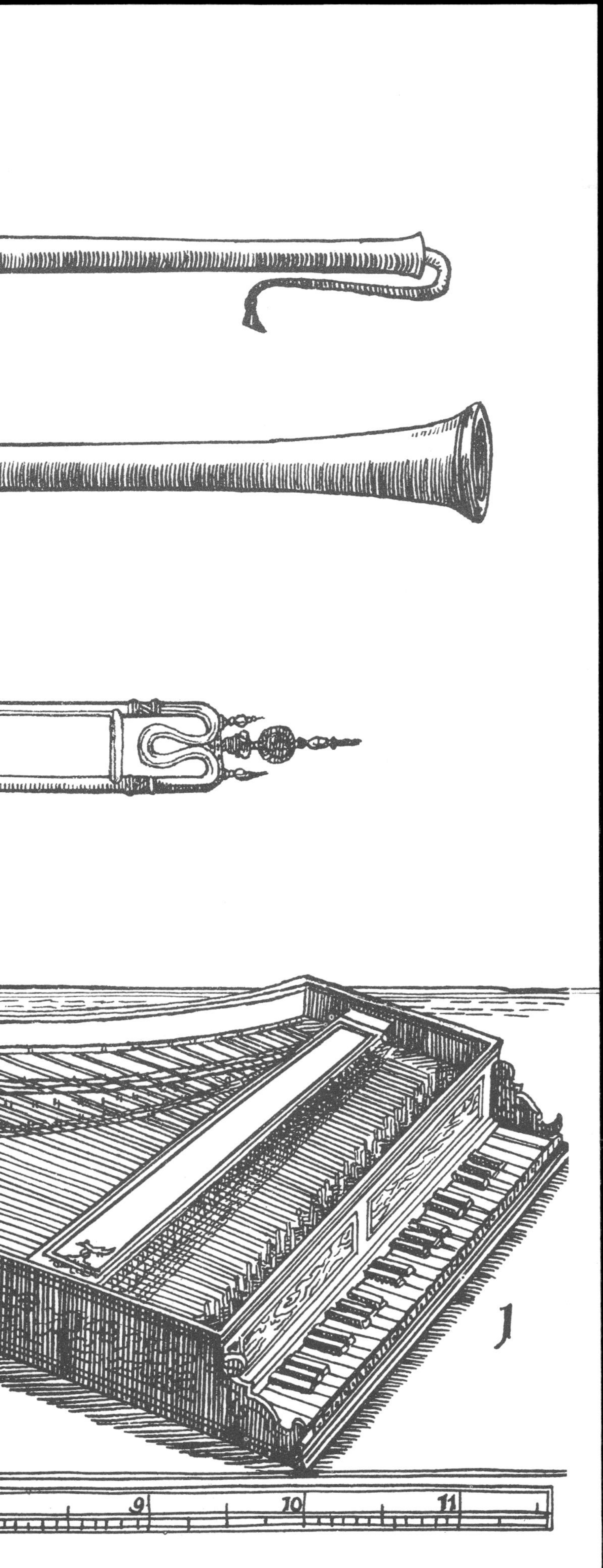

111 Music-Makers

It is remarkable that so many of the musical instruments we now regard as "modern" and distinctly Western European are in fact nothing of the sort. Even the principles on which our ultra-sophisticated grand pianos function can be traced back to the ancient dulcimer, brought from the Middle East in the eleventh century. Shapes have changed, refinements have been introduced, but basically the component instruments of the symphony orchestra of today have changed little in the last few centuries. Moreover, their counterparts may be found all over the world, wherever the materials from which they are constructed – wood, metal and gut, in the main – are available.

Illustration from the appendix of Michael Praetorius's *Syntagma Musicum*, showing recorders, sackbut, harpsichord and viol.

Stringed Instruments

Any instrument in which sound is produced by string-vibration is a *chordophone*. The four members of the modern bowed strings are the violin, viola, cello and double-bass. Though in shape and proportion they are not dissimilar to the older viol family, they are different both structurally (for example, they have no frets), and musically (they produce a far brighter sound than the viols).

The violin

The violin is among the best loved of all instruments. Its beauty of tone and its outstanding range of emotional expressiveness make it an ideal solo instrument, popular for centuries with performers and audiences alike. No less important, however, is its role as an orchestral and chamber instrument. In combination with the larger and deeper-sounding members of the same family, the violins form the nucleus of the modern symphony orchestra and the classic chamber ensemble, the string quartet.

Of all modern instruments, the violin is apparently one of the simplest. It consists in essence of a hollow, varnished wooden sound-box or resonator, and a long neck or finger-board, along which four strings are stretched at high tension. The beauty of design, shape and decoration is no accident: the proportions of the instrument are determined almost entirely by acoustical considerations. Its simplicity of appearance is deceptive. About seventy parts are involved in the construction of a violin.

The violin has been in existence since about 1550. Its importance as an instrument in its own right dates from the early 1600s, when it first became standard in Italian opera orchestras (see page 126). Its stature as an orchestral instrument was raised further when in 1626 Louis XIII established at his court the orchestra known as *Les vingt-quatre violons du Roy*, which was to become widely famous later in the century under Lully.

In its early history, the violin had a dull and rather quiet tone resulting from the fact that the strings were thick and were attached to the body of the instrument very loosely. During the eighteenth and nineteenth centuries, exciting technical changes were inspired by such composer-violinists as Vivaldi and Tartini. Their concertos and solo sonatas demanded a fuller, clearer and more brilliant tone (which was produced by using thinner strings) and a far higher string tension to make possible brilliant passage work. Small changes had to be made to the violin's internal structure and to the finger-board so that they could withstand the extra strain.

Accordingly, a higher standard of performance was achieved, in terms of both facility and interpretation. Left-hand technique was considerably elaborated, and new fingerings were developed for very high notes.

In the early part of the eighteenth century, the practice of holding the violin under the chin instead of against the chest or collar bone was established. Later in the century, the bow was considerably improved: it was strengthened, and made both longer and wider. This facilitated the long, smooth strokes of the bow so necessary in lyrical music, of which composers such as Haydn and Mozart produced a good deal.

The violin was established in its modern form, therefore, by the late eighteenth century, by which time the viol had largely fallen out of use. The high point of violin virtuosity came in the nineteenth century with Niccolò Paganini, the archetypal romantic. He used his remarkable gifts to excite his audiences to a state of near-hysteria. Paganini also wrote a quantity of complex and brilliant music for the violin which remains a challenge and an inspiration even for today's virtuoso performers.

The violin has an extensive solo repertoire, perhaps second only to that of the piano in its range and quality. Among those who in the present century have made this repertoire known to audiences the world over are Jascha Heifetz, Yehudi Menuhin, Isaac Stern, David Oistrakh, Pinchas Zukermann and Kyung Wha Chung.

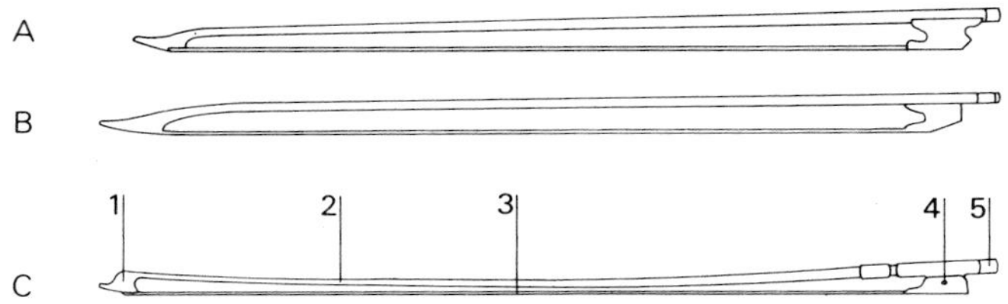

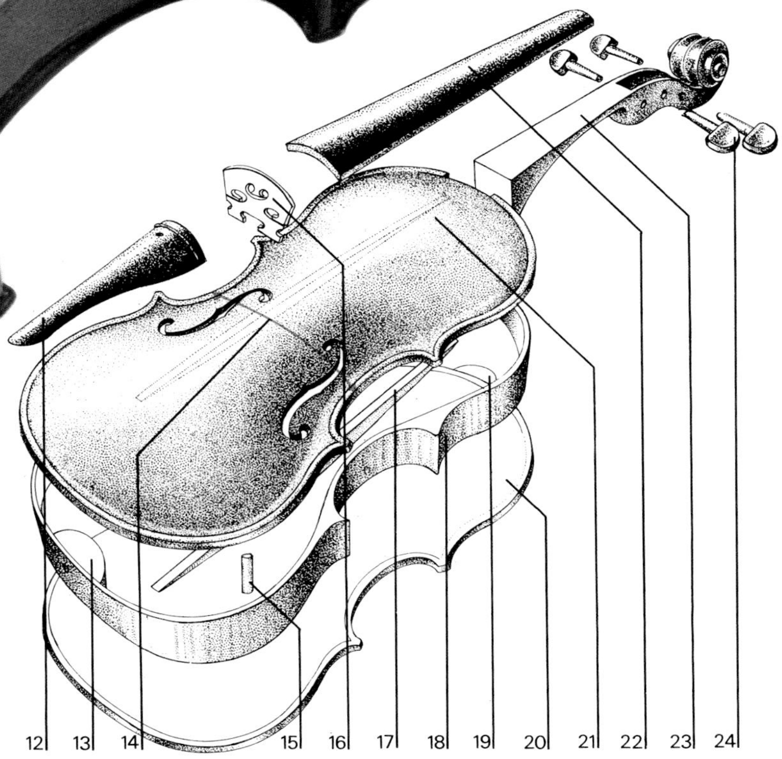

Left The elegant lines of the violin conceal several important constructional features, both internal and external, that fundamentally affect the acoustical qualities of the instrument. The back, neck, scroll and ribs are made of a hardwood, usually maple, while the belly is of a softwood, often a piece of European spruce with a close, straight grain. The finger-board and tailpiece are of the hardest wood, such as ebony, or of a hard plastic, and the chinrest too is made of hardwood, such as rosewood, or of a plastic called vulcanite. The materials from which the violin strings are made have a marked effect on the tone the violinist produces. Originally, all strings were gut, but modern strings have cores of finely drawn steel wire, gut, nylon or some other synthetic material, closely wound with aluminium, silver or stainless steel. The top or E string is now generally made of steel. The delicate adjustments essential to tuning the strings of the violin, where tolerances are extremely fine, can be achieved easily by adding a small lever device operated by turning a screw. The violinist fits the tuning adjustment to the tailpiece of the instrument. The parts of the violin are called: **1** chinrest; **2** end-pin (or tail-pin); **3** tailpiece loop; **4** saddle; **5** body or sound-box; **6** purfling; **7** f-hole; **8** nut; **9** peg-box; **10** scroll; **11** scroll eye; **12** tailpiece; **13** end-pin block; **14** waist; **15** sound-post; **16** bridge; **17** brass bar; **18** neck plate or button; **19** sides or ribs (called "bouts" in the waist of the violin); **20** back; **21** belly; **22** finger-board; **23** neck; **24** tuning peg.

Top left Violinists have employed various styles of bow over the centuries. The late seventeenth-century bow (**A**) was short, rather inflexible and loosely strung; the eighteenth-century bow (**B**) was longer and more springy. The most important characteristic of the modern bow (**C**), pioneered by François Tourte in the early nineteenth century, is the long, tapering, inward-curving stick, balanced at a point about 22cm from the nut. Bows for the viola, cello and double-bass are similar to the violin bow but successively heavier. The parts of the modern bow are: **1** point; **2** stick; **3** hair; **4** nut; **5** screw.

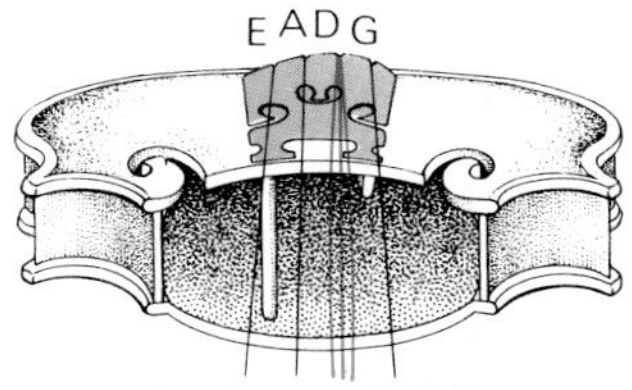

When a string is sounded, it transmits vibrations to the bridge and from there to the belly.

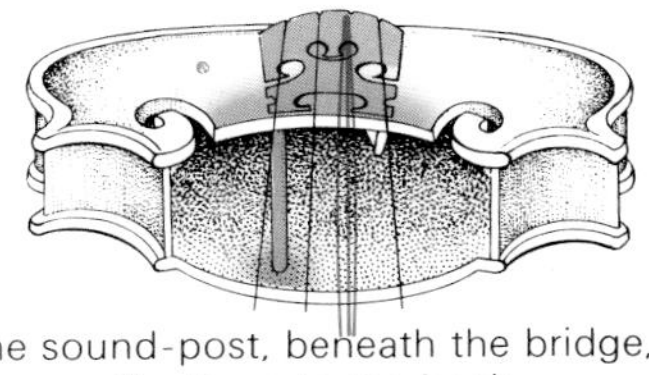

The sound-post, beneath the bridge, passes vibrations to the back.

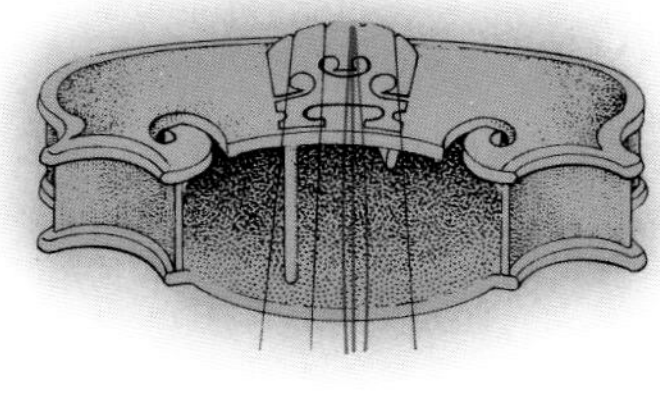

The tone of the single violin string, amplified and enhanced, is modified by the whole sound-box.

Viola, violoncello and double-bass

In addition to the violin itself, the violin family has three other important members – the viola, the violoncello (usually shortened to cello), and the double-bass. The instruments share the same appearance and basic playing method, but the cello and double-bass are held vertically for playing while the viola, like the violin, is held under the chin.

The viola is the alto member of the family. It is only slightly larger than the violin (in the region of 7·5cm) but the extra size gives it a characteristically gentle and mellow tone. Its history and development follow very closely those of the violin, though it has never shared the violin's popularity as a solo instrument. Lacking the latter's flexibility and brilliance in passage work, the viola was most commonly used in an accompanying capacity, filling in and enriching the harmonies. During the last two decades of the eighteenth century musicians gradually recognized the peculiar beauty of the viola's tone colour; this is clearly heard in the string quartets of Haydn and Mozart. Musicians grew increasingly aware of the viola's qualities in the nineteenth century – Berlioz's orchestral piece *Harold in Italy* includes a substantial part for solo viola – and since 1900 the viola has acquired an increasingly important solo role.

The history of the cello is very different. Roughly twice the size of the violin, its deep body produces a rich resonance that carries well. It first appeared in the sixteenth century but its importance dates from the early seventeenth century when it was first used as a continuo instrument, joining with the harpsichord to play the bass line and support the harmonies in early orchestras and smaller ensembles.

After the early eighteenth century almost every composer contributed to the cello's repertoire, which includes J. S. Bach's suites for solo cello, and the concertos by Haydn, Dvořák and Elgar. Virtuoso players carried cello technique forward in the romantic period when the instrument's expressive qualities were exploited. Outstanding cellists of the twentieth century include Pablo Casals, Jacqueline du Pré, Pierre Fournier, Paul Tortelier and Mstislav Rostropovitch.

The double-bass is the deepest member of the violin family. It is constructed slightly differently from the other members, inheriting some features from an older bowed stringed instrument, the bass viol. Though its somewhat muffled sound makes it rather unsatisfactory as a solo instrument, the double-bass's role in large

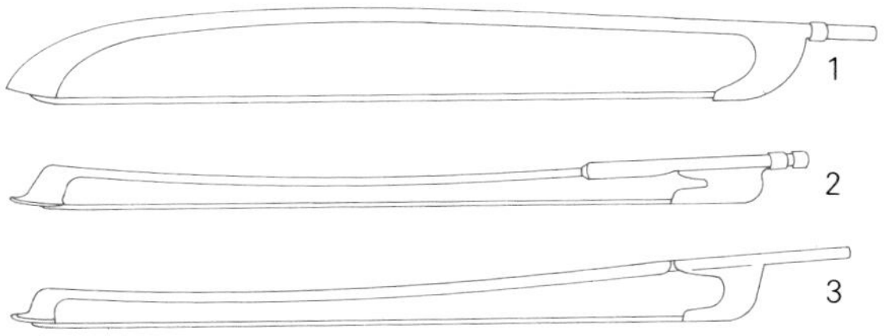

Above Double-bass bows: **1** early nineteenth-century English bow; **2** modern French bow; **3** Simandl bow, used by players who prefer a palm-upwards grip. **Below** The viola and violin share the same body shape and construction but the viola (**B**) is about 7·5cm longer than the violin (**A**). Its extra size makes it more awkward to hold, and rapid passage work is considerably harder. During this century, the first true virtuoso viola-players, William Primrose and Lionel Tertis, have carried the instrument's prestige to new technical and musical heights. **Right** The cello, roughly twice the length of the violin, provides the bass part for the string quartet. It is fitted with a retractable spike so that its height can be adjusted for the player's convenience. The cello is played with a shorter, thicker bow than that used for the violin.

Far right The double-bass stands about 1·8m high. There are two main body shapes – one with sloping shoulders (**A**), the other based on that of the violin (**B**). The size of the double-bass forces the player to span considerable distances between stopping positions on the finger-board. In order to train and strengthen their students' fingers, some teachers have been known to recommend practising with matchboxes between the fingers of the left hand to stretch the muscles!

Viola

Cello

Double-bass

Playing positions for violin and viola, cello and double-bass.

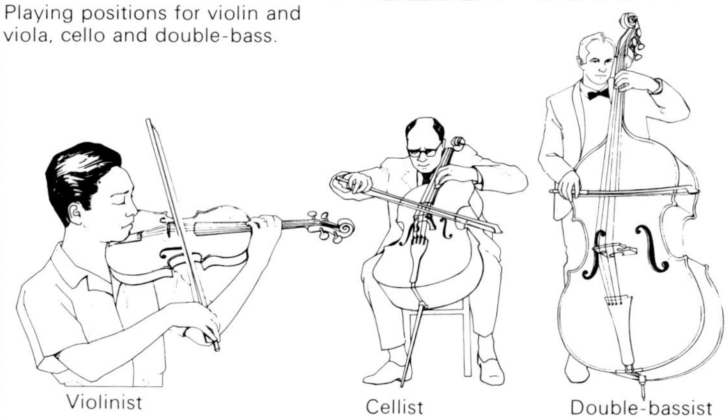

Famous works for violin
J. S. Bach: partitas for solo violin
L. van Beethoven: Violin Concerto in D, *Spring* sonata in F, *Kreutzer* sonata in A
A. Berg: Violin Concerto
J. Brahms: Violin Concerto in D
M. Bruch: Violin Concerto in G minor
A. Corelli: *concerti grossi*
W. A. Mozart: violin concertos and sonatas
G. Tartini: *Devil's Trill* sonata in G minor
P. Tchaikovsky: Violin Concerto in D
A. Vivaldi: violin sonatas

Famous works for viola
H. Berlioz: *Harold in Italy*
W. A. Mozart: *Sinfonia concertante* for violin, viola and orchestra
R. Strauss: *Don Quixote*
W. Walton: Viola Concerto

Famous works for cello
J. S. Bach: Six Suites for cello
L. Boccherini: cello concertos
B. Britten: *Cello Symphony*
E. Elgar: Cello Concerto
J. Haydn: Cello Concerto in C
S. Prokofiev: *Ballad*
C. Saint-Saëns: "The Swan", from *Carnival of the Animals*
P. Tchaikovsky: *Variations on a Rococo Theme*
A. Webern: *Three Little Pieces*

Famous works for double-bass
A. Dubensky: Fugue for eight double-basses
S. Koussevitsky: Double-bass Concerto
E. Varèse: *Octandre*

Pitch ranges

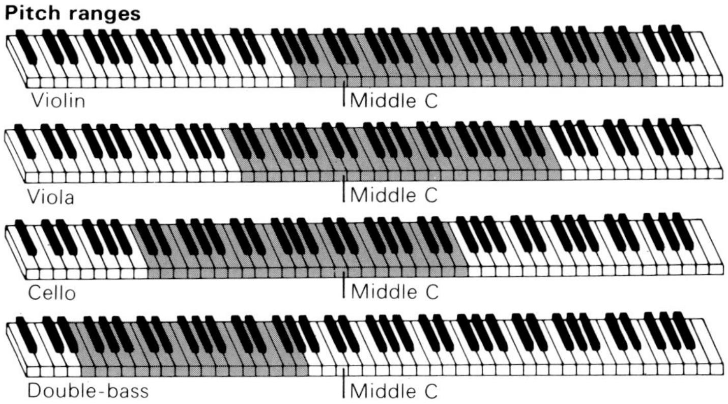

Positions in the orchestra
1 First violins
2 Second violins
3 Violas
4 Cellos
5 Double-basses

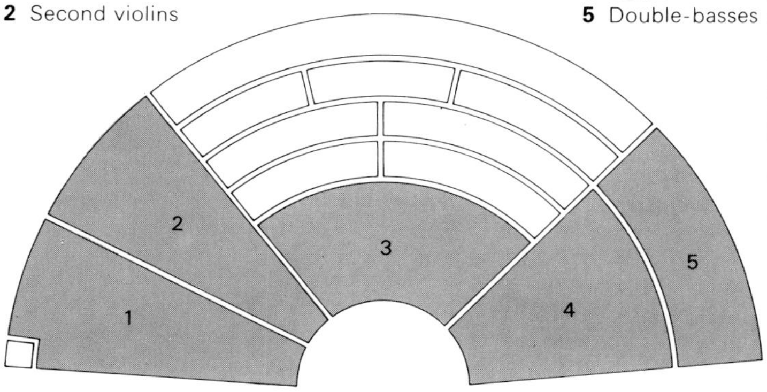

ensembles and orchestras is vital. It is used to play the lowest notes and to provide the bass line for harmonies. It often plays one octave lower than the cellos, and adds considerable richness and depth to the instrumental texture.

Development of the orchestral strings

About 350 years ago, the long period of polyphony (music expressed through the combination of several melodic parts) declined before the advance of homophony (in which the melody is generally concentrated in one part). This change demanded greater tonal brilliance from the orchestral strings than the viol family could offer so the violin family supplanted viols in large ensembles. The development of the orchestral string family became inseparable from the history of Western music, its composers and its performers. There are three important reasons for this: firstly, the violins, violas, cellos and double-basses are richly expressive and responsive instruments capable of an enormous range of tonal subtleties; secondly, the tone qualities of all four instruments are complementary, giving a varied blend of sounds to act as a background for or a contrast to other instrumental sonorities; thirdly, the bow allows players to sustain the sound and to control its intensity.

The violin family as we know it dates from the late sixteenth century but various kinds of bowed instruments were played in Europe as far back as the Middle Ages. Of these instruments three had a decisive influence on the development of members of the violin family.

The first of the violin's ancestors was the rebec, the European version of the ancient Arab *rebab*. The second was the medieval fiddle, an instrument with a finger-board, a slightly waisted body, sound holes, and five strings – four on the finger-board to be stopped by the fingers, and one off the finger-board to act as a drone. The third instrument was the lira da braccio ("arm lyre"), with a body similar to a violin's. It had seven strings, five on the finger-board and two drones.

The first recognizable members of the violin family emerged around 1550. While the "invention" of the instruments cannot be attributed to any one maker, some of the earliest violins, violas and cellos were the work of the Italians Gasparo da Solo (1540–1609) and Giovanni Paolo Maggini (1580–*c*.1632), both of Brescia. These early instruments had thick, rather loose strings, giving a quieter, duller sound than modern equivalents.

More or less at the same time, Andrea Amati (*c*.1505–*c*.1580) founded the

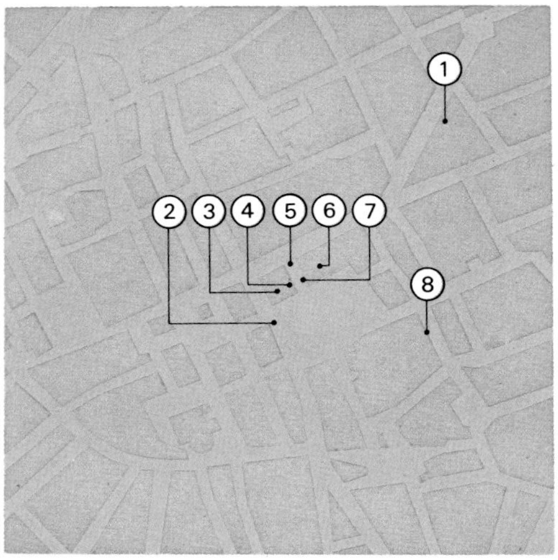

Above Street map of Cremona showing the location of some famous violin-makers' workshops.

1 Antonio Stradivari
2 Carlo Bergonzi
3 Giuseppe Guarneri del Gesù
4 Antonio and Hieronymus Amati
5 Lorenzo Storioni and G. B. Ceruti
6 Francesco Pescaroli
7 Gio Maria Cironi
8 Nicola Amati

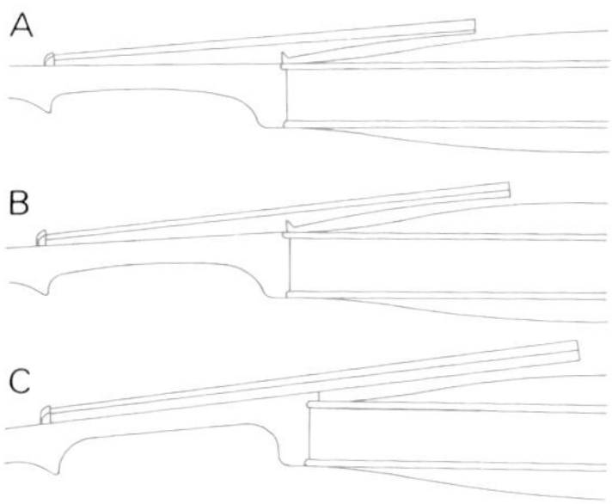

Above A diagram showing the evolution of the tilt of the violin neck and the elongation of the finger-board. Before 1750 the neck was in line with the body and the finger-board was short (**A**). In the late eighteenth century a slight tilting back of the neck and elongation of the finger-board facilitated the execution of passages of difficult fingerwork (**B**). Increasingly taxing demands on performers in the nineteenth century resulted in a profile like that of the modern violin (**C**). **Right** A rebec (**1**), one of the ancestors of the violin, and a kit (**2**), a pocket-sized fiddle used by dancing masters in the eighteenth and nineteenth centuries.

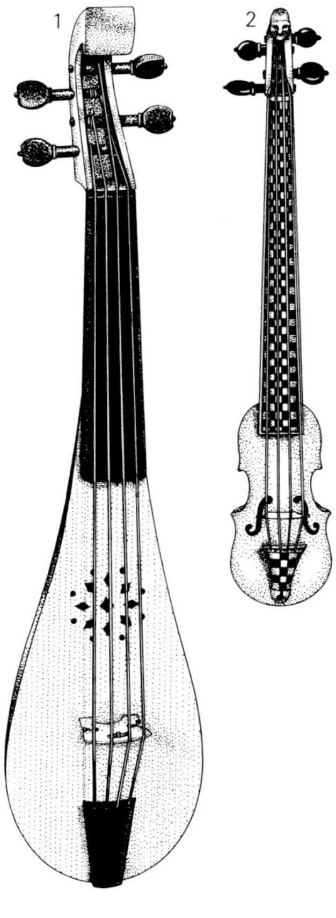

Below Illustration from *Epithome Plutarchi* (1501) of a poet with a lira da braccio hanging from a nearby tree. **Right** A lira da braccio. It has five bowed strings and two sympathetic strings which vibrate "in sympathy" when the instrument is played. An offshoot of the fiddle, and about the size of the viola, it was played resting on the shoulder. The earliest examples were unfretted, so this lira da braccio is probably a seventeenth-century instrument.

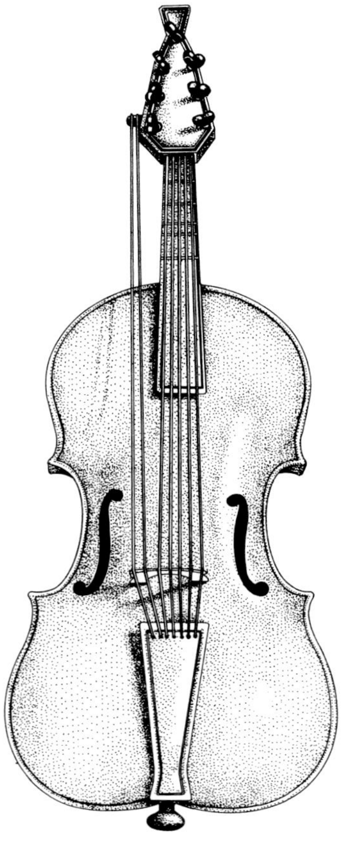

renowned workshops at Cremona, and his work was continued by his sons and his grandson Nicola (1596–1684), the finest craftsman in the family. The Amatis brightened the tone of the violin and developed its classic shape. They made the body flatter, the curve of the bouts deeper, the corners sharper, increased the string tension and improved the varnish.

Nicola Amati's supreme pupil, Antonio Stradivari (*c.*1644–1737), also worked in Cremona. Throughout his long life, he changed the design of his instruments several times, but in 1698 he adopted a model 35cm long and 20cm wide for his basic design, and built most of his finest violins to this pattern. Stradivari's workmanship was rivalled by another great Cremonese, Giuseppe Guarneri del Gesù (1698–1744).

By about 1800, craftsmen had made several small but significant changes to the violin. The bridge was higher, the strings were thinner and secured at a higher tension to improve the tone, the bass bar was made stronger and longer to withstand the greater strain, the neck and finger-board were lengthened, tilted back slightly and made narrower at the pegbox end to facilitate rapid fingerings, and a chinrest was added to enable the player to hold the violin securely. These modifications proved so successful that the structure of the violin has scarcely changed since then.

The double-bass was first known in the late sixteenth century in Italy and Germany. Like all very large instruments, its design was altered many times without becoming standardized. Perhaps the most significant difference between the double-bass and the rest of the violin family is that it has never been an important solo instrument, except in jazz. Its main importance has been its function as the bass instrument of orchestras and chamber ensembles.

The bow

The modern bow is longer than earlier bows, can be screwed to greater tension and is of a more springy construction. String-players have developed the art of bowing considerably over the last four centuries. From the predominance of dance music in the sixteenth century early players initiated a tradition of establishing a strong beat by using a down-bow for emphasis – that is, the performer would draw the bow across the string from heel to point. String-players developed many subtle variations of bowing technique for all members of the violin family, and the modern player must be familiar with at least a dozen ways of bowing to produce the wide range of nuances required.

The growth of interest in playing the instruments of the violin family in the nineteenth and twentieth centuries has led to the establishment of centres in Europe, Japan and the United States of America where mass-production techniques have been adapted to the manufacture of instruments. This development has made instruments available at a low cost to thousands of aspiring players.

Harp, zither and guitar

The instruments of the plucked string family have several important modern representatives. The three best-known – the harp, the zither, and the guitar – are entirely different from each other in appearance, method of playing and function.

The harp This is the only plucked stringed instrument that has held a regular place in the symphony orchestra since Beethoven. It is one of the world's oldest instruments and is still found in a variety of forms as a folk instrument in many parts of Africa, the East and Europe. The European medieval harp suffered from the severe limitation of being tuned to one scale. If accidentals were required the

Right Stringed instruments can be sounded in many different ways. The overhand bow-hold (**1**) is now used commonly on the violin, viola, and cello. Some double-bass-players prefer to hold the bow with the palm outwards, a hold used by all viol players (**2**). Plucking the strings – *pizzicato* – shown here on violin (**3**), is a technique possible on all the orchestral strings. A mute (**4**) is a device clamped over the strings to limit their vibrations and so give a quiet sound. **Left** The viol was an important fretted stringed instrument of the Renaissance and early Baroque. It was made in several sizes, and played in an upright position. Its tone is much less "bright" than that of the violin. **Below** The deeply curved medieval viol bow (**1**) was superseded by the less unwieldy Renaissance version (**2**).

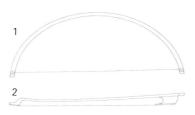

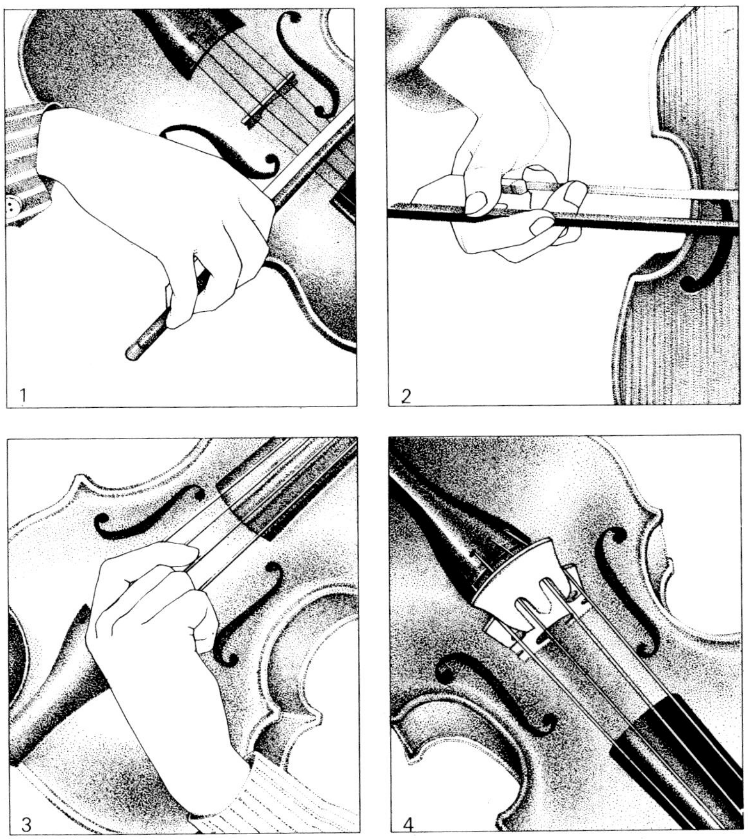

harpist had to press a string with his fingers while playing, an unacceptably clumsy system. Between 1600 and 1800 makers devoted their attention to trying to provide the "missing" notes without unduly complicating the playing technique. The most satisfactory solution was reached in about 1810 with the perfection of the double-action pedal harp by Sebastien Érard (1752–1831). This design is still used for most modern harps.

Though used quite widely in the orchestral music of the romantic era, the repertoire of solo music for the harp is sadly limited. It was, however, a favourite instrument with some late-nineteenth- and twentieth-century French composers, such as Ravel and Debussy, who used its delicate tones to enrich the impressionistic colouring of much of their music.

The zither This popular plucked instrument is traditionally associated with Austria and Bavaria. The history of the European zither dates back to the late Middle Ages when the psaltery, an instrument similar to the modern zither, was introduced from the Middle East. An alternative method of playing, by striking the strings with small hammers, was also established, rather later; when played like this the instrument was, and still is, referred to as a dulcimer.

In the last two centuries, the zither has enjoyed popularity not only as a folk instrument but also as a concert instrument. The concert zither has between thirty and forty-five strings, four or five of which are melody strings that run over a fretted finger-board and can be stopped with the fingertips of one hand and plucked with a plectrum. The other strings are used for accompaniment. For playing, the zither is set horizontally on a table or across the player's lap.

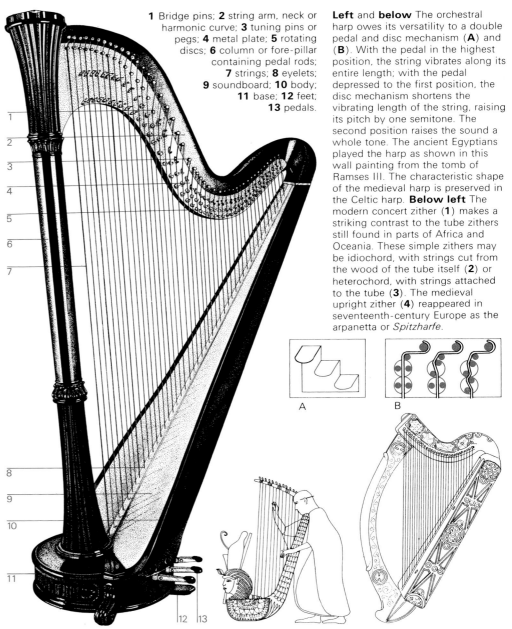

1 Bridge pins; **2** string arm, neck or harmonic curve; **3** tuning pins or pegs; **4** metal plate; **5** rotating discs; **6** column or fore-pillar containing pedal rods; **7** strings; **8** eyelets; **9** soundboard; **10** body; **11** base; **12** feet; **13** pedals.

Left and **below** The orchestral harp owes its versatility to a double pedal and disc mechanism (**A**) and (**B**). With the pedal in the highest position, the string vibrates along its entire length; with the pedal depressed to the first position, the disc mechanism shortens the vibrating length of the string, raising its pitch by one semitone. The second position raises the sound a whole tone. The ancient Egyptians played the harp as shown in this wall painting from the tomb of Ramses III. The characteristic shape of the medieval harp is preserved in the Celtic harp. **Below left** The modern concert zither (**1**) makes a striking contrast to the tube zithers still found in parts of Africa and Oceania. These simple zithers may be idiochord, with strings cut from the wood of the tube itself (**2**) or heterochord, with strings attached to the tube (**3**). The medieval upright zither (**4**) reappeared in seventeenth-century Europe as the arpanetta or *Spitzharfe*.

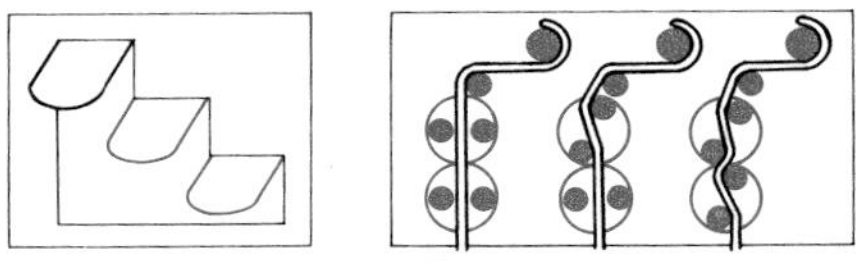

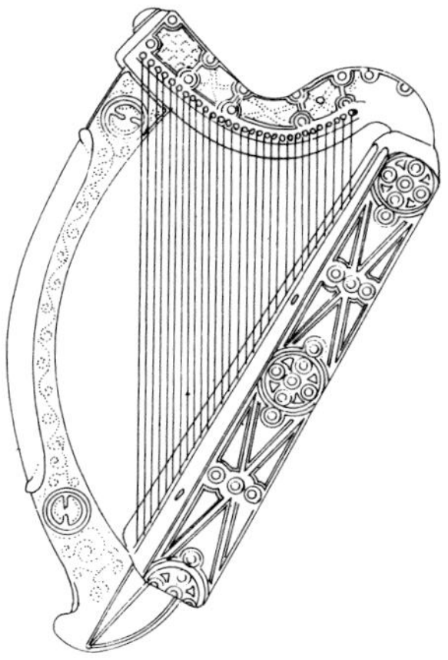

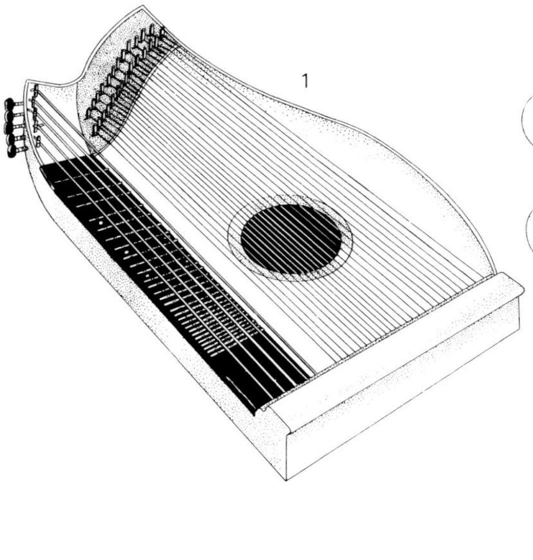

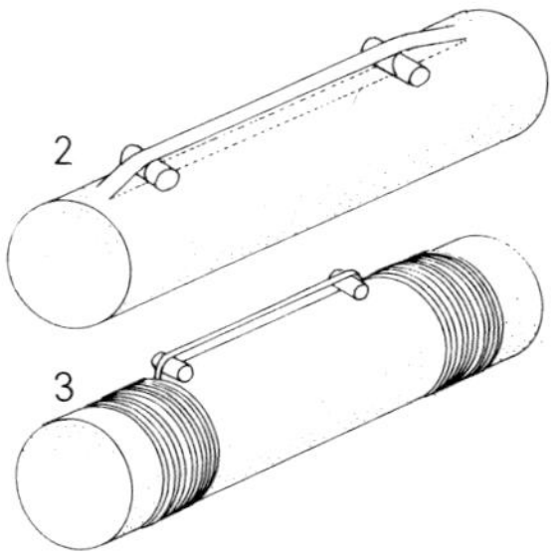

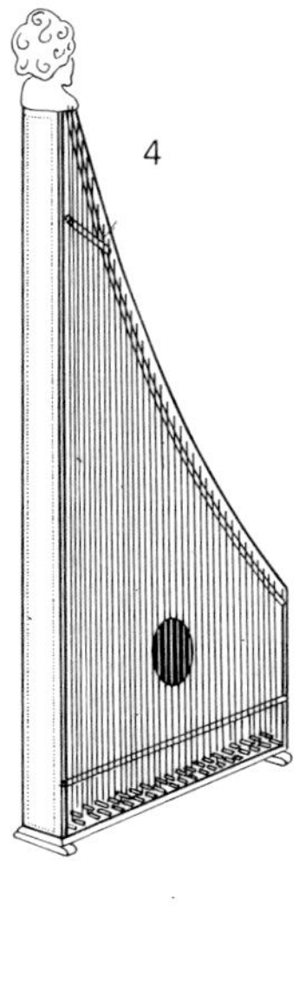

1 Concert zither
2 Idiochord tube zither
3 Heterochord tube zither
4 Upright board zither

The guitar The guitar's enormous popularity is not a recent phenomenon: as contrapuntal music gave way to music of a more chordal style at the end of the sixteenth century, the Spanish version of the guitar rose to a position of eminence as a solo instrument, and as one used to accompany singing and dancing. It has two essential characteristics that may account for its popularity: it is easily portable, and it can play both melodies and chordal accompaniments equally effectively. The player stops the strings by putting the fingers of his left hand against the fretted finger-board, and plucks them with his right hand, using his finger-nails or a plectrum.

The appearance of the guitar has changed little in three centuries. The body has become larger and deeper and more waisted, and the number of strings has in most cases been standardized to either six or twelve. The most important development took place in the nineteenth century when the wooden supporting struts that had been glued from side to side on the underside of the instrument's table were rearranged to radiate outwards from the sound hole. This not only strengthened the instrument a good deal but also helped to increase the resonance by transmitting vibrations through the body. Alongside the guitar in more recent years have developed other instruments, such as the ukulele, that share the same playing technique and are similar in appearance.

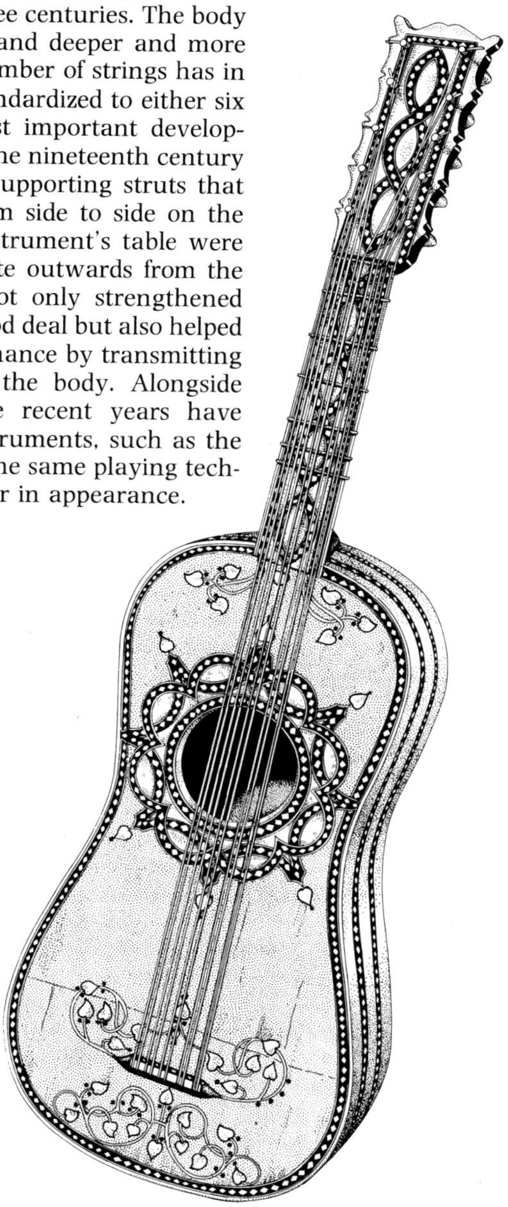

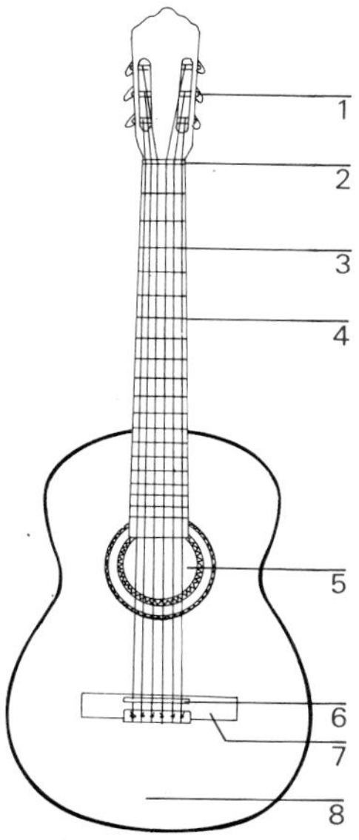

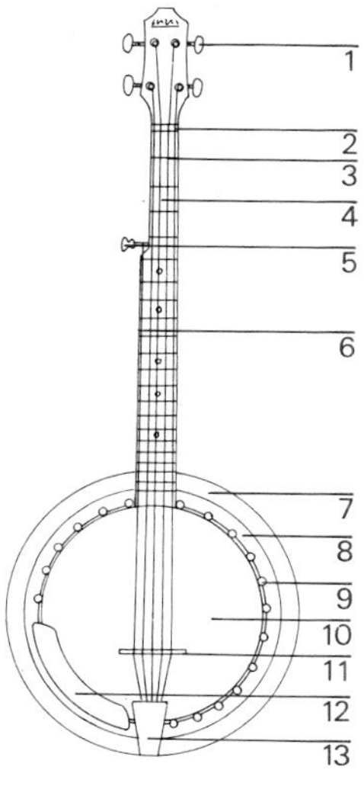

Above This beautifully decorated Spanish guitar dates from the seventeenth century. **1** Machine head; **2** nut; **3** fret; **4** neck; **5** sound-hole; **6** bridge saddle; **7** bridge; **8** table.
Left the banjo, similar to the guitar but not historically related, has a circular wooden frame and a parchment belly. The short "thumbstring" plays the melody, the other strings the accompaniment. The finger-board may be fretted. The banjo may have gut or metal strings. **1** Machine head; **2** nut; **3** fret; **4** finger-board; **5** thumbstring peg; **6** thumbstring; **7** resonator; **8** metal frame; **9** tension screw; **10** parchment belly; **11** bridge; **12** sleeve protector; **13** tailpiece.

1
Harpist

The harp-player sits forward on her chair and plucks the strings from both sides of the instrument. Guitarists usually place a low stool under the right foot.

2
Guitarist

Famous works for the guitar
M. Castelnuovo-Tedesco: Concerto for guitar
S. Dodgson: Concerto for guitar
M. de Falla: *Homenaje pour le tombeau de Claude Debussy*
N. Paganini: Six Sonatas for violin and guitar
M. Ponce: Concerto for guitar
A. Roussel: *Segovia*
J. Turina: Sonata in D minor, *Sevillana*, *Fandaguillo*
H. Villa-Lobos: Preludes

Works for zither
The zither is occasionally included in orchestral works to supply local colour, but remains primarily a folk instrument.

Famous works for harp
A. Bax: Sonata for viola and harp
C. Debussy: Sonata for flute, viola and harp, *Danse sacrée et danse profane* for harp and strings
D-E. Inghelbrecht: Sonata for flute and harp
W. A. Mozart: Concerto in C for flute and harp
M. Ravel: *Introduction and Allegro* for harp, string quartet, flute and clarinet, *Impromptu*
A. Roussel: *Serenade* for flute, violin, viola, cello and harp
C. Saint-Saëns: *Fantasie* for violin and harp, *Fantasie* for solo harp
F. Schmidt: *Andante and Scherzo* for harp and string quartet

Pitches

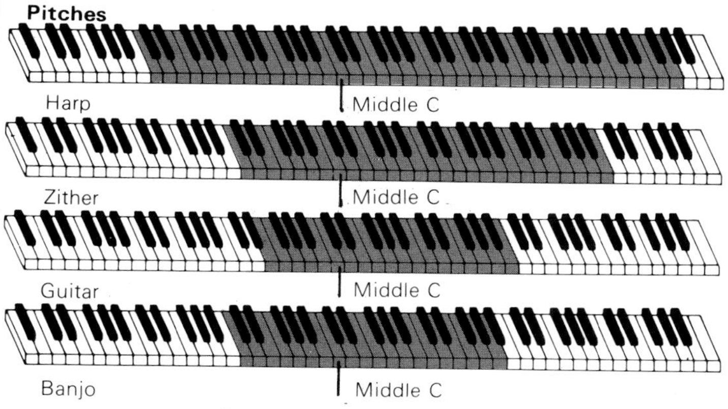

Position in the orchestra

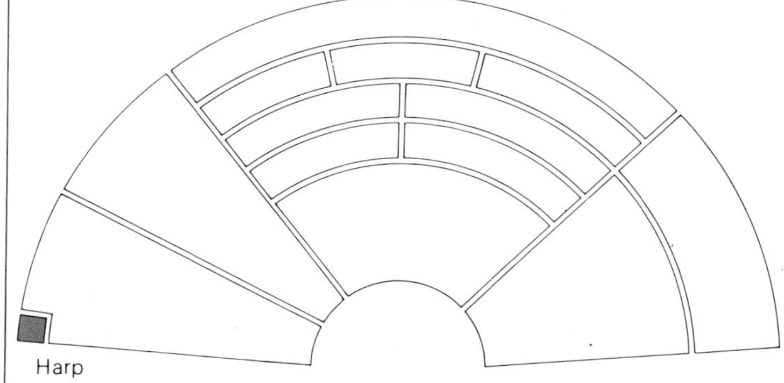

Keyboard Instruments

A musician playing a keyboard instrument can produce a wide range of musical responses. The modern piano, with its range of about seven octaves, allows the pianist to encompass the harmonic range of an orchestral score. That other and more complex keyboard instrument, the organ, can surpass it in tonal variety and dynamic range. Franz Liszt wrote in 1838:

"Perhaps I am deluded by this mysterious feeling which binds me to the piano, but I regard its importance as enormous. To my mind, the piano occupies the highest place in the hierarchy of instruments; it is the one most widely cultivated, the most popular of all, and it owes this importance and popularity to the harmonic resources which it alone possesses, and, because of this, to its ability to epitomize and concentrate the whole musical art within itself. Within the compass of seven octaves it covers the spectrum of the orchestra, and the ten fingers of one man are enough to reproduce the sounds created by a hundred musicians in concert. It is thanks to the piano that we have an opportunity to become familiar with works that would otherwise be little known or completely unknown because of the difficulty of assembling an orchestra to perform them. It has the same relationship to orchestral music as engraving does to painting: it multiplies it and makes it available to all: if it does not reproduce its colours at least it reproduces its light and shade."

Family traits

The principal members of the keyboard family are the clavichord, the harpsichord, the piano (whose full name is the pianoforte) and the organ. With the exception of the organ each of these instruments consists in essence of a boxed-in harp with a complete set of strings – one or more for each semitone throughout its range – and a soundboard to amplify the vibrations. But instead of being plucked with the fingers like the strings of the harp or struck with little hammers like the strings of a dulcimer, the strings are set vibrating by means of a more or less complex mechanism – or action – of bars and levers.

The mechanism of the clavichord presses small brass blades or *tangents* to the strings; in the harpsichord the strings are plucked by *plectra* made of quill, leather or (nowadays) delrin; the strings of the modern piano are struck by felt-covered hammers. Of the three types of mechanism it is that of the piano which is much the most complicated. Because the leather- or felt-covered hammers must

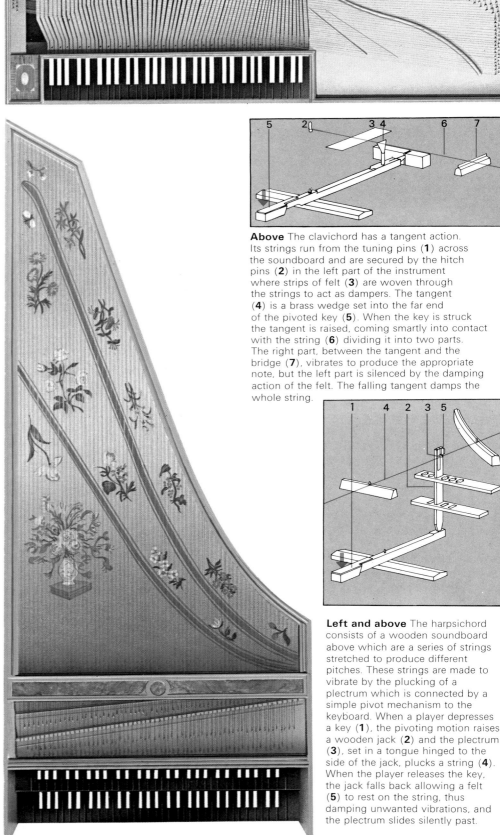

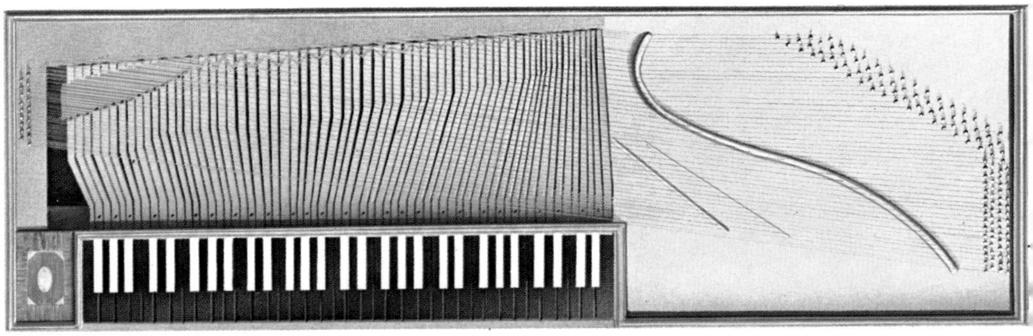

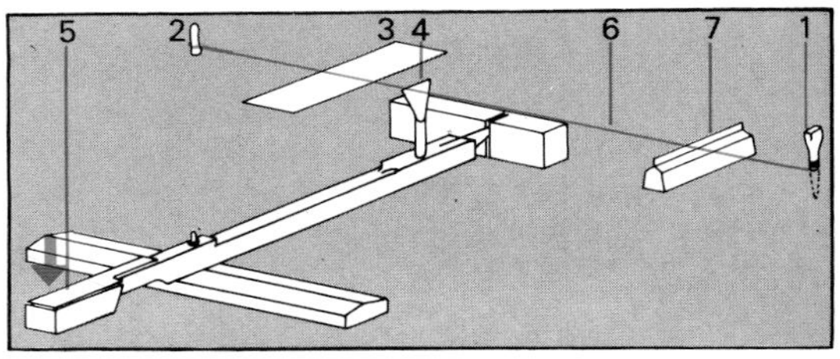

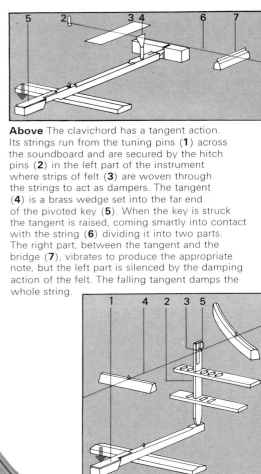

Above The clavichord has a tangent action. Its strings run from the tuning pins (**1**) across the soundboard and are secured by the hitch pins (**2**) in the left part of the instrument where strips of felt (**3**) are woven through the strings to act as dampers. The tangent (**4**) is a brass wedge set into the far end of the pivoted key (**5**). When the key is struck the tangent is raised, coming smartly into contact with the string (**6**) dividing it into two parts. The right part, between the tangent and the bridge (**7**), vibrates to produce the appropriate note, but the left part is silenced by the damping action of the felt. The falling tangent damps the whole string.

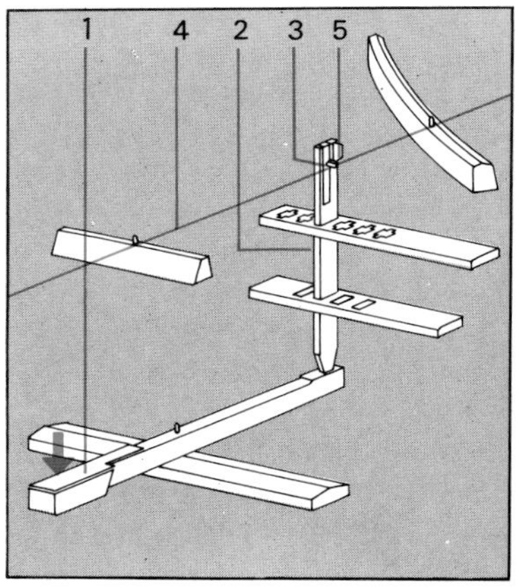

Left and above The harpsichord consists of a wooden soundboard above which are a series of strings stretched to produce different pitches. These strings are made to vibrate by the plucking of a plectrum which is connected by a simple pivot mechanism to the keyboard. When a player depresses a key (**1**), the pivoting motion raises a wooden jack (**2**) and the plectrum (**3**), set in a tongue hinged to the side of the jack, plucks a string (**4**). When the player releases the key, the jack falls back allowing a felt (**5**) to rest on the string, thus damping unwanted vibrations, and the plectrum slides silently past.

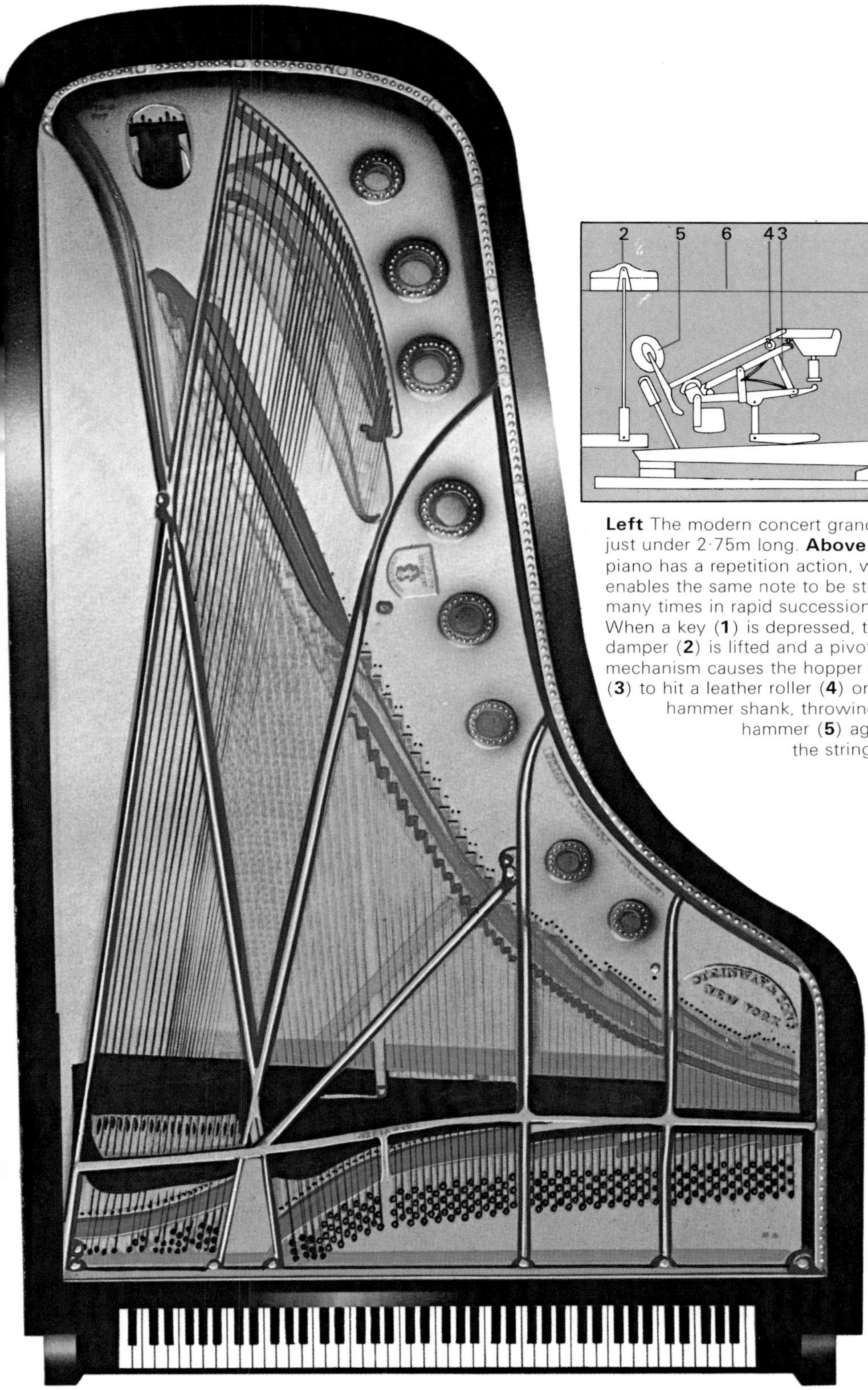

Left The modern concert grand, just under 2·75m long. **Above** The piano has a repetition action, which enables the same note to be struck many times in rapid succession. When a key (**1**) is depressed, the damper (**2**) is lifted and a pivot mechanism causes the hopper end (**3**) to hit a leather roller (**4**) on the hammer shank, throwing the hammer (**5**) against the string (**6**).

not be allowed to remain in contact with the strings after plucking them (since that would have the effect of cutting off the sound before it had properly begun), pianos generally include an escapement device for disengaging the hammers as soon as they have delivered their blow.

As soloists, as accompanists in songs, and as participants in chamber music, modern pianists have a very important role to play in music, as did their predecessors in the baroque and early classical periods. The earliest orchestras needed the harmonic support of a harpsichord and were often directed by a harpsichordist seated at his instrument: the tones of the keyboard instruments of the period made them suitable for reinforcing both rhythm and harmony. Later the pianoforte became the darling of the drawing-room and the *soirée* – the pivot around which much nineteenth-century social life revolved.

Distant relatives

The family of keyboard instruments includes some eccentric members. One is the freakish claviorganum, a cross between a harpsichord and an organ. Then there is the celesta, invented in 1886, which looks like a small upright piano but has tuned bars instead of strings: Tchaikovsky makes effective use of its bell-like tones in the "Dance of the Sugar-Plum Fairy" in his ballet *The Nutcracker*. Another version of the same instrument, with tuning forks instead of steel bars, is called the dulcitone.

Electronic instruments are another important group. They include two inventions of the 1920s, the American Hammond organ, which works by means of a rotating tone wheel and a permanent magnet, and the French ondes-martenot, which has five octaves of notes produced by oscillating radio tubes.

There have been many attempts, some of them extraordinarily successful, to apply automatic mechanisms to the piano. Music was recorded on rolls of punched paper which controlled the instrument pneumatically. The "player piano" is also known by various trade names, such as "Pianola", and, in more sophisticated versions, as the "reproducing piano" because piano rolls made by famous virtuosi, among them Paderewski and Rachmaninov, could simulate great performances. The ever-improving record-player, tape-recorder and radio have largely taken the place of the player piano, and today we can only imagine the amount of diversion and instruction these inventions brought to Victorian listeners.

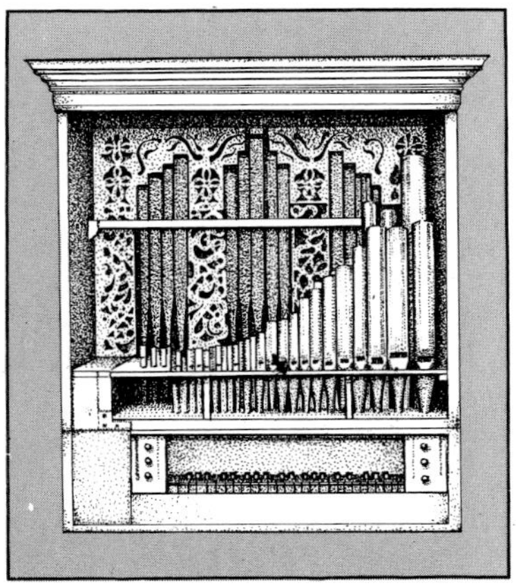

Left and right The organ is divided into three main parts: the mechanism, the keyboard or console, and the pipes. When a key (**1**) is depressed, the valve (**2**) is opened, letting air flow into the flue-pipe (**3**). Wind passes through a reservoir appropriately weighted to keep the supply at a constant pressure. The wind passes from the windchest (**4**) into the flue and strikes the upper lip (**5**), producing an audible frequency, the pitch and resonance of which is determined by the "speaking" length of the pipe: the longest pipe makes the deepest note, the shortest pipe the highest note.

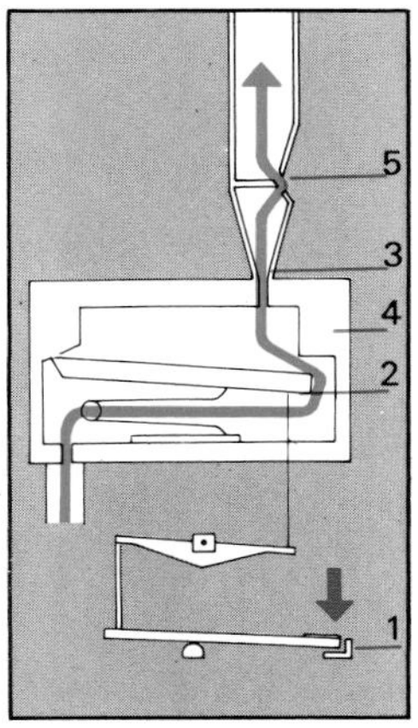

Early keyboard instruments

Stringed keyboard instruments have been of major importance in music-making of every kind for over three centuries. The clavichord and harpsichord reigned supreme until about 1800 when they were largely superseded by the more versatile piano. This century has seen the revival of interest in both the music and the instruments of the Baroque. The harpsichord, in particular, is frequently heard in performances of music of the period. Fine reproduction harpsichords can be obtained, but sadly only a handful of contemporary composers have written music for them.

The clavichord is the oldest of the stringed keyboard instruments. It was developed in the twelfth century from the monochord – a simple device, consisting of a single stretched string with movable bridges, used for demonstrating musical intervals. With the addition of a keyboard the clavichord was born. Most early clavichords clung to the monochord principle by using only one string or, on "double-strung" instruments, two unison strings, for several different notes. (Such economy was feasible since the point at which the tangent strikes the string determines its vibrating length and therefore its pitch.) On these instruments, called "*gebunden*" or "fretted", it was often impossible to play certain adjacent notes at the same moment, for groups of two to four adjacent notes could share the same pair of strings. Later clavichords, called "*bundfrei*" or "unfretted", had a string for each note.

The clavichord is essentially an instrument for personal music-making. Many baroque composers, notably J. S. Bach, valued its uniquely expressive and responsive tone. Its sound, however, is exceptionally quiet and usually unsuitable for performances in large rooms or concert halls. The young Handel was able to learn the clavichord in secret by practising it in the attic of his father's home.

The harpsichord occupied a prominent position in almost every aspect of music-making in the seventeenth and eighteenth centuries. It was an important part of every musical ensemble, supporting and reinforcing the harmonies, and its bright, clear sound made it an ideal solo instrument. It remains the perfect medium for the performance of the contrapuntal music of the period as the lower lines in the musical texture stand out with extraordinary clarity. Many larger instruments had more than one keyboard or manual, and a few had stops for altering the tone colour so that contrasts could be made between one manual and the other.

Two other baroque instruments shared the harpsichord's plucking mechanism. The virginal (often referred to in the plural), small and rectangular in shape, was particularly popular in England and was reputed to be the favourite instrument of Elizabeth I. The spinet, with its characteristically wing-shaped case, was more common in Italy.

1

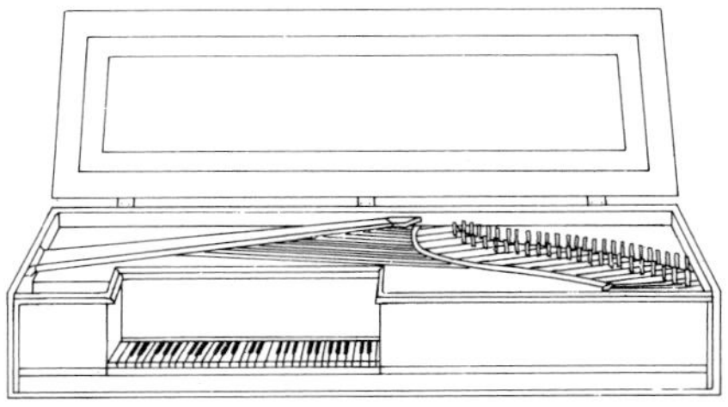
2

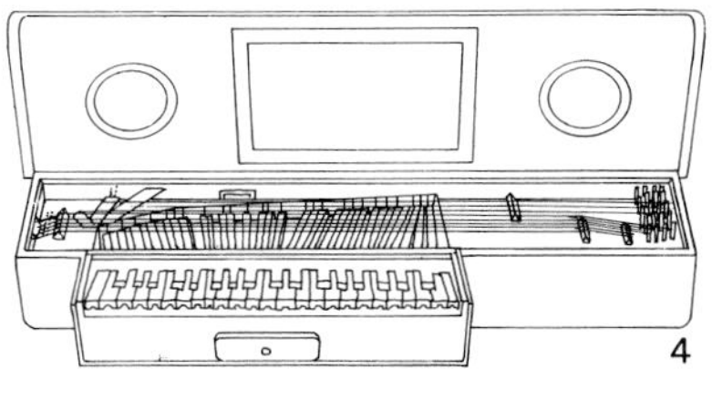
4

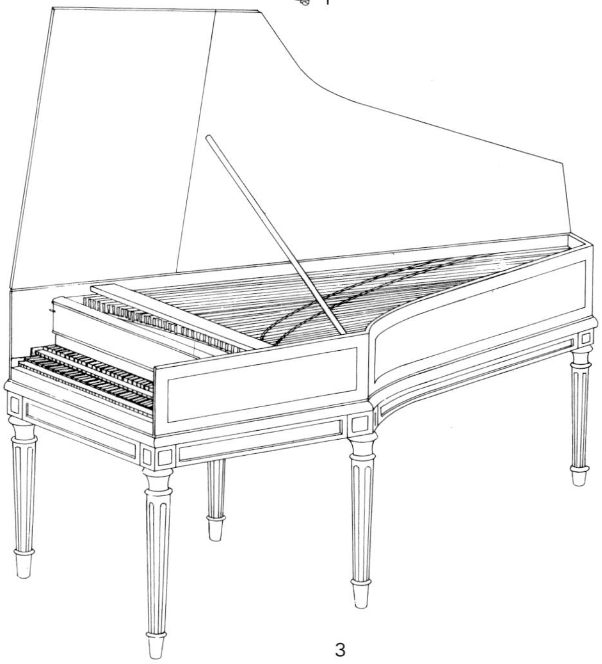
3

5

6

Right Some important predecessors of the piano. Though the spinet (**1**), virginal (**2**) and harpsichord (**3**) share the same plucking mechanism, they differ in size, shape and capabilities. The harpsichord, the largest of the three, was the favourite ensemble instrument. In addition to octave stops, some harpsichords had a lute or "buff" stop that gave a gentle, muted sound—a strong contrast to the instrument's normally bright tone. In common with the piano, organ and many other instruments, the pitch range of the stringed keyboard instruments was gradually extended over the years and it is impossible to quote a standard for any of them. Many harpsichords were made in Europe between the sixteenth and seventeenth centuries. Many of those which survive are elaborately decorated; some have cases and lids covered in paintings of pastoral scenes while others have exquisitely inlaid keys. The clavichord (**4**) is the real predecessor of the piano, which began to oust the clavichord in about 1700. The giraffe piano (**5**) and upright grand (**6**) are examples of some eccentric case shapes produced in the nineteenth century in an attempt to economize on the amount of floorspace occupied by the instrument. They are distantly linked with today's upright pianos (**7**), but have string arrangements similar to those of the modern grand piano (**8**).

The modern piano

The first piano was made in Florence in about 1700 by Bartolomeo Cristofori (1655–1731). It represented an attempt to produce an instrument more responsive to the player's touch than the harpsichord – indeed Cristofori referred to it as a "*gravicembalo col piano e forte*", or "harpsichord with soft and loud". The new instrument's extra sensitivity of touch relied on the fact that its strings were struck by hammers rather than plucked with plectra. Thus the degree of force with which the key was struck determined the volume of the note produced.

It was about one hundred years later, however, that the piano finally ousted the harpsichord in popularity. From 1800 onwards, many improvements were made to the piano mechanism. The frame was considerably strengthened and the "double escapement" mechanism allowing for rapid repetition of notes was incorporated.

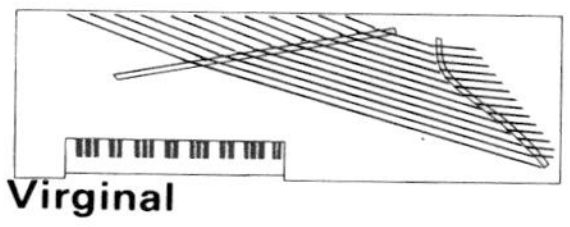

Virginal

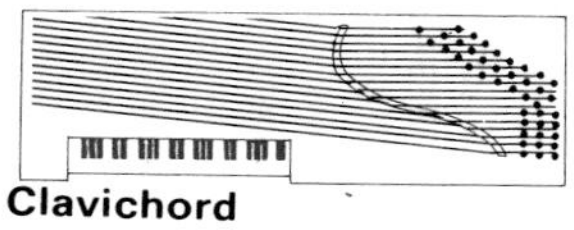

Clavichord

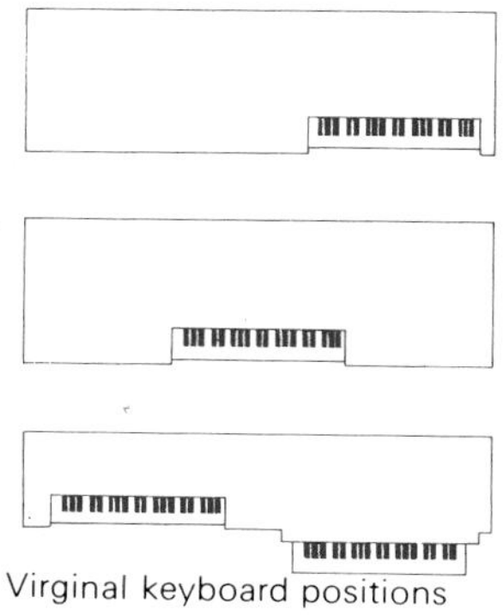

Virginal keyboard positions

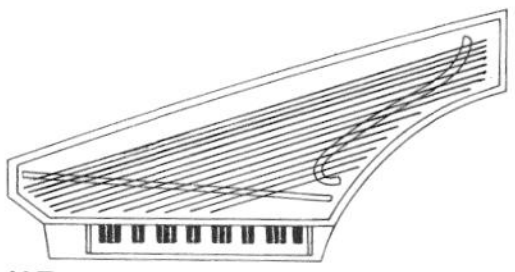

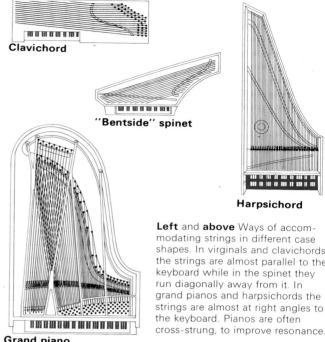

"Bentside" spinet

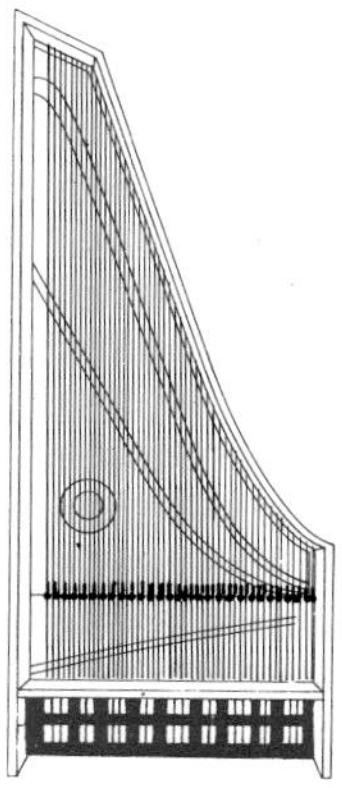

Harpsichord

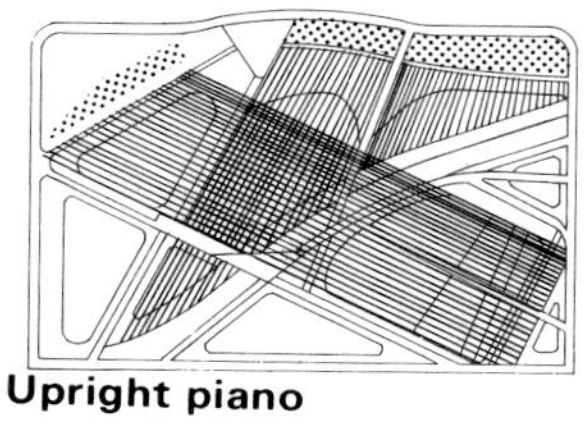

Upright piano

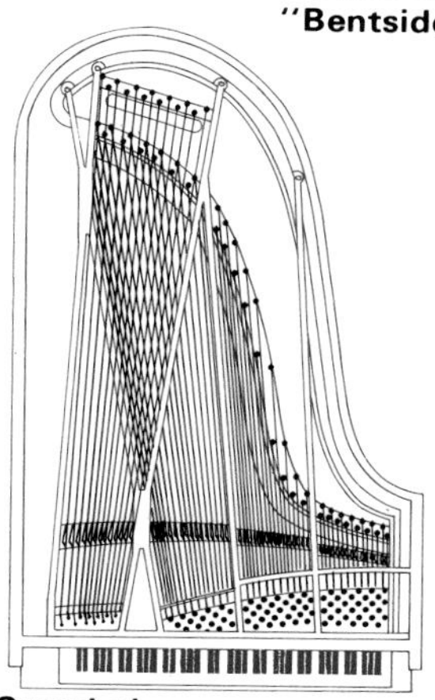

Grand piano

Left and **above** Ways of accommodating strings in different case shapes. In virginals and clavichords, the strings are almost parallel to the keyboard while in the spinet they run diagonally away from it. In grand pianos and harpsichords the strings are almost at right angles to the keyboard. Pianos are often cross-strung, to improve resonance.

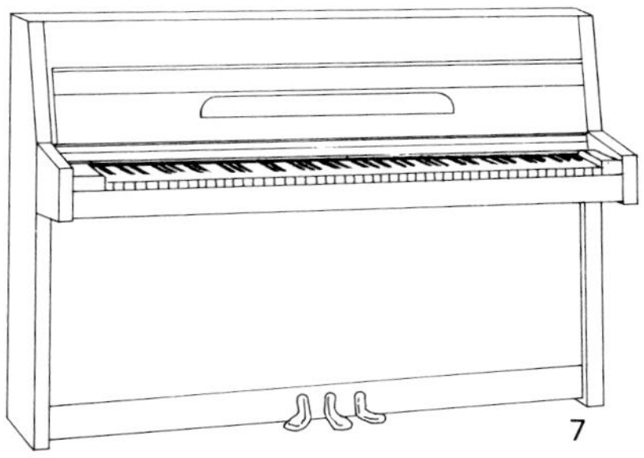

7

8

Pianist

Famous works for piano

- B. Bartók: *Romanian Dances, Mikrokosmos*
- L. van Beethoven: piano sonatas and concertos
- J. Brahms: ballades, rhapsodies, concertos
- F. Chopin: waltzes, nocturnes, scherzos, polonaises, mazurkas, piano sonatas, *études*
- M. Clementi: piano sonatas
- C. Debussy: *Preludes, Children's Corner Suite, Estampes, Images, Suite bergamasque*
- J. Haydn: piano sonatas
- F. Liszt: *Transcendental Studies, Années de pèlerinage, Hungarian Rhapsodies*
- O. Messiaen: *Vingt Regards sur l'enfant Jésus*
- W. A. Mozart: piano sonatas and concertos
- S. Rachmaninov: preludes, *Etudes-tableaux*, piano concertos
- F. Schubert: piano sonatas, *Moments musicaux*
- R. Schumann: *Carnaval*, Piano Concerto in A minor
- A. Scriabin: preludes, nocturnes, studies, sonatas

Famous works for harpsichord, virginal, spinet and clavichord

- J. S. Bach: *The Well-tempered Clavier* (*Forty-eight Preludes and Fugues*), *Two-* and *Three-part Inventions, Goldberg Variations, Brandenburg Concerto* no. 5
- J. Bull: pavanes, galliards, fantasias (virginal)
- W. Byrd: *The Battell* (virginal)
- F. Couperin: *Ordres*
- G. F. Handel: suites
- F. Martin: Concerto for harpsichord and small orchestra

Famous works for organ

- J. S. Bach: chorale preludes, preludes and fugues, toccatas
- G. F. Handel: organ concertos
- P. Hindemith: organ sonatas
- F. Liszt: *Fantasia on B.A.C.H.*
- F. Mendelssohn: organ sonatas
- O. Messiaen: *Messe de la Pentecôte*
- F. Poulenc: Concerto for organ, strings and percussion
- M. Reger: *Symphonic Fantasia and Fugue*

The piano's advantages over the harpsichord are, firstly, that the player's touch can vary the intensity of volume as required; and secondly, that it can sustain a "singing" tone very well, because the sound is not damped until the player's finger leaves the note. Moreover, it is equipped with two pedals, the left for decreasing the volume of sound, the right for sustaining the sound.

The organ

Unique among keyboard instruments – indeed among all instruments – is the organ. Dating from over two thousand years ago, it is one of the world's oldest instruments. The principle on which the organ works has remained unchanged: a modern organ, just like the earliest organs, has a wind chest or reservoir, and a means of admitting air into selected pipes. Though the principle is simple, the operating mechanism of the modern organ is ex-

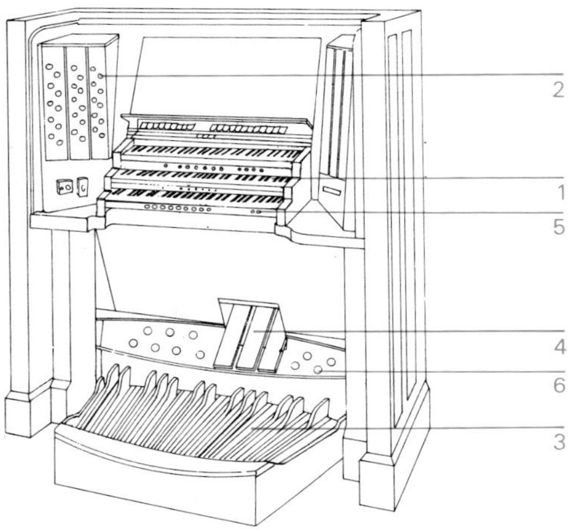

Above A typical modern organ console with three manuals (**1**), several sets of drawstops (**2**), a pedalboard (**3**) and foot pedals (**4**) for controlling the "swell" effect, (**5**) thumb pistons and (**6**) foot pistons for selecting drawstops.

Right A magnificent baroque organ, at the Klosterkirche in Birnau, Bodensee, Germany, surmounted by paintings by G. B. Götz and J. A. Feuchtmayr. The pipes seem to soar to the celestial realms suggested by the decor.

tremely complex. Most organs are now electrically operated, but in older instruments the action is purely mechanical and takes its name from the "trackers" or rods that operate the sliders.

Most organs have a pedalboard and at least two manuals or keyboards – some have as many as five, six or even seven. Each manual controls its own "division" of the whole organ – in itself a complete small organ. To vary the tone colour the player can select by means of drawstops different sets or "ranks" of pipes from within each division of the organ. The tone colour depends on the types of pipes to which the particular stop admits air. There are two main sorts of pipes – flues and reeds. A flue-pipe has a lip like a large recorder and produces a flute-like sound; a reed-pipe contains a single beating reed and gives a more strident, penetrating sound.

Controlling the many aspects of the organ's mechanism demands the complete coordination of eyes, mind, hands and feet and is a challenging and strenuous task. This task is further complicated by the fact that very few instruments are absolutely alike. The date of building has much to do with the size and capabilities of a particular organ, and these factors are themselves closely linked with the predominating musical style of the period. Probably the best-known type of instrument is the baroque organ. This is usually fairly small, with two or three manuals, a pedal organ and between twelve and thirty-five stops. The baroque organ is ideal for the performance of the organ works of J. S. Bach. The "romantic" organ is altogether a larger and more elaborate piece of musical equipment, with a wide variety of stops and other devices. Most romantic composers found the organ a less than ideal vehicle for their works, for they sought a multiplicity of tone colours perhaps better provided by the orchestra.

Relatives of the organ

Similar in appearance to the organ is the harmonium, a small portable instrument. Generally regarded as a humble substitute for the organ, it is traditionally associated with Victorian parlours and chapels and has mostly been used to accompany hymns. In common with the accordion and non-keyboard instruments such as the mouth-organ and concertina, the harmonium produces a sound by the vibration of a free reed – a metal tongue fixed over an accurately cut aperture. The length and thickness of the tongue determines the pitch of the note.

Among the most recent developments in electronic instruments is the keyboard synthesizer. The synthesizer has been in use for some years but the addition of a keyboard makes it easier to control the almost limitless variety of tones it emits.

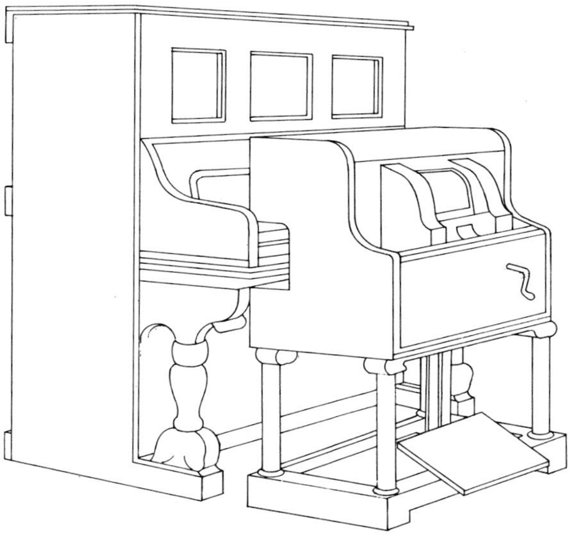

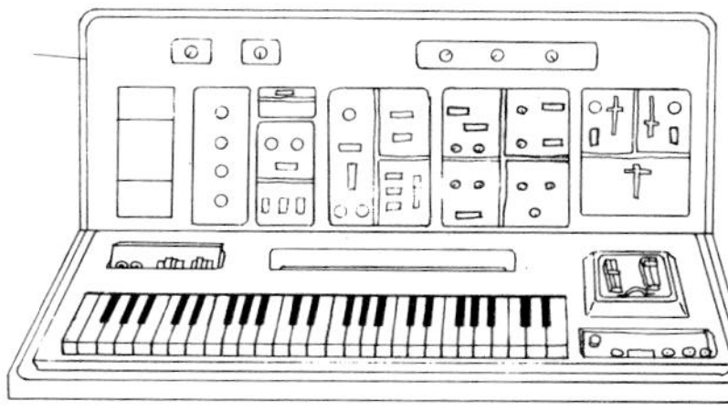

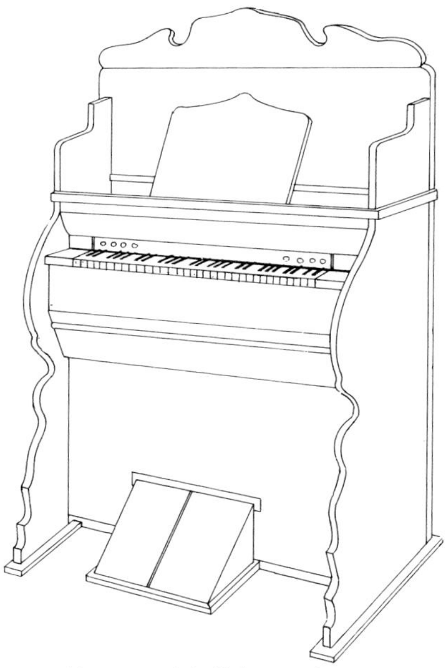

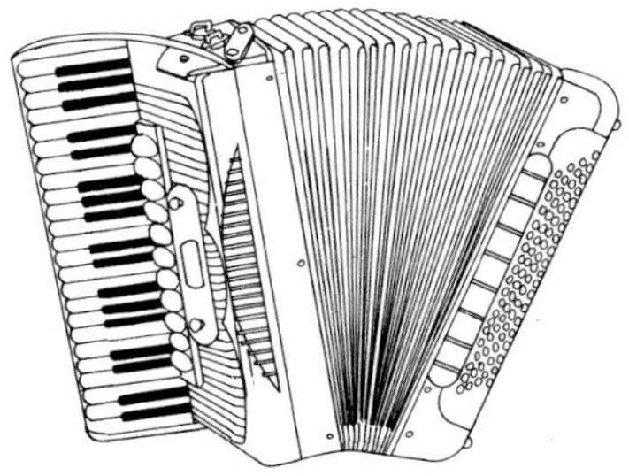

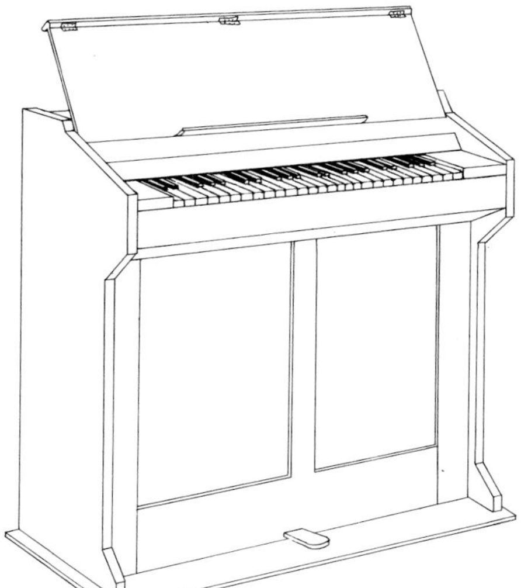

Above and **left** Lesser-known keyboard instruments. The piano player (above left) was a mechanism, contained in a cabinet, which could be pushed up to the keyboard of an ordinary piano so that felt-covered hammers projecting from the case could strike the piano keys in response to a punched music roll. Such a roll was also used for the piano player's important successor, the player piano (below right). The harmonium (above right) was a favourite Victorian domestic instrument. The celesta (below left) is the only keyboard instrument to have a regular place in the symphony orchestra while the keyboard synthesizer (above centre) and piano accordion (centre) are used mostly in popular music.

Woodwind Instruments

Woodwind instruments belong to the group of musical instruments known as *aerophones*, meaning that the sound is produced by the vibration of a column of air within a pipe. Brass instruments and organ pipes are also aerophones, but differ from woodwind in that the pipe is open only at each end whereas a woodwind instrument has a set of finger-holes along the pipe. In addition, they are blown in different ways. The basic kinds of woodwind instruments are the recorder, flute, clarinet, oboe, bassoon and saxophone. They are called woodwind because, the saxophone apart, they were once all made of wood and the name is still used even though some are now made of metal or plastic.

The column of air is set vibrating, and thereby made to sound, in several ways. In the flute, the player blows across a hole at the end of the pipe and, as the moving air strikes the edge of the hole, it sets the air column vibrating. Other woodwind instruments have a mouthpiece into which the player blows. This usually contains a single reed, as in the clarinet, or a pair of reeds (a double reed), as in the oboe and bassoon. The reed vibrates to make the air column sound. The air column extends from the end of the instrument in the mouth to the first open hole, and its length varies as the player opens and closes the holes with the fingers. Keys and pads are normally used to help the performer play easily. As the length of the air column varies, so the pitch of the note changes – getting higher the shorter the air column and vice versa. The action of the fingers gives a basic scale of notes extending over an octave or more that make up the low register of the instrument.

Another scale of notes, the middle register, can be obtained by slight adjustment of the fingering or by blowing harder. These notes are harmonics of the first scale of notes and are usually an octave higher. Finally, a higher scale of notes making up the high register can be obtained by a combination of special fingering and blowing. The complete range usually extends about three octaves, but extra high notes are often produced by good players.

The history of the woodwind family

The origins of the woodwind family date back some 20,000 years to prehistoric times, when people realized that a sound could be produced by blowing across the end of a hollow bone or horn, a piece of bamboo cane, a shell or a gourd with a hole in it. Such "instruments" are primi-

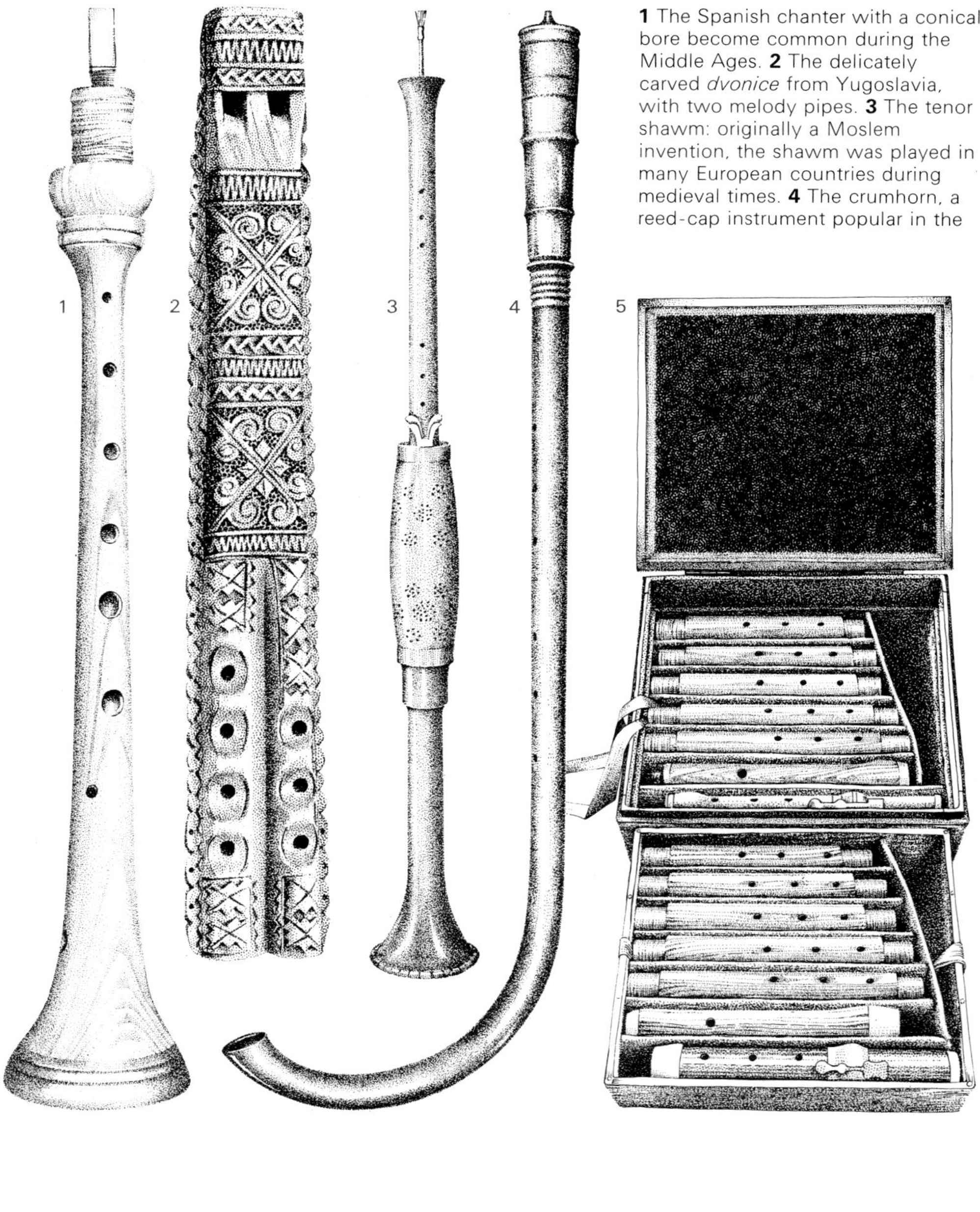

1 The Spanish chanter with a conical bore become common during the Middle Ages. **2** The delicately carved *dvonice* from Yugoslavia, with two melody pipes. **3** The tenor shawm: originally a Moslem invention, the shawm was played in many European countries during medieval times. **4** The crumhorn, a reed-cap instrument popular in the

Left Woodcut from *The Triumph of Maximilian I* (1526). The nearest riders are playing fifes, with instrument cases hanging from their waists. Those on the far left are playing shawms, those in the middle *Rauschpfeifen*, which were "haut" or loud shawms with reed-caps. The principle on which reed-cap instruments work is outlined on page 109.

Middle Ages, was usually made from boxwood that had been turned and bored. **5** A case containing a pair of transverse flutes made of wood with ivory mounts. One has a silver key, the other a gold one, indicating that they were used by a nobleman and his tutor. **Below** Pitch is altered by the length of a pipe, the shorter being higher in pitch, the longer lower. To vary the pitch in a pipe, holes are bored along its length, effectively shortening it. When a hole is covered, a lower-pitched note results. **Bottom** Two types of end-blown flute. The third, with a hole bored in its casing, is a side-blown or transverse flute, held against the lower lip.

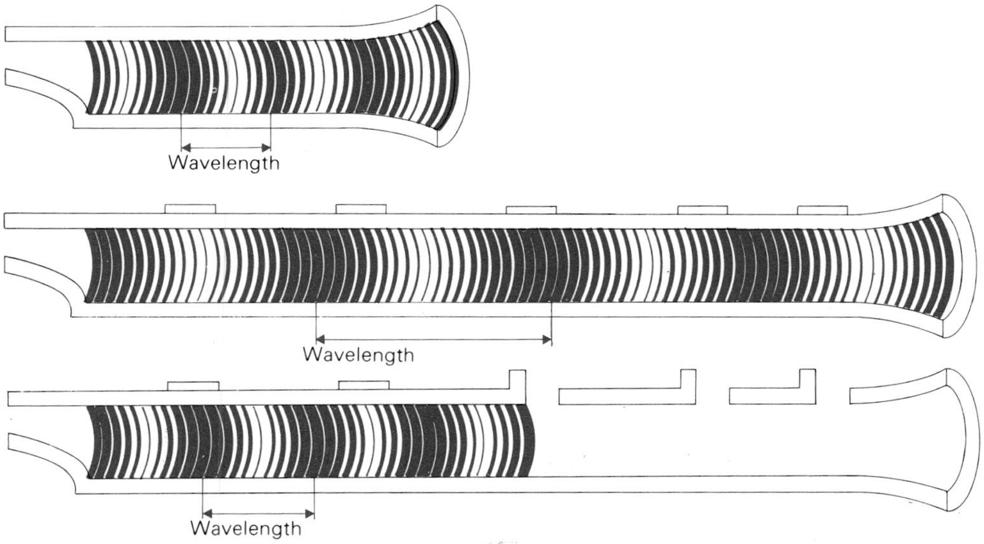

tive flutes and produce a sound in the same way as blowing across the neck of a bottle. They are found among most primitive peoples, though not in all; the aborigines of Australia are one exception. These flutes would have been used in rituals and perhaps to give a summons or warning call. Several different kinds of primitive flutes existed (and still exist in today's ethnic music). End-blown flutes were held vertically and blown across the open end, whereas transverse flutes were held horizontally and sounded by blowing across a hole in the tube itself, as with the modern flute. Globular flutes were simply round shells, bones or hollow stones with a blow hole.

It was no doubt discovered in very early times that a sound can easily be obtained by blowing into the end of a pipe if a notch is cut in the side. The moving air strikes the edge of the notch and sets the air column vibrating in the same way as blowing across a hole. This notched flute was the ancestor of the recorder, which makes a sound in this way.

Another way of making sound that was probably discovered in ancient times is to stretch a blade of grass between the thumbs and blow into it, producing a loud squawk. This method of exciting an air column is rarely found among primitive peoples and its early history is uncertain. The first reed-pipes were probably made by cutting a cane so as to produce a vibrating reed at one end. Anyone can easily make such an "instrument" by cutting the end of a straw into a V, putting this end into the mouth and blowing. However it originated, the reed-pipe was well established by the beginnings of civilization.

These early woodwind instruments had no finger-holes. The flutes could be blown harder to achieve various harmonics and a limited range of notes obtained, but the reed-pipes would have given only a single note. By the time civilizations had begun to emerge in the East and the Mediterranean, finger-holes had been added to increase the number of notes available. Another early development was the double pipe: notched flutes and reed-pipes could easily be played in pairs with each hand playing a separate melody. A double reed-pipe was the most played wind instrument of the ancient Greeks and Romans, who called it "aulos" and "*tibia*" respectively.

The ancient civilizations of the West came to favour reed-pipes while flutes remained the principal wind instruments of primitive peoples. But, by the Renaissance, both had become popular in the West as they had long been in the East. Woodwind instruments now began to evolve towards the forms they have today. Keys were added to extend the range of notes obtainable, and consorts or families of instruments of different sizes and ranges developed. As musicians began to travel from one country to another, so the pitches of the notes became standardized. The recorder was the first instrument to attain its present form, though this is because it is an archaic instrument that has not been developed, unlike the other members of the woodwind family. It has remained virtually unchanged since the baroque era, when it was ousted by the flute – a louder and more brilliant instrument.

However, baroque composers did not really exploit the sound qualities of instruments in an expressive way. It was not until the romantic era that woodwind instruments, with their great variety of tone colour, came into their own. The woodwind section of the symphony orchestra was standardized at two flutes, two clarinets, two oboes and two bassoons. During the nineteenth century, key systems were redesigned to make the instruments much easier to play, particularly by the German flute-maker Theobald Boehm (1794–1881). Other improvements were made, too, producing instruments substantially like those of today, which can give a wide range of subtle effects. By 1900, members of the woodwind section were expected to perform as a prominent ensemble within the orchestra as well as being soloists in their own right.

Transposing instruments

As families of woodwind instruments have developed, many musicians have become proficient on more than one member of a family. However, because each member has a different range of notes, problems arise in that each instrument demands a different fingering to produce a note of the same pitch. A player switching from, say, the concert flute to the alto flute should not have to learn a whole new set of fingerings. This problem is overcome by transposing the music, so that the player reads the music in a different key depending on the instrument. He or she can then use the same fingering for every instrument in the family.

The recorder

The popularity of the recorder today is due principally to the work of Arnold Dolmetsch and his son Carl, who were born in France but lived mainly in England. Arnold Dolmetsch began to make recorders in 1919, using an English instrument of the 1700s as a model. Carl Dolmetsch and other members of the family became virtuoso players and encouraged people to take up the instrument.

It is not difficult to get a sound out of the recorder, but the fingering is not so easy. Except for a few low keys on the larger members of the family, all the notes have to be obtained without mechanical assistance. To play a chromatic scale involves cross-fingering, which may be awkward at first, and half-covering some holes. The family has six members, but the highest and lowest are not often played. The highest is the octave or sopranino recorder, followed by the descant or soprano, the treble or alto, the tenor, the bass and the great bass recorders. The lowest note of the first, third and fifth member is F; for the others it is C. The music is written either at the pitch that it sounds or at an octave below.

The flute

The modern flute was developed by the German flute-maker Theobald Boehm from 1832 onwards. He placed the holes in the correct positions to obtain notes in tune – which are not necessarily the positions covered by the fingers. He also made the holes larger to produce a loud sound, and developed a system of keys and pads so that the instrument could be fingered easily. He gave the flute a cylindrical bore, though the head is conical inside, to produce a full and clear tone. Most flutes are now made of metal to give a bright sound, though some performers prefer the mellow quality of a wooden flute.

The main member of the family is the concert flute or flute in C. The piccolo is a small flute sounding an octave above the concert flute. The alto flute, which is a transposing instrument pitched in G, sounds below the concert flute and the lowest member is the bass flute, which sounds an octave below the concert flute. The piccolo can often be heard piping away above the other instruments of the orchestra, but the deep, woolly sounds of the softer alto and bass flutes are much less evident in orchestral music.

Many composers have written pieces for the flute. Among the best-known are the Suite in B minor by Bach, the flute concertos by Mozart, the *Serenade* for flute, violin and viola by Beethoven, and *Syrinx* for solo flute by Debussy.

The clarinet

The clarinet has a cylindrical bore widening to a flared bell at the lower end; a

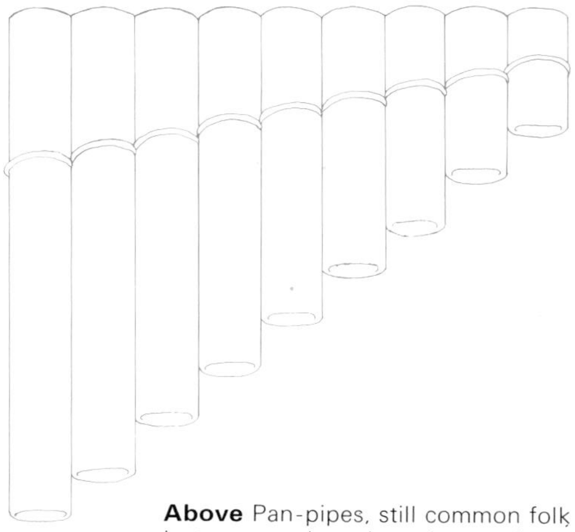

Above Pan-pipes, still common folk instruments, have been known for over two thousand years and are associated with the god Pan of Greek mythology. They consist of a set of pipes without finger-holes, joined together. They are blown either by the mouth or, occasionally, by the nostrils.

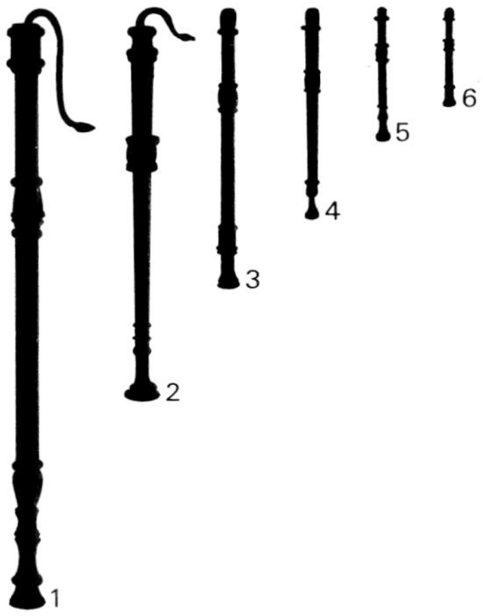

Above Playing recorders in groups was popular in the sixteenth and seventeenth centuries. A consort of recorders consisted at first of six instruments, but the sopranino and great bass were later dropped. A revival of interest in the instrument was begun by Arnold Dolmetsch in 1919. **1** Great bass recorder; **2** bass recorder; **3** tenor recorder; **4** treble or alto recorder; **5** descant recorder; **6** octave or sopranino recorder.

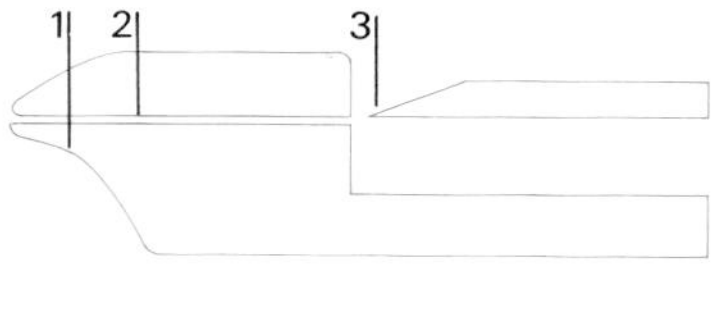

Above The recorder endpiece consists of a block of wood called a fipple (**1**), and the slit (**2**) between the fipple and the mouthpiece itself forms the channel for the air, which is directed against the sharp edge of the lip (**3**).

Right Comparative sizes of the flute, piccolo, clarinet and alto saxophone, and the identification of their parts. **Flute: 1** embouchure (mouthpiece); **2** head joint; **3** key; **4** foot joint. **Piccolo: 1** embouchure; **2** head joint; **3** key; **4** foot joint. **Clarinet: 1** single-reed mouthpiece; **2** body; **3** key; **4** rod mechanism; **5** bell. **Saxophone: 1** mouthpiece; **2** rod mechanism; **3** key; **4** brace; **5** bell.

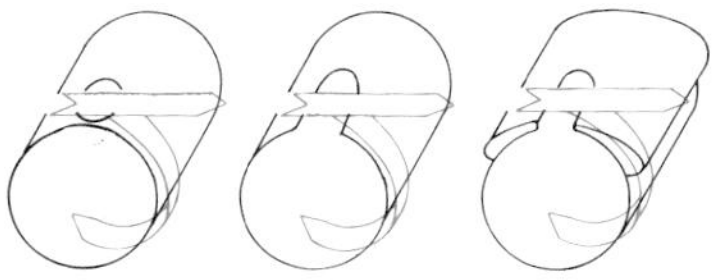

Above Blow holes were originally round, but it was later found that an oval hole produced a more vibrant sound. The modern flute also has a lip plate to direct the air.

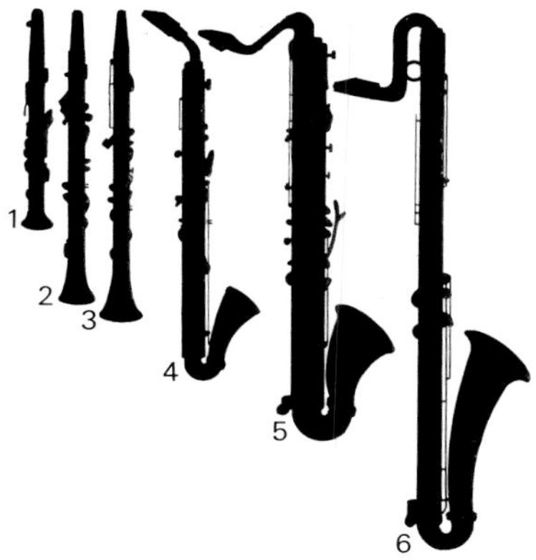

Above The six main instruments of clarinet family. The alto in E♭ is not in general use, the standard B♭ and A being most used professionally. The Boehm system of keys is still in use today. **1** E♭ clarinet; **2** B♭ clarinet; **3** A clarinet; **4** alto clarinet in E♭; **5** bass clarinet in B♭; **6** contrabass clarinet in B♭.

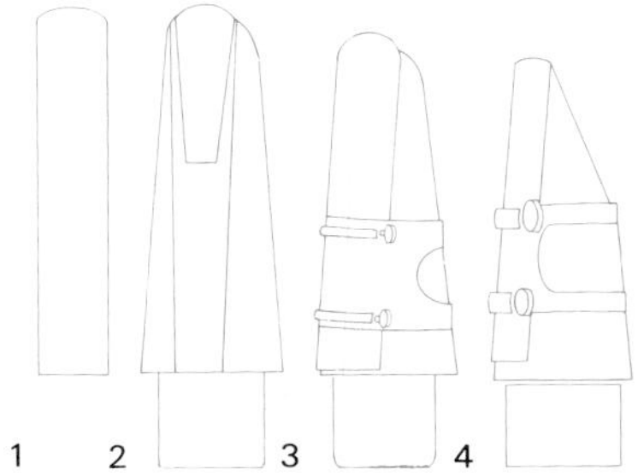

Above The clarinet reed (**1**) is usually of natural cane, and is strapped to the mouthpiece (**2**) by a metal band (**3**). Plastic and fibreglass reeds are also used. The mouthpiece is made of wood or ebonite. **4** Saxophone mouthpiece.

mouthpiece containing a single reed is attached to the upper end. It is usually made of wood. The instrument was developed from the chalumeau, a primitive forebear, by the German instrument-maker Johann Denner (1655–1707) in about 1700. The key system was radically improved in the late 1800s by adopting the Boehm system of the flute.

There are several members of the clarinet family, but only four are commonly played. The standard clarinet is pitched in B♭, but some musicians also play a clarinet in A pitched a semitone lower where fingering is difficult on the B♭ clarinet. A small clarinet in E♭ is often called for to provide high penetrating notes, and the deep reedy sound of the bass clarinet in B♭, which sounds an octave below the standard B♭ clarinet, is common in orchestral music of the last hundred years.

Perhaps the best-known pieces for clarinet are the Clarinet Quintet and Clarinet Concerto by Mozart. In this century, the instrument has been well served by jazz musicians, notably the virtuoso Benny Goodman.

The oboe and cor anglais

The oboe has a conical bore with a slightly flared bell, and the mouthpiece consists of a tube ending with a double reed. It is constructed of wood. Its forebear is the folk instrument generally known as the shawm, and it was probably invented in about 1650 by the French instrument maker Jean Hotteterre (its name comes from the French *hautbois*, meaning "high wood"). Improvements have been made gradually since then. The standard oboe is not a transposing instrument. The only other member of the family to be widely used is the English horn or cor anglais. It is lower than the oboe and is pitched in F.

Many concertos and much chamber music were written for the oboe in the baroque era. This tradition has been continued, notably in the Oboe Concerto by Richard Strauss.

The bassoon

The bassoon also developed from the shawm, gradually evolving from about 1700. It consists of a conical wooden tube folded back on itself with a double-reed mouthpiece. Modern key systems and other improvements have not succeeded in retaining the bassoon's distinctive sound, and it remains a rather awkward instrument to play. Experiments are taking place to simplify the fingering by using electrically-driven keys. The bassoon is not a transposing instrument. The only

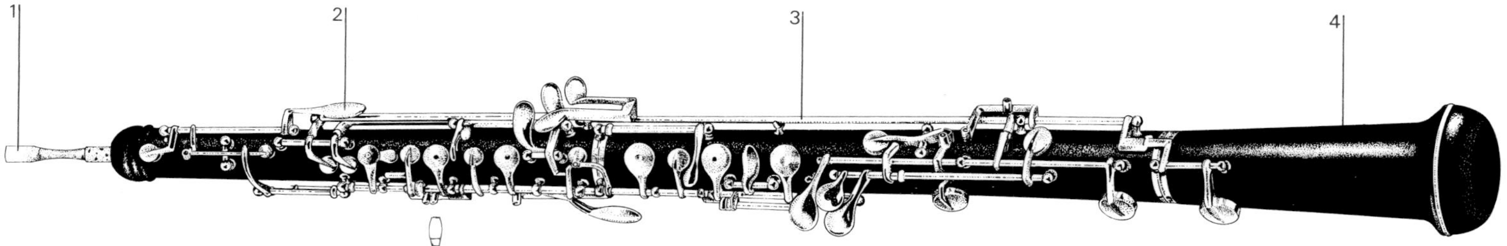

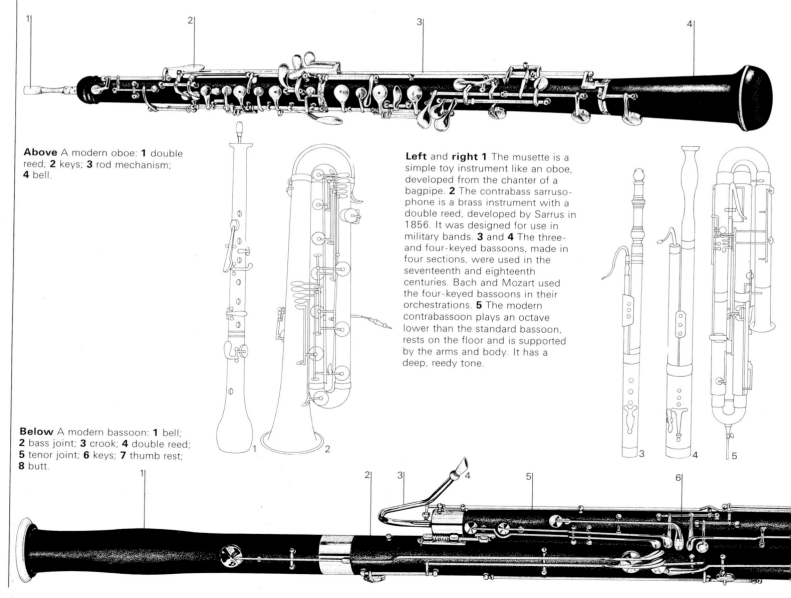

Above A modern oboe: **1** double reed; **2** keys; **3** rod mechanism; **4** bell.

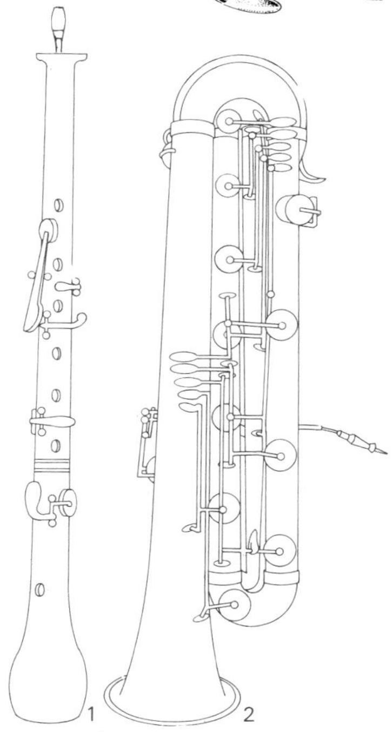

Left and **right 1** The musette is a simple toy instrument like an oboe, developed from the chanter of a bagpipe. **2** The contrabass sarrusophone is a brass instrument with a double reed, developed by Sarrus in 1856. It was designed for use in military bands. **3** and **4** The three- and four-keyed bassoons, made in four sections, were used in the seventeenth and eighteenth centuries. Bach and Mozart used the four-keyed bassoons in their orchestrations. **5** The modern contrabassoon plays an octave lower than the standard bassoon, rests on the floor and is supported by the arms and body. It has a deep, reedy tone.

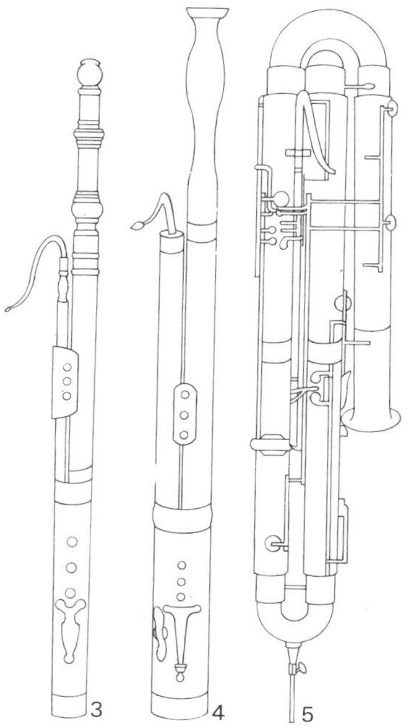

Below A modern bassoon: **1** bell; **2** bass joint; **3** crook; **4** double reed; **5** tenor joint; **6** keys; **7** thumb rest; **8** butt.

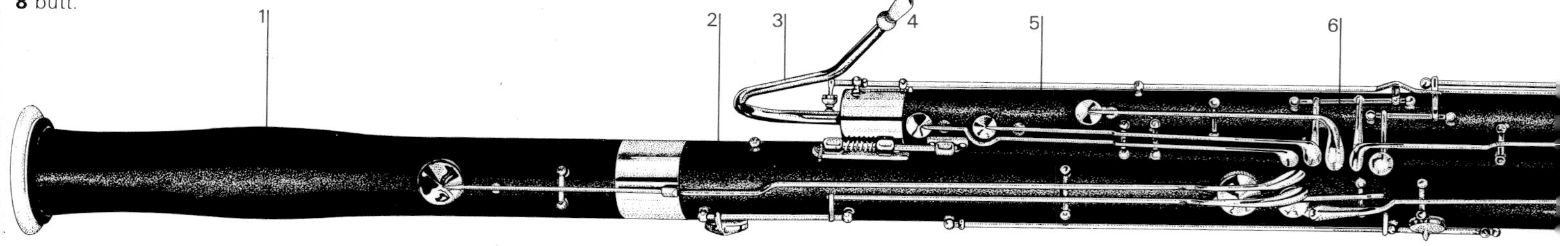

other member of the family is the contra-bassoon, which is pitched an octave lower.

Few composers have written for the bassoon in a solo role but it is important as a low voice in the orchestra.

The saxophone

The saxophone is a hybrid woodwind instrument, having the conical bore of the oboe but the single-reed mouthpiece of the clarinet. It is made of brass. The saxophone family was invented by the Belgian instrument-maker Adolphe Sax in the 1840s. There are four principal members: the soprano in B♭, alto in E♭, tenor in B♭ and baritone in E♭.

The saxophone has never become standard in the symphony orchestra, and is to be heard more in military bands and dance bands. Jazz musicians have made far greater use of the instrument.

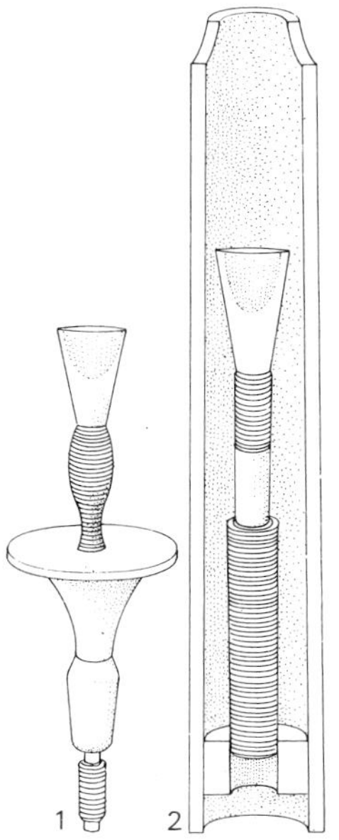

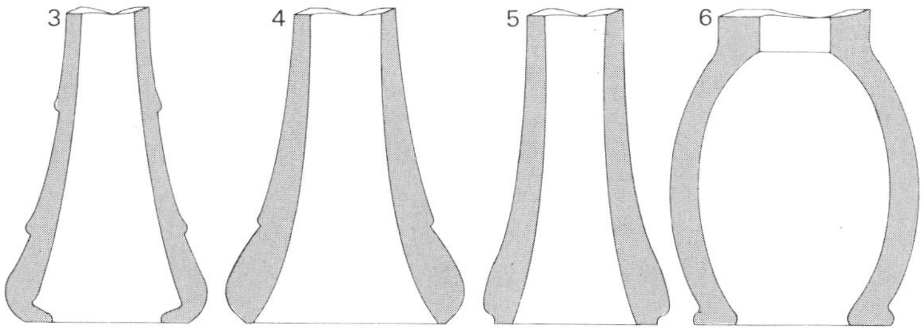

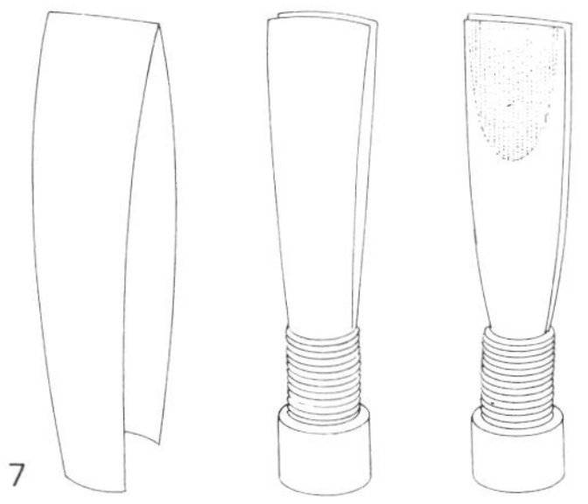

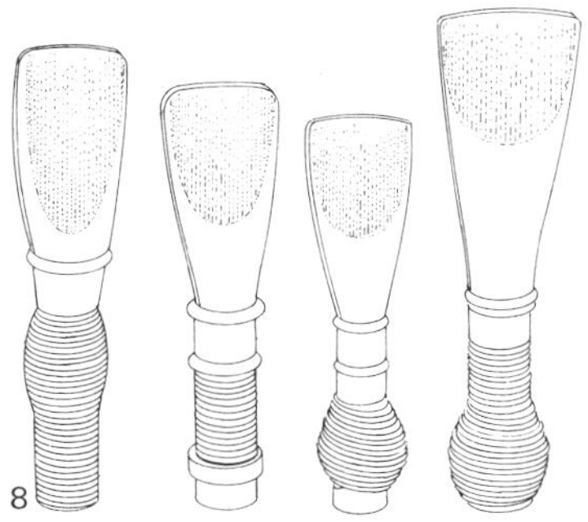

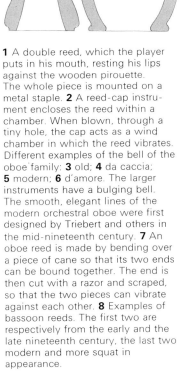

1 A double reed, which the player puts in his mouth, resting his lips against the wooden pirouette. The whole piece is mounted on a metal staple. **2** A reed-cap instrument encloses the reed within a chamber. When blown, through a tiny hole, the cap acts as a wind chamber in which the reed vibrates. Different examples of the bell of the oboe family: **3** old; **4** da caccia; **5** modern; **6** d'amore. The larger instruments have a bulging bell. The smooth, elegant lines of the modern orchestral oboe were first designed by Triebert and others in the mid-nineteenth century. **7** An oboe reed is made by bending over a piece of cane so that its two ends can be bound together. The end is then cut with a razor and scraped, so that the two pieces can vibrate against each other. **8** Examples of bassoon reeds. The first two are respectively from the early and the late nineteenth century, the last two modern and more squat in appearance.

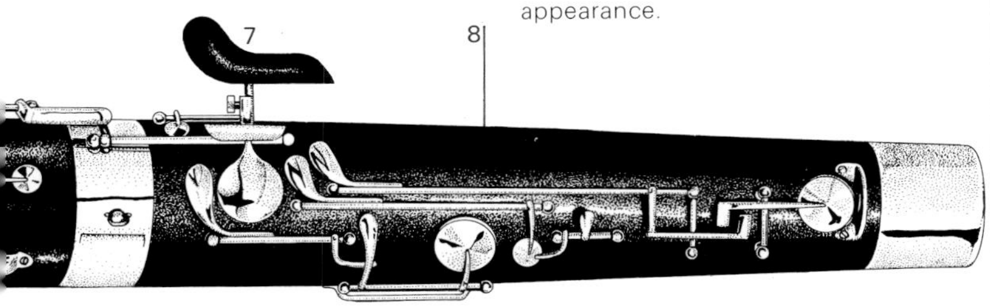

Famous works for wind instruments

J. Brahms: Clarinet Quintet
A. Copland: Clarinet Concerto
C. Debussy: *Syrinx*
G. Handel: oboe concertos
W. A. Mozart: flute, oboe, clarinet and bassoon concertos, Clarinet Quintet
C. Nielsen: Flute Concerto
R. Strauss: Oboe Concerto
C. M. von Weber: Bassoon Concerto

Pitch ranges

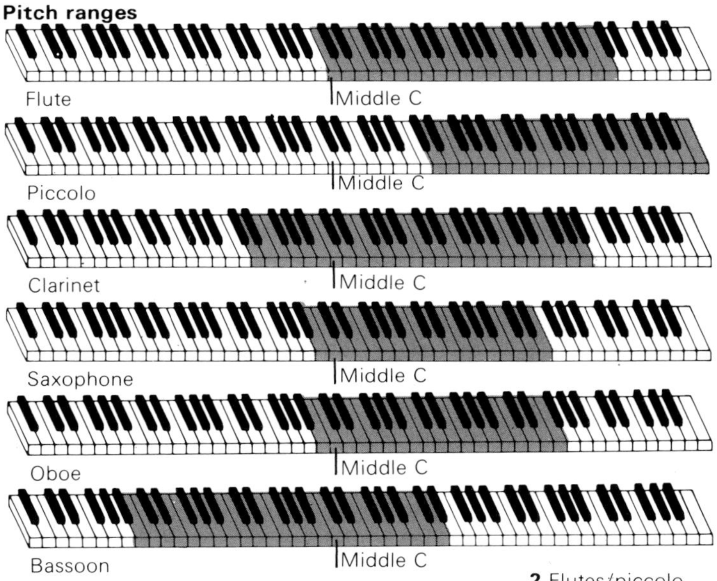

Positions in the orchestra

1 Clarinets
2 Flutes/piccolo
3 Bassoons
4 Oboes/cor anglais

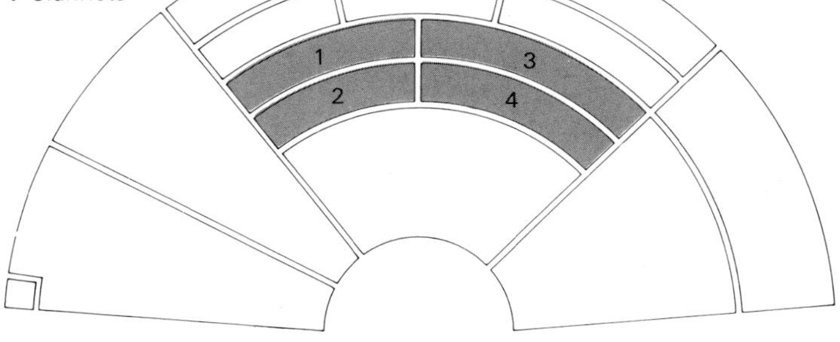

Brass Instruments

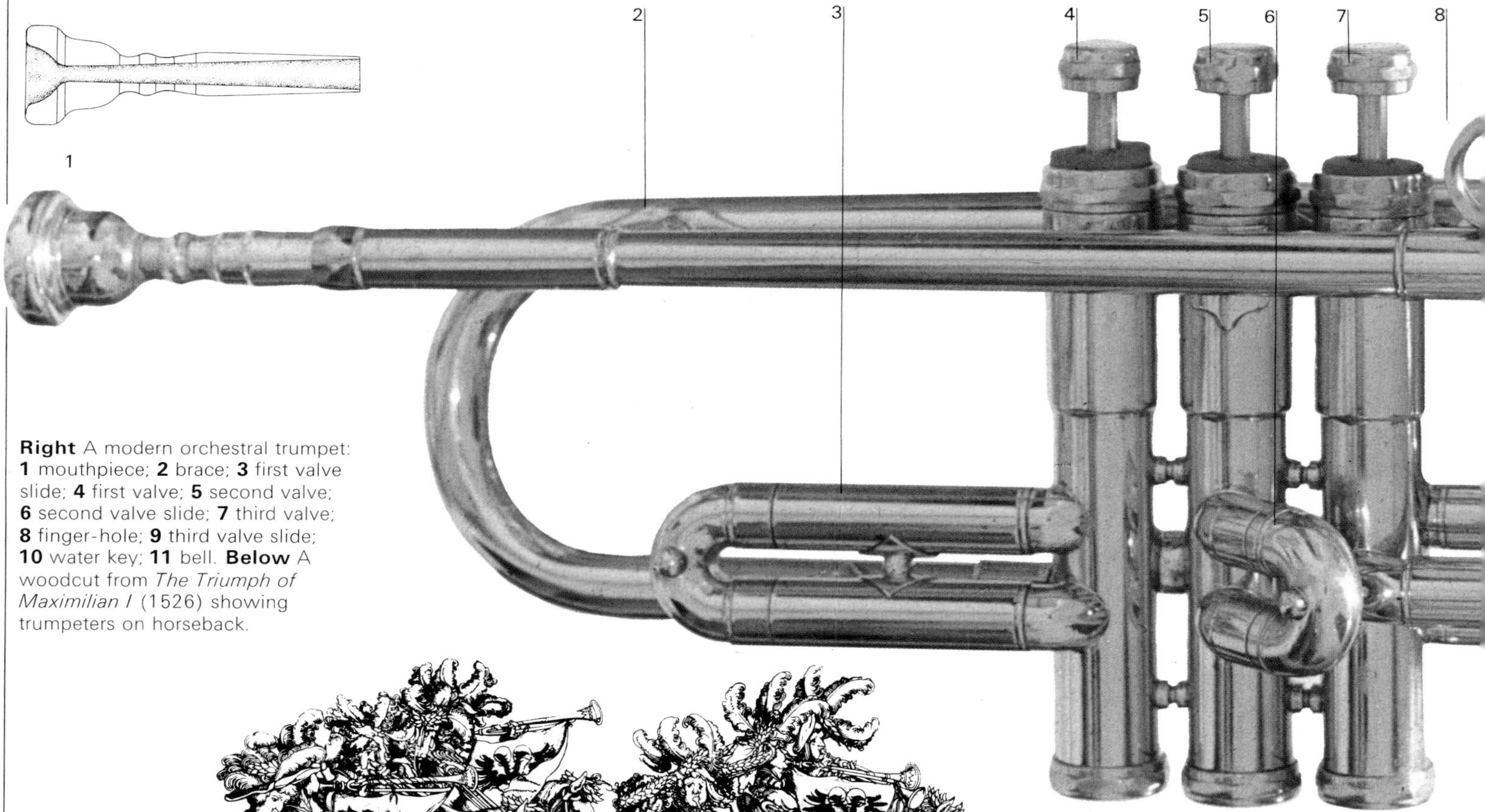

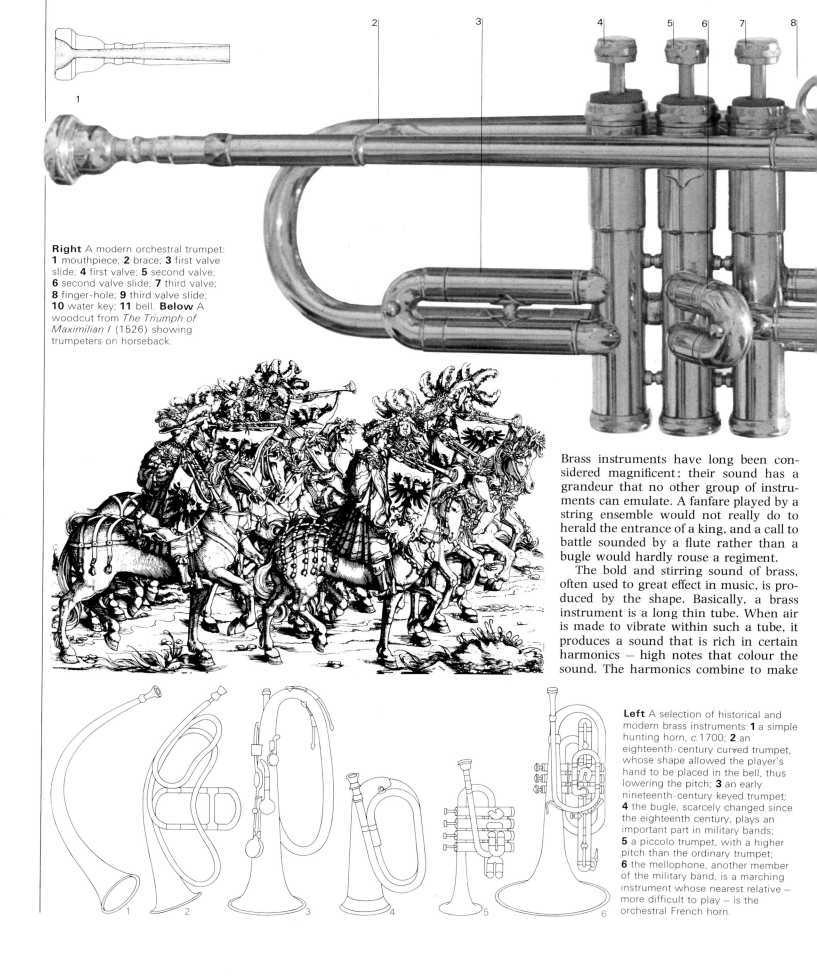

Right A modern orchestral trumpet: **1** mouthpiece; **2** brace; **3** first valve slide; **4** first valve; **5** second valve; **6** second valve slide; **7** third valve; **8** finger-hole; **9** third valve slide; **10** water key; **11** bell. **Below** A woodcut from *The Triumph of Maximilian I* (1526) showing trumpeters on horseback.

Brass instruments have long been considered magnificent; their sound has a grandeur that no other group of instruments can emulate. A fanfare played by a string ensemble would not really do to herald the entrance of a king, and a call to battle sounded by a flute rather than a bugle would hardly rouse a regiment.

The bold and stirring sound of brass, often used to great effect in music, is produced by the shape. Basically, a brass instrument is a long thin tube. When air is made to vibrate within such a tube, it produces a sound that is rich in certain harmonics – high notes that colour the sound. The harmonics combine to make

Left A selection of historical and modern brass instruments: **1** a simple hunting horn, *c.*1700; **2** an eighteenth-century curved trumpet, whose shape allowed the player's hand to be placed in the bell, thus lowering the pitch; **3** an early nineteenth-century keyed trumpet; **4** the bugle, scarcely changed since the eighteenth century, plays an important part in military bands; **5** a piccolo trumpet, with a higher pitch than the ordinary trumpet; **6** the mellophone, another member of the military band, is a marching instrument whose nearest relative – more difficult to play – is the orchestral French horn.

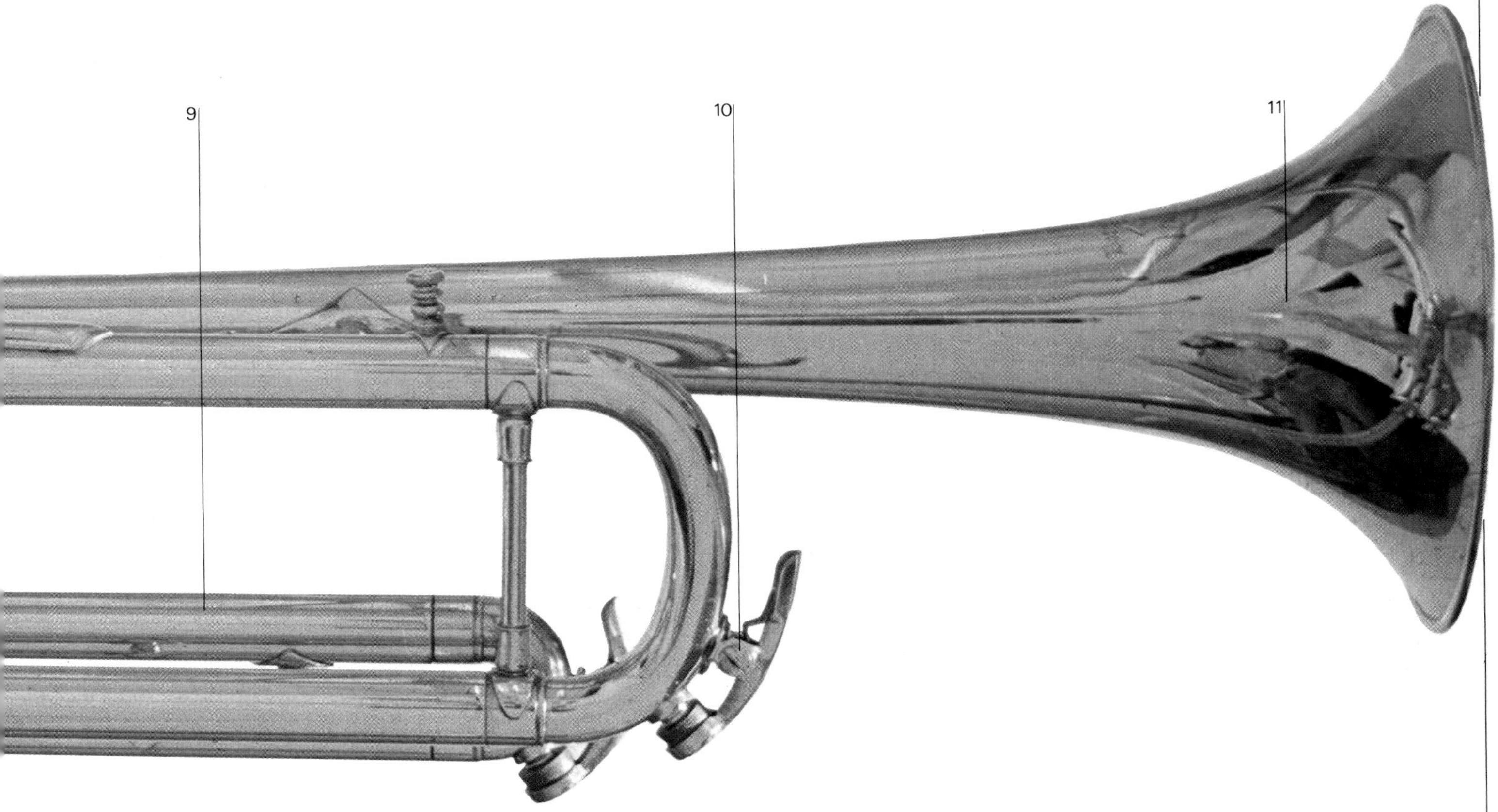

the bright but full sound characteristic of brass instruments.

The air column in a brass instrument is set vibrating by the lips of the player. He or she blows into a mouthpiece attached to one end of the tube, pressing the lips into a cavity in the mouthpiece and forcing air through them to make the lips vibrate. This vibration causes the air in the instrument also to vibrate and a sound issues from the other end of the tube, which widens into a bell. The tone depends on the length and shape of the tube, for widening the bore and shortening the tube robs the sound of some of its harmonics and therefore some of its bright quality. However, several brass instruments do have a conical bore and the higher instruments are not very long because this makes them easier to play.

The shape of the mouthpiece also influences the sound, the cup-shaped opening of a trumpet mouthpiece helping to produce a brilliant tone and the funnel-shaped mouthpiece of the horn giving a more mellow sound. When sounded by vibrating lips, a long narrow tube will give out a set of notes forming the harmonic series, each being a harmonic of the lowest note obtainable. By tensing the lips, higher notes in the series are obtained. Notes outside the series cannot be obtained, but enough notes are present to perform simple tunes – bugle calls consist of notes in the harmonic series, for example.

However, this limited range of notes is insufficient for most music and a brass instrument must be able to produce all the notes of the chromatic scale, as can all keyboard, string and woodwind instruments. This is done by changing the length of the tube as a player sounds a certain harmonic, so that the pitch of the note changes. Most brass instruments have a set of valves that, when pressed, open extra pieces of tubing and divert the air column of the instrument, usually making it longer and lowering the note produced. Most have three valves connected to pieces of tubing of different lengths; when pressed in various combinations, six lower notes each a semitone apart are obtained. This is enough to fill up any of the gaps in the harmonic series, and so a complete chromatic compass is obtained. The trombone has a slide to lengthen the tube instead of valves, but otherwise works in the same way.

The total range of a brass instrument is

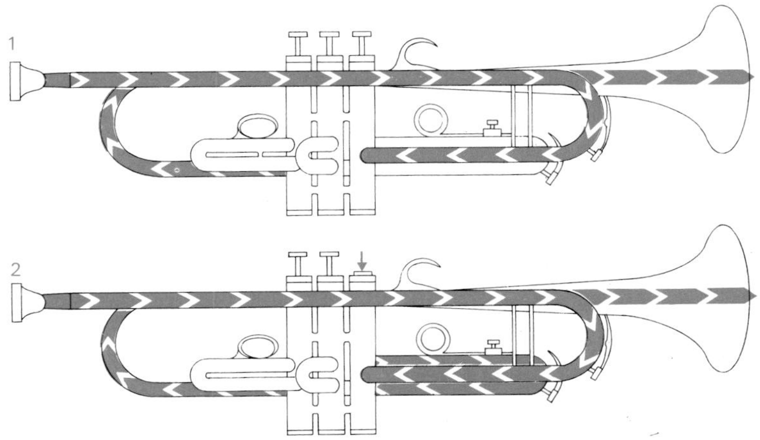

Left The valve action of the trumpet. The three valves lower the instrument's pitch by two, one or three semitones respectively, and, when more than one valve is depressed, by four, five or six semitones. When the valves are at rest (**1**) the air passes directly through the main tubing. When a valve is depressed (**2**), the air is diverted through an extra piece of tubing, thus lengthening the air column.
Right A selection of mutes which, when fitted into the bell of the trumpet, can diminish its volume or produce novel effects. Mutes, made of wood, metal, rubber or plastic, are more frequently used by jazz musicians.

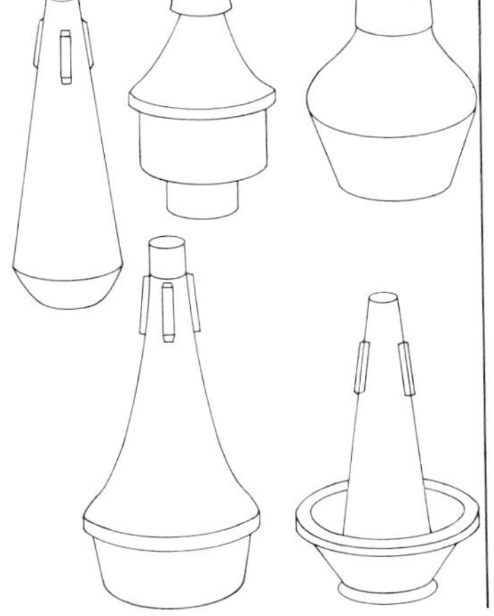

about three octaves, but many players can extend the range higher. It is easier to obtain high notes on an instrument such as a horn that has a very long and narrow tube, but it is also hard to make certain of getting a particular high harmonic. This is why inexpert brass players are more prone to "fluff" notes than other musicians. Playing in tune is also difficult, because some of the harmonics are not in tune with the tempered scale. Varying the lip pressure can help to correct poor intonation in valved instruments; with the trombone, the player has simply to adjust the slide.

All orchestral brass instruments are made of metal and are usually silver-plated. Like woodwind instruments, some of them are transposing instruments.

The history of brass instruments

The origins of brass instruments lie far back in prehistory when it was discovered that a tube can be used to amplify the voice like a megaphone or distort it. People shouted or sang into tubes to ward off evil spirits and to make calls and signals. Soon it was found that sounds could be obtained by blowing into bamboo canes, hollow horns and shells, or tubes carved in wood. Such "instruments" still exist among primitive peoples. The aborigines of Australia have such an instrument in the didgeridoo, which is basically a long wooden tube, and conch shells are still used to make signals in many parts of the world. The Swiss, being far from the sea, bored out a log to make a signalling instrument called the alpenhorn; only in recent times has it been used for music.

With the coming of civilization and the discovery of metals, brass instruments could begin to advance towards those we know today. A silver trumpet was discovered in the tomb of the ancient Egyptian pharaoh Tutankhamun, who died in 1352 BC, and bronze trumpets dating back to about 1000 BC have been found in Danish peat bogs. An inventory of gifts presented to another pharaoh in about 1400 BC lists forty horns, all covered with gold and some studded with precious stones.

By the Middle Ages, trumpets were still associated with royalty and players had cultivated the brilliant high notes of the instrument for playing fanfares. The horn was principally a signalling instrument used when hunting. The trombone first appeared in Europe in about 1400, when it was known as the sackbut. Its use of a slide showed a way of extending the range of brass instruments away from the harmonic series, but this method was not adopted at the time. Instead, instrument-makers provided crooks – additional

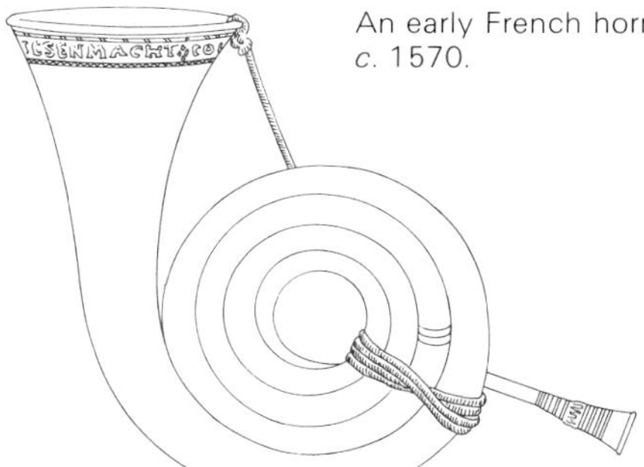

An early French horn, *c.* 1570.

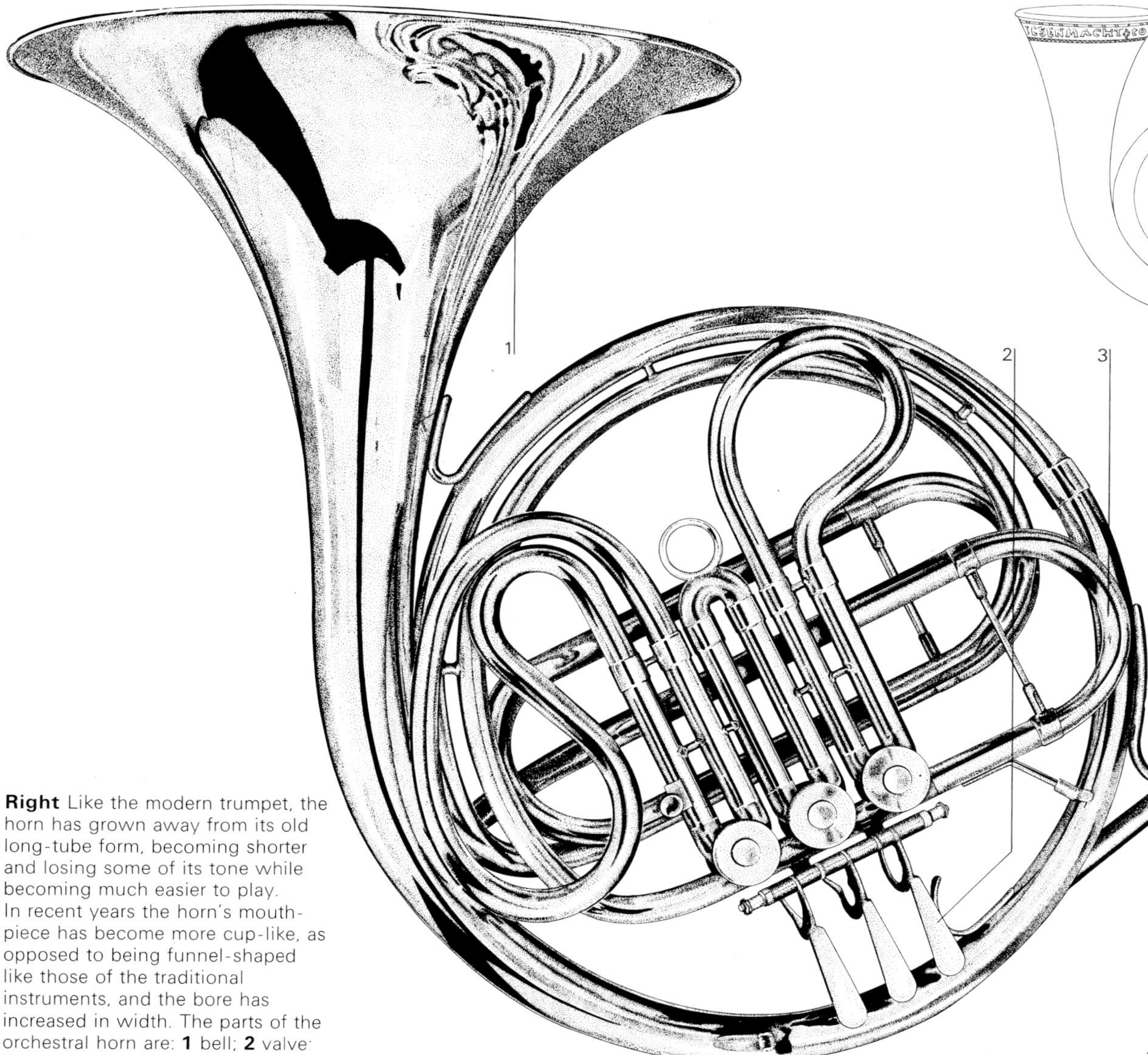

Right Like the modern trumpet, the horn has grown away from its old long-tube form, becoming shorter and losing some of its tone while becoming much easier to play. In recent years the horn's mouthpiece has become more cup-like, as opposed to being funnel-shaped like those of the traditional instruments, and the bore has increased in width. The parts of the orchestral horn are: **1** bell; **2** valve; **3** crook; **4** brace; **5** mouthpiece.

Horn mouthpiece

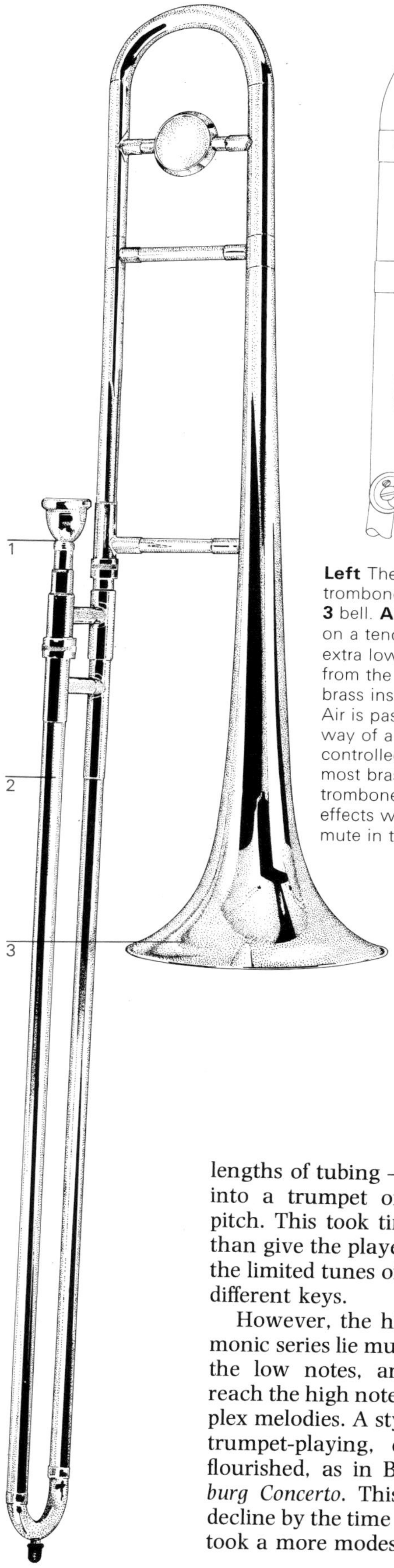

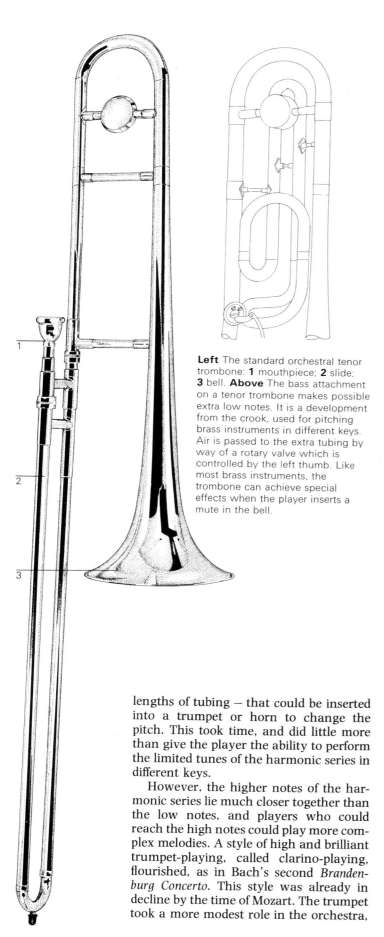

Left The standard orchestral tenor trombone: **1** mouthpiece; **2** slide; **3** bell. **Above** The bass attachment on a tenor trombone makes possible extra low notes. It is a development from the crook, used for pitching brass instruments in different keys. Air is passed to the extra tubing by way of a rotary valve which is controlled by the left thumb. Like most brass instruments, the trombone can achieve special effects when the player inserts a mute in the bell.

lengths of tubing – that could be inserted into a trumpet or horn to change the pitch. This took time, and did little more than give the player the ability to perform the limited tunes of the harmonic series in different keys.

However, the higher notes of the harmonic series lie much closer together than the low notes, and players who could reach the high notes could play more complex melodies. A style of high and brilliant trumpet-playing, called clarino-playing, flourished, as in Bach's second *Brandenburg Concerto*. This style was already in decline by the time of Mozart. The trumpet took a more modest role in the orchestra,

Trombonist

Tuba-player

Horn-player

Trumpeter

Famous works for trumpet
- J. Clarke: Suite in D, *Trumpet Voluntary*
- A. Copland: *Quiet City*
- J. Haydn: Trumpet Concerto
- J. N. Hummel: Trumpet Concerto
- F. Mendelssohn: *Trumpet Overture*
- S. Prokofiev: Concerto for piano, trumpet and strings
- H. Purcell: Trumpet Sonata
- D. Shostakovich: Trumpet Concerto
- A. Vivaldi: Concerto for two trumpets

Famous works for horn
- B. Britten: *Serenade for tenor, horn and strings*
- J. Haydn: Horn Concerto
- W. A. Mozart: horn concertos, Horn Quintet
- R. Strauss: horn concertos

Famous works for tuba and trombone
- N. Rimsky-Korsakov: Trombone Concerto
- R. Vaughan Williams: Concerto for bass tuba

Pitch ranges

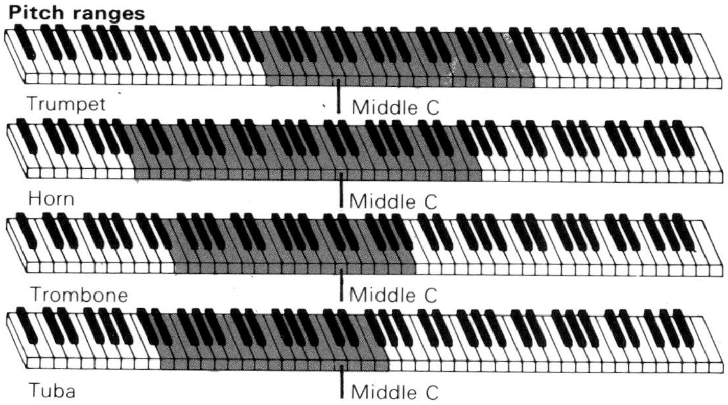

Positions in the orchestra
1 Horns
2 Trumpets
3 Trombones and tubas

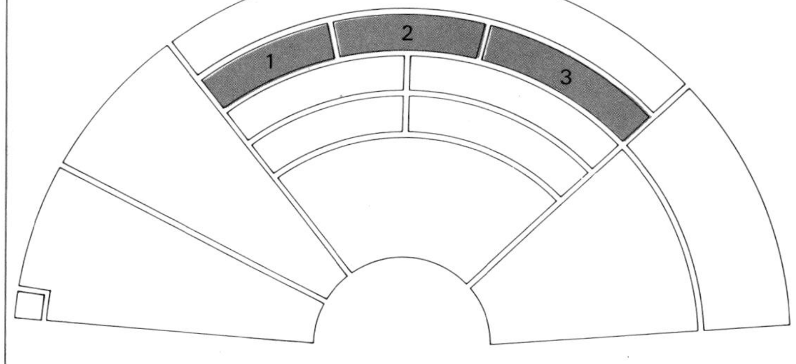

while the horn was still capable of little more than hunting calls. The invention of the valve in about 1815 changed all this, putting the trumpet and horn on a melodic footing with the other instruments of the orchestra. The trombone gained favour as a bass voice in the brass family, and the tube took the range deeper still from the mid-1800s. The brass section of the symphony orchestra became standardized at four horns, three trumpets, three trombones and a tuba. Other brass instruments, such as cornets and saxhorns, were invented during the 1800s. These are mostly confined to military and brass bands.

The trumpet

The standard trumpet has a thin cylindrical bore for most of its length, widening over the last quarter into a flared bell. The three valves work with pistons, unlike the horn, which has rotary valves. It is pitched in B♭, which may be changed to A and sometimes to C by adjusting the tubing. It is designed to be a flexible instrument, producing a bright and full sound over a wide range. The sound can be adjusted by placing mutes in the bell. A straight mute, which is shaped like a cone, gives a piercing and sinister sound, whereas a bucket mute, which clips in front of the bell, makes the instrument sound mellow. The cup mute and harmon mute produce soft and buzzy sounds. Over all, the trumpet has more variety of tone than any other instrument of the orchestra, but the exploitation of its wide range of sound has been confined mainly to popular music, especially jazz.

Two other trumpets may be heard in orchestral music: a small high trumpet in D and a large bass trumpet in E♭.

The horn

The horn mainly used in the orchestra is the double horn, which is in fact two horns in one. It is often called the French horn, an archaic and misleading term. The bore of the horn is narrow and very long, widening to a funnel-shaped bell at the end. There are four valves. Three are used to obtain a chromatic scale, as in the trumpet, although the valves are rotary in action and do not contain pistons. The fourth valve opens an extra-long length of tubing, effectively converting the instrument into a deeper horn; this is why it is called a double horn. The longer section is used to give a warm, dark sound, while the shorter horn is brought into play when brilliant high notes are required. In this way, the horns can create a glowing veil

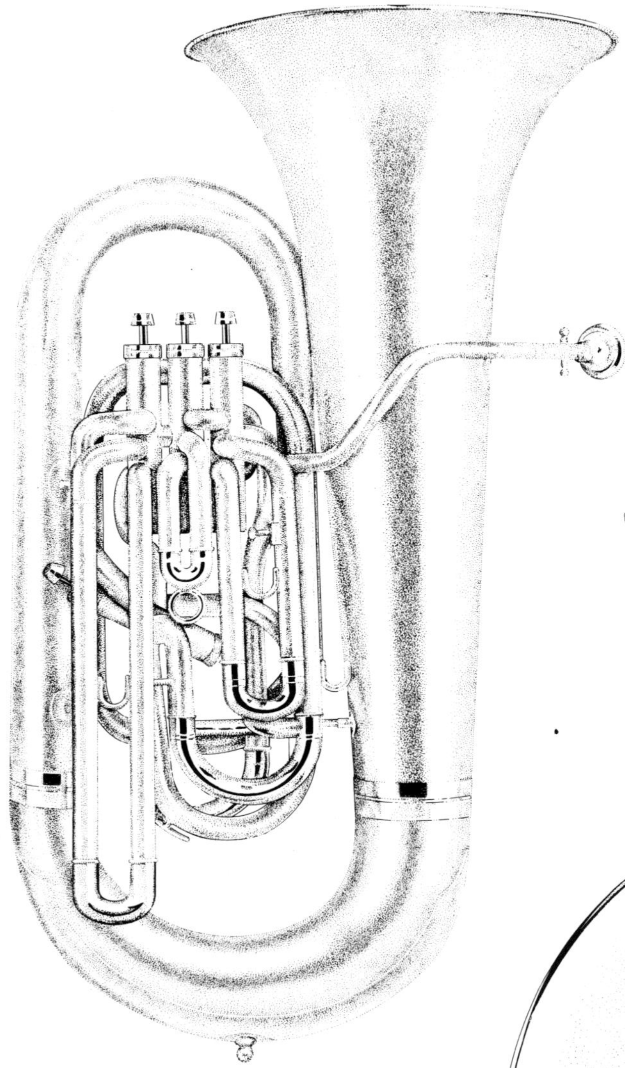

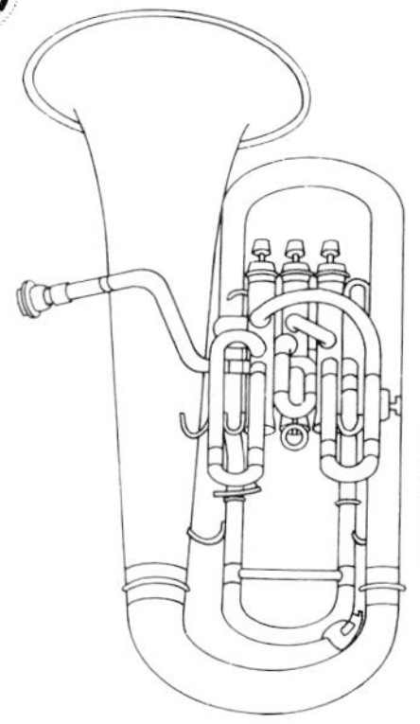

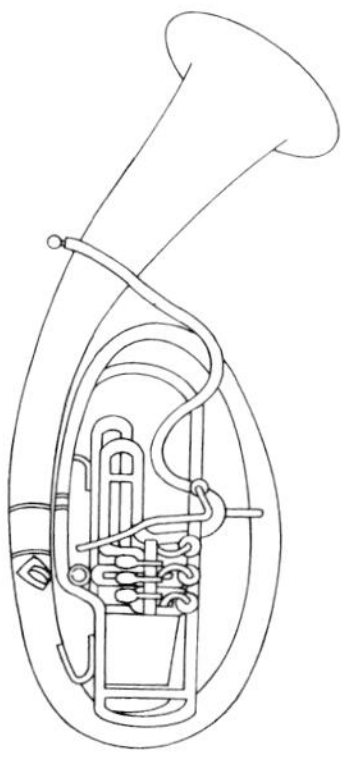

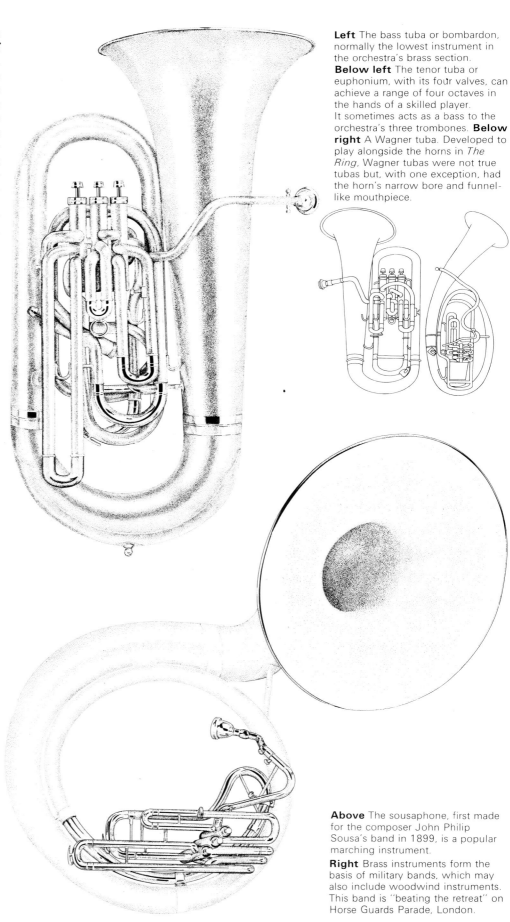

Left The bass tuba or bombardon, normally the lowest instrument in the orchestra's brass section. **Below left** The tenor tuba or euphonium, with its four valves, can achieve a range of four octaves in the hands of a skilled player. It sometimes acts as a bass to the orchestra's three trombones. **Below right** A Wagner tuba. Developed to play alongside the horns in *The Ring*, Wagner tubas were not true tubas but, with one exception, had the horn's narrow bore and funnel-like mouthpiece.

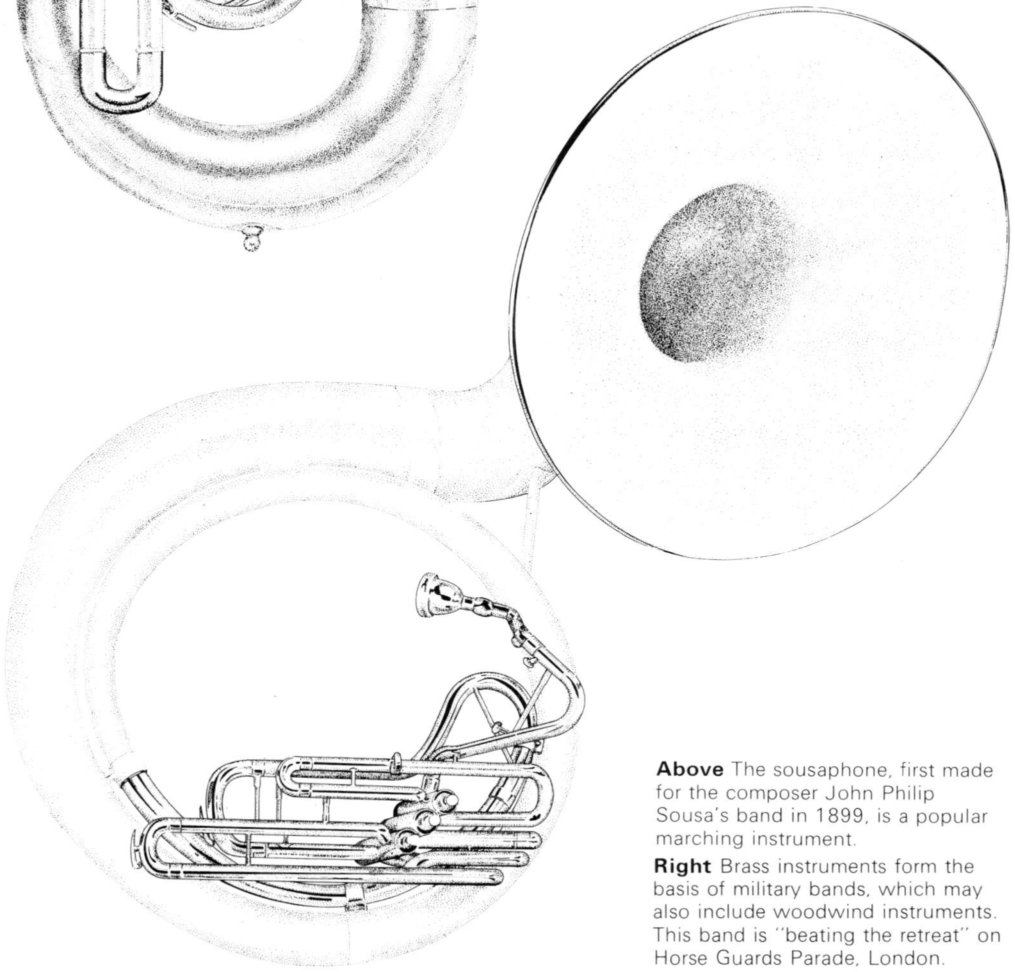

Above The sousaphone, first made for the composer John Philip Sousa's band in 1899, is a popular marching instrument.

Right Brass instruments form the basis of military bands, which may also include woodwind instruments. This band is "beating the retreat" on Horse Guards Parade, London.

of tone colour but also cut through with a bright flare of sound.

The right hand is placed in the bell, where it can control tuning and also the tone. If the hand is thrust up the bell, the horn produces a soft, metallic but piercing sound. Mutes are therefore rarely used. The horn is a transposing instrument pitched in F.

The trombone

The trombone has a cylindrical bore for about two-thirds of its length and then widens into a flared bell, giving a rich and powerful sound. All notes away from the harmonic series are obtained by moving the slide to various positions. Continuous movement of the slide gives a glissando very characteristic of the instrument. The same kinds of mutes are used as with the trumpet. The trombone is not a transposing instrument.

Most orchestral players use the tenor trombone. A bass trombone capable of deeper sounds is often called for, and many trombonists have an attachment that brings an extra length of tubing into play to reach the lower notes, rather like the double horn. Trombones have been made with valves instead of a slide, but in these the majestic sound is lost so the valve trombone has not been widely used.

The tuba

Tubas are the lowest brass instruments. They come in various sizes and ranges and are equipped with a varying number of valves. The tuba has a reputation as a musical elephant, but its sound is not always weighty and it can be played with grace and agility. Many tubas have a wide conical bore and are played with a cup mouthpiece. Wagner tubas, developed by the German composer Richard Wagner, are more horn-like in shape and sound, and are played with a funnel mouthpiece.

The bugle

The bugle has a wide conical bore, giving a broad sound without the brilliance of the trumpet. The military bugle has no valves and is used to give signals, but several instruments have been made with valves to exploit the bugle's sound. The highest-valved bugles are called flugelhorns and have much the same range as the trumpet. The flugelhorn produces a beautiful mellow sound, which has best been exploited in jazz, especially by Miles Davis. The lower members of the family are played with the bell pointing upwards. They are the tenor horn, baritone horn and euphonium or tuba. All are used in brass bands, giving these ensembles their distinctive mellow sound. The tuba is one of those played in the symphony orchestra.

Valved bugles were developed in the early 1800s. In 1845, Adolphe Sax, the Belgian instrument-maker best-known for the saxophone, patented a complete family and called them saxhorns, a name that still survives today.

The cornet and the cornett

These two brass instruments, so alike in name, are in fact totally different. The cornet is a descendant of the post-horn, the horn used by coachmen to signal their coming. It was invented in about 1825 in France and is like a trumpet with a narrow conical bore. Its sound is round, not so brilliant as the trumpet and not so mellow as the flugelhorn. It is often played with great agility in brass bands.

The cornett is an obsolete instrument that was popular from the late 1400s to about 1800. It solved the problem of obtaining notes outside the harmonic series by having a row of finger-holes along the tube, like a woodwind instrument. Furthermore, it was made of wood. Nevertheless, it is considered a brass instrument because it was blown with the lips. The longest-lasting were the low members of the family – the serpent, so called because of its shape, and the ophicleide.

Percussion

The term "percussion" covers all musical instruments which produce their sound when struck, either with an implement or with the hand. They have a place in all musical cultures, and in some they are the dominant, sometimes the sole, form of musical expression. Percussion instruments are of two kinds: *idiophones* and *membranophones*. Each type includes both tuned and untuned instruments.

Percussion in the orchestra

The percussion section of the modern symphony orchestra contains examples of all categories. The most prominent are the tuned membranophones known as timpani or kettledrums. They consist of a hemispherical metal shell over the open end of which is stretched a skin, secured by a wooden hoop. The tension on this skin can be varied by means of screws or a foot-pedal, thereby altering the pitch of the note. Orchestral timpani derive from military kettledrums and were probably introduced into Europe by the Crusaders. Nowadays they are rarely used as generators of rhythm, but to add colour and emphasis to a piece of music. In the symphony orchestra they are usually used in pairs and tuned to the tonic and dominant.

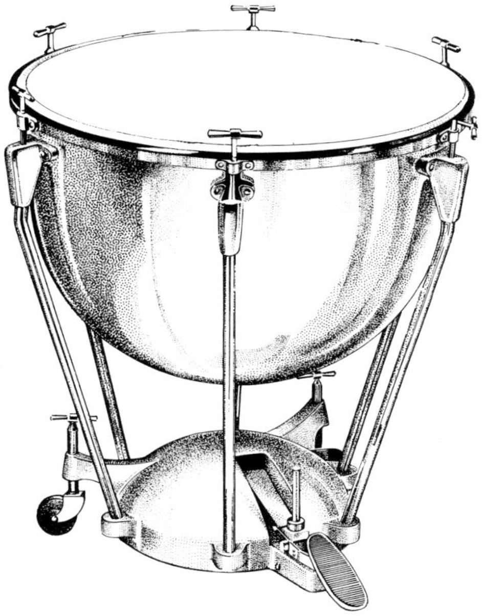

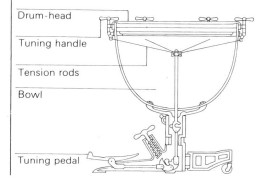

A pedal-operated kettledrum. To raise the drum's pitch the drummer depresses the pedal. This pulls the metal rim to which the drumhead is attached, which in turn increases the head's tension.

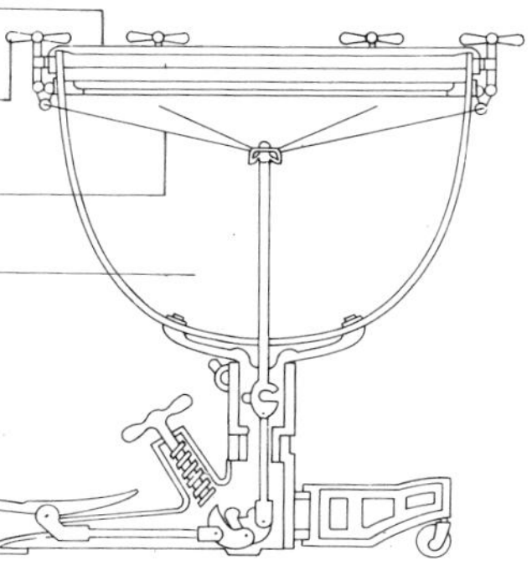

A mounted German kettledrummer of 1584, by Jost Amman.

The other principal orchestral membranophones are cylindrical double-skin drums of various sizes, once again adapted from military originals. The bass drum is the largest and is played with a single soft-headed stick, while the smaller side drum has wires (known as "snares") attached to the lower skin, which produce a rattling sound when the playing skin is struck. Other drums of similar shape but intermediate size are sometimes used too. The tambourine, a small wooden hoop with a single skin, is the smallest membranophone regularly used in the symphony orchestra. Attached to the hoop are pairs of small metal discs. The instrument is struck, shaken or rubbed by the player's moistened thumb.

Among the idiophones, the various types of cymbals are most commonly used. These discs of thin metal range from tiny "finger cymbals" to plates of 60cm or more in diameter. In the orchestra they are normally played in pairs – clashed together and damped by being held against the player's body. A cymbal can also be suspended from a stand and beaten with a soft-headed stick.

The other principal metal instruments are the gong and the tubular bells. Gongs are common in Asia, particularly China, and there they take numerous forms. In the orchestra the gong, a disc of metal with a turned-in rim, is suspended and beaten with a soft-headed beater. A gong, known as the tam-tam, is also used. Tubular bells consist of a graded series of metal tubes, hung vertically on a frame and beaten with a hard mallet.

An orchestral percussion section often includes a few instruments used to provide "colour". Castanets, for instance, are employed to give a Spanish flavour to certain compositions. They consist of two hollow shell-shaped pieces of ebony, attached to the thumb and middle finger and clicked together, or mounted on a piece of wood and shaken. There are also the rattle (similar to the football variety) and the anvil. There is an endless variety of such "colouristic" instruments, including the typewriter, used by Erik Satie in his ballet-score *Parade* (1917). Composers often devise their own instruments of this kind.

Apart from the tubular bells and the timpani, there is a number of other tuned percussion instruments. The dulcimer, a stringed instrument similar to a zither but struck with hammers rather than plucked, is not used orchestrally, but parts are often written for the glockenspiel, which consists of a set of steel plates corresponding to the notes of the chromatic scale and arranged like a keyboard. The notes are struck with hard mallets to produce a bright, penetrating sound which carries above the whole orchestra. A similar instrument, although larger and with wooden keys, is the xylophone, an instrument which occurs in many forms through the world (see pages 122–3).

Percussion in Latin-American music and jazz

Percussion instruments do not play a leading part in the symphony orchestra, but are used principally for emphasis and colour. Musical cultures in which the interplay of rhythm takes a central role yield a greater variety of percussion instruments and have developed a far more expressive and subtle use of them. The two Western forms which exemplify this are Latin-American music and jazz.

In South America, particularly Brazil, large groups of rhythm instruments combine to produce complex structures, although individual parts may be simple. The fluid beat of the mambo, baion, samba and other dance rhythms derives its effect not only from the intermingling of patterns but also from the tonal variety obtained by the battery of percussion upon which they are played. The principal treatise, by Humberto Morales, lists eleven main types, and there are many others.

The simplest instrument is the claves, two small, solid cylinders of resonant wood struck together to produce the highest note of the rhythm ensemble. The cowbell, either held in the hand or mounted on a stand is capable of a variety of timbre, depending upon how it is held and where it is struck. Other simple instruments are the *cabaza* – a large round gourd covered with rows of strung beads which are slapped while the gourd is rotated, the *chocallo*, a hollow cylinder containing beads or dried seeds, and the well-known maracas, a pair of gourd shells with handles and filled with seeds or buckshot. These last two are shaken.

The virtuoso instrument of Latin America is the timbales, a pair of copper-shelled drums, played with sticks. The drums are struck on the skins, the metal rims or the shells themselves. They pro-

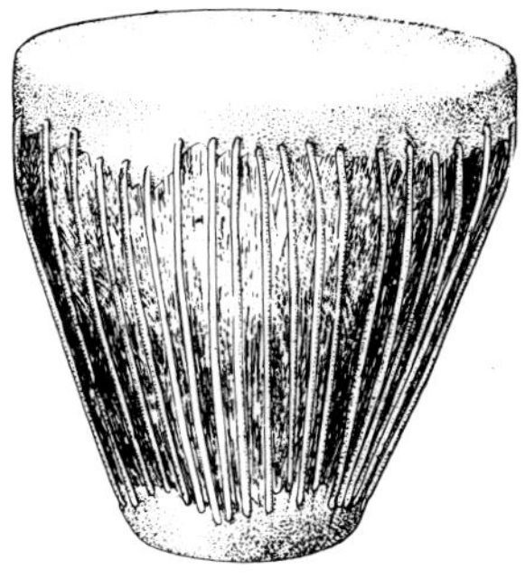

Above An African double-headed drum, the *ntenga*, from Uganda. It is often played in pairs. **Left** Latin-American dance-band drums: **1** bongos, played with the fingers; **2** cocktail drums, a sophisticated version of the conga drum; **3** conga drums are played with the hands while regulating the pitch by arm pressure on the skin; **4** timbales, copper-shelled drums played with thin sticks.

1 Hi-hat
2 Cymbal
3 Side(snare) drum
4 Bass drum
5 Tom-tom
6 Tenor drum

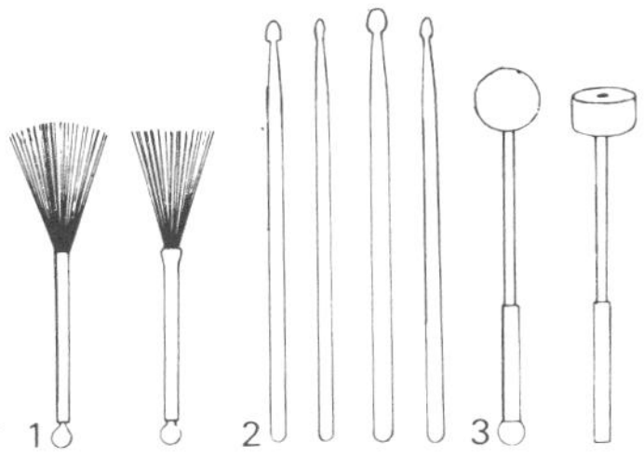

Above 1 Wire brushes, which are used for special effects in the orchestra and play an important role in jazz drumming. **2** Side-drum sticks, usually made of hickory or lance wood. **3** Kettledrum (timpani) sticks. Berlioz recommended three types of head: wood, leather and sponge, but nowadays heads are principally made of wood and felt. To meet the demands of modern composers the heads vary considerably in shape, size, weight and texture.

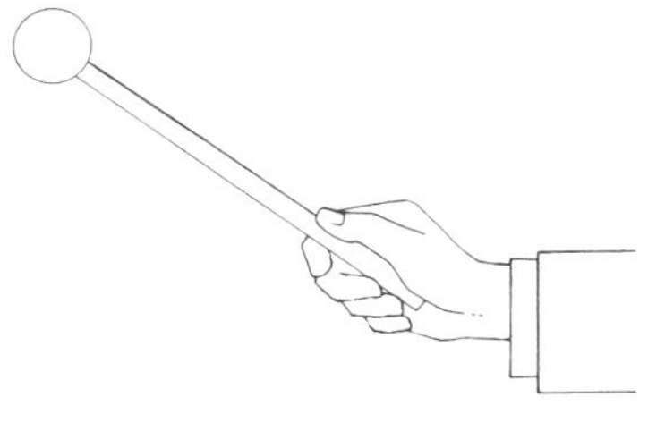

Above The grip of the kettledrum stick. **Left** A set of modern dance-band drums. The hi-hat is played by depressing the pedal at the bass of the stand; a similar pedal operates the bass drum.

duce a sharp, commanding sound. The other principal drums are the bongos, a pair of small hand-drums, and the conga, a large, barrel-shaped drum, also played with the hands. All these drums have a specific and complicated technique and well-defined parts to play in the ensemble.

Unlike the South American ensemble, which plainly evolved out of common natural objects or household implements, the jazz drum kit derives from a series of orchestral or military originals. Starting as a makeshift assemblage of random bits and pieces, it has developed into a complex, precision-built multiple instrument. It contains a snare drum, a series of tom-toms (double-skin drums without snares), a foot-operated bass drum, suspended cymbals and a hi-hat. The latter consists of a pair of cymbals mounted horizontally, the lower one attached to a foot-controlled spring device which brings it into contact with its partner.

The drum kit requires the use of both hands and both feet. When played by a master it is capable of endless variety of sound and enormous rhythmic complexity. Great jazz drummers like Jo Jones, Elvin Jones and Max Roach are able to provide not only a basic beat for the other musicians but, at the same time, a series of rhythmic interjections and comments. Jazz and rock drummers all make their individual selection of parts for their kits, particularly where cymbals are concerned. Recent developments have included electronic attachments which to modify an instrument's sound.

Another percussion instrument adopted for jazz use is the vibraphone. This resembles a large glockenspiel with a vertical tube fixed beneath each note to provide resonance. At the top of each tube is a small electric fan which imparts vibrato to the sound. The vibraphone was introduced into the orchestra in the 1920s, but was developed as a virtuoso instrument first by Lionel Hampton (in about 1936) and subsequently by Milt Jackson, Bobby Hutcherson and others. A similar instrument, the marimba – with wooden bars and without fans – is used in the popular music of Mexico. A cross-bred version, the vibra-marimba, has been made, but is little used.

Development of percussion proceeds, sometimes in the most unlikely manner. The so-called "steel drum" of Trinidad is a good example. This is not strictly a drum at all but an idiophone, a form of gong. It is made by cutting a section through a steel oil-drum. The top is divided into sections, each section being heated and beaten out until it produces a specific note. The resulting tone is extremely mellow and whole orchestras of steel drums can be assembled.

Percussion is perhaps the only field in which such basic innovation can still take place, leaving aside electronics. Any resonant object, when struck, gives out a sound. One has only to look at the enormous variety of percussion instruments in the world to realize that the possibilities are limitless.

Above A modern orchestral xylophone, a far cry from its prehistoric ancestors—rough slabs of wood laid across a seated player's legs. **Below** The marimba, a deeper-pitched cousin of the xylophone, takes its name from a folk instrument of Africa and Central America.

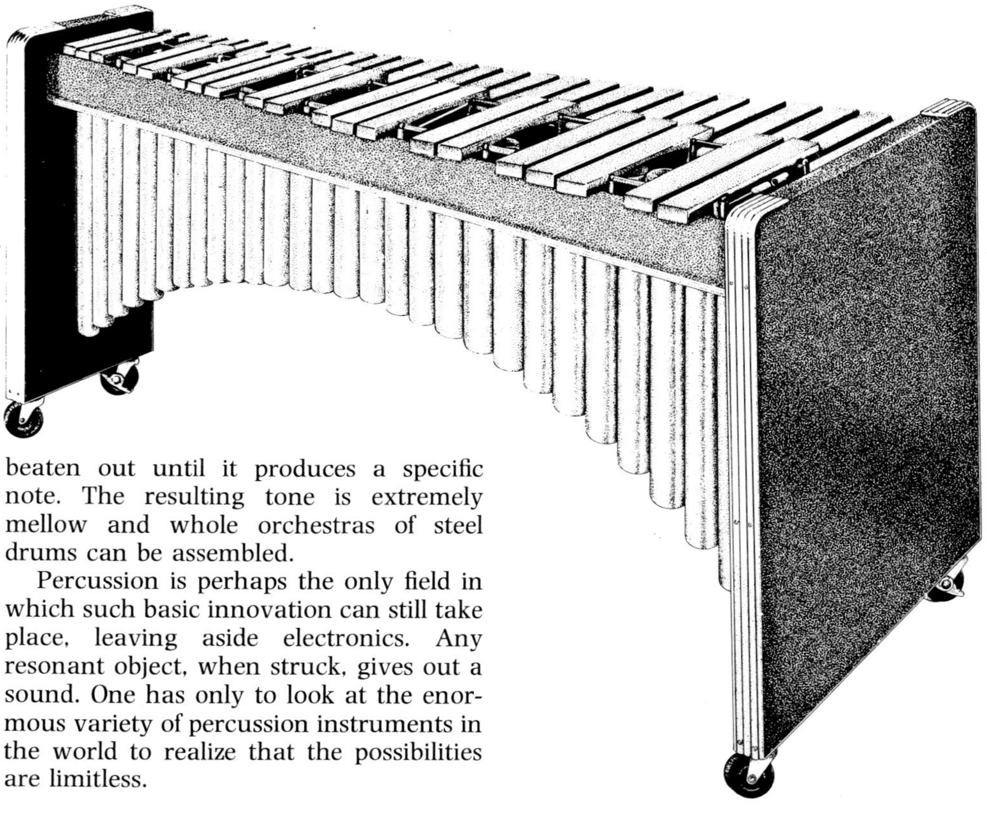

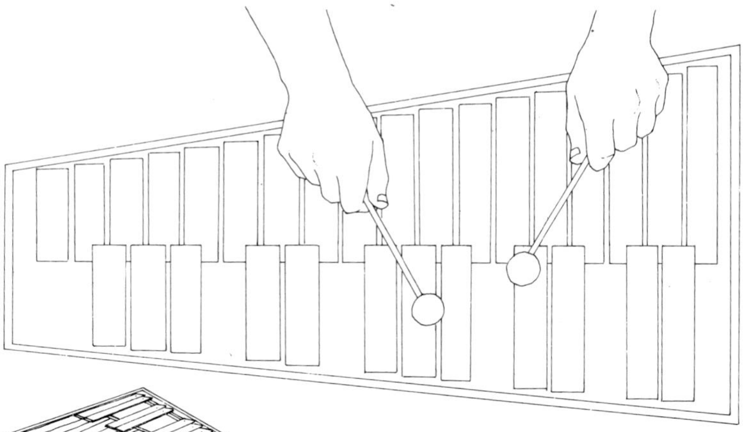

1

A selection of orchestral percussion instruments: **1** a glockenspiel, played with hard beaters to produce a bell-like tone; **2** Latin-American maracas; **3** tubular bells, which are struck with drum-sticks; **4** a tam-tam, or orchestral brass gong; **5** castanets, usually made of wood, although sometimes plastic is used. As few orchestral percussionists have mastered the art of playing castanets in the hand, they are often mounted on a central handle and shaken or struck on the knee or palm. **6** A triangle, usually 16–17 cm long and suspended by a thin gut string.

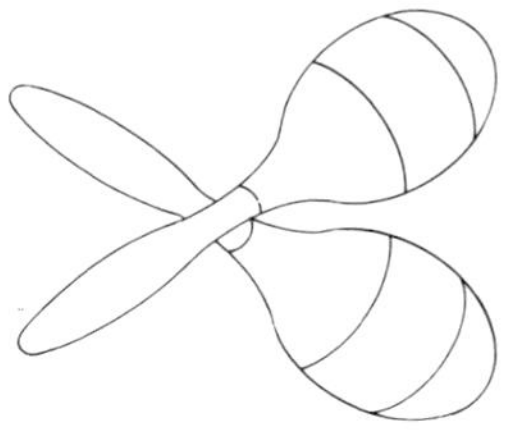

2

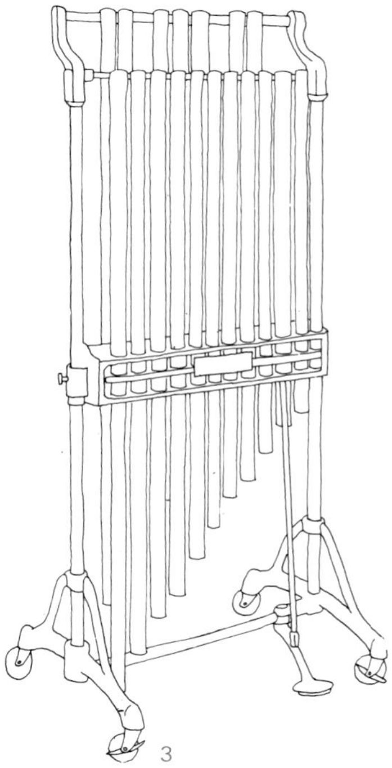

3

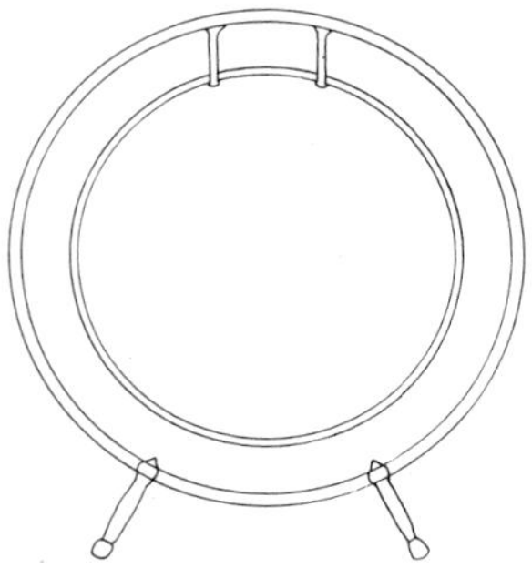

4

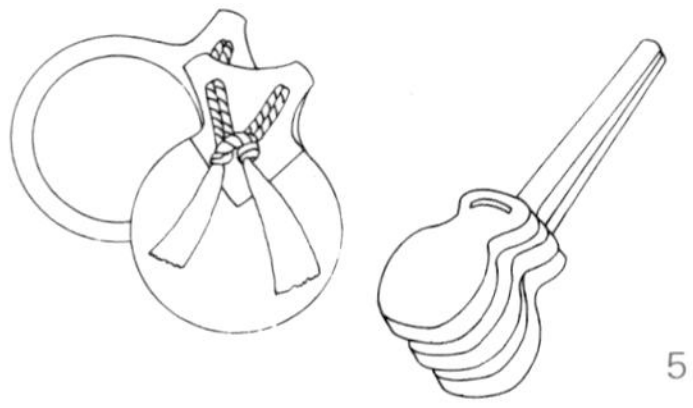

5

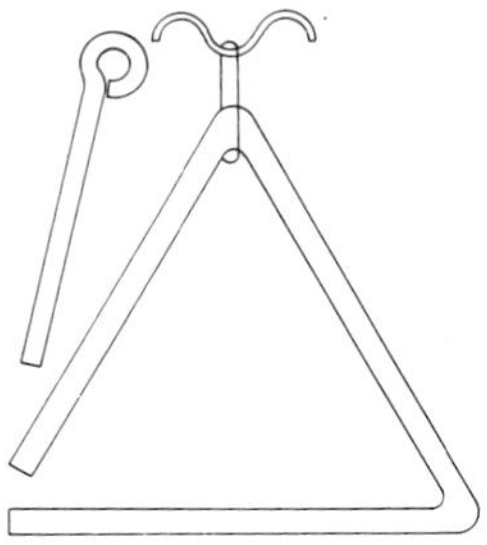

6

Drummer

Famous works for percussion

B. Bartók: *Music for strings, percussion and celesta,* Sonata for two pianos and percussion
L. van Beethoven: *Battle* symphony ("Wellington's Victory")
L. Berio: *Tempi concertati, Circles*
P. Boulez: *Le Marteau sans maître, Pli selon pli*
J. Cage: *Construction in Metal*
E. Carter: *Six Pieces for Kettle-drums, Canto, Adagio*
C. W. Gluck: *Concerto upon Twenty-six Drinking-glasses*
G. Holst: *The Planets*
E. Lutyens: *Scena for violin, cello and percussion*
D. Milhaud: Concerto for percussion and small orchestra
L. Nono: *Diario Polacco '58*
M. Ravel: *Bolero*
W. Russel: Concerto for eight percussion instruments
C. Saint-Saëns: *Danse Macabre*
K. Stockhausen: *Zyklus*
I. Stravinsky: *Les Noces, The Soldier's Tale*
E. Varèse: *Ionization*

Pitch ranges

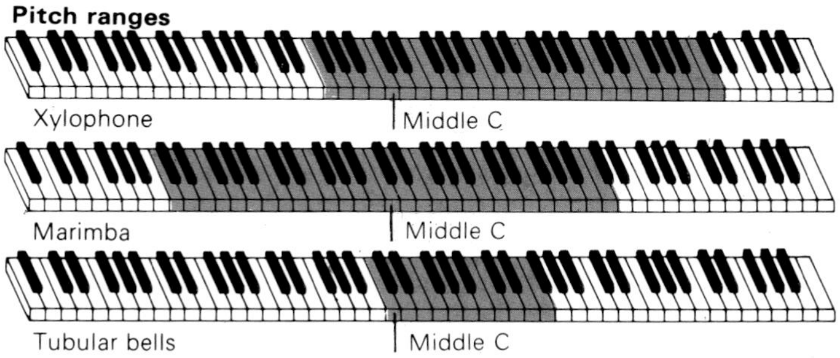

Position of percussion instruments in the orchestra

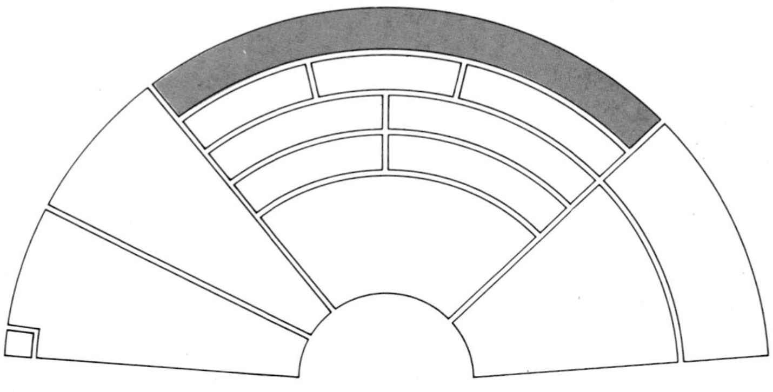

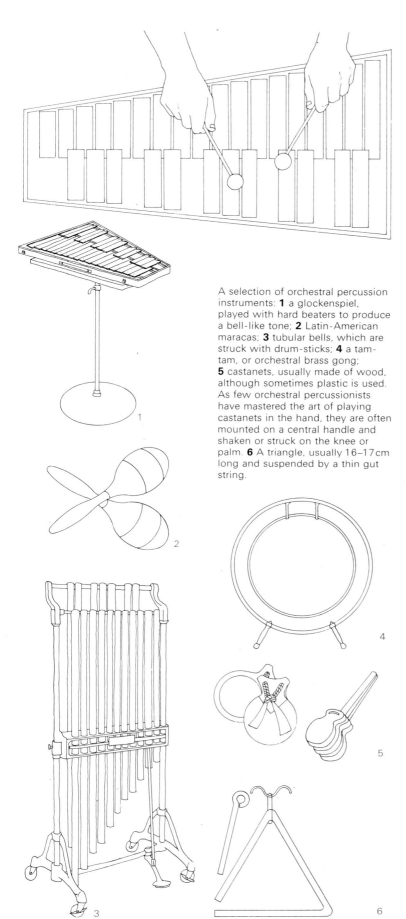

Instruments around the World

The materials available to a society will naturally determine the kinds of musical instrument that can be made. The life-style of the people will also determine the kinds of instrument it uses. Pastoral peoples tend to play flutes and reed-pipes, which can be made by shepherds and herdsmen with time on their hands; nomadic tribes make small, portable instruments; complex settled societies establish bands or orchestras of skilled players with an elaborate range of resources, and so on.

A common type of instrument in primitive cultures is the idiophone, a "self-sounding" instrument made of resonant material. Archaeology has revealed the remains of idiophones, usually stone rattles, dating as far back as the European paleolithic, while chimes made of stone, and specifically tuned to the pentatonic scale, have been discovered at neolithic sites in Indo-China. Being made of durable materials, they have survived; there is good reason to assume that other musical instruments, constructed from wood, skin and other perishable substances, were also played in that period.

Idiophones are found in all societies. The simplest are rattles and clappers. They take many forms and have a variety of purposes, some of them practical – like the wooden bird-scarer depicted in Egyptian art and still widely used today – or ceremonial, such as the shaman's gourd rattle.

A common form of struck idiophone is the hollowed log. The most impressive instrument of this type is probably the log drum of the Naga people of Assam. These can be up to thirteen metres long. They are hollowed out through a longitudinal slit and placed on a framework above the ground for maximum resonance. The whole community shares the labour of making these instruments and they are an important part of Naga village life. Their great size means that they can be heard over long distances, and they are used for sounding alarms as well as in celebrations and festivities. The community also builds a house for the drum, and gives it a ceremonial name. The drum's importance in daily life is typical of many tribal societies, although details of the rituals associated with it vary from tribe to tribe.

Idiophones can also be plucked, in which case they incorporate a tongue, usually of metal, that the player twangs. Because the natural sound produced is very quiet, plucked idiophones always include a resonator. The *sansa*, or African thumb-piano, consists of a series of metal tongues fixed on to a hollow box. The player holds the box and plucks the tongues with his thumbs, producing a gentle, plangent sound. The other main form is the jew's harp (or jaws harp), in which the metal tongue is held between the player's teeth, his mouth cavity acting as resonator. The plucked idiophone is one of the few primitive instruments with no modern orchestral descendants, the nearest European equivalent being the musical-box.

Perhaps the most common form of tuned idiophone is the xylophone, consisting of bars of wood of different lengths which are struck with hammers. Xylophones are common throughout Africa and are often combined into orchestras. The Chopi of Mozambique, in particular, have developed ensemble xylophone-playing into an art of great subtlety. The Chopi band is similar in many ways to the *gamelan* orchestras of Java and Bali, except that the Indonesians use metal bars and bamboo resonators. This gives a clangorous, insistent sound unlike that of any other ethnic music. Western developments of these instruments can be seen in the orchestral xylophone, the marimba and the glockenspiel.

Gongs, metal discs struck with hammers, are particularly associated with Asia. They have been known from very early times in China, Tibet, India and Burma.

Closely related to idiophones are membranophones, instruments in which a stretched membrane vibrates to produce sound. The most common form of membranophone is the drum. Musicologists assume that drums date back to very early times because of their almost universal distribution. Certainly the Greeks and Romans used them and the *Rig-Veda*, one of the ancient books of Hindu scripture, mentions drums being used in India in about 1000 BC.

Drums have either one membrane, which is beaten, or two, the second acting as resonator. They come in a variety of

Few instruments are confined to any one country or even one continent. Some of the most important ethnic instruments are found over vast areas of the world.

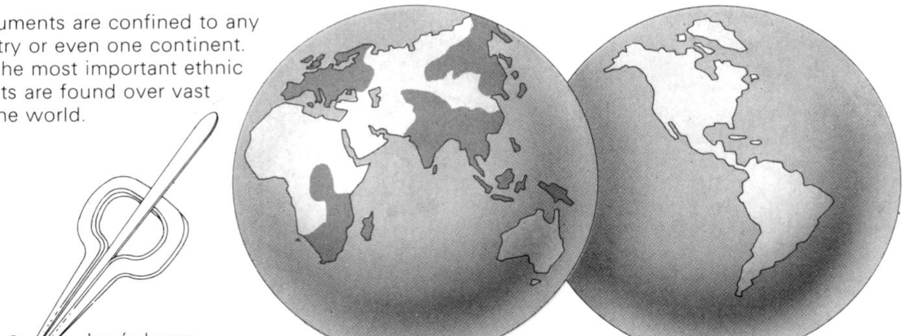

Jew's harps

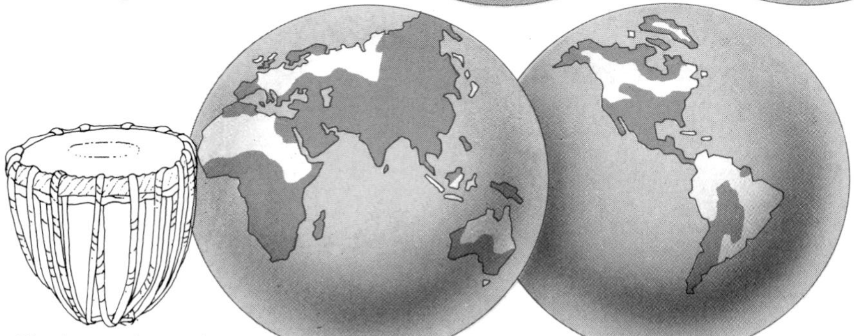

Single-membrane drums

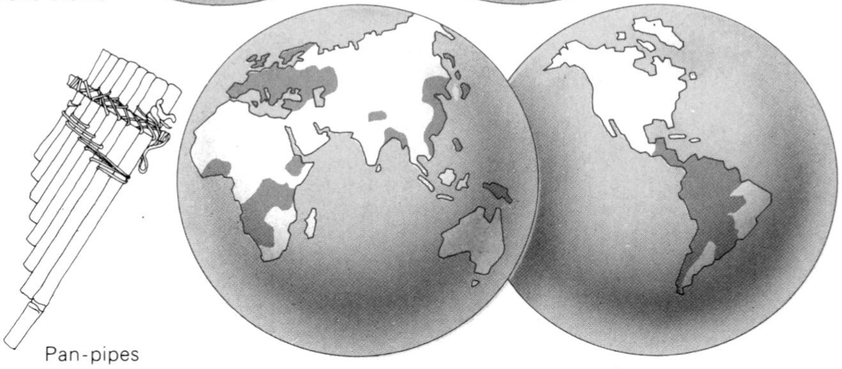

Pan-pipes

shapes: tubular drums often have a double membrane; kettledrums have some kind of pot or bowl as the body; and frame drums, as their name suggests, are without a solid body. The tubular type is the most common.

Many peoples attribute supernatural powers to their drums. Criminals in certain East African tribes can obtain sanctuary by running to the drum enclosure; drums are used for blessing marriages, banishing spirits and controlling the weather. In many African monarchies the drum has been the symbol of the king.

The waisted drum is shaped like an hourglass and the upper and lower membranes are laced together with thread. If the threads are squeezed at the waist they increase the tension on the skins and raise the pitch of the drum's note. This is the form of the famous "talking drum" of Nigeria. Skilled control of the pressure on the cords can produce inflexions very similar to those of the Yoruba language.

Versions of all the main categories of aerophone, or wind instrument, can be found throughout the world. Edge-tone pipes (flutes) occur in many forms, the most common probably being the end-blown flute, played by blowing across the open top of the instrument. Frequently groups of these simple tubes are bound together to make pan-pipes, each pipe having a separate note. These instruments are widely used in Balkan folk music and among the Basque people, while examples of pottery pan-pipes appear in ancient Peruvian remains.

It is easier to produce a note from an end-blown flute if the blowing end is cut into a V-shaped notch. The *quena* of South America is a typical notched flute and, like most flutes, it has finger-holes for varying its note. Related to the notched variety is the duct flute, of which the European recorder is a good example, in which the air is blown through a small aperture on to a prepared edge. Instruments made to imitate bird calls are usually duct flutes, which are often shaped in the form of birds.

Transverse or cross-blown flutes are less common outside Europe, although they are used extensively in China.

There are ethnic examples of both single- and double-reed instruments, sometimes with multiple pipes. A typical single-reed, single-pipe example is the Tunisian *zummara*, which has a bell made of cow-horn. Double-reed ancestors of the modern oboe (the shawm, for example) have been common in Europe for centuries. Similar instruments are found elsewhere, from Tibet to Nigeria.

Objects such as cow-horns and conch shells are played all over the world, by lip-compression. Most lip-compression instruments are end-blown, like the Jewish *shofar*, but side-blown examples are known in Africa.

Chordophones, in which strings are held at tension and either plucked, bowed or struck, are the fourth basic category of instrument. Because the sound is naturally quiet, most string instruments have some form of resonator, in primitive societies often made from a dried gourd or shell. The hunting bow is probably the origin of many such instruments, but there is no hunting people today which uses its bows to make music. Nevertheless, many simple forms of harp and lyre bear a striking resemblance to the bow in shape.

The word "lute" derives from the Arabic *'ud*. This is a short-necked stringed instrument with sound-box and bridge which is still used throughout the Islamic world. In North Africa the same instrument is known as a *quitara*, which points to the origin of the word "guitar". The complex musical systems of Islam and the Indian subcontinent developed alongside the predominating lute-type instruments. The sophisticated theories of tuning and rhythm which characterize these cultures, together with the enormous technical expertise required, have resulted in instruments which are both complicated and delicate in construction. Perhaps the most impressive of these is the *sitar*, which has a range of sympathetic strings as well as those which are plucked.

Bowed instruments, a comparatively late development, are found throughout Europe and Asia and in parts of Africa. In form they vary from the one-stringed *gusle* of Yugoslavia to the multiple-stringed folk violins of China, Persia and North Africa. The modern European violin has been adopted in recent years by Indian musicians – an untypical development.

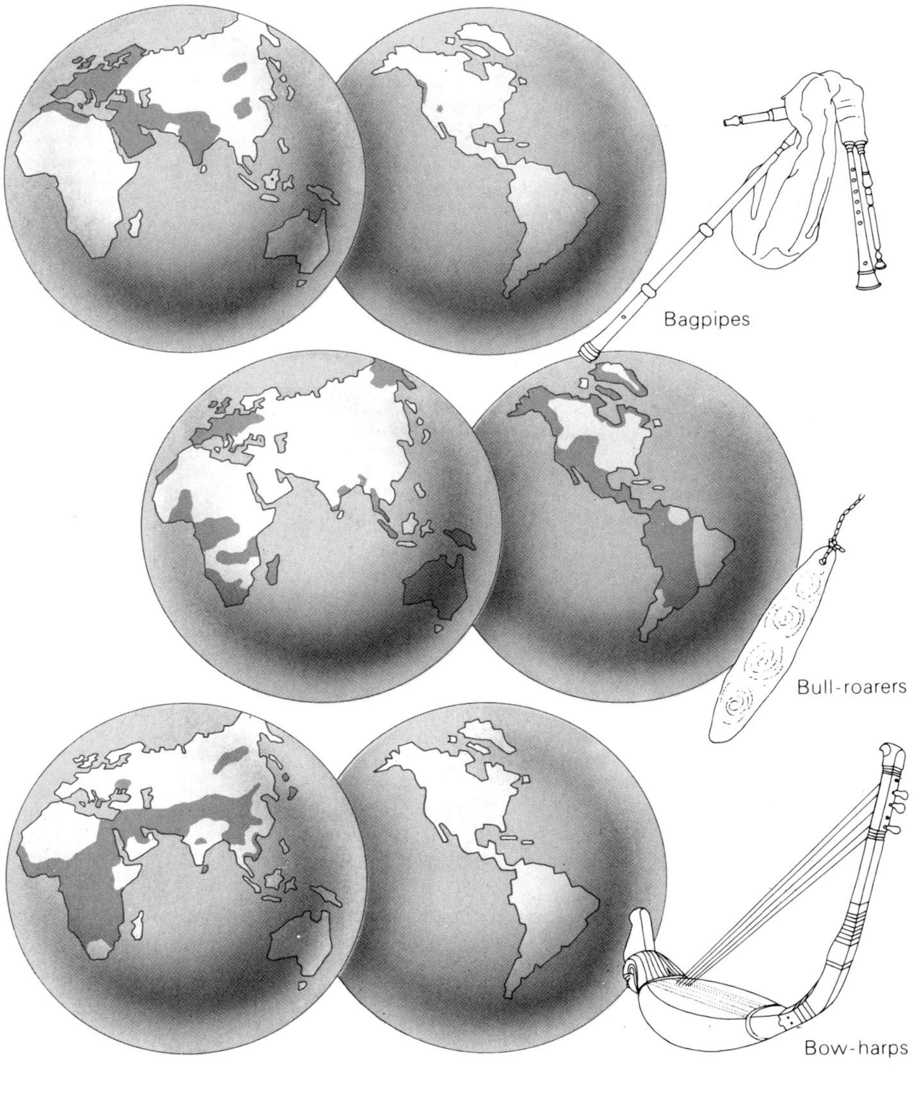

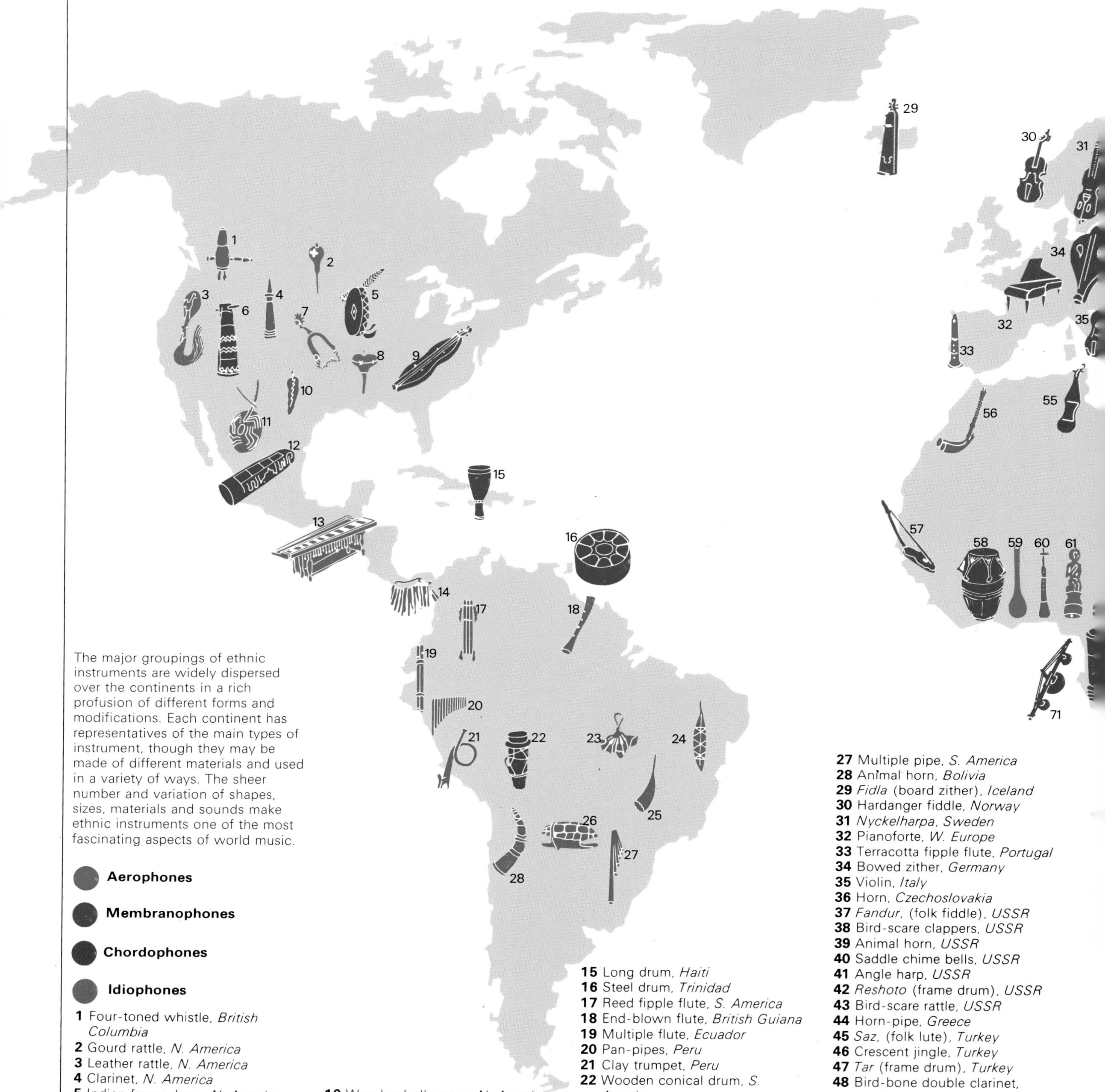

The major groupings of ethnic instruments are widely dispersed over the continents in a rich profusion of different forms and modifications. Each continent has representatives of the main types of instrument, though they may be made of different materials and used in a variety of ways. The sheer number and variation of shapes, sizes, materials and sounds make ethnic instruments one of the most fascinating aspects of world music.

Aerophones

Membranophones

Chordophones

Idiophones

1 Four-toned whistle, *British Columbia*
2 Gourd rattle, *N. America*
3 Leather rattle, *N. America*
4 Clarinet, *N. America*
5 Indian frame drum, *N. America*
6 Apache fiddle, *Arizona*
7 Spur jingle, *N. America*
8 Gourd rattle, *N. America*
9 Appalachian dulcimer, *N. America*
10 Wooden bull-roarer, *N. America*
11 *Papago* (Red Indian wood scraper), *N. America*
12 Slit drum, *Mexico*
13 Marimba, *Guatemala*
14 Bird-bone flutes, *Panama*
15 Long drum, *Haiti*
16 Steel drum, *Trinidad*
17 Reed fipple flute, *S. America*
18 End-blown flute, *British Guiana*
19 Multiple flute, *Ecuador*
20 Pan-pipes, *Peru*
21 Clay trumpet, *Peru*
22 Wooden conical drum, *S. America*
23 Jingle, *S. America*
24 Wooden bull-roarer, *Brazil*
25 Horn-pipe, *S. America*
26 Tortoise-shell friction drum, *S. America*
27 Multiple pipe, *S. America*
28 Animal horn, *Bolivia*
29 *Fidla* (board zither), *Iceland*
30 Hardanger fiddle, *Norway*
31 *Nyckelharpa*, *Sweden*
32 Pianoforte, *W. Europe*
33 Terracotta fipple flute, *Portugal*
34 Bowed zither, *Germany*
35 Violin, *Italy*
36 Horn, *Czechoslovakia*
37 *Fandur*, (folk fiddle), *USSR*
38 Bird-scare clappers, *USSR*
39 Animal horn, *USSR*
40 Saddle chime bells, *USSR*
41 Angle harp, *USSR*
42 *Reshoto* (frame drum), *USSR*
43 Bird-scare rattle, *USSR*
44 Horn-pipe, *Greece*
45 *Saz*, (folk lute), *Turkey*
46 Crescent jingle, *Turkey*
47 *Tar* (frame drum), *Turkey*
48 Bird-bone double clarinet, *Israel*
49 Bagpipe, *Arabia*
50 *'Ud* (lute), *Syria*
51 *Rebab* (fiddle), *Iraq*
52 *Tanbur* (lute), *Iran*
53 *Kemange* (spike fiddle), *Iran*

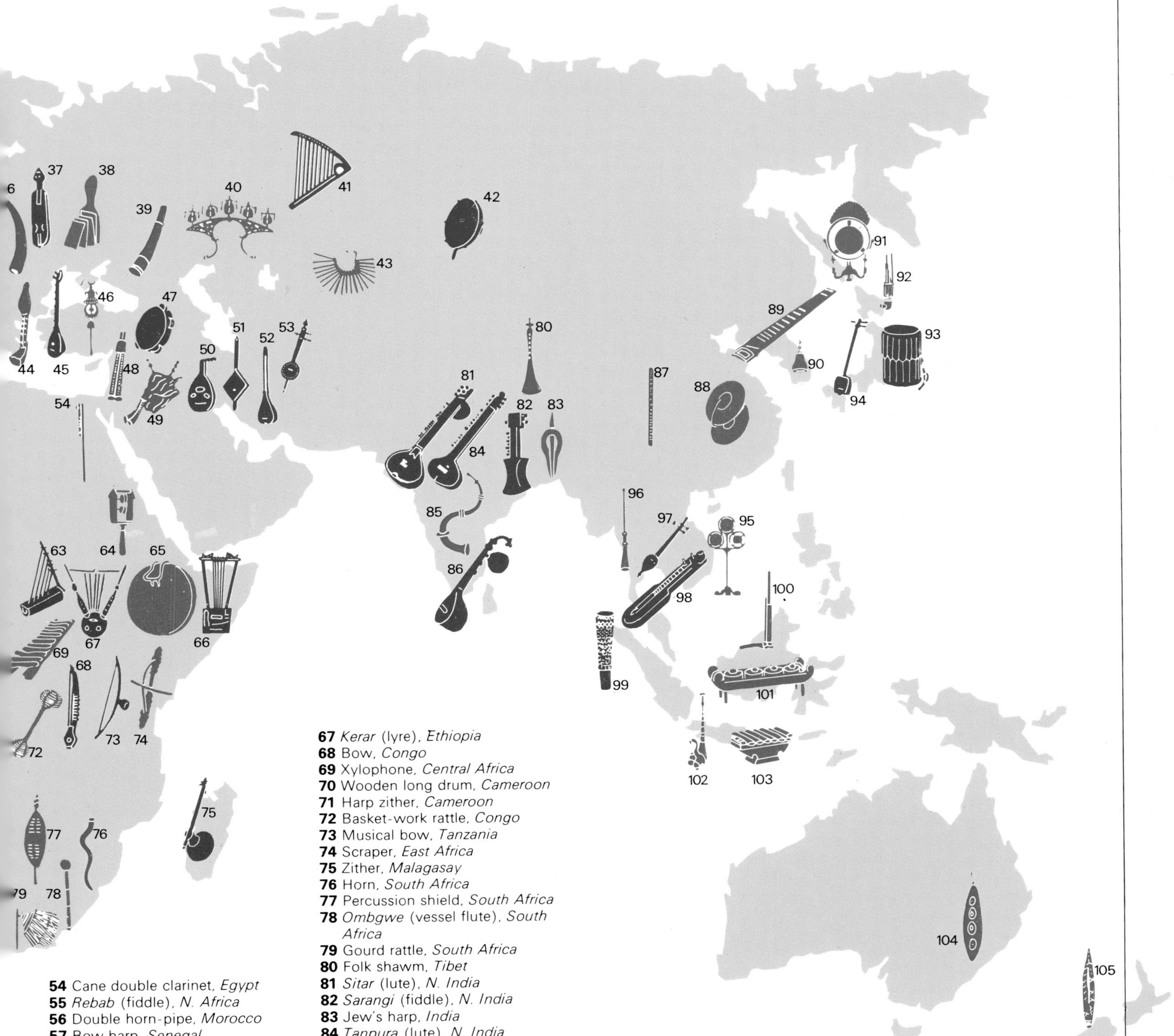

54 Cane double clarinet, *Egypt*
55 *Rebab* (fiddle), *N. Africa*
56 Double horn-pipe, *Morocco*
57 Bow harp, *Senegal*
58 Barrel drum, *Ghana*
59 *Adenkum* (stamping stick), *Ghana*
60 *Alghaita* (shawm), *Nigeria*
61 Wooden bell, *Nigeria*
62 Mirliton horn, *Nigeria*
63 Angle harp, *Congo*
64 *Sistrum* (rattle), Ethiopia
65 Gong, *Ethiopia*
66 *Bagana* (lyre), *Ethiopia*
67 *Kerar* (lyre), *Ethiopia*
68 Bow, *Congo*
69 Xylophone, *Central Africa*
70 Wooden long drum, *Cameroon*
71 Harp zither, *Cameroon*
72 Basket-work rattle, *Congo*
73 Musical bow, *Tanzania*
74 Scraper, *East Africa*
75 Zither, *Malagasay*
76 Horn, *South Africa*
77 Percussion shield, *South Africa*
78 *Ombgwe* (vessel flute), *South Africa*
79 Gourd rattle, *South Africa*
80 Folk shawm, *Tibet*
81 *Sitar* (lute), *N. India*
82 *Sarangi* (fiddle), *N. India*
83 Jew's harp, *India*
84 *Tanpura* (lute), *N. India*
85 *Ranasringa* (horn), *India*
86 *Veena* (lute), *S. India*
87 Bamboo *ti-tzu* (flute), *China*
88 Cymbals, *China*
89 *Komungo* (zither), *Korea*
90 Wind bell, *Korea*
91 Wooden *tsuri daiko* (drum), *Japan*
92 Bamboo and wood *shô* (mouth-organ), *Japan*
93 *Okedo* (drum), *Japan*
94 *Ko-kiu* (fiddle), *Japan*
95 *Tam âm la* (chime), *Vietnam*
96 Large trumpet, *Burma*
97 *Saw-thai* (spike fiddle), *Thailand*
98 *Chakay* (zither), *Thailand*
99 Conical drum, *Nias Island*
100 Bamboo and gourd mouth-organ, *Borneo*
101 Gong chime, *Borneo*
102 Shawm, *Java*
103 *Gansa* (metallophone), *Bali*
104 Wooden bull-roarer, *Australia*
105 Maori *putorino* (trumpet), *New Zealand*

IV
Listening to Music

Our familiarity with music may begin in any number of ways – hearing performances on records, radio or television, sitting in the auditorium of one of the world's great concert halls, singing in the school or the church choir, or learning to play an instrument (and, all too often, wondering in later years why we ever "gave it up"). No book can ever bring alive the experience of listening to music: the reader must seek the means himself. A love of music is something that can be nurtured and developed for a lifetime. The purpose of a book such as this is to encourage the reader *not* to read, but to go away and listen.

The symphony orchestra as depicted
by the cartoonist Hoffnung

Orchestra and Conductor

The orchestra that concert-goers have come to regard as the central element of musical life is a comparatively recent development in the history of Western music. In the sixteenth century, when the transition from polyphony to homophony began, orchestras were chance groupings of available instruments. In Italy large instrumental bodies were sometimes used in comic interludes in plays and also in large-scale vocal works, but rarely was there any specific indication of orchestration.

A notable early example of explicit orchestration is Monteverdi's opera *Orfeo* (1607), scored for viols, violins, lutes, harp, harpsichords, chamber organs, reed-organ, descant recorder, cornetts, trumpets and kettledrums: the current resources of the Duke of Mantua's court. The bowed strings were the most prominent element of this orchestra's sound, comprising over half the total number of instruments. This emphasis on string sound has remained constant. The most famous orchestra of the later seventeenth century was that of Louis XIV, "*Les vingt-quatre violons du Roy*", which had no permanent wind section until about 1700.

During the time of Bach and Handel, instruments were improved and composers experimented with different combinations. A bass instrument, together with either harpsichord or organ, would supply the *basso continuo* and so hold the performance together. Viols had generally given way to violins – the backbone of most ensembles. The woodwind included flutes, oboes and bassoons, the brass section usually horns, trumpets and, rarely, trombones.

In the mid-eighteenth century, a generation of composers, headed by Johann Stamitz (1717–57), laid the foundations of the classical orchestra with its paired flutes, oboes, bassoons and horns. Later, pairs of clarinets, trumpets and kettledrums were often added. Trombones sometimes featured in opera and church music but not – before Beethoven – in symphonies or concertos.

The role of the keyboard as background accompaniment diminished as the eighteenth century progressed and the orchestra grew in size, though Haydn habitually "presided at the instrument" when conducting his symphonies. A typical "classical" orchestra had about thirty-five players. The strings remained paramount, each line of music in that section being played by several players. Wind instruments gradually developed their own functions, instead, for example, of merely

doubling the first violins' melody: now, their parts began to reflect the special qualities and capacities of each instrument. Skilful combinations of different instruments produced orchestral "colour".

Beethoven's first symphony (1800) is scored for first and second violins, violas, cellos and double-basses, a pair each of flutes, oboes, clarinets, bassoons, trumpets and horns, and two kettledrums (timpani). This constitutes the nucleus of the standard romantic/modern symphony orchestra, the forces of which otherwise may vary considerably. The massed strings still comprise two-thirds to three-quarters of the total forces. Unbowed strings may include one or two harps. To the wind section may be added a piccolo, a bass clarinet, a double-bassoon and perhaps a third flute, oboe and bassoon. There may be two extra horns, one extra trumpet and possibly a tuba (tenor, bass or both). The modern percussion section will differ most from its 1800 counterpart, almost certainly including a bass drum and side drum, a pair of cymbals and a triangle in addition to the kettledrums (of which there may now be as many as five). There may also be a military drum, a tambourine, bells (tubular and/or sleigh, for example), a glockenspiel, a xylophone, a celesta and possibly a piano.

During the nineteenth and twentieth centuries, orchestral forces such as these have allowed for a greater range of sound and dynamics than previously possible.

Some composers, such as Mahler in his eighth symphony, the *Symphony of a Thousand* (1910), and Britten in his *War Requiem* (1961), have employed massive forces: the former, for example, is scored for orchestra, brass group, seven solo singers, one boys' and two mixed choirs.

In recent decades composers have shown a renewed interest in writing works for chamber and string orchestras, and for brass ensembles, perhaps in reaction against the mammoth symphony orchestra. Moreover, works of the classical period are now performed with fewer players, to produce something nearer the authentic volume of sound.

The Vienna Symphoniker in the Musikverein, Vienna. The great symphony orchestras of the world are supported by some or all of the following: government subsidy, income from recordings, public performances and private donations. The lives of the players are divided between orchestral rehearsals, travelling, recording sessions – with their own orchestra or perhaps in another capacity – and performances.

Below The development of the orchestra. (**A**) Handel commemoration in Westminster Abbey, 1784. The choir of 264 singers is situated in galleries on either side and in front of the conductor. (**B**) An orchestra as arranged by Wagner in the nineteenth century. (**C**) A modern arrangement of the orchestra.

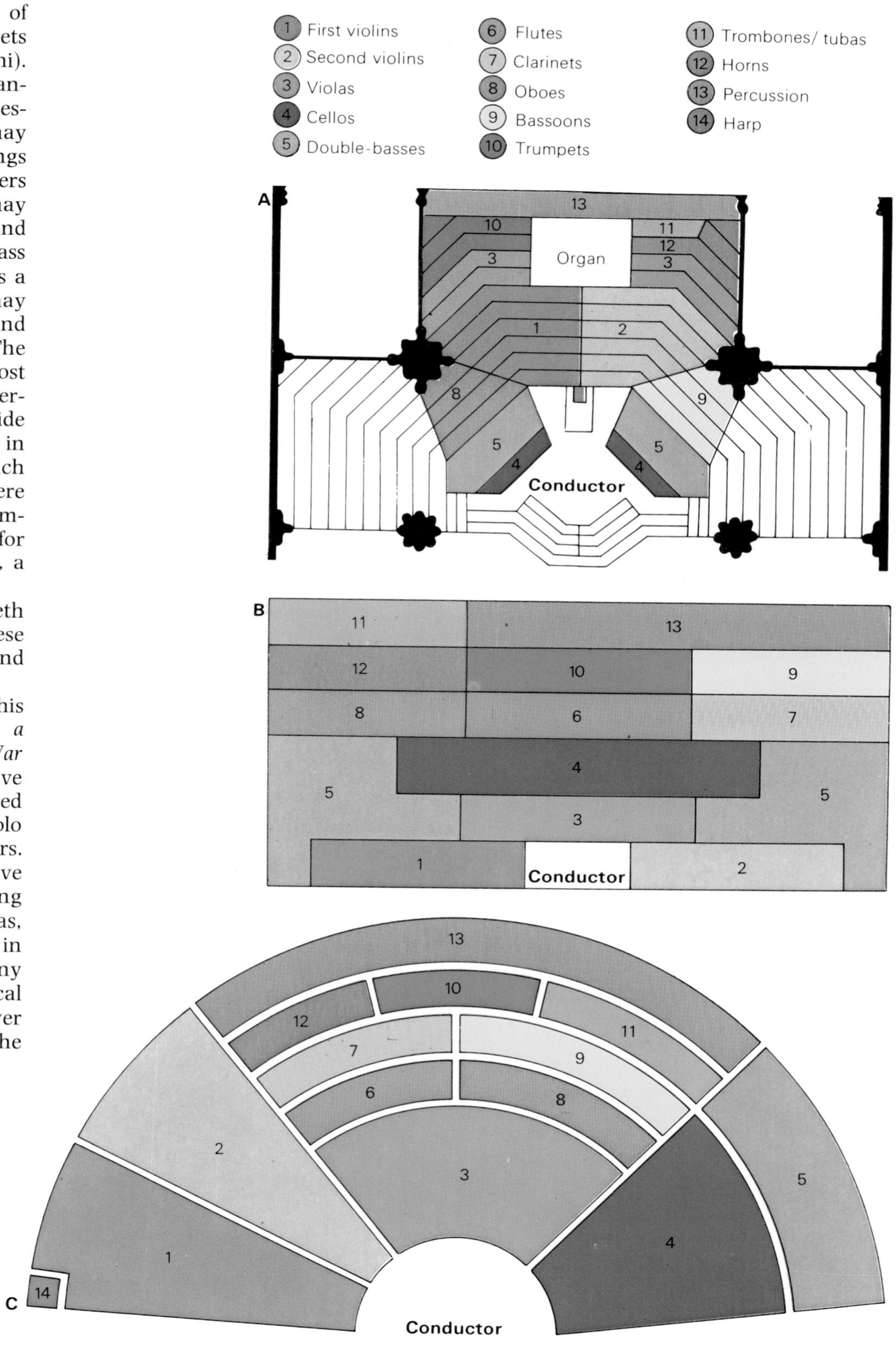

When in the early baroque period music became complex and was performed by a large-ish group of people, it became necessary to develop a method of keeping the performers together. This was sometimes achieved by the director or *maestro di cappella* beating time with his hand. When it became customary to have a *basso continuo*-player, in the early seventeenth century, he would indicate the speed at the beginning of a piece in this way, before starting to play. Sometimes, particularly in churches, the beat would have to be audible rather than visual because the view of some of the players would be obscured by features of the building. In such cases, the director might tap on the floor to keep time.

In the later seventeenth century, as the violin came to prominence, the first violinist often took over the director's function. Louis XIV's orchestra, "*Les vingt-quatre violons du Roy*", was conducted by the violinist Jean-Baptiste Lully, who was known to thump out the beat on the floor with a stick. In 1687, however, during a performance of a *Te Deum* which Lully had written to celebrate the king's recovery from illness, Lully accidentally struck his foot with the staff. He later died of the resulting abscess.

In the eighteenth and early nineteenth centuries, performances were directed by the first violinist, the keyboard-player or, sometimes, both. The first violinist had the advantage of being able to stand during a performance, but the normal manner of conducting – playing a few bars then breaking off to conduct with the bow – was distracting and inelegant. A seated keyboard-player, on the other hand, could not provide a clearly visible beat. As *basso continuo*-players became unnecessary during the eighteenth century, the way was paved for professional conductors. Johann Stamitz (1717–57) is generally regarded as the founder of modern conducting technique. To Hans von Bülow (1830–94) is attributed the art of "virtuoso conductorship", for which he was celebrated both in Germany, where baton conducting was first established, and abroad. Batons were not used in London concert halls until the end of the nineteenth century.

The conductor's principle function in an orchestral performance is to establish tempo, by beating time, in such a way that his players are perfectly synchronized. Most music is divided into bars containing a fixed number of beats, and the movements of the conductor's baton-hand (most frequently his right) must unambiguously sustain the music's beat, or rhythmic pulse.

The first, and strongest, beat of each bar is indicated by a firm downstroke. The last beat of the bar is a weak one, shown by an upstroke. Intermediate beats, if any, are shown by small sideways thrusts.

The conductor must also indicate changes of tempo, whether momentary

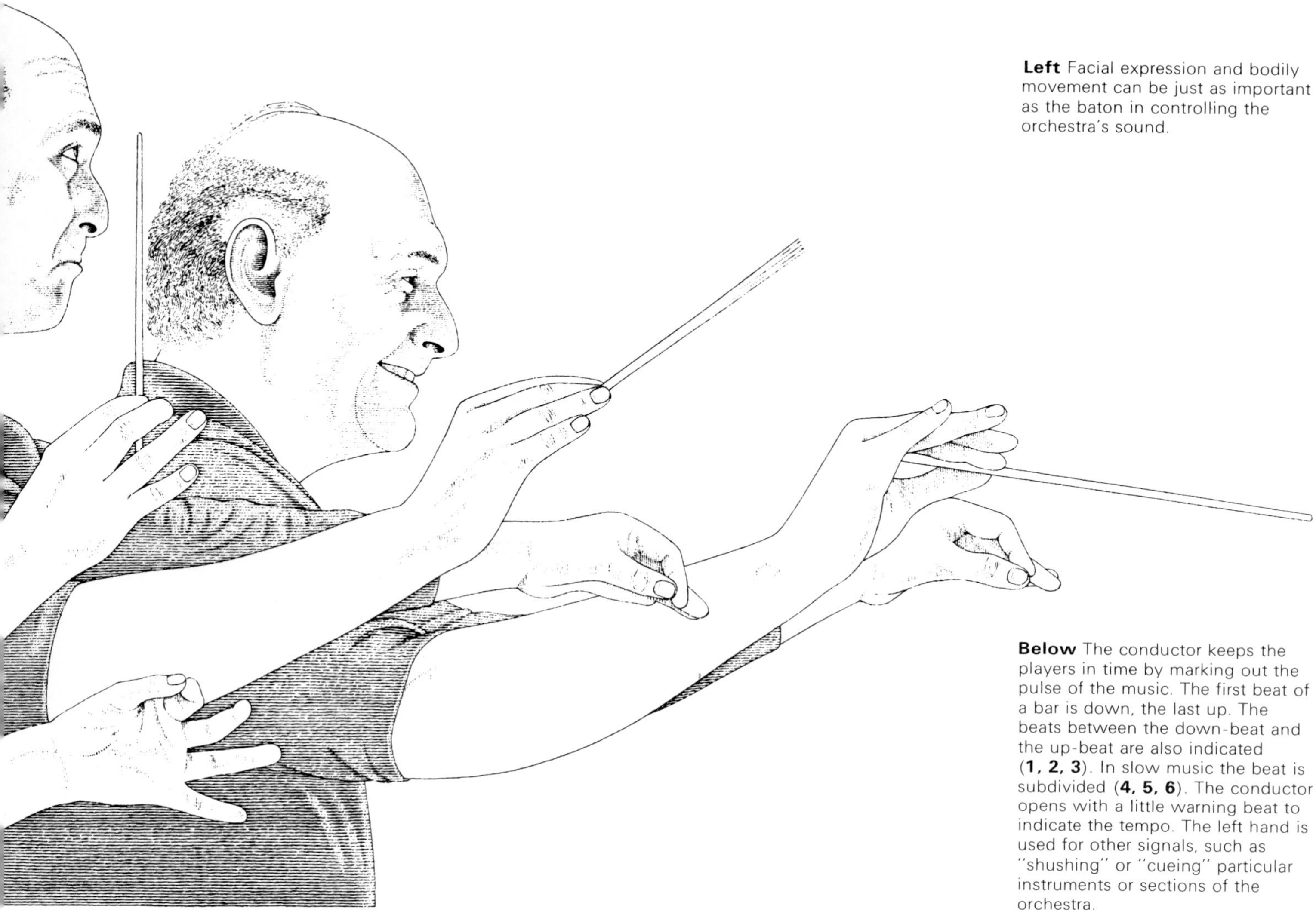

Left Facial expression and bodily movement can be just as important as the baton in controlling the orchestra's sound.

Below The conductor keeps the players in time by marking out the pulse of the music. The first beat of a bar is down, the last up. The beats between the down-beat and the up-beat are also indicated (**1, 2, 3**). In slow music the beat is subdivided (**4, 5, 6**). The conductor opens with a little warning beat to indicate the tempo. The left hand is used for other signals, such as "shushing" or "cueing" particular instruments or sections of the orchestra.

(as shown in the score by such markings as *ritenuto, accelerando* and *stringendo*) or more permanent (shown by more prominent markings such as *allegro, andante* or *lento*). To ensure that the various instruments enter at the right moments in the score, he uses his free hand to cue in, or beckon to, different players or sections of the orchestra.

Dynamics (degrees of loudness and softness) are shown by expressive motions either of the left hand or of both hands: extravagant, wide-reaching movements of the arms, for example, will mean that the orchestra should play loudly; more circumspect gestures, that the orchestra should play quietly.

Some conductors use not only their hands and faces but their whole bodies, in a sort of dance or mime: Beethoven would crouch behind his desk like a mouse during soft passages and spring into the air like a lion for the loud ones. Another of Beethoven's idiosyncracies was to shout at the players by way of encouragement during a *forte* passage. He was never aware of doing this, however.

Whatever the conductor's method, his aim will be to make the orchestra play not as a gathering of talented individuals, each with his own ideas on expression, tempi, etc., but as one great instrument. Hence the need for a single sensitive intelligence to be in control.

The conductor will have made a detailed study of the scores of the works for which he is responsible. In addition, he must ensure that every moment of costly rehearsal time is put to the best use. He will aim to establish in rehearsal a perfect consistency of style and interpretation. To this end, he must be a thorough musician, with an understanding not only of music in general but of the peculiarities of every orchestral instrument, a natural teacher, able to explain what effect he wants and why, and, preferably, a model of diplomacy and tact.

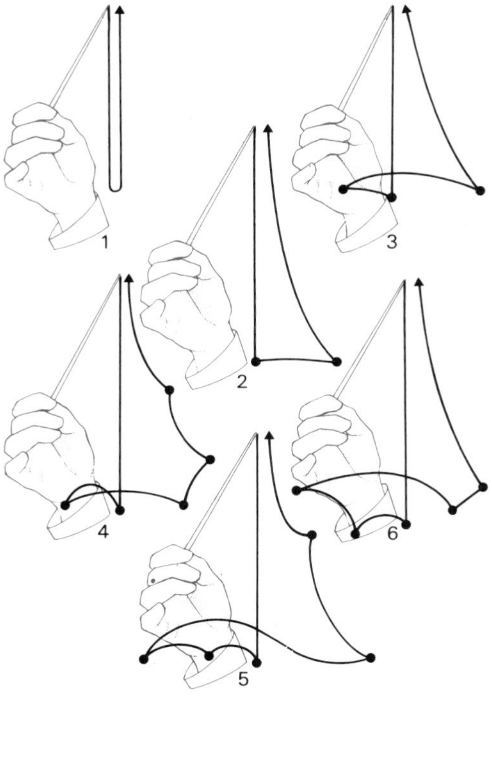

Instrumental Groups

For all instrumentalists, one of the most challenging and rewarding of all musical experiences is to play with others. The name given to music for a small number of players, each having his own line of music to play, is chamber music – literally "room" or domestic music. The performance of chamber music requires long and careful rehearsal since inaccuracies of any kind show up very clearly in the instrumental texture. The performers therefore have to rely on each other to regulate the tempo, balance, and light and shade of the piece. The difficulties of playing chamber music are the very aspects that most musicians enjoy. Many groups meet rather in the spirit of the early chamber musicians – that is, to make music principally for their own enjoyment rather than with any thought of a specific public performance.

One of the most popular instrumental groups is the duo. The various duo combinations are many, but the commonest is that of a "melody" instrument, such as a violin or clarinet, with an "accompanying" one, such as a harpsichord or piano. In many ways combinations of this type are ideal; a keyboard instrument, capable of supplying a full, rich accompaniment, is a perfect foil for single-note instruments, but can also take the role of soloist when a contrast is required.

A natural extension of the duo is the trio. A trio can be any combination of three instruments, but one of the most popular has been that of a keyboard instrument with treble and bass melody instruments – a grouping that provides a very wide melodic and tonal range.

The string quartet is probably the best-known of all chamber ensembles. As instrumental groups go, it is a comparatively new grouping – the first important examples of string-quartet writing date from the end of the eighteenth century. It consists of two violins, a viola and a cello (similar to the instrumental formation of the orchestral strings, but without the double-bass). The string quartet's homogeneity of tone colour makes it an outstandingly successful combination. Some of the very finest chamber music, notably works by Haydn, Mozart, Beethoven and Dvořák, are for string quartet. Debussy, Ravel and Bartók also wrote for this ensemble, exploiting the different sonorities of the instruments and combining them to produce unusual textures.

The standard formation of the wind quintet is flute, oboe, clarinet, bassoon and horn. This grouping lacks the unified tone colour of the string quartet but can offer a composer five completely contrasting

Duo

Trio

String quartet

timbres. In larger groups – particularly those involving woodwind and brass instruments – attention has to be paid to the seating of players. In the absence of a conductor the players need to be able to see each other easily. Also, the balance of the different instrumental sounds needs to be just right; the flautist, for instance, usually directs his flute towards the audience to maximize the volume while the horn-player ensures that the bell of his horn is directed slightly away from the audience. Arrangements obviously change according to the acoustics of the room or hall, but the seating plan shown here is most common for the wind quintet.

The sextet has been less popular with composers than smaller ensembles. Composers have tended to favour using pairs of instruments; this grouping (right) of two clarinets, two horns and two bassoons is for Beethoven's Sextet op. 71.

Combinations of seven or more instruments are comparatively rare, though septets, octets and nonets have been written by several composers, including Ravel, Mendelssohn and Spohr. Writing for such combinations is very difficult and, with some exceptions, composers have tended to use techniques more usually associated with the composition of orchestral music than chamber works. An exceptionally large group of instruments was used by Mozart in his *Serenade*, K. 361, scored for two oboes, two clarinets, two basset horns, two bassoons, four horns, and a double-bass (or contrabassoon); for large ensembles such as these, a conductor is usually necessary.

Wind quintet

Sextet

Instrumental group for Mozart's Serenade in B-flat, K.361

Recording and Broadcasting

It was in 1877, at Menlo Park, New Jersey, USA, that Thomas Alva Edison invented the primitive phonograph. While trying to find a method of automatically recording telegraph messages on a paper disc, he discovered how to make a diaphragm that would respond to sound vibrations. He incorporated such a diaphragm in a small toy which had a funnel at one end and a model of a man with a saw at the other. When Edison shouted into the funnel, the little man started sawing. Sound was thus transformed into movement.

After some experimentation, he designed a machine consisting of a shaft bearing a grooved cylinder covered in tin foil. As the shaft was turned by a hand crank, the cylinder travelled across the machine. On one side of it was a recording diaphragm and stylus, on the other a reproducing stylus and diaphragm, each of which could be brought into contact with the cylinder as required. Slowly turning the handle, Edison recited "Mary had a little lamb" into the recording diaphragm. He then wound back the cylinder, put the reproducing stylus into position and turned the handle. His voice was heard quite distinctly repeating the rhyme. Edison patented the device in December 1877 and a company was formed to manufacture phonographs.

Edison regarded his invention primarily as a *talking*-machine: a novelty to record the voices of great men and an adjunct to the telephone. The device was marketed as an office dictating machine, the "ideal amanuensis". But the early models had many limitations: reproduction was poor, the cylinders played for little more than a minute and quickly wore out.

In 1885 Alexander Bell, the inventor of the telephone, patented an improved machine (the "graphophone") incorporating a wax-coated cylinder. Edison then developed a solid wax cylinder for recording sounds. He also developed a floating stylus and an electroplated "master record" from which copies could be pressed. Though he at first concentrated on perfecting cylinders for office dictation, the Victor and Columbia companies were convinced that there was a market for discs which could record from two to four minutes of music. Such discs were initially made for the Victor company's talking-machine, or "gramophone", invented by Emile Berliner in 1897.

The musical possibilities of the new invention were scarcely realized before the 1890s. There exists, however, an earlier (and extremely indistinct) cylinder recording, made in Vienna, of Johannes Brahms shouting, "I am Doctor Brahms," and then playing one of his own Hungarian dances on the piano. The earliest surviving example of serious musical recording derives from the first Paris performance of Wagner's opera *Parsifal* in 1882.

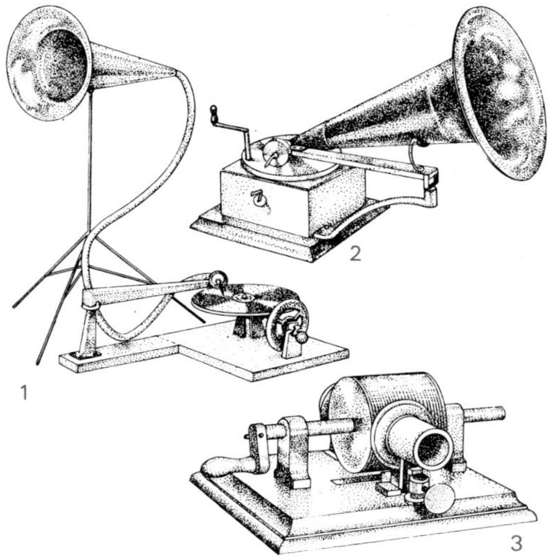

Above Early phonographs: **1** a Berliner gramophone of 1888; **2** His Master's Voice gramophone, *c.*1900; **3** the original tin-foil phonograph by Thomas A. Edison, 1877.

Below Sir Edward Elgar opening the EMI studios at Abbey Road, conducting Verdi's *Falstaff*, with the London Symphony Orchestra, in November 1931.
Bottom Leonard Bernstein with the record-producer John McClure in the no. 1 control room at the CBS studios in London.

By 1896 disc records were being issued commercially in competition with the Edison cylinders. The cylinders were musically more satisfactory than the early disc recordings, but were virtually impossible to mass-produce. Discs, less bulky to store and less awkward to handle than cylinders, were first made of metal, then of a shellac mixture, a resinous substance which made multiple pressings from a "master" disc very easy. In the case of cylinders, the performer would have to repeat his song or monologue perhaps several hundred times in order to satisfy the demand, each performance producing only ten or a dozen cylinders.

In the 1890s, both cylinders and discs were considered novel. Music-hall monologues and sketches, band music and sentimental songs were the staple fare of the early recordings. It was found that certain wind instruments and above all the human voice reproduced best. Hence, from about 1900 onwards, many distinguished opera-singers recorded solos. At first they sang with piano accompaniment, later (from about 1905) with small instrumental groups. The recording-machines of those days, being more sensitive to some instruments than to others, necessitated careful positioning of the players. For example, trombonists had to sit on a raised platform and oboists on low stools. In 1903 the Italian branch of the Gramophone and Typewriter Company made the first virtually complete opera recording (Verdi's *Ernani*, on forty single-sided records). The first complete symphony (Beethoven's fifth) was recorded in 1909.

Short films with soundtracks began to appear from about 1923. The first "talkie" with music, *The Jazz Singer*, was produced in 1927. Magnetic tape which could record music was developed in Germany during the Second World War. Long-playing (L.P.) microgroove records, made of vinylite, an unbreakable plastic, were introduced in 1948. They increased the total playing time of a record from eight minutes to almost an hour. Until "stereophonic" sound was introduced in 1958, recordings had been made with a single signal and channel of sound, the "monaural" system. Stereophonic reproduction produces a solid, three-dimensional sound,

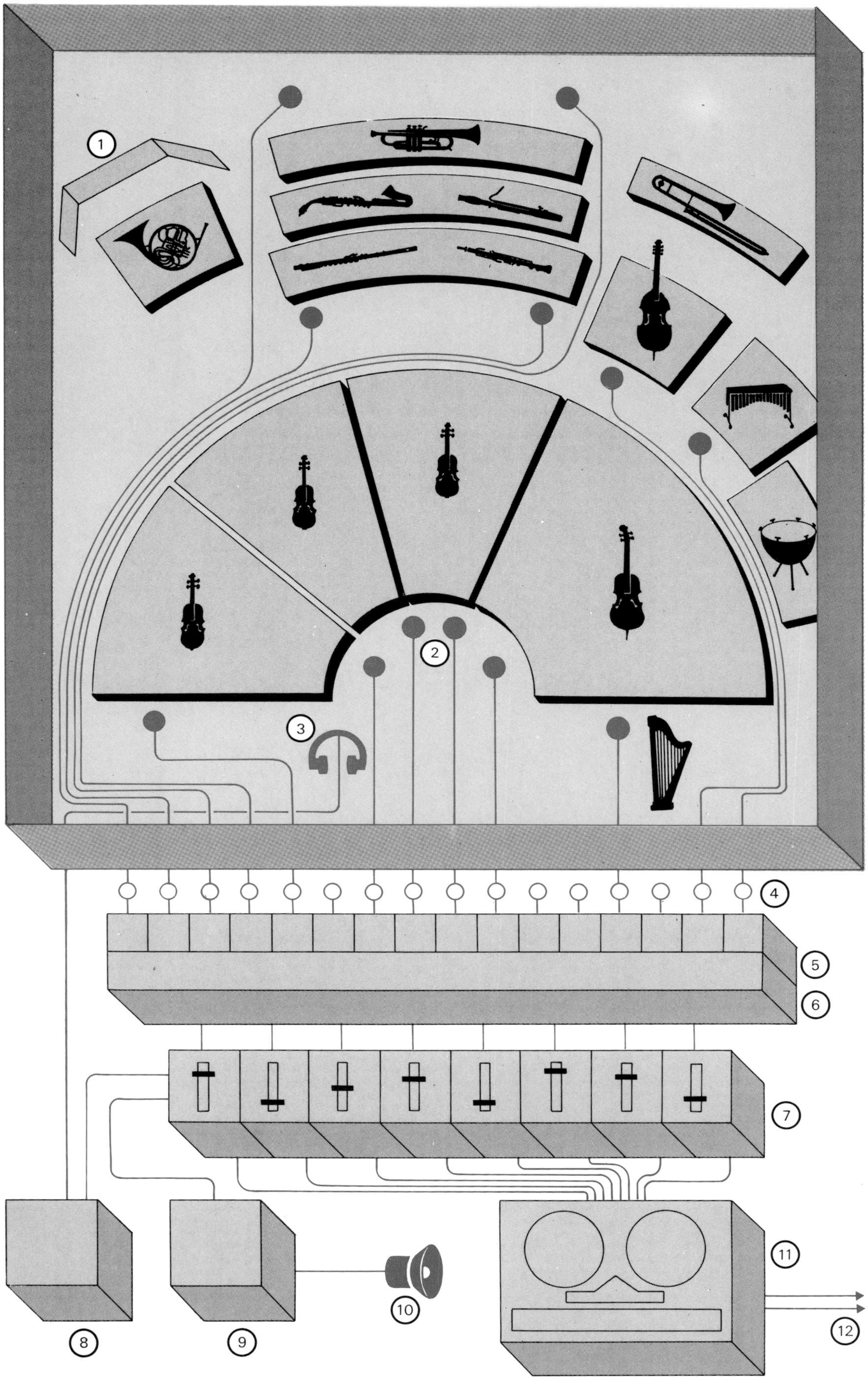

Left The recording studio. Today, records are made by recording the separate component sounds on different tracks of a multi-track tape recorder. Up to twenty-four tracks can be recorded on a single tape. From this is made the master tape from which the record is produced. A mixing desk puts one or two microphone signals on to each track of the tape. This permits the sounds on each track to be manipulated independently. The multi-track tape is then replayed into the mixing deck and the output from each track is fed into a separate input channel of the mixer. The signals are then mixed together to one or two channels and recorded on to the tape from which the record is cut. This process allows each component of the music to be recorded separately. Re-mixing can be carried out many times in order to achieve the final version.
1 Reflecting screen. **2** As many microphones as desired are placed in suitable positions. **3** Studio headphone. **4** Input channels. **5** Amplifiers and equalizers. **6** Routing unit. **7** Output mixing groups. **8** Feedback mixer. **9** Monitor mixer. **10** Monitor loudspeaker. **11** Eight-track tape recorder.

achieved usually by two channels of sound. More recently, "quadrophonic" recording has been developed; this uses four channels of signal to produce a 360° field of sound.

Tape recordings in cassette form have become popular in recent years with the introduction of small tape and cassette recorders. The Dolby system has greatly improved reproduction from tape: by compressing the signal before it is recorded and expanding it on replay, background noise and tape hiss are both minimized.

Broadcasting

In 1830 Michael Faraday discovered that electrical energy could pass between two circuits without them being in direct contact. In 1863 the existence of electromagnetic "waves" was demonstrated for the first time, and by the end of the century such waves were being produced artificially, though it is not known for certain who was the first to do so. In 1895–96 Marconi developed a method of

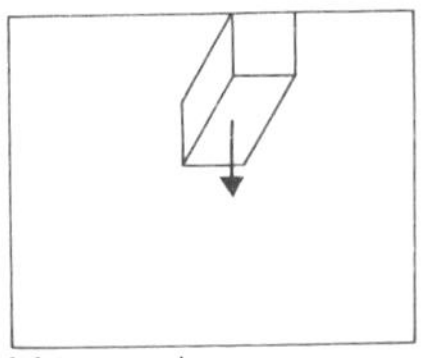

Monaural

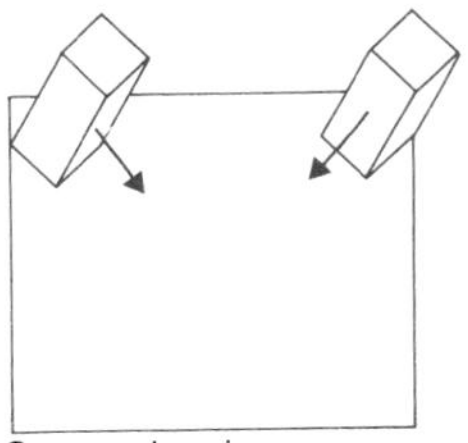

Stereophonic

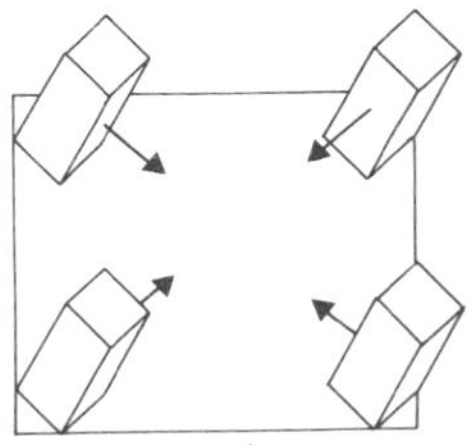

Quadrophonic

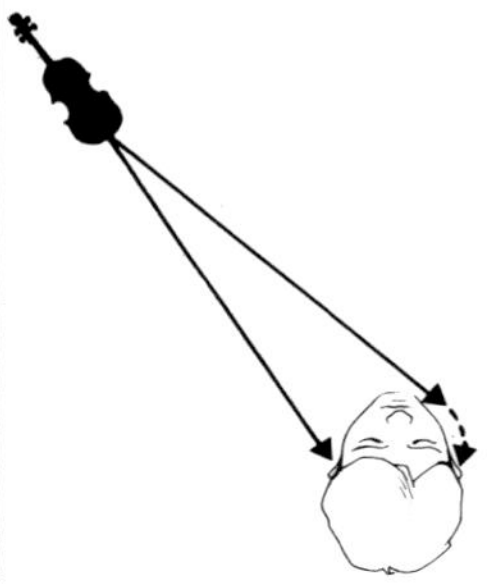

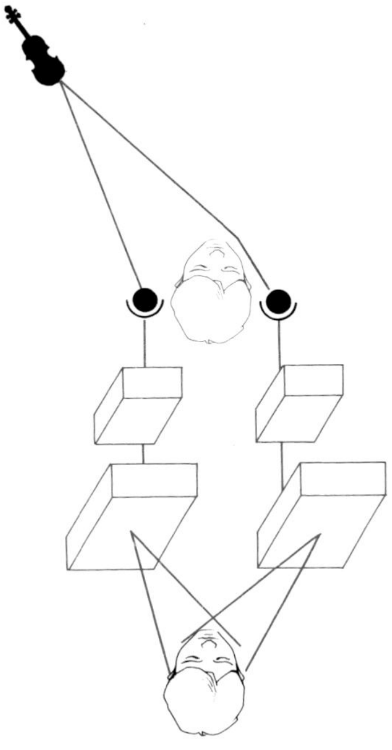

Top right The positions and quantities of loudspeakers required for various types of sound reproduction. **Above** Real stereo effect is the result of time delay between sound reaching the left and right ears. **Right** Modern stereo used in the recording of music mimics the spatial effect of the human system of hearing.

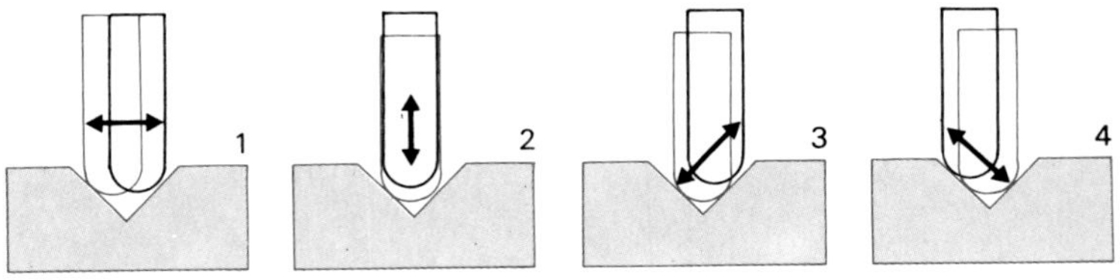

Above At first, stereo reproduction on records was achieved by applying a lateral movement of the stylus to produce a left signal (**1**), and a "hill-and-dale" movement (the method originally used by Edison in his phonograph) to produce the right signal (**2**). However, the method adopted for commercial reproduction of stereo sound is the 45°/45° principle, in which the left signal appears on the inner wall of the groove (**3**), and the right signal on the outer wall (**4**).

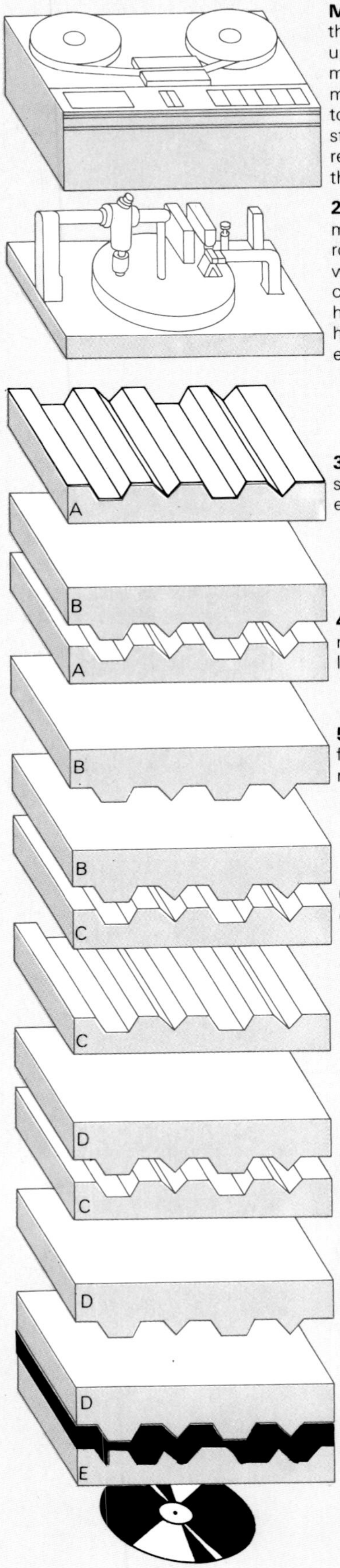

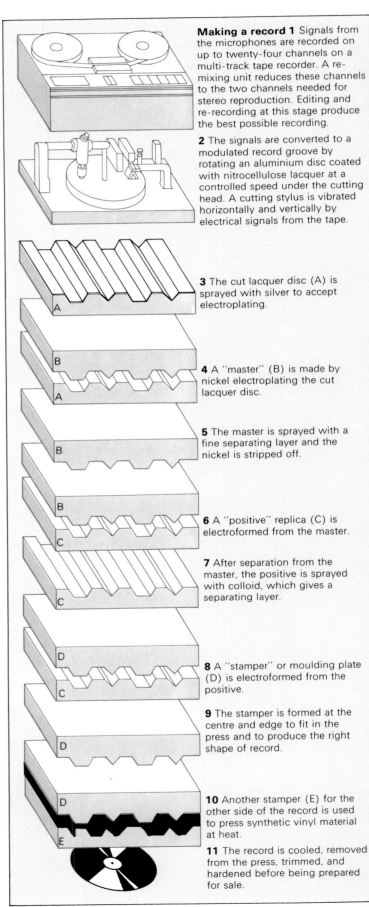

Making a record 1 Signals from the microphones are recorded on up to twenty-four channels on a multi-track tape recorder. A re-mixing unit reduces these channels to the two channels needed for stereo reproduction. Editing and re-recording at this stage produce the best possible recording.

2 The signals are converted to a modulated record groove by rotating an aluminium disc coated with nitrocellulose lacquer at a controlled speed under the cutting head. A cutting stylus is vibrated horizontally and vertically by electrical signals from the tape.

3 The cut lacquer disc (A) is sprayed with silver to accept electroplating.

4 A "master" (B) is made by nickel electroplating the cut lacquer disc.

5 The master is sprayed with a fine separating layer and the nickel is stripped off.

6 A "positive" replica (C) is electroformed from the master.

7 After separation from the master, the positive is sprayed with colloid, which gives a separating layer.

8 A "stamper" or moulding plate (D) is electroformed from the positive.

9 The stamper is formed at the centre and edge to fit in the press and to produce the right shape of record.

10 Another stamper (E) for the other side of the record is used to press synthetic vinyl material at heat.

11 The record is cooled, removed from the press, trimmed, and hardened before being prepared for sale.

producing and receiving the waves. The experiments were patronized by the British Post Office. In 1898 transmitted messages were received at a distance of twelve miles. In 1901 Marconi was able to relay "wireless" messages across the Atlantic, and by the outbreak of the First World War a wireless service was in operation on a number of ships.

It was not until 1919, however, that the first radio broadcasts (of music) took place, in the USA. The first broadcasting station in America was at Pittsburgh, Pennsylvania, and the first in Britain was near Chelmsford in Essex. The first broadcast opera was Mozart's *The Magic Flute*, transmitted from Covent Garden in 1923. In 1936 the first television service in the world was opened in Britain. Both popular and serious music were important elements of early television programmes.

The broadcasting process begins with a microphone, which converts sound into an electric signal varying according to the sound it represents. These variations alter a radio signal transmitted from high-transmission masts. A radio receiver picks up this signal and converts it back into an alternating current which, when amplified, can be heard through a loudspeaker. The frequency of the vibrations which reach the loudspeaker is the same as that which reached the microphone in the transmitting station. This system of sound transmission is called "amplitude modulation" (AM). Another common system is "frequency modulation" (FM), in which the frequency of the alternating current is varied by the frequency of the sound to be broadcast.

Television (literally "far vision") extends the principle of radio communication to the transmission and reception of a visual image. The image to be transmitted is projected on to a light-sensitive surface through each point of which is passed an electric current. The resulting varying electric signal has a wave-form corresponding to the intensity of the light at the various points of the image. This varying signal is transmitted on a radio wave, and is reconstituted as an image by the television receiver in a similar manner.

Radio and television provide an invaluable service for music-lovers. Radio broadcasts, in particular, cater for almost every musical taste. Although the sound quality of television may not be up to the standards of the best possible radio reception, it has other advantages. For example, close-up shots reveal details of performance that would be denied to a live audience, even that part of it sitting in the best seats. Television cameras can also show the conductor in action.

Through television, vast audiences are able to see a range of fine operatic productions without the expense of visiting an opera-house. Some composers have written operas especially for television: the first was Menotti's *Amahl and the Night Visitors* (1951), which greatly impressed American audiences; another, Britten's *Owen Wingrave* (1971) was based on a Henry James story, and uses televisual effects to enhance the strange, sinister atmosphere of the story.

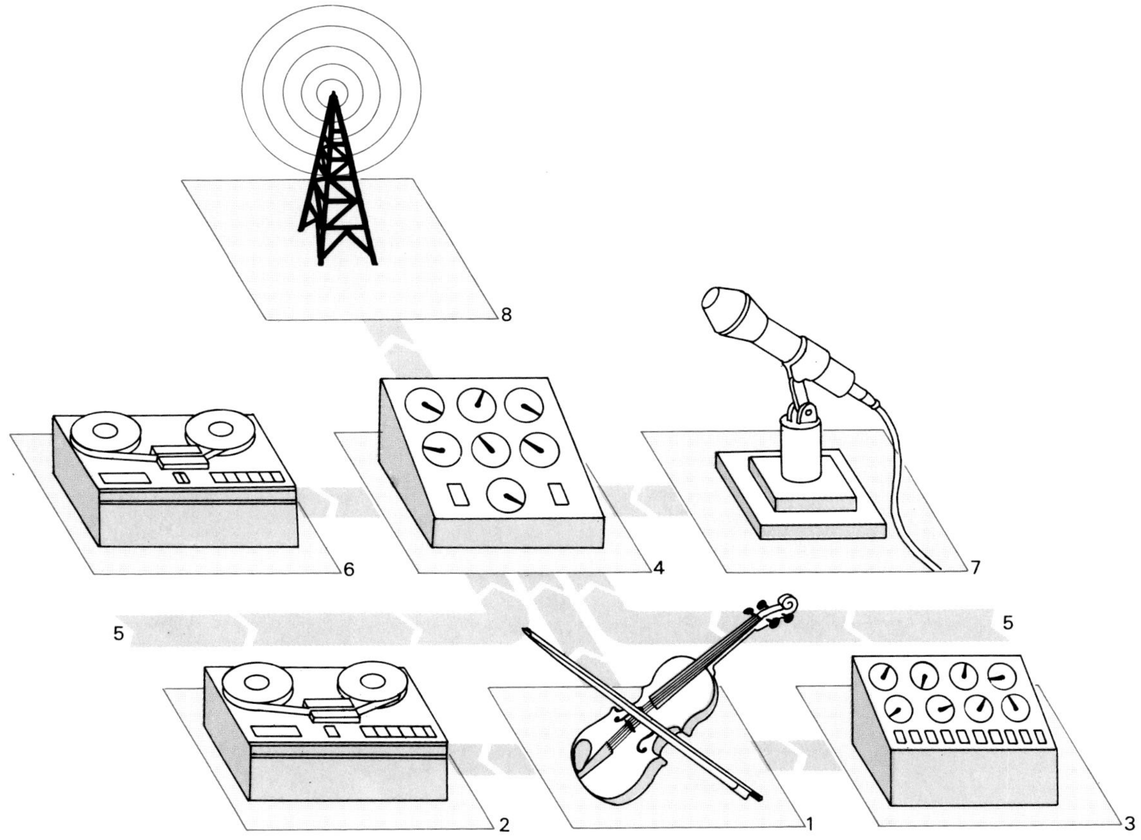

Above The "broadcasting chain" is a sequence of events which starts in a studio (**1**) and ends with a signal in the listener's home. A performance can be recorded for editing or storage (**2**), directed to a remote studio for inclusion in another programme (**3**), or it may go straight to a continuity mixer for live broadcast (**4**). The continuity mixer can combine the input from the studio with others from separate studios (**5**) or previously recorded programmes (**6**). A continuity announcer (**7**) is usually responsible for running the service, and must intervene if anything goes wrong. From the continuity mixer the signal is beamed out by a transmitter (**8**) to a receiving aerial in the listener's home.

Just as light waves are reflected from polished surfaces, so radio waves are reflected from certain layers of charged (or ionized) particles in the atmosphere, as well as from the earth's surface itself. A radio wave is thus able to travel directly from the transmitter to a receiver which is hidden from it by the earth's curvature. Radio waves of different lengths are reflected from different ionized layers.

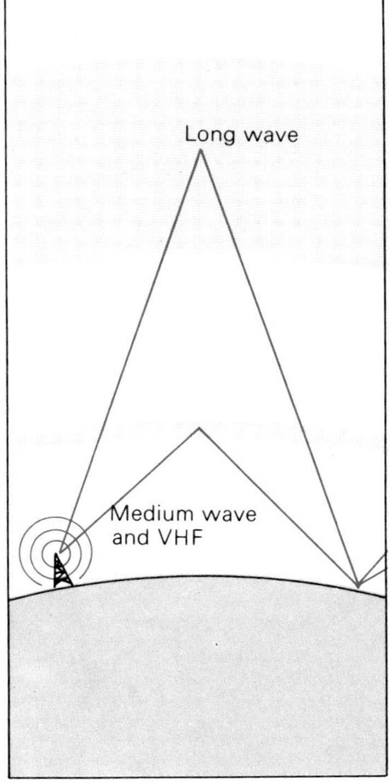

Buildings for Music

The design of a concert hall or opera-house may affect the success of the works performed inside it almost as much as the quality of the works and performances themselves. The architect's job is to ensure that within the auditorium musical sound will transfer from performers to audience without any loss of definition, balance, dynamic range, timbre and tone colour. Among performers and critics there is considerable agreement as to which buildings have good acoustics, but there are also many false beliefs – for example, that the acoustics of a building improve with age.

Acoustic qualities of buildings

Terms such as "intimate", "full", "brittle", "brilliant", "responsive" and "muddy" are amongst those frequently used by musicians in describing various concert halls. Intimacy and fullness are the most important attributes of an auditorium. Reverberation is the only acoustical factor that can be calculated and is defined as the length of time it takes for the level of sound which persists in a room after the note that created it has been stopped to decay by sixty decibels. (Musical compositions have an average range of sixty decibels between their loudest and softest sounds.)

A hall which is reverberant is called a "live" hall. One that reflects too little sound back to the audience is called "dead" or "dry". Liveness in an auditorium gives fullness of tone to music. Bach was well aware of the difference between the live acoustics of St Jacob's church, Lübeck, and the dry ones of St Thomas's, Leipzig, and endeavoured to compose works for each in accordance with this realization.

The reverberation time is governed by the volume of an auditorium, by the amount of absorptive materials in it and, to a lesser extent, by the shape of it. Reverberation times range from 1·1 seconds for London's Royal Opera House, Covent Garden, through 2·05 seconds for the Grosser Musikvereinssaal, Vienna, to 7 seconds for medieval churches. However, this time-span can be modified by introducing absorptive surfaces, or by electronic means such as "assisted resonance". One acoustical quirk that churches with long reverberation times often have is a "sympathetic note". This is a region of pitch, between G♮ and A♯, in which tone is apparently reinforced by the vibration of the structure itself.

It is traditionally held that each par-

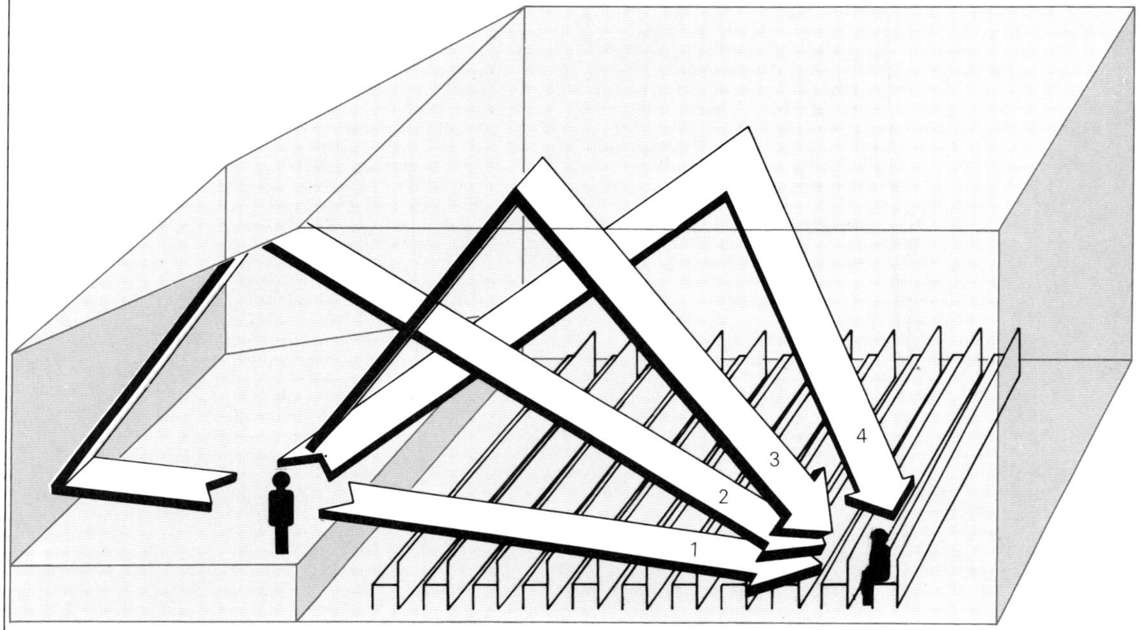

Sound paths There are four basic paths between performer and listener: **1** the direct path; **2** the path reflected from the stage; **3** the path reflected from the ceiling; **4** the path reflected by the walls. The order in which the reflected sound reaches the listener after the sound is made (the "direct sound") is determined by the distance between the listener and the reflecting surface. The delay between the direct sound and the first reflected sound is known as the "initial time-delay gap". The length of this gap determines the degree of intimacy afforded by an auditorium. The initial time-delay gap is second in importance only to reverberation time in an over-all acoustic appraisal of an auditorium. For concert performances it should be 10–20 milliseconds and for opera 24. Auditoria with excessively long initial time-delay gaps can be modified to acceptable levels by introducing canopies and "clouds".

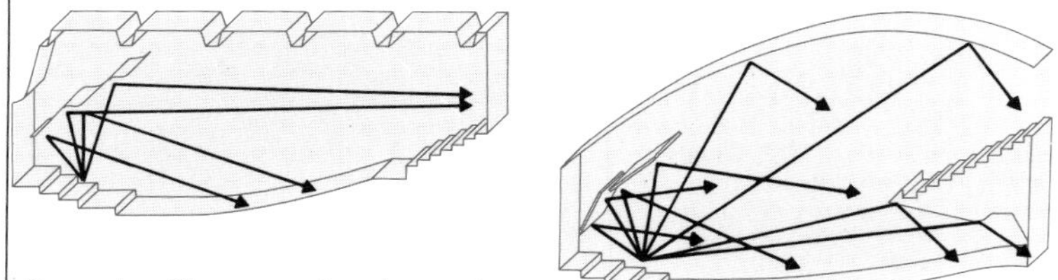

Canopies These are placed over the stage area in order to reduce the initial time-delay gap. This increases musical intimacy and also projects sound to the rear of the auditorium, as well as under balconies and boxes. In an auditorium with a balcony, members of the audience sitting underneath it will be shielded from much of the sound reflected from the ceiling. A canopy over the stage will help to reflect sound into this zone (see second diagram). The underside of the balcony should also act as a reflector. A further important function of the canopy is to maintain a balance between the sections of the orchestra. Some canopies are adjustable. Interesting examples can be seen at the Royal Festival Hall, London and the Tanglewood Music Shed, Lenox, Mass., USA.

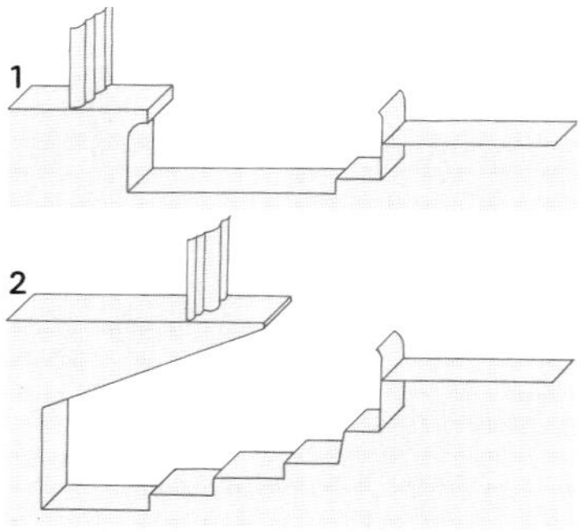

Orchestra pits The traditional Italian pit design (**1**) was abandoned when Wagner built his opera-house at Bayreuth (**2**). This design created a better balance between singers and orchestra, and also made the audience watch the stage, the orchestra being invisible.

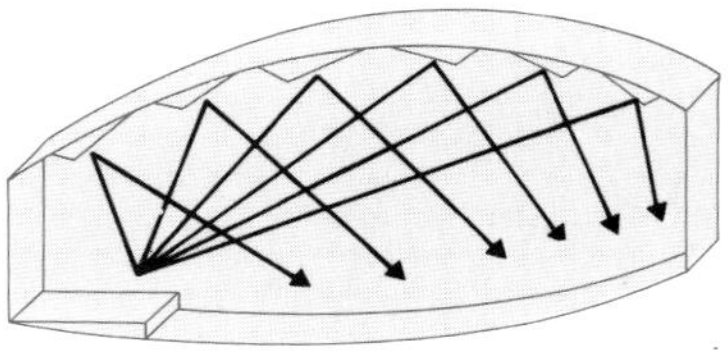

Clouds Many old concert halls with bad echo problems have been improved by suspending sound-reflecting "clouds" or "flying saucers" from the ceiling. One hall where this has been done is the Royal Albert Hall, London. In modern concert halls, "clouds" are often integrated into the original design – often in tandem with a stage canopy. A good example of this is the Philharmonic Hall, Lincoln Centre, New York.

ticular style of musical composition has an optimum acoustical environment for its performance. For example Bach's Toccata in D minor for organ should be performed in an auditorium with a reverberation time of 4 seconds and a Mozart piano concerto in one where it is 1·3 seconds. However, with the exception of operas and certain works for organ, most international concert halls are suitable for a wide repertoire.

The development of the concert hall

Early music was played at home, in churches, or at court. In the eighteenth century, however, concert halls grew up in fashionable towns and capital cities to meet the needs of a better-educated and more prosperous public. This coincided with the height of the classical period, when many of Mozart's and Haydn's works were scored for medium-sized orchestra and therefore needed purpose-built premises for performance. Nonetheless, the first concert halls were small, usually seating about 400 persons. By the end of the eighteenth century, halls were being built all over Europe and by the middle of the nineteenth century the need for much larger halls had been recognized.

Generally, the music of the romantics, from Beethoven and Schubert to Tchaikovsky and Mahler, requires auditoria providing high fullness of tone and low definition. The Concertgebouw in Amsterdam, built in 1887, is a good example of a concert hall designed for music of this period.

With the completion of the Boston Symphony Hall in 1900, the first concert hall designed on established acoustic principles had appeared. A knowledge of acoustics is now considered essential for all architects involved in auditorium design, yet, although Boston is judged by many to have very fine acoustics, they are no better than the acoustics of many halls designed before scientific methods were employed.

Opera-house design has changed very little since La Scala was built in Milan in 1778. The Royal Opera House, Covent Gàrden, the Vienna Staatsoper and the Opéra, Paris (completed in 1875) follow a similar plan. However, the recently completed Sydney Opera House is a radical departure from traditional forms. Opinions have been mixed, but generally the design is considered to be successful.

The three basic plan shapes for audi-

La Scala, Milan Built in 1778, La Scala is horseshoe-shaped. Its design was widely adopted for other opera-houses but has not been used for concert halls, since it results in too short a reverberation time – La Scala's is only 1·2 seconds.

La Scala has 2,289 seats, including 154 from which the stage is not visible. Sound reflection is excellent, except for listeners at the rear of the boxes – the side boxes in particular. This style of opera-house is suitable for most of the standard operatic repertoire, though less sympathetic to the works of Wagner.

The theatre, with its plush tiers of boxes, was designed for social as well as musical pleasure, but most conductors and signers praise its acoustics. Toscanini, Karajan, Caruso, Gigli and Maria Callas are just a few of the famous musicians who have been associated with this beautiful opera-house.

La Scala was bombed in 1943 but is now happily restored to its former grandeur.

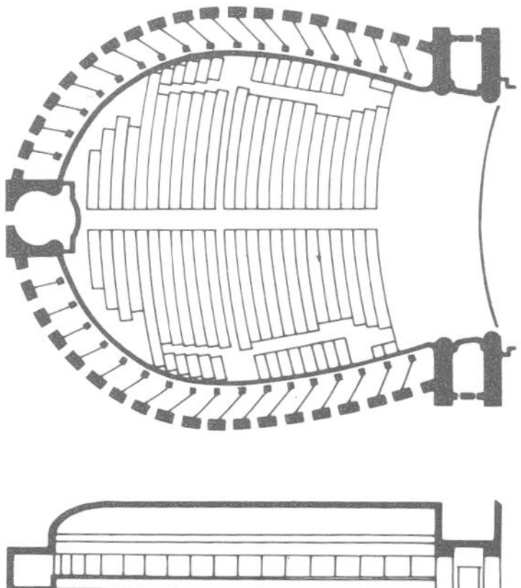

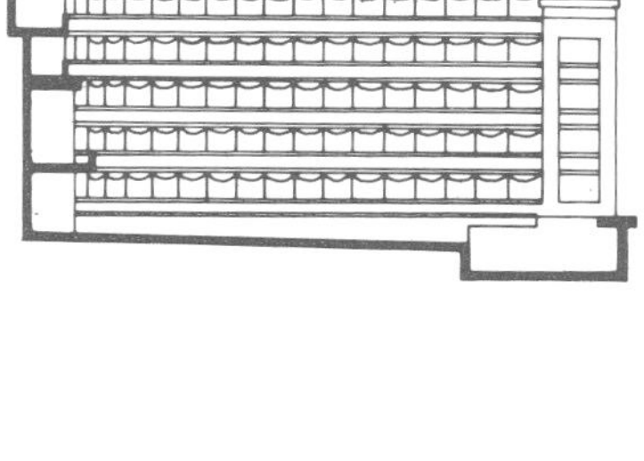

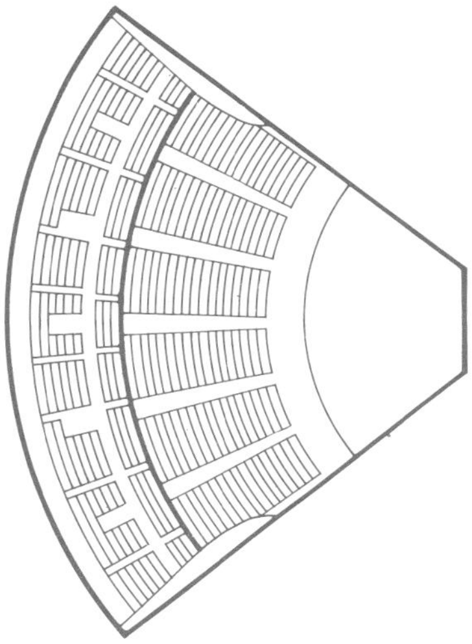

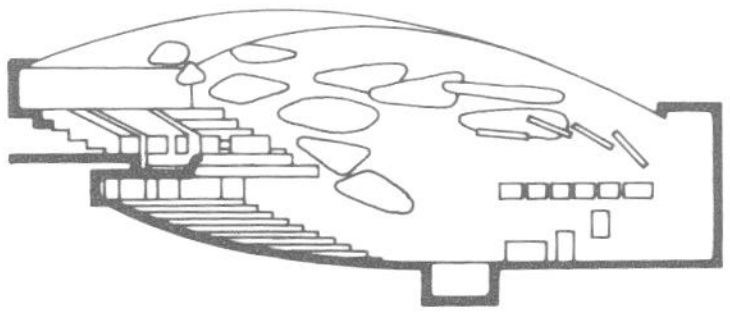

Aula Magna, Carácas Aula Magna, completed in 1954, is an interesting example of the fan-shaped auditorium. Inherent to the design is the problem of focused echoes, created by a curved rear wall. The hall also has a domed ceiling, and therefore an additional echo problem. The solution adopted was an attractive array of coloured "stabiles", designed by sculptor Alexander Calder, which have the same effect as the "clouds" described opposite.

The hall seats 2,660 people and is considered to be one of the best in South America. Its relatively short reverberation time, resulting in clear, distinct tones, makes it ideal for chamber music, piano and modern compositions.

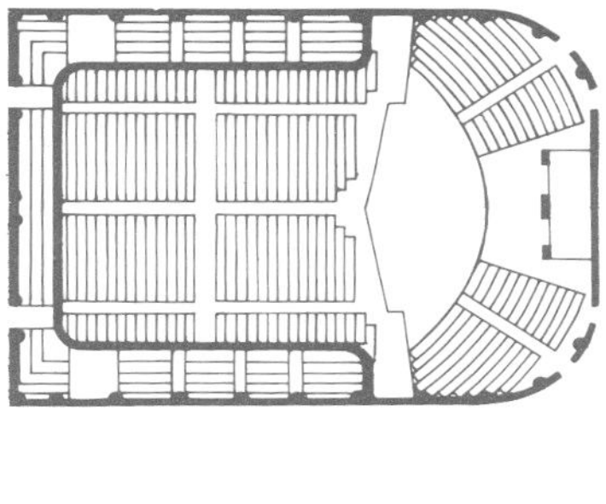

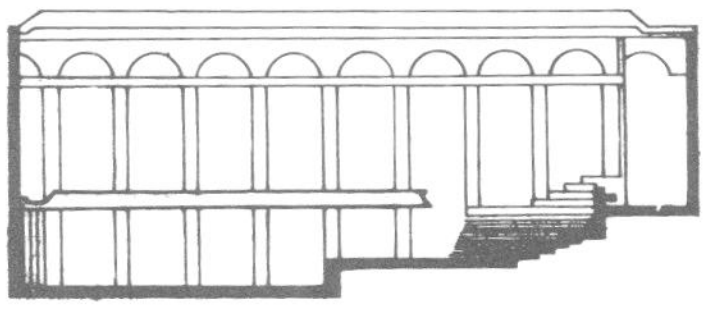

Concertgebouw, Amsterdam This auditorium has an excellent reputation among most musicians, though it has some imperfections.

A traditional rectangular hall, it was built in 1888. With a width of about 30 metres, it is considerably wider than most comparable halls, such as those at Leipzig and Vienna. It seats 2,206 people, some of them on the steep steps behind the orchestra. These were originally provided to accommodate a chorus, for large-scale works such as Mahler's eighth symphony, Beethoven's ninth symphony and J. S. Bach's *St Matthew Passion* have been presented there annually.

The Concertgebouw is now mainly used for orchestral concerts, both chamber and symphonic. It has a reverberation time of 2 seconds. The wall niches aid sound diffusion. The balcony does not inhibit the reflection of sound to the seats underneath it, though the hall's high ceiling and great width create a long initial time-delay gap and lessen presence.

toria are the horseshoe, the fan and the rectangle, as shown on page 137.

From about 1950 there has been a noticeable loosening up of architectural form in relation to public buildings. The time-honoured Greek-temple appearance of many of the older opera-houses and concert halls, from the Bolshoi in Moscow to the Concertgebouw in Amsterdam, has given way to architectural forms as widely divergent as those shown opposite.

Conversions

In addition to new buildings, there are conversions of existing buildings into concert halls. Conversions are usually cheaper than new constructions and of course support the policies of conservation which have recently gained great favour.

Two notable English examples, in strong contrast to each other, are in Suffolk and London. The Maltings at Snape, originally built for the making and storing of malt, is now a first-class auditorium which serves as base for the Aldeburgh Festival. The first conversion, completed in 1967, was gutted by fire and the hall has since been rebuilt exactly as before. The acoustics are of high quality and the restored building blends well with its rural surroundings.

The second notable example is the conversion of St John's, a magnificent baroque church in Smith Square, London, into a concert hall, with full radio broadcasting facilities, for solo recitals and ensemble performances.

The interior alterations are not extensive but have included the replacement of the altar by a platform, the construction of a control-room for broadcasting, and the conversion of the crypt into a restaurant and bar for concert-goers.

Integration and social change

Just as styles in music and architecture have changed, the style of concert-going has altered greatly since about the turn of the century. Previously, concert-going was considered by many people to be as much a social function as a musical experience. It was important to "be seen" by one's acquaintances at the opera, and essential to "dress" for the occasion. Attitudes have changed; now, the immediacy of being present at a live performance is the main attraction for concert-goers. The vitality and tensions – and, one hopes, the spontaneity – of the live performance can never be replaced by recordings.

Any attempt to make listening to live music a regular part of everyday life and to integrate auditoria into the urban fabric must therefore be welcome. One such development can be seen at Lenox, Mass., USA, where the Tanglewood Music Shed, a vast steel shed with seating for six thousand inside and a further six thousand outside, has been built. The building sits in a landscaped "saucer" which helps to create favourable acoustics for the audiences sitting outside.

Such a venue encourages an informality and spontaneousness often lacking in old-established halls where complicated booking procedures (and usually, owing to the restricted number of seats available, far higher ticket prices) tend to prevail.

The changing social aspects of concert-going are also reflected in plans for the Music Centre at Utrecht, in the Netherlands. The auditorium will form part of a complex which sits within the existing townscape – almost an adjunct to the shopping centre, and equally accessible.

Building for the music of the future

Musical experimentation, a particularly active area of twentieth-century music, has in the past been limited, very often, by the architectural facilities available. However, the new Pompidou Arts Centre in Paris includes a musical research centre called IRCAM (Institute for Research and Co-ordination into Acoustics and Music), comprising four main departments: instrument and voice, electro-acoustic, computer and co-ordination. Its auditorium is an acoustic-research concert hall seating up to 400 people. The complex, a revolutionary blend of architecture and music, is directed by Pierre Boulez.

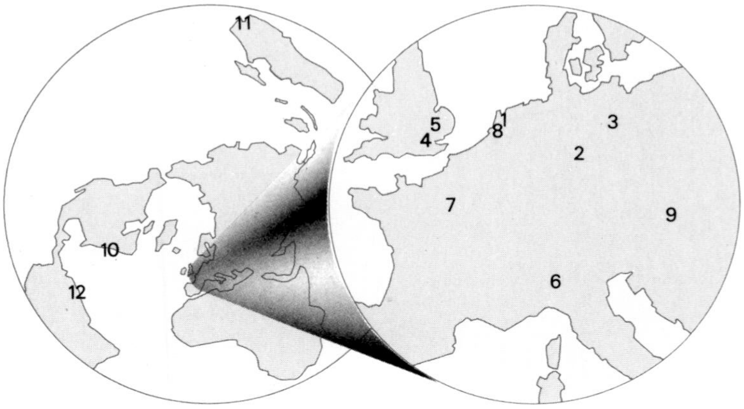

Above The Maltings at Snape, Suffolk. The increasing attendance at the Aldeburgh Festival made it necessary to convert some disused malt houses on the banks of the River Alde. This concert hall was completed in 1967. **Right** Locations of some major concert halls and opera-houses: **1** *Concertgebouw*, Amsterdam; **2** *Festspielhaus*, Bayreuth; **3** *Philharmonic*, Berlin; **4** *Royal Opera House*, Covent Garden, *Royal Albert Hall*, *Festival Hall*, London; **5** *Maltings*, Snape; **6** *La Scala*, Milan; **7** *Théâtre National de l'Opéra*, *IRCAM*, Paris; **8** *Music Centre*, Utrecht; **9** *Staatsoper Grosser Musikvereinssaal*, Vienna; **10** *Philharmonic Hall*, *Lincoln Centre*, *Carnegie Hall*, New York, USA; *Symphony Hall*, Boston, USA; *Tanglewood Music Shed*, Lenox, Mass., USA; **11** *Opera House*, Sydney, Australia; **12** *Aula Magna*, Carácas, Venezuela.

Sydney Opera House Originally designed by Danish architect Jørn Utzon in 1956, the building's interior was designed in 1966–8 by the Australian architects Hall Todd and Littlemore together with British engineers to a revised brief. The complex, opened in October 1973, comprises a concert hall seating 2,700, an opera-house auditorium seating 1,500, a drama theatre seating 550, a cinema seating 400 and a recital room seating 200. There is also a rehearsal room/recording studio which can accommodate a full orchestra. The soaring forms of the roof shells are a dominant feature of Sydney Harbour.

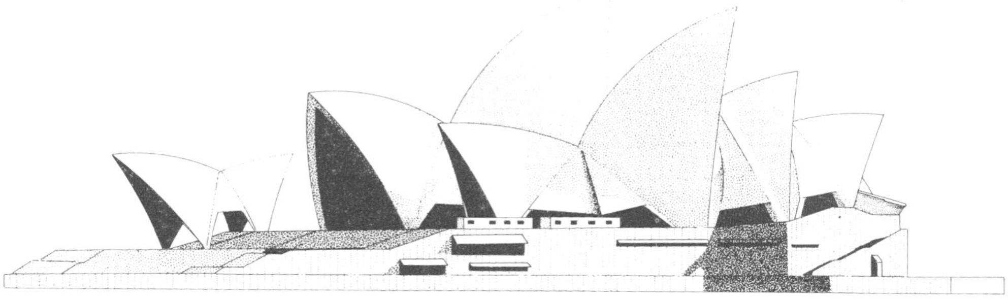

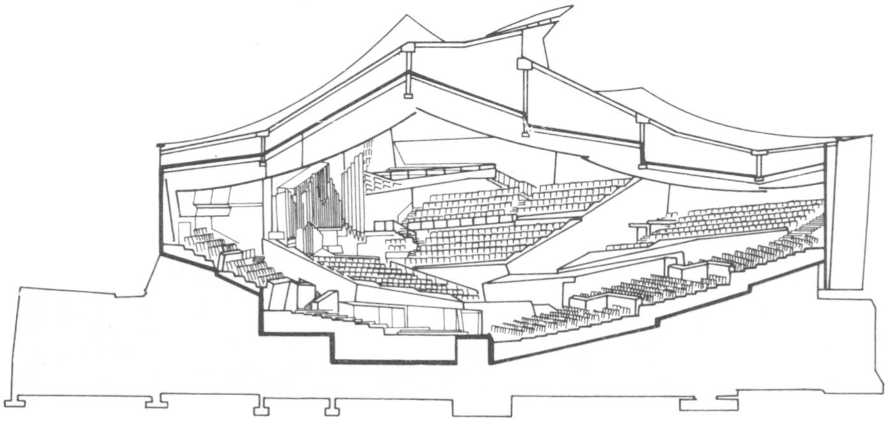

Berlin Philharmonic Completed in 1963, this was the winning design, by Hans Scharoun, in a competition held for the purpose. The building seems to exemplify a definition sometimes used of architecture, namely that it is "frozen music". The building forms part of the encompassing landscape, rather than dominating it like the monumental Sydney Opera House. Inside, there has been an attempt to maintain a human scale in the vast auditorium by using alternating planes of seating which, like the roof and the building's exterior, are irregular.

The Music Centre, Utrecht This building illustrates the idea of integrated, accessible auditoria. The Centre includes shops, offices, resting places and cafés in internal streets which are part of the complex. The internal streets are extensions of the town's existing street pattern. The architect, Herman Hertzberger, has said that in designing this building he aimed to "de-mystify the ritual elements" – that is, to dispel the aura of sanctity which tends to predominate in some of the world's great temples of the arts. The illustration shows the informal nature of the interior.

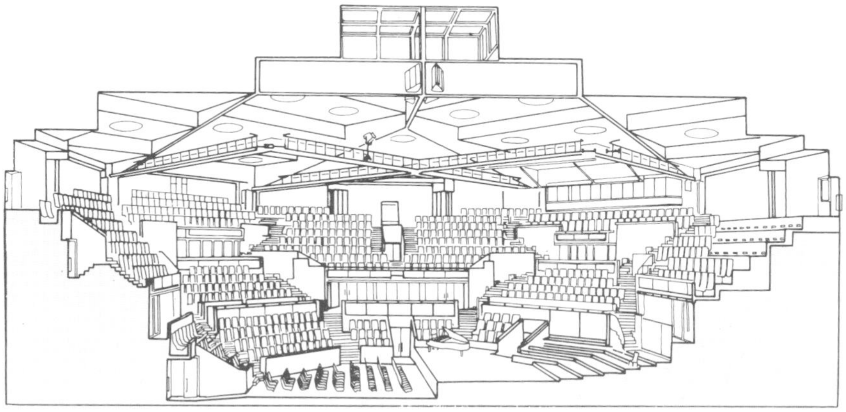

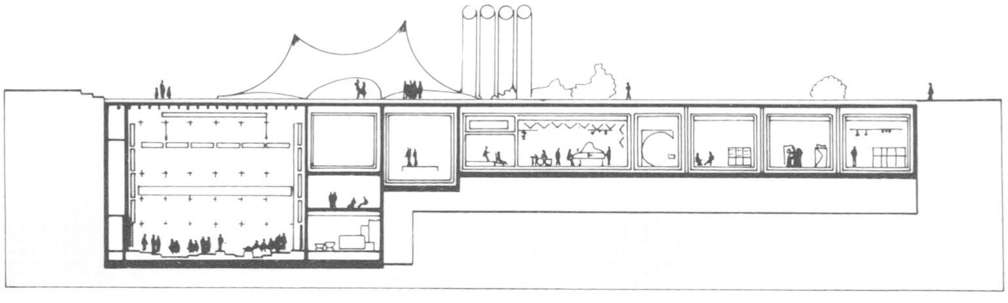

IRCAM, Centre Pompidou, Paris The building is divided into four zones: an acoustical zone which includes a reverberation chamber, an anechoic chamber, studios, control rooms, laboratories, electro-acoustic research and computer rooms; a second acoustical zone containing the acoustic-research concert hall, which has movable walls, floor and ceiling together with changeable surfaces for visual and acoustic effects; a third zone for administration, conferences and library facilities; the fourth zone is the roof (the building is essentially underground) which is used for public events.

Music and Education

Music has always had a place – sometimes a central place – in Western education. The Mesopotamians believed that musical intervals mirrored the harmony of the universe, and we can surmise that music was studied together with astronomy and mathematics in the Mesopotamian temples. To the Greeks, music meant intellectual culture in general, including literature and art as well as music in the modern sense; music and physical culture were the two main branches of education, and also two of the prime attributes of the Greek gods.

In the Middle Ages, the Church had monopolized education; the chief importance of practical musical training at that time was to ensure the correct singing of plainsong. The first choristers' schools, or *scholae cantorum*, were founded in the early Middle Ages and continued to play a major part in European musical education for many centuries.

The old association of musical theory with mathematics and astronomy was maintained in the medieval and Renaissance university curricula, which were divided into the *quadrivium* of geometry, arithmetic, music and astronomy, and the *trivium* of grammar, dialectic and rhetoric. During the Renaissance, the ability to play or sing was an indispensable social accomplishment, and every artist and thinker had a knowledge of musical theory.

The Protestant churches which emerged from the sixteenth-century Reformation emphasized music in education. This was particularly true of the Lutheran Church. Martin Luther, himself a lutenist and composer, did much to establish a lasting tradition of musical education in Germany.

Music had a significant role in the thinking of many educational reformers in the eighteenth and nineteenth centuries. Many of them took their cue from the French philosopher Jean-Jacques Rousseau (1712–78), who had a lifelong interest in music. In his book *Emile*, in which he described a boy's ideal education, Rousseau included detailed proposals for musical training. He suggested that an interest in music could be awakened if pupils learnt simple songs by ear, much as we learn to speak, and that reading music should come later. He also felt that children should be encouraged to create their own simple compositions. Many modern music teachers would agree with these ideas.

A similar approach to Rousseau's lay behind the development of the tonic sol-fa method of sight-singing by the English

Above In developed societies, an academic approach to music learning can begin at an early age. These little girls are playing a piano duet from written music. If the desired result is competence in playing written pieces, the validity of this approach is not in doubt. Yet it is a mistake to define musicality in terms of musical literacy and sophisticated instruments—as the picture on the left shows.

Left Zulu women singing and drumming as their children dance. In tribal societies such as this, small children take part in music-making as a communal, informal activity, rather than on an individual, formal basis as in the Western music lesson. In this way, music is acquired without conscious application, much as we learn to speak.

Left A class of Japanese infants learning violin by the world-famous method developed by the violinist Shinichi Suzuki. Children begin to play small violins as soon as they can hold them. No music reading is involved at this stage, and the emphasis is on acquiring technique as a natural physical action related to aural perception. Suzuki's method is based on his belief that musical talent is something that can be developed in most people, rather than an inherited special ability, and that music is best learned at the same stage that a child learns its first language—rather than as a "second language" studied by eye rather than by ear. The soundness of these principles has been shown by their international success. A further advantage of the Suzuki method is that it can be used to teach large classes of fifty to sixty children, making it much cheaper and more widely available than the traditional one-to-one relationship of instrumental teaching.

Below The Italian Renaissance theorist Gafurio (1451–1522) lecturing to students. The picture shows that simple proportions of the lengths of pipes (left) or strings (right) give the basic intervals of octave (6 : 3 or 2 : 1), fifth (6 : 4 or 3 : 2) and fourth (4 : 3). This "rational" approach to the foundations of music is accessible to any numerate person but is infrequently used today. Instead, the theoretical side of music all too easily appears as a set of half-understood rules without apparent foundation. Nevertheless, an understanding of theory is a necessary part of creating rather than recreating music.

congregational minister John Curwen (1816–80). The simplicity of this system, based, like that of Guido d'Arezzo, on named degrees of the scale (*doh, re, mi . . .*) led to a great spread of choral singing among the less educated section of British society. Tonic sol-fa has had a worldwide impact because of its use by missionaries.

Rousseau's successors Johann Pestalozzi (1746–1827) and Friedrich Froebel (1782–1852) both stressed the value of music in education. Pestalozzi held that music helped "harmonize" the character and Froebel held that music helped the child to realize its full potential. The connection between music and movement, and their joint contribution to a balanced education, was the basis of the system of eurhythmics developed by the Swiss teacher Emile Jaques-Dalcroze (1865–1950).

In the twentieth century, major contributions to the musical education of younger children have included those made in Germany and Hungary by the composers Carl Orff and Zoltán Kodály, and in Japan by the violinist Shinichi Suzuki.

Orff's system uses tonally simple and rhythmically lively music for specially designed class sets of tuned and untuned percussion instruments. In Hungarian schools, the use of Kodály's methods of carefully graded musical concept-building has led to almost universal musical literacy. In the system of violin teaching developed by Suzuki, infants start on small violins as soon as they can hold them. Technique is developed as a natural physical response to aural perception and no music reading is involved at the outset.

Methods and aims

Specialized musical education is mainly geared to turning out professional musicians, composers and teachers, most of whom are destined to function in the area of "serious" or "classical" music. For a young musician to reach orchestral standards (and still more to become a concert soloist), lessons must begin early. A costly one-to-one relationship is necessary between pupil and teacher, which not everyone can afford.

This situation inevitably tends to an élitism which may conflict with the need

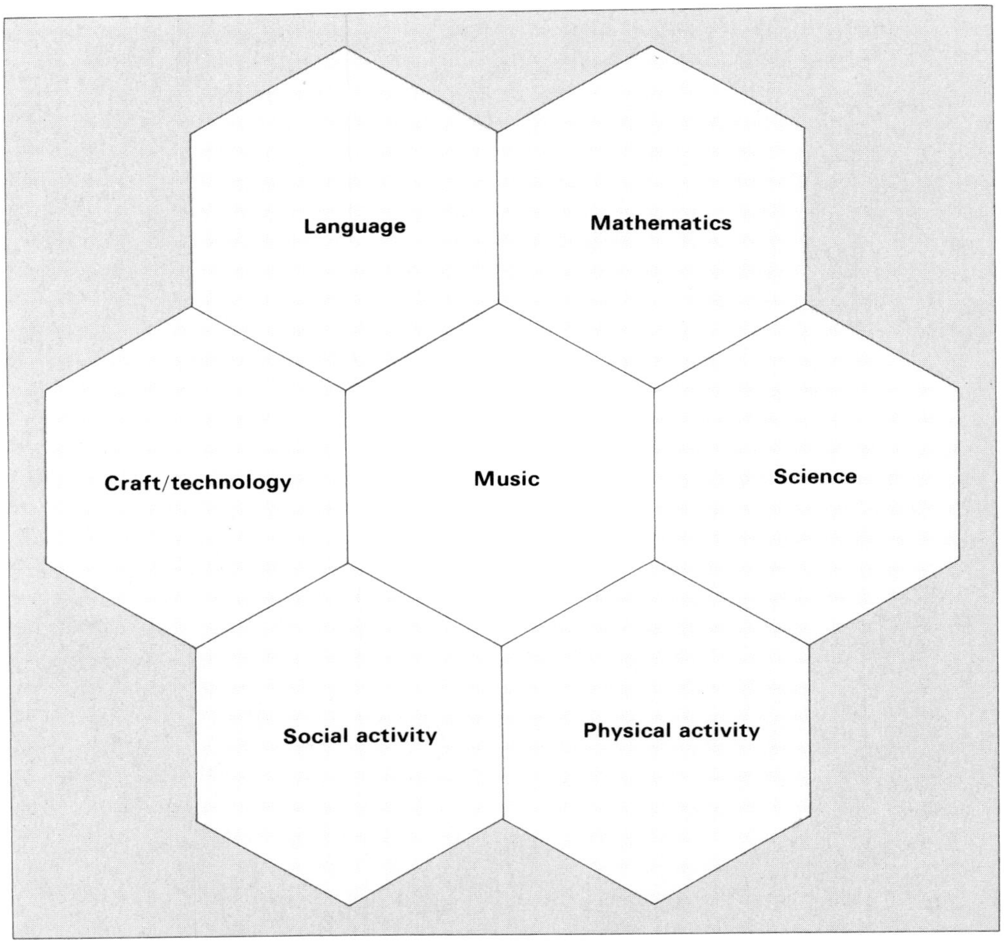

Above right Music has general as well as particular educational value, overlapping with other key subject areas. **Below right** Trouble with fans at a pop concert. Uninspired school music may be partly to blame for the excesses of pop.

to give as many young people as possible the opportunity to participate in and appreciate music – and not necessarily classical music. Furthermore, the classical training system is not without disadvantages for those who benefit from it. The job of creating as opposed to recreating music falls to the small minority who become composers. For the rest, emphasis on reading and performing the classical repertoire may stifle individual creativity. Improvisational skill is often neglected, despite the fact that it is a starting point for composition and despite the importance attached to it by the virtuosi of the classical and romantic periods.

Not without reason, many traditionalist teachers deplore the banality and excesses of much of today's pop music. However, they themselves bear some of the responsibility for a situation in which many young people are put off classical music by the uninspired teaching of music in schools.

A pluralist, open-ended approach to musical education probably provides the best solution to these problems. Such an approach starts from the assumption that musical basics (rhythm, melody, harmony and form) are not the exclusive property of one style or idiom, and that once learned, the basics can be applied in many directions.

Above An open-air concert at a summer school of music. Summer schools, such as the one held at Dartington Hall in Devon, are an increasingly popular feature of musical life in Britain and some other countries. Amateur musicians and music-lovers can attend them and benefit from contact with and tuition from internationally famous teachers, instrumentalists and composers.

Britain has a number of music schools and colleges, including the Royal College, Royal Academy, Guildhall School and Trinity College in London, the Royal Scottish Academy in Glasgow, the Royal Manchester College and the Birmingham School of Music. **Left** The composer Sir Michael Tippett talks to students at the Royal College, where he himself studied.

The USSR and other Eastern European countries have extremely high standards of higher musical training. **Above** The late Heinrich Neuhaus, an outstanding pianist who taught for more than forty years at the Moscow Conservatory. Neuhaus, seen here with Alexander Slobodyanik in 1960, was the teacher of the internationally famous pianists Sviatoslav Richter and Emil Gilels.

Above A student string quartet rehearses at New York's Juilliard School, one of the United States' leading centres for the performing arts, which caters for music, dance and drama. The school was established in 1926 with funds from a foundation endowed by the French-American financier and philanthropist Augustus Juilliard (1836–1919). Many leading instrumentalists, singers, conductors and composers have received training there.

Austria's capital Vienna, once the home of Haydn, Mozart and Beethoven, has probably had more influence on the history of Western music than any other city and, not surprisingly, its tradition of musical education is outstanding. **Above** A chamber group of young string musicians rehearse at the Vienna Conservatory.

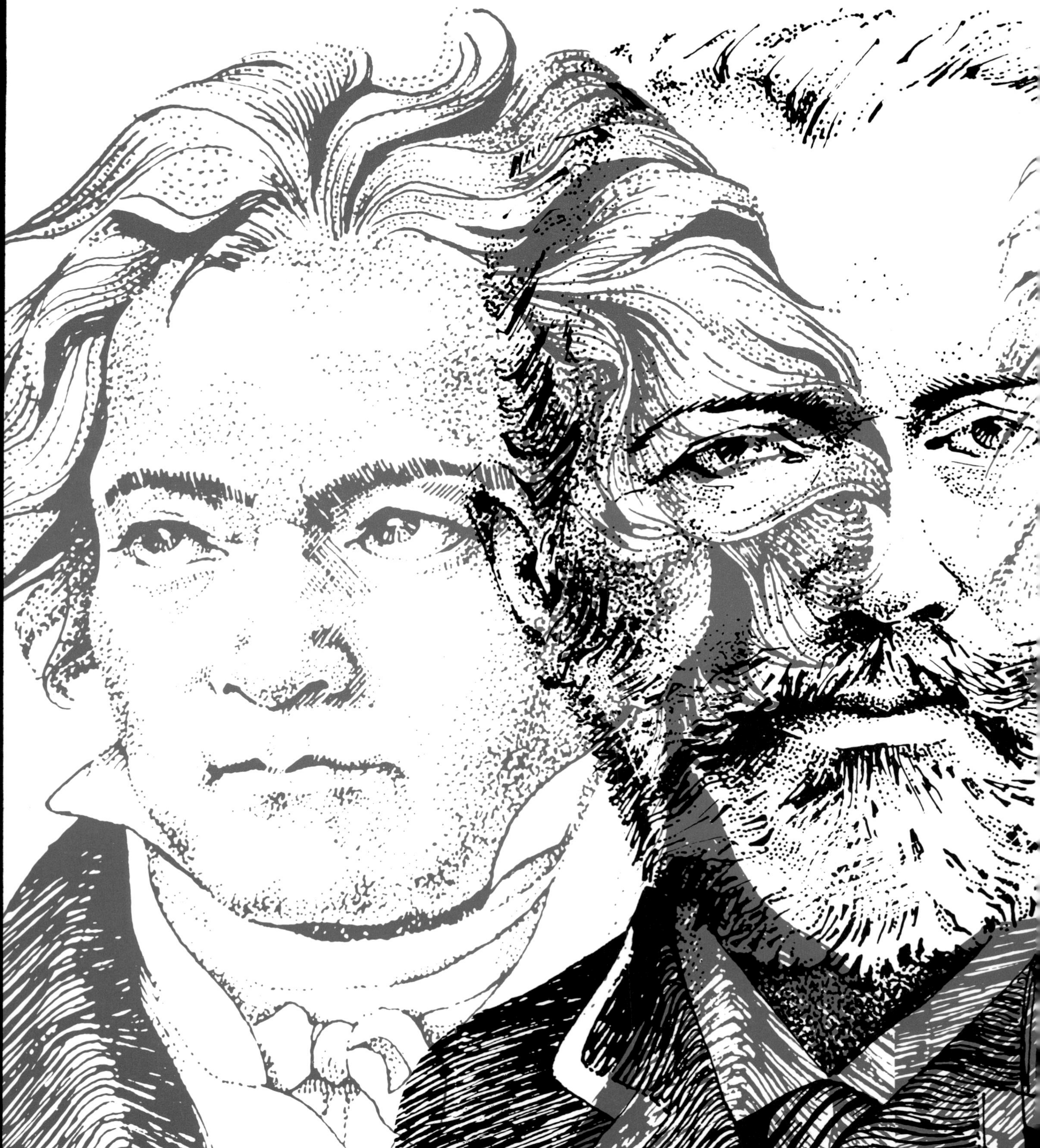

V

A Chronology of Music

The following may be regarded as a sort of ordnance survey of the progress of music from the earliest times until the present day. Though it cannot claim to be comprehensive, it may perhaps help to focus some of the movements and main events of musical history in the mind of the reader. For example, the importance of religion in the everyday life of the Middle Ages strongly influenced the course of musical development. In later times, political matters were to affect the musical output of such giants as Beethoven and Liszt as much as that of many of the composers who have come to wear the "nationalist" label. The juxtaposition of works, composers and other landmarks in music highlights such cross-currents as the effect made on music by – say – a new dance or the improvement of a musical instrument, and, of course, by one composer on another.

Beethoven, Tchaikovsky and Grieg

Pre-1000

4000 3000 2000 1000

Pindar, G
500 BC P

● *4000* BC Flute and harp in Egypt. Accompanied liturgical chant in Mesopotamia
● *3500* BC Lute and double clarinet in Egypt
● *3000* BC Bamboo pipe in China
● *700* BC Terpander,
● *2000* BC Trumpet in Denmark
● *2000* BC Percussion instruments and lyre in Egyptian orchestral music
● *1700* BC Secular music of growing importance in Mesopota
● *1500* BC Female musicians entertain at feasts in Gree
● *1500* BC Hittites use harp, lyre, guitar, tambourine
● *1500* BC Harp used for court dances in Egypt
● *950* BC Music at relig
● *800* BC Scales of five
● *800* BC Music for dr
● *600* BC Clas
● *500* BC
● *400* BC

● Music history dates
○ General history dates
♩ Musical compositions
All dates in italics are approximate

○ 336
○ 490 BC Battle
○ *850* BC Homer writes *Iliad*
○ *4000* BC City of Susa founded. Sumerian civilization begins in "Fertile Crescent"
○ *1400* BC Knossos burnt. Temple of Luxor built in Egy
○ *3000* BC First Egyptian dynasty.
○ 960 BC Solomon succeeds Da
○ 214
○ *753* Rome founded

Limestone relief showing musicians at a feast. Egypt, 5th Dynasty.

Girl playing an angle harp. Egypt, 850 BC.

100 200 300 400 500 600 700 800 900 1000

ser and poet, 520–447 BC
writing Odes

of Greek music", develops accompanied monody

● AD *350* Schola Cantorum founded in Rome for the teaching of liturgical song
et
● *386* Ambrose, Bishop of Milan, introduces hymn-singing
● 350 "Hallelujah" hymns sung in Christian churches
onies in Israel, e.g. at Solomon's temple
● *450* Flutes, tubas and drums in Peru. Call-and-response singing in Roman Church
notes used in Babylonian music
● *500* Boëthius's musical treatise *De Institutione Musicae* establishes Greek letter-names of scale in Europe
oped in Greece
drama at its height
● *590–600* Pope Gregory I compiles collection of plainsong chants
goras founds musical theory in Greece: demonstrates intervals on monochord.
● *610* Celtic bowed lyre, the crwth, developed. Flutes, gongs, guitars, bells and drums in China
pet-playing competitions held in Greece
C *Hydraulis* or water organ in Roman Empire
● *619* Orchestras with hundreds of players formed in China
Earliest form of oboe introduced in Rome
● *750* Wind organs replacing *hydraulis*. Gregorian chant sung in Germany, France and England
Aristoxenus, Greek philosopher, defines natural intervals, writes musical treatise
Chinese divide octave into sixty notes

● *650* Neumes, early form of musical notation, developed
● *790* Schola Cantorum establishes schools in Paris, Cologne, Soissons and Metz

● *800* Poems sung to musical accompaniment at Charlemagne's court

● *850* Church modes established

● *800* Organum (plainsong in fourths, fifths and octaves) develops

Winchester Abbey: 400-pipe organ built *980* ●

Secular fauxbourdon style (singing in parallel 3rds and 6ths) adopted in plainsong *900* ●

○ 527 Justinian becomes Emperor of Byzantine (East Roman) Empire
○ 306 Constantine becomes Roman Emperor. Christianity becomes Empire's "official" religion
○ 117 Hadrian becomes Roman Emperor. Roman Empire reaches greatest extent under his rule
960 Sung dynasty founded in China ○
Julius Caesar murdered
○ 410 Alaric the Goth sacks Rome. End of West Roman Empire
nder the Great becomes king of Macedon
○ 395 Roman Empire divided into East and West
○ 732 Battle of Tours: Charles Martel halts Moslem western advance
thon: Athenians defeat Persians
BC Carthage destroyed by Romans. Rome becomes dominant Mediterranean power
○ 800 Charlemagne becomes first Holy Roman Emperor: a cultural revival begins
○ AD *30* Jesus Christ crucified
s Yahweh temple in Jerusalem
ruction of Great Wall of China begins
○ 570 Mohammed, founder of Islam, born
○ 874 Norsemen settle in Iceland

Impressed brick with design showing pan-pipers and dancers. China, Han Dynasty, 200 BC– AD 200.

Impressed brick with design depicting *ch'in*- and panpipe-players and dancers. China, Han Dynasty, 200 BC–AD 200.

1000~1500

1000 1050 1100 1150 1200

Guido d'Arezzo ● Italian musical theorist and teacher 995–1050
1026 Establishes syllable names for notes

Bernard de Ventadour troubadour *c.*1130–1195

● *1100 Ars Antiqua* begins: elaboration of organum at St Martial of Limoges, France
● *1150* Notre Dame School founded in Paris: **Léonin** (2-part) and **Pérotin** (3-part) composers of organ
● *1200* German *Minnesä*
● *1050* Proportional time values given to notes
● *1125* Rise of troubadours and trouvères (S. and N. France)
● *1100* Portative organ invented

○1147 Second Crusade launched
○1215 King J
○1066 William of Normandy conquers England, becomes king
○1189 Third Crusade launched
○1095 Urban II initiates First Crusade
○1206 Genghis Khan becc

"Christ Glorified in the Court of Heaven" by Fra Angelico (*c.*1400–1455).

1300 | 1350 | 1400 | 1450 | 1500

de la Halle
ère *c.*1240–87

Philippe de Vitry French composer 1291–1361

Guillaume de Machaut Flemish composer 1300–1377

Francesco Landini Italian composer and organist 1325–97

John Dunstable English composer *c.*1375–1453

Guillaume Dufay Flemish composer *c.*1399–1474

Gilles de Binchois Flemish composer *c.*1400–1460

Johannes Okeghem Flemish composer *c.*1430–*c.*1495

Alexander Agricola Flemish composer 1446–1506

0 Earliest extant round, "Sumer is icumen in", in 6 parts

ished. Boys' choir founded in Dresden

●*1300* German *Meistersinger* established

0 First *Meistersinger* school established in Mainz

●*1300* *Jongleurs*, wandering entertainers, active in France. *Chansons de geste*, e.g. *"Chanson de Roland"*, sung

●1322 Pope John XXII prohibits elaborate harmonization of plainsong.

●*1325* Pedals added to organ mechanism

●*Tournai* Mass, earliest extant polyphonic mass, composers unknown

●*1350* Clavichord begins to be developed

●1385 First court ball in France, for royal wedding

●*1390* Rise of choral polyphony

Jacob Obrecht Flemish composer 1452–1505

Taverner

Josquin Després Flemish composer *c.*1450–1521

Willaert

●1400 First reference to dulcimer's appearance in Europe

●*1430* First Flemish school of music begins, represented by Binchois and Dufay

Ballet starts to develop in Italian courts *1490* ●

Jean Mauburnus writes first treatise on musical instruments, *Rosetum exercitiarum spiritualium* 1494 ●

Degrees in music introduced at Oxford University 1499 ●

Constantinople taken by Turks: Byzantine Empire ends 1453 ○

○1368 Ming dynasty established in China

Mongol hordes invade Europe

First printing from movable type, at Gutenberg's works 1453 ○

○1338 Hundred Years War between England and France begins

s Magna Carta

○1294 Kublai Khan, Mongol Emperor of China, dies

○1378 Disputed papal election: Great Schism begins

○1321 Dante, Italian poet, dies

Columbus makes first voyage to New World 1492 ○

○1274 Thomas Aquinas, Italian philosopher, dies

○1363 Tamerlane, Mongol conqueror, begins conquest of Asia

gol Emperor

○1348 Black Death sweeps through Europe

Vasco de Gama finds sea route to India 1498 ○

Earliest known printed music, *c.*1473.

Fool playing bagpipes. Italy, sixteenth century.

1500~1600

1500 1510 1520 1530 1540

Giovanni Pierluigi da Palestrina Italian composer *c.*1525–1594

Cyprien de Rore Flemish composer 1516–65

Giaches de Wert Dutch composer *c.*153

Agricola

Thomas Tallis English composer *c.*1505–1585

William Byrd En

Obrecht

John Taverner English composer *c.*1495–1545

Roland de Lassus Flemish composer *c.*1530–1594

Desprès

Adriaan Willaert Flemish composer *c.*1480–1562 ●1527 *Maestro de cappella* at St Mark's, Venice

Vincenzo Galilei Italian lutenist and composer *c.*1520–91

Richard Edwards English composer and poet *c.*1522–66

Andrea Amati First of Italian violin-making family 1530–15

● 1500 Ottavio de' Petrucci prints music with movable type in Venice

●1502 Petrucci publishes masses by Deprés

●1537 First musical conservatories foun

●1524 Johann Walther and Martin Luther produce Protestant hymnal

●1523 First manual on lute-playing, by Hans Judenkünig

○1533 Ivan IV ("the Terrible") becomes Tsar of R

○1520 Suleiman the Magnificent becomes Sultan of Turkey: Ottoman power reaches its height

○1524 Peasants' War in Germany

○1542 Portuguese are

○1517 Martin Luther formulates 95 Theses: Protestant Reformation begins

○1545 Co

○1519 Magellan begins first circumnavigation of world. Leonardo da Vinci, Italian artist, philosoph

○1513 Balboa discovers Pacific Ocean

○1529 Turks besiege Vienna

Title page from *Stramotti fioretti. . . rulce fiorentino*, 1524.

"Street musicians" by Crispin de Passe, sixteenth century.

1560 1570 1580 1590 1600

Johannes Eccard German composer 1553–1611

Scheidt

1551 *Maestro de cappella* at St Peter's, Rome ●1565 Writes *Missa Papae Marcelli*

Michael Praetorius German composer, organist and musicologist 1571–1621

Claudio Monteverdi Italian composer 1567–1643 ●1587 First book of madrigals

Heinrich Schütz German composer 1585–1672

Schein

ulio Caccini Italian composer and singer 1545–1618

ás Luis de Victoria Spanish composer of church music *c.*1549–1611

ooser 1543–1623 ●Organist at Lincoln cathedral ●1572 Byrd and Tallis employed as organists at Chapel Royal

Orlando Gibbons English composer 1583–1625

John Bull English organist and composer *c.*1562–1628

Jacopo Peri Italian composer 1561–1633 *Dafne*, first known opera (music lost) 1597

Jan Pieterszoon Sweelinck Dutch composer 1562–1621

John Dowland English lutenist and composer 1562–1626

●1556 Publishes first book of motets

Frescobaldi

Giovanni Gabrieli Italian composer 1557–1612

Gregorio Allegri Italian composer 1582–1652

Thomas Morley English composer and theorist 1557–1602 *A Plaine and Easie Introduction to Practicall Musick* 1597●

●1572 Makes one of earliest cellos

aples and Venice ●1570 High point of unaccompanied vocal polyphonic church music

●*1555* Development of violin in Cremona

Elizabeth I sends an organ to the Sultan of Turkey 1594 ●

●1558 Gioseffo Zarlino defines major and minor scales

Nicola Amati, greatest member of violin-making family, born 1596●

Musica transalpina, madrigal collection, published in England by Nicholas Yonge 1588 ●

○1562 First religious war in France: Huguenots massacred at Vassy ○1588 English defeat Spanish Armada

opeans in Japan ○1571 Battle of Lepanto: Christian league defeats Turks

rent: Catholic Counter-Reformation begins ○1572 Huguenots massacred on St Bartholomew's Day, France

engineer, dies ○1564 Shakespeare, English dramatist and poet, born. Michelangelo, Italian artist, dies

Edict of Nantes ends French religious wars 1594○

Title page from a four-part setting of *The Psalms of David*, 1579.

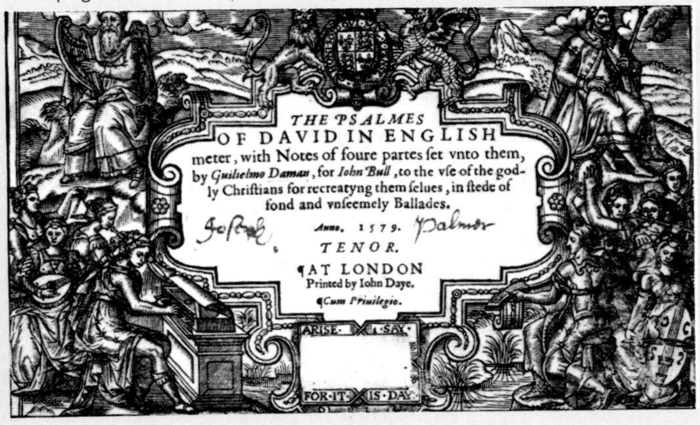

Monteverdi

Frescobaldi

1600~1700

1600 1610 1620 1630 1640

Eccard

Samuel Scheidt German composer 1587–1654

M. Praetorius ● 1618 *Syntagma Musicum*,

Monteverdi ♩1607 *Orfeo*, opera ●1613 *Maestro de cappella*, St Mark's, Venice ●1632 Takes holy orders

Schütz ●1617 *Kapellmeister* at Dresden ♩1629 *Sinfonie Sacrae* ♩1645 *S*

Johann Schein German composer 1586–1630

Francesco Cavalli Italian composer 1602–1676 ♩1643 *Egisto*, ope

Caccini

De Victoria

Jean-Baptiste Lully Italian composer 1632–1687 ●

Byrd ♩1611 *Parthenia*

Gibbons ♩1611 *Parthenia*

Bull ♩1611 *Parthenia*, collection of virginal music

Heinrich von

Peri

Sweelinck

1605 *Lachrymae*, collection of instrumental pieces

Dietrich Buxtehude Danish compos

Girolamo Frescobaldi Italian composer and organist 1583–1643 ♩1630 *Aire Musicale*

G. Gabrieli

Giacomo Carissimi Italian composer 1605–1674

Johann Jacob Froberger German composer 1617–67

Allegri

♩ **Morley** 1601 *Triumphs of Oriana*, madrigal collection

Marcantonio Cesti Italian composer 1623–1669

●1637 First public opera-house, Teatro

●1645 Ven

●1636 *Harmonie universelle* published in Fr

●*1600* Recorder becomes popular in England ●1619 *Fitzwilliam Virginal Book*, collection of keyboard pieces ●*1644* French

○1608 Quebec founded by Champlain

○1611 Authorized version of Bible published

○1616 Shakespeare dies. Cervantes, Spanish writer, dies

○1618 Bohemian Revolt begins Thirty Years War

○1620 Pilgrim Fathers settle in New England

○1624 Cardinal Richelieu becomes chief minister of France

○1632 Gustavus Adolphus defeats Wallenstein and di

○1636 Japanese forbidden to go abroad

○1642 English Civil War be

○1643 French defeat Sp

○1644 Mar

John Playford's *The Dancing-master*; 7th edition, 1686, London.

Schütz

1660 1670 1680 1690 1700

ds from the Cross, oratorio 1664 *Christmas Oratorio*
Henry Purcell English composer 1659–1695 1689 *Dido and Aeneas,* opera
1660 Writes opera *Serse* for marriage of Louis XIV **Jean Philippe Rameau** French composer 1683–1759
n **Blow** English composer 1649–1708 ●1670 Organist at Westminster Abbey
Alessandro Scarlatti Italian composer 1660–1725 1679 *Gli equivoci nell'amore*, opera 1693 *Teodora*, opera
nist at court of Louis XIV 1661 Director of music to Louis XIV 1674 *Alceste*, opera **Tartini**
Sammartini
Arcangelo Corelli Italian composer 1653–1713
trian composer 1644–1704
Zipoli
Johann Pachelbel German composer 1653–1706
Nicola Porpora Italian composer 1686–1767
7–1707 ●1668 Organist at St Mary's, Lübeck
J. S. Bach
Handel
D. Scarlatti
Giuseppe Torelli Italian composer 1658–1709
Georg Philipp Telemann German composer 1681–1767
Quantz
François Couperin French composer 1668–1733
Johann Fux Austrian composer and theorist 1660–1741
●1666 *Kapellmeister* in Vienna **Metastasio**
Antonio Vivaldi Italian composer *c*.1685–1741

siano, opens in Venice ●*1660* French horn used in orchestra ●1678 First German opera-house opens in Hamburg
ra company gives first opera in Paris ●1680 Musical entertainment begins at Sadler's Wells, London
Marin Mersenne, with descriptions of all contemporary musical instruments
omes orchestral instrument ●1661 *Académie Royale de Danse* founded by Louis XIV in France
0 French and Italian overtures develop ●1680 Ballet arrives in Germany from France
●*1652* The minuet becomes fashionable at French court ●1672 First public concert (violin recital) in London given at Whitefriars

asty established in China ○1669 Rembrandt, Dutch artist, dies ○1683 Turks besiege Vienna but are repulsed
le of Lützen ○1661 Mazarin dies: Louis XIV begins rule in France ○1688 "Glorious Revolution" in England
○1652 Dutch colony founded at Cape of Good Hope, South Africa ○1673 Molière, French dramatist, dies
dinal Mazarin succeeds Richelieu ○1664 English take New York from Dutch Peter I ("the Great") becomes Tsar of Russia 1696 ○
Rocroiz 1653 Cromwell becomes Lord Protector of England ○1672 William of Orange leads Dutch against French invaders

Street procession.

Corelli

Purcell

Vivaldi

1700~1800

1700 1710 1720 1730 1740

Nicola Piccini Italian composer 1728–1800

William Boyce English composer 1710–1779

Rameau ●1722 *Traité de l'harmonie* ♩1735 *Les Indes galantes*, opera-ballet

Blow

Christoph Gluck German composer 1714–1787 ♩1744 *Iphigénie*

A. Scarlatti

Joseph Haydn Austrian composer 1732–1809

Giovanni Pergolesi Italian composer 1710–1736 ♩1733 *La serva padrona*, opera

Giuseppe Tartini Italian composer 1692–1770

Giovanni Battista Sammartini Italian composer 1698–1775

Corelli ♩1712 Twelve *concerti grossi*

Biber

Thomas Arne English composer 1710–1778 ♩1740 Song "Rule Britann

Domenico Zipoli Italian composer 1688–1726

Luigi Boccherini

Pachelbel

Porpora

Buxtehude

Johann Stamitz Bohemian violinist, conductor and composer 1717–1757 ●1745 *Kapellme*

Johann Sebastian Bach German composer 1685–1750 ♩1721 Brandenburg Concertos ♩1729 *St Matthew Passion* ♩1738 Mass in B minor

George Frideric Handel German-born composer 1685–1759 ♩1717 *Water Music* suite ●1726 Becomes British subject ♩1741 *Messiah*, oratorio ●

●1740 Visits Dublin and Lon

Domenico Scarlatti Italian composer 1685–1757

Carl von Dittersdorf Austrian

Torelli

Telemann ●1721 Director of music, Hamburg

Giovanni Paisiello Ita

Johann Quantz German composer and flautist 1697–1773 ●1741 Joins court of Frede

Couperin ●1716 *L'Art de toucher le clavecin* ("The Art of Harpsichord-playing")

André Grétry Bel

Charles Di

Fux ●1725 *Gradus ad Parnassum*

Pietro Metastasio opera librettist 1698–1782

Vivaldi

●*1707* Gottfried Silbermann builds first organ in Saxony

●*1709* Bartolomeo Cristofori makes first piano

●1710 Marie de Camargo, French ballerina, appears at Paris Opéra

●1711 Hasse's opera *Croesus* includes first orchestral part for clarinet

●1715 Musical comedies (vaudeville) given in Paris

●1728 John Gay's *The Beggar's Opera*

●1731 First public concerts held in Boston and Charleston,

●1732 Opera-house opens at Covent Garden, London

●1735 Imperial Ballet Schools founded in

●1744 Madrigal Soc

○1700 Great Northern War between Sweden, Denmark and Russia begins

○1701 War of Spanish Succession begins

○1713 Peace of Utrecht ends War of Spanish Succession

○1715 Louis XIV dies

○1739 Persian Army takes Delhi

○1740 Frederick II ("the Gre

○1745 Jaco

Rameau

Soldiers in the courtyard of St James's Palace, London, *c.*1790.

Handel

0 1760 1770 1780 1790 1800

menico Cimarosa Italian composer 1749–1801

Niccolo Paganini Italian composer 1782–1840

lide, opera ♩1770 *Paride ed Elena*, opera ♩1777 *Armide*, opera

● 1761 *Kapellmeister* to Paul Esterházy ♩1780 *Toy* symphony ♩*The Creation*, oratorio 1799

Muzio Clementi Italian composer 1752–1832

Wolfgang Amadeus Mozart Austrian composer 1756–1791 *Don Giovanni*, opera 1787 ♩1791 *Magic Flute*, opera

n *Alfred*, a masque **Schubert**

Daniel Steibelt German composer 1765–1823

ian composer 1743–1805 ●1787 Court composer in Berlin

org Vogler German music teacher 1749–1814

Mannheim court **Ludwig van Beethoven** German composer 1770–1827 ●1792 Taught by Haydn

Rossini

19 *Firework Music* **Carl Friedrich Zelter** German composer 1785–1832

Donizetti

John Field English composer 1782–1837

mposer 1739–99

nposer 1740–1816 ♩1780 *The Barber of Seville*, opera

Great

Luigi Cherubini Italian composer 1760–1842 ♩1791 *Lodoiska*, opera

nposer 1741–1813

glish composer 1745–1814

Ignaz Pleyel French-Austrian composer and piano-maker 1757–1831

Sébastien Erard French piano-maker 1752–1831 ●1780 Makes the first modern pianoforte, Paris

Thomas Attwood English composer 1765–1838

●1751 *La guerre des bouffons*, quarrel between supporters of Italian and French opera

●1760 Noverre publishes his reforming *Letters on Dancing and Ballet* **Weber**

750 Johann Breitkopf prints music with movable type in Leipzig ●1783 John Broadwood patents piano pedals, London

Petersburg and Moscow by Empress Anne ●1775 The waltz becomes fashionable in Vienna

unded in London ●1762 Franklin improves harmonica

●1758 First guitar manual published, in England ●1778 La Scala opens in Milan

stroys Mogul power in India ○1776 American Declaration of Independence

comes king of Prussia ○1759 British capture Quebec. ○1770 James Cook lands in Botany Bay, N.S.W. ○1789 French Revolution begins

bellion defeated in Britain ○1773 Americans protest against tea duty: "Boston Tea-party"

○1755 Lisbon earthquake: 30,000 killed France becomes a republic 1792○

Haydn

Gluck

Frontispiece of *The Modern Musickmaster* by Prelleur, 1731.

Beethoven

1800~1900

1800	1810	1820	1830	1840

Fryderyk Chopin Polish composer 1810–1849 ♩1833 Twelve *études*, op. 10

Mikhail Glinka Russian composer 1804–1857 ♩1836 *A Life for the Tsar*, first Russian opera

Ferencz Liszt Hungarian composer 1811–1886 ♩1845 *Les Prélu*

Anton Bruckner Austrian composer 1824–1896

César Franck Belgian composer 1822–1890

Cimarosa

Jacques Offenbach French composer 1819–1880

Paganini ●1805 Tours Europe **Jules Massenet** Fren

Giacomo Meyerbeer German composer 1791–1864 ♩1831 *Robert le diable*, opera ●1842 Director of mu

Haydn ♩1801 *The Seasons* **Richard Wagner** German composer 1813–1883 ♩1843 *The Fly*

Clementi

Albert Lortzing German composer 1801–51

Otto Nicolai German composer 1810–49

Peter Tchaikovsky Russ

Franz Schubert Austrian composer 1797–1828 ♩1819 *Trout* quintet **Johannes Brahms** German composer 1833–1897

Steibelt **Léo Delibes** French composer 1836–189

Boccherini **Giuseppe Verdi** Italian composer 1813–1901 *Macbeth*, opera 1847 ♩

Vogler **Anton Rubinstein** Russian pianist and composer 1829–1894

Vincenzo Bellini Italian composer 1801–1835 ♩1831 *Norma*, opera **Nikolai Rimsk**

Johann Strauss II Austrian composer 1825–1899

Bedřich Smetana Czech composer 1824–1884

Beethoven ♩1804 *Eroica*, symphony ♩1809 *Emperor* piano concerto ♩1824 *Choral* symphony **Alexander Borodin** Russian composer 1833–1887

Gioacchino Rossini Italian composer 1792–1868 ♩1816 *The Barber of Seville* ♩1829 *William Tell*, opera ♩1841 *Stabat Mater*, cho

Zelter

Gaetano Donizetti Italian composer 1797–1848 *Anna Bolena*, opera 1830 ♩ ♩1832 *L'elisir d'amore*, opera ♩1840 *La Fille du régiment*. o

Field ♩1814 Nocturnes

Hector Berlioz French composer 1803–1869 ♩1832 *Symphonie fantastique* ♩1846

Paisiello **Georges Bizet** French composer 1

Charles Gounod French composer 1818–1893

Cherubini ♩1800 *Les Deux Journées*, opera **Gabriel Fau**

Grétry **Arthur Sullivan** Eng

Dibdin **Modest Mussorgsky** Russ

Pleyel ●1807 J. G. Pleyel starts piano factory in Paris **Camille Saint-Saëns** French composer 183

Robert Schumann German composer 1810–1883 ♩1830 *Abegg Variations* ♩1841 *Spring* symphony

Erard

Felix Mendelssohn German composer 1809–1847 ♩1833 *Italian* symphony

Attwood **Anton Dvořák** Cze

Edvard Grieg

Carl Maria von Weber German composer 1786–1826 ♩1821 *Der Freischütz*, opera

●1834 Fanny Elssler, Austrian ballerina, at Paris Op

●1818 Christmas carol "Silent Night" written by Franz Huber and Joseph Mohr

●1822 Royal Academy of Music founded in London ●*1841* Adolphe Sax, Belg

●1814 J. N. Maelzel invents metronome in Vienna ♩1832 *La Sylphide*, ballet ● 1842 New Y

●1812 San Carlo opera-house completed in Naples ●1829 Charles Wheatstone patents the concertina

○1800 Alessandro Volta invents electricity ○1829 Greece secures independence from Turkey

○1805 Battle of Trafalgar 1812 Napoleon invades and retreats from Russia ○1830 Revolutions in France and Belgium ○18

○1807 Slave trade abolished in British Empire ○1825 Spanish colonies in Latin America gain independence

Poster by Jules Chéret advertising
La Princesse de Trébizonde.

Donizetti

Chopin

Bruckner

0 1860 1870 1880 1890 1900

Arnold Schoenberg Austrian composer 1874–1951 *Verklärte Nacht* 1899
Giacomo Puccini Italian composer 1858–1924 ●1880 Enters Milan conservatory 1894 *La Bohème*, opera
Gustav Mahler German composer 1860–1911 ●1888 Musical director of Budapest Opera
phonic poem **Pijper**
1873 Second symphony 1884 Seventh symphony
Symphonic Variations 1885 **Prokofiev**
1864 *La Belle Hélène*, operetta **Béla Bartók** Hungarian composer 1881–1945
poser 1842–1912 1884 *Manon*, opera
a House, Berlin **Jean Sibelius** Finnish composer 1865–1957 *Finlandia*, orchestral piece 1894
hman, opera ●1855 Conducts in London 1876 *Ring* cycle performed **Alban Berg** Austrian composer 1885–1935
Edward Elgar English composer 1857–1934 *Enigma Variations*, 1899
Arturo Toscanini Italian conductor 1867–1957 Appears at La Scala, Milan 1898 ●
Ignacy Paderewski Polish pianist, composer and statesman 1860–1941 ●1887 Gives first recital in Vienna
poser 1840–1893 1868 First symphony 1875 First piano concerto 1882 *1812* overture 1892 *The Nutcracker*, ballet
1868 *A German Requiem* 1881 *Academic Festival* overture
1870 *Coppélia*, ballet 1876 *Sylvia*, ballet 1883 *Lakmé*, opera
851 *Rigoletto*, opera 1862 *The Force of Destiny*, opera 1874 Requiem 1887 *Otello*, opera 1893 *Falstaff*, opera
Poulenc
sakov Russian composer 1844–1908 *The Snow-maiden*, opera 1882 1888 *Scheherazade*, symphonic suite
1874 *Die Fledermaus*, operetta 1885 *The Gypsy Baron*, operetta
1866 *The Bartered Bride*, opera 1874 *Má Vlast*, cycle of symphonic poems **Hindemith**
Bliss
Igor Stravinsky Russian composer 1882–1971
Serge Rachmaninov Russian pianist and composer 1873–1943
Maurice Ravel French composer 1875–1937
Ernest Bloch Swiss composer 1880–1959
Claude Debussy French composer 1862–1918 *L'Après-midi d'un faune*, orchestral piece 1894
nation of Faust, cantata 1863 *Les Troyens*, opera **Gustav Holst** English composer 1874–1934
Ralph Vaughan Williams English composer 1872–1958
'5 1863 *The Pearl-fishers*, opera 1875 *Carmen*, opera
1859 *Faust*, opera
ch composer 1845–1924
poser 1842–1900 1875 *Trial by Jury*, first operetta 1885 *The Mikado*, operetta
poser 1839–1881 1874 *Boris Godunov*, opera **Percy Grainger** Australian composer 1882–1961
1871 *Le Rouet d'Omphale*, symphonic poem
●1854 Attempts suicide **Frederick Delius** English composer 1862–1934
Richard Strauss German composer 1864–1949
ert Parry English composer 1848–1918
poser 1841–1904
vegian composer 1843–1907
Charles Ives American composer 1874–1954
Honegger
Erik Satie French composer 1866–1925
Leoš Janáček Czech composer 1858–1928

ument-maker, invents the saxophone ●1871 Royal Albert Hall opens in London ●1883 Metropolitan Opera House opens in New York
armonic Society founded ●1860 Eisteddford re-inaugurated in Wales
●1853 Heinrich Steinweg starts Steinway piano factory in New York ●1876 Purcell Society founded ●1886 The celesta invented by Charles Mustel

○1854 Crimean War begins ○1865 American Civil War ends. Lincoln assassinated Henry Ford makes his first car 1893 ○
lutions in France, Germany, Italy and Central Europe ○1869 Suez Canal opened ○1876 Bell invents telephone ○1889 Second Socialist International
○1859 Darwin's *Origin of Species* published ○1884 French protectorate established in Indo-China

Borodin

Tchaikovsky

Brahms

Dvořák

After 1900

1900 1910 1920 1930 1940

Schoenberg ♩1906 *Chamber Symphony* ♩1920 *Five Orchestral Pieces* ●1933 Emigrates to USA ♩19
Puccini ♩1900 *Tosca*, opera ♩1910 *The Girl of the Golden West*, opera ● **Peter Maxwell Davis** English composer born 1
Mahler ● **Leonard Bernstein** American composer, pianist and conductor born 1918 ♩1944 **Bernstein**
Willem Pijper Dutch composer 1894–1947
Aaron Copland American composer born 1900 ♩1925 **Copland** Symphony for organ and orchestra ♩1944 **Copland**
Serge Prokofiev Russian composer 1891–1953 ♩1917 *Classical* symphony ♩1935 *Romeo and Juliet*, ballet ♩1944 *War and Pe*
Bartók ♩1908 First string quartet ♩1926 *The Miraculous Mandarin*, mime-play ●1940 Moves to USA
Massenet ● **Pierre Boulez** French composer and conductor born 1925
Sibelius ♩1902 Second symphony ♩1915 Fifth symphony ♩1923 Sixth symphony
Berg ●1904 Studies with Schoenberg ♩1925 *Wozzeck*, opera ● **John Lennon** English singe
Elgar ♩1901 *Cockaigne*, overture ♩1910 Violin Concerto ♩1919 Cello Concerto ● **Richard Rodney Bennett** English compo
Toscanini ●1928 Conductor of New York Philharmonic Orchestra
Paderewski ●1909 Directs Warsaw Conservatory
● **Olivier Messiaen** French composer born 1908 ● **Yannis Xenakis** Greek composer born 1922 ♩1941 **Messiaen** Quartet
● **Michael Tippett** English composer born 1905 ● **Thelonious Monk** American jazz musician born 1920 ♩1941 **Tippett** *A Child of O*
● **Dmitri Shostakovich** Russian composer 1906–1975 ♩1925 First symphony ♩1934 *Lady Macbeth of Mzensk*, opera ♩1944 Eig
● **William Walton** English composer born 1902 ♩1923 **Walton** *Façade*, entertainment ♩1941 **Walton** *Scapi*
Francis Poulenc French composer 1899–1963 1923 *Les Biches*, ballet
Rimsky-Korsakov **Benjamin Britten** English composer 1913–1976 *Fantasy Quartet* 1934♩ *The Rape of Lucretia*, opera 1946 ♩
●**Hans Werner Henze** German composer born 1926
Paul Hindemith German composer 1895–1963 ♩1938 *Mathis der Maler*, opera ♩1945 *Lu*
Arthur Bliss English composer 1891–1975 ♩1922 *Colour Symphony* ♩1
Stravinsky ♩1910 *The Firebird*, ballet ♩1918 *The Soldier's Tale*, stage work ♩1930 *Symphony of Psalms*, choral work
Rachmaninov ♩1901 Second piano concerto ●1918 Moves to USA ♩1934 *Rhapsody on a Theme of Paganini*, for piano a
Ravel ♩1901 *Jeux d'eau*, piano piece ♩1912 *Daphnis and Chloe*, ballet ♩1928 *Bolero*, orchestra work
Bloch ♩1916 *Schelomo*, for cello and orchestra
Debussy ♩1905 *La Mer*, orchestral piece ● **Charlie Parker** American jazz musician 1920–1955 ● **Elvis Presley** American rock 'n' roll sing
Holst ♩1920 *The Planets*, orchestral suite ● **Paul McCartney** Engl
Vaughan Williams ♩1910 *Sea* symphony ♩1922 *Pastoral* symphony ♩1943 Fifth symphor
George Gershwin American composer 1898–1937 ♩1923 *Rhapsody in Blue* ♩1935 *Porgy and Bess*, opera
● **John Cage** American composer born 1912
Fauré ● **Malcolm Williamson** Australian composer born 1931
● **Lennox Berkeley** English composer born 1903 ● **Ella Fitzgerald** American jazz singer born 1918
Grainger ●1901 Moves to London ●1914 Settles in USA
Saint-Saëns ● **Maria Callas** Greek-Italian singer 1923–1977
Delius ♩1902 *Appalachia*, choral work ♩1912 *On Hearing the First Cuckoo in Spring*, orchestral work
Richard Strauss ♩1905 *Salome*, opera ♩1911 *Der Rosenkavalier*, opera ♩1948 *F*
Parry ● **Margot Fonteyn** English ballerina born 1919
Dvořák ♩1901 *Russalka*, opera ● **Yehudi Menuhin** American violinist born 1916
Grieg ● **Herbert von Karajan** Austrian conductor born 1908 ● **Karlheinz Stockhausen** German composer born 1928
Ives ♩1906 *The Unanswered Question*, chamber work
Arthur Honegger Swiss composer 1892–1955
Satie ●1905 Enters Schola Cantorum ♩1919 *Socrate*, symphonic drama
Janáček ♩1904 *Jenůfa*, opera ♩1926 *Glagolitic Mass* ●1935 Electronic Hammond organs popular in U
●1901 Wigmore Hall opens in London ●1916 Jazz becomes widely popular in USA ●1935 Swing develops from jazz
●1907 Ziegfeld Follies staged in New York ●1924 Lev Theremin (USSR) invents first electronic musical instrument ●19
●1901 Ragtime develops in USA ●1919 Los Angeles Symphony Orchestra gives first concert ●1944 Oxford Univer
○1911 Roald Amundsen reaches South Pole ○1926 General Strike in Great Britain ○1939 Second World War begins
○1903 Wright brothers make first controlled flight, in USA ○1929 Wall Street Crash, USA: world economic crisis
○1907 First exhibition of Cubist painting, Paris ○1920 Treaty of Versailles: League of Nations established ○1941 Hitler invades USS
○1914 First World War begins ○1924 Lenin dies: Stalin assumes power

Rimsky-Korsakov

Satie

Ravel

Prokofiev

) 1960 1970

-vivor from Warsaw, orchestral piece

Town, musical ♩1957 **Bernstein** *West Side Story*, musical ♩1972 **Bernstein** Mass

palachian Spring, ballet

ra

♩1958 **Boulez** *Le Visage nuptial*, cantata

gwriter, member of the Beatles born 1940

1936 ♩1965 **Bennett** *The Mines of Sulphur*, opera

●1954 Retires

e, oratorio ♩1962 **Tippett** *King Priam*, opera

phony ♩1962 Twelfth symphony ♩1972 Fifteenth symphony

rture ♩1957 **Walton** Cello Concerto

951 *Billy Budd*, opera ♩1961 *War Requiem* ♩1974 *Death in Venice*, opera

alis, piano work

Olympians, opera

51 *The Rake's Progress*, opera

nestra

5–1977

er/songwriter, member of the Beatles, born 1942

♩1953 *Sinfonia Antarctica*

♩1954 **Berkeley** *Nelson*, opera

Songs

♩1952 **Stockhausen** *Electronic Study 1* ♩1971 **Stockhausen** *Hymnen*, electronic work

●1958 First commercial stereophonic records produced

●1965 Pirate radio stations broadcasting pop music 24 hours a day

●1954 First Newport Jazz Festival, USA ●1969 Woodstock Pop Festival: 300,000 in audience

●1954 First rock 'n' roll hit record: "Rock around the Clock", Bill Haley and the Comets

long-playing record produced in USA ●1963 "Beatlemania" begins

tutes a faculty of music ●1967 Monterey International Pop Festival

○1952 First hydrogen bomb exploded, by Americans ○1971 American astronauts land on Moon

○1957 European Economic Community formed

enters War ○1961 Yuri Gagarin (USSR) first man in space. Cuban missile crisis

0 India becomes a republic. Korean War begins ○1968 Student unrest in France, Germany, USA and Japan. Soviet armies invade Czechoslovakia

Sibelius

Stravinsky

Shostakovich

Stockhausen

8
molto
riten.
p
1 2 3 4 5 6 7 8 9 10 11 12 13 14 15 16
21 22 23 24 25 26 27

VI The Glossaries

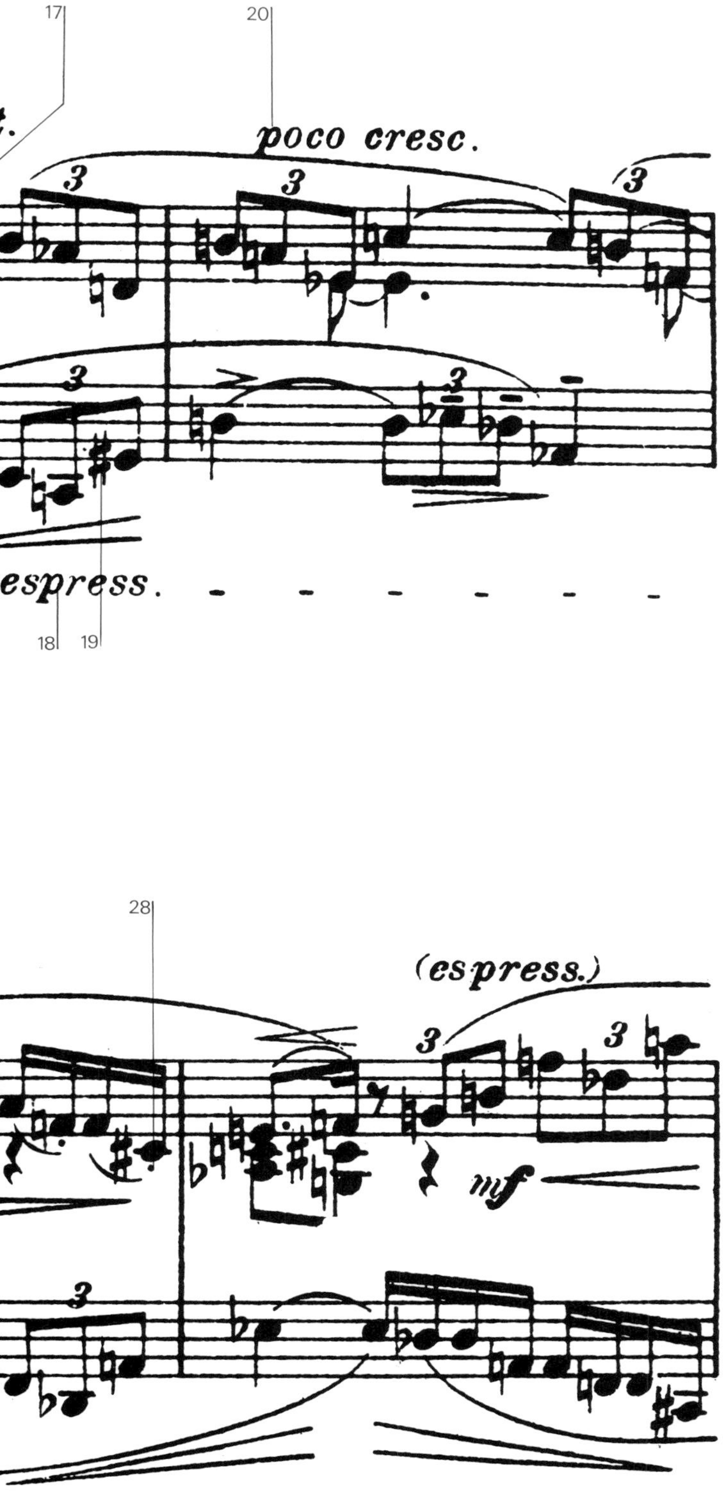

The glossaries which follow provide summaries of composers' lives and works, explanations of technical terms and basic descriptions of most of the musical instruments referred to in the main text. Used as a point of reference, the entries will clarify and in some cases amplify any points which for reasons of space may have been too briefly dealt with earlier in the book.

1 Treble clef
2 Bass clef
3 Key signature
4 Stave
5 Play an octave higher
6 Accent
7 Natural
8 Flat
9 Bar line
10 Phrase mark
11 *Diminuendo*: get softer
12 *Ritenuto*: hold back the tempo
13 Quaver triplet
14 Pause
15 Make a slight break between phrases
16 *Piano*: soft
17 *Pianissimo*: very soft
18 *Molto espressivo*: very expressively
19 Sharp
20 *Poco crescendo*: get slightly louder
21 Quaver rest
22 Crotchet rest
23 *Crescendo*: get louder
24 Weight touch
25 Tie
26 *Mezzo-forte*: moderately loud
27 Ledger lines
28 *Staccato*: detached

Extract from Alban Berg's Piano Sonata, op. 1 (bars 67–75) by permission of the publishers Robert Lienau, Berlin.

Glossary of Composers

J. S. Bach

Bartók

Bellini

Berlioz

Adam de la Halle (*c.*1230 or 1240–*c.*1287) French trouvère, poet, dramatist and composer. The best-known of his many surviving works is the pastoral drama *Le Jeu de Robin et de Marion* ("The Play of Robin and Marion", dialogue and songs). His other works include chansons, rondeaus and three-part motets.

Albéniz, Isaac (1860–1909) Spanish nationalist composer who first appeared as a pianist at the age of four. As well as operas and orchestral pieces he wrote 250 piano works. His masterpiece is the *Iberia* suite.

Albinoni, Tommaso (1671–1750) Italian violinist, singer and composer of operas and *concerti grossi*. Bach is said to have studied his work with interest.

Arnold, Malcolm (1921–) British composer, formerly principal trumpeter with the London Philharmonic Orchestra. His works include six symphonies; concertos for horn, clarinet, piano, oboe and harmonica; overtures *The Smoke* and *Tam o'Shanter*; ballets, chamber music and film music.

Auric, Georges (1899–) French composer, the youngest of "The Six". Besides film music, his works include ballets, operas and piano music.

Bach, Carl Philipp Emanuel (1714–88) German composer, the third son of J. S. Bach. He was a noted keyboard performer and an important pioneer of sonata form and the symphonic style of composition perfected by Haydn and Mozart. As court musician to Frederick the Great and later director of music in Hamburg, his prolific output included many symphonies and keyboard compositions.

Bach, Johann Christoph (1735–82) German composer, the eleventh and youngest son of J. S. Bach. Known as "the English Bach", he lived nearly twenty-five years in London as music teacher to the royal family and an opera and concert director. His compositions include operas, symphonies and keyboard works.

Bach, Johann Sebastian (1685–1750) German composer, born at Eisenach; the most distinguished of a long line of musicians, in whom the baroque era reached its peak. In his lifetime, Bach was chiefly famous as an organist and his style of composition was regarded as rather dated. Only later was the universal appeal of his music recognized. Before he became cantor at the school of St Thomas's church, Leipzig, Bach had been church organist at Arnstadt and Mülhausen and later court musician at Weimar. Twice married, he had twenty children, several of whom became famous musicians in their own right. He died in Leipzig, having gone blind a year earlier. Bach's vast output as a workaday composer can be divided into three groups: organ works; instrumental and orchestral works (including concertos, suites and keyboard works); and religious choral works (including motets, cantatas, Passions, oratorios and masses).

Balakirev, Mily (1837–1910) Russian composer, a founder of the group of pioneer nationalist composers called "The Five". His best-known compositions are the symphonic poem *Thamar* and the oriental piano fantasy *Islamey*. He also wrote two symphonies, and an overture and incidental music to Shakespeare's *King Lear*.

Barber, Samuel (1910–) A leading neo-romantic American composer. Born in Pennsylvania, he studied at the Curtis Institute in Philadelphia and won the American Rome Prize in 1935. He later won two Pulitzer Prizes for his opera *Vanessa* and his first piano concerto. Among the best-known of his earlier works are the *Adagio for Strings* and overture to *The School for Scandal*.

Bartók, Béla (1881–1945) Hungarian composer, one of the leading nationalists and modernists of the earlier twentieth century. He studied at the Budapest Conservatory and became known as a brilliant pianist. Bartók's earlier style was influenced by the German romantics, but his interest in East European folk music led him to develop a new, tonally original style. He emigrated to the USA in 1940, where he died in poverty five years later. Bartók's many compositions include stage works, orchestral and choral music, string quartets, violin sonatas and piano works and folk-song arrangements. He also collected thousands of folk-tunes.

Bax, Arnold (1883–1953) British composer who studied at the Royal Academy of Music. A prolific composer, his works include seven symphonies, the symphonic poems *The Garden of Fand* and *Tintagel*, concertos for violin and cello, chamber music and piano works.

Beethoven, Ludwig van (1770–1827) German composer, one of the outstanding figures of Western music, whose work is a unique testimony to the human spirit. He is often considered to have been the last classical and the first romantic composer. The son of a court singer, Beethoven was born in Bonn, where he became a teenage court musician. Visiting Vienna when seventeen, he had some teaching from Mozart. At twenty-two he settled there, continuing composition studies with Haydn and Albrechtsberger. Viennese society welcomed Beethoven as Mozart's heir, first as pianist and then as composer. In Vienna Beethoven never had a paid post, becoming history's first "freelance" composer. Troubled by failing hearing from about thirty, he nevertheless produced his greatest string quartets after he became totally deaf at forty-five. Though attractive to and attracted by many women Beethoven never married. His stormy character made life difficult, particularly in his relations with his ward and nephew Karl. As a composer he worked ceaselessly and with constant revision, sometimes throwing water over himself to revive his energies. His symphonies, overtures, concertos, piano sonatas and string quartets are considered some of the world's greatest, as is his Mass in D and his single opera *Fidelio*.

Bellini, Vincenzo (1801–35) With Donizetti and Rossini, Bellini was one of the three greatest Italian opera composers of the earlier nineteenth century. His flowing melodies showed off the voice to great advantage, and gained him immediate popularity. He was much admired by Chopin and other romantics. Bellini's best-known operas include *La sonnambula*, *Norma*, *I puritani* and *Beatrice di Tenda*.

Bennett, Richard Rodney (1936–) A leading younger British composer who studied at the Royal Academy of Music and under Pierre Boulez. He composed, in dissonant style, a successful melodramatic opera *The Mines of Sulphur*. His other works include the operas *The Ledge* and *Victory*, symphonies, chamber music and film scores.

Berg, Alban (1885–1935) Austrian twelve-note composer and uncompromising modernist who was a student and associate of Schoenberg. Berg's best-known work is the opera *Wozzeck*. His other compositions include the *Chamber Concerto* (violin, piano and wind), the *Lyric Suite* for strings, the unfinished opera *Lulu* and the posthumous violin concerto.

Berlioz, Hector (1803–69) Leading French romantic composer; also a brilliant writer and critic whose memoirs are a case-study in romantic sensibility. The son of a doctor, Berlioz gave up medical studies and took up composition, first privately and then at the Paris Conservatoire, where despite the hostility of the director, Cherubini, he won the Prix de Rome after five attempts. His compositions are mostly programmatic, and notable for their range of literary derivation, often massive scale and imaginative orchestral colour. A characteristic unifying feature is his use of a recurring theme or *idée fixe*, as in his *Symphonie fantastique*. Berlioz's many works include overtures, symphonies, choral works, operas and songs. He was well-known as a conductor and critic, and his *Treatise on Orchestration* remains a standard work.

Bernstein, Leonard (1918–) Leading American conductor, pianist and composer. He studied at Harvard and the Curtis Institute, and became conductor of the New York Philharmonic Orchestra in 1958. His compositions include the ballet *Fancy*

Free, the musicals *West Side Story*, *On the Town* and *Candide*, the symphonies *Jeremiah* and *The Age of Anxiety*, and some chamber music.

Bizet, Georges (1838–75) French composer mainly famous for his Spanish gypsy opera *Carmen*. He studied at the Paris Conservatoire and won the Prix de Rome with an operetta, *Doctor Miracle*, but subsequent recognition was slow. Bizet died soon after the première of *Carmen* in 1875. His other works include the successful overture *La Patrie*, *L'Arlésienne* and other suites, and several little-heard operas.

Bliss, Arthur (1891–1975) British composer noted for his bold and unusual instrumental and vocal combinations. He studied at Cambridge University and at the Royal College of Music with Vaughan Williams. From 1941–4 he was musical director of the BBC, was knighted in 1950 and became Master of the Queen's Music in 1953. His works include the *Colour* symphony, opera, ballet and film music, and a piano concerto.

Bloch, Ernst (1880–1959) Swiss-born Jewish-American composer, much of whose work was based on Jewish themes. Born in Geneva, he studied there and elsewhere in Europe before entering the family clock business and composing in his spare time. His opera *Macbeth* was performed in Paris in 1910, and in 1915 Bloch emigrated to the USA, where he taught and composed. His works include the *Concerto Grosso* for piano and strings, symphonies, symphonic poems, a violin concerto, choral music and chamber music.

Blow, John (1649–1708) English composer, organist at Westminster Abbey from 1668–79 and (after Purcell's tenure) from 1695–1708. Blow's works include English and Latin anthems, the operatic masque *Venus and Adonis*, keyboard pieces and songs.

Boccherini, Luigi (1743–1805) Italian composer and near-contemporary of Haydn, who lived most of his life in Madrid. He was an outstanding cellist and a prolific composer of string trios, quartets and quintets (more than 460 pieces in all).

Borodin, Alexander (1833–87) Russian composer, one of the nationalist group called "The Five". A doctor and professor of chemistry, Borodin founded a women's medical school and was a spare-time composer. His works included two symphonies, the symphonic poem *In the Steppes of Central Asia*, three string quartets, songs and piano music. An unfinished opera, *Prince Igor*, was completed by Rimsky-Korsakov and Glazunov. The song "Stranger in Paradise" from the Hollywood musical *Kismet* was based on a theme by Borodin.

Boulanger, Nadia (1887–) French composer and internationally famous teacher of composition.

Boulez, Pierre (1925–) A leading French conductor and *avant-garde* composer. He studied with Messiaen, and his compositions show the influence of Schoenberg and Webern, and also of oriental music. Boulez also uses aleatoric (chance) techniques and electronic sounds.

Brahms, Johannes (1833–97) German composer whose work, in contrast to Wagner's, represents the more classical aspect of romanticism. The son of a Hamburg pit-musician, Brahms began his career as a café pianist. His talent as a composer was noticed and encouraged by the violinist Joachim and by Liszt and Schumann. Brahms allowed himself time to mature, writing his first symphony when middle-aged. His works include four symphonies, two piano concertos, a violin concerto and double concerto (violin and cello), chamber music, piano music and many songs and choral compositions, including the *German Requiem*.

Britten, Benjamin (1913–76) Perhaps the outstanding twentieth-century British composer, and a brilliant pianist, Britten was especially noted for his operas, choral music and songs, which showed a talent for word-setting that rivalled Purcell's. A boy prodigy, he studied at school with Frank Bridge and at the Royal Academy with John Ireland. With singer Peter Pears and others, Britten founded the English Opera Group and the Aldeburgh Festival after World War II. His compositions, evolutionary rather than *avant-garde* in style, include eight operas (e.g. *Peter Grimes* and *The Turn of the Screw*), many choral works and songs, and orchestral and film music.

Bruch, Max (1838–1920) Long-lived German composer who was well known for his choral and orchestral works and violin and cello concertos. He conducted the Liverpool Philharmonic Society from 1880–83.

Bruckner, Anton (1824–96) Austrian composer especially noted for his nine symphonies. Like Brahms, he was a classic-romantic in style, but showed some Wagnerian influence. At first a village church organist, Bruckner became a famous soloist before settling in Vienna and concentrating on composition. Apart from his symphonies, Bruckner wrote several masses and other choral works as well as songs, chamber music and organ works.

Busoni, Ferruccio Benvenuto (1866–1924). Italian-Austrian composer and pianist. Busoni's compositions, which became "anti-romantic" in style, included songs, orchestral, chamber and piano music and four operas. He was considered one of the finest pianists of his time.

Buxtehude, Dietrich (1637–1707) Danish-born composer who, as *Kapellmeister* at Lübeck, was the most famous organist of his time; the young J. S. Bach walked 200 miles to hear him. Buxtehude's compositions include cantatas, chorale preludes and organ works.

Byrd, William (1543–1623) English composer, with Palestrina and Victoria one of the greatest of the later polyphonists, whose varied outpost included sacred and secular choral music and instrumental music. Byrd excelled as a madrigalist and was a major pioneer of keyboard composition.

Caccini, Giulio (*c*.1546–1618) Italian composer who, with Monteverdi and others, marked the shift from polyphony to homophony. His *Euridice*, staged in 1602, was one of the first operas, and he pioneered the monodic song style in his collection *Le nuove musiche*.

Cage, John (1912–) A leading American *avant-gardist*, some of whose works emphasize random natural sounds and silence. He studied with Henry Cowell and Arnold Schoenberg. Cage's compositions include music for "prepared piano" and twelve radio sets, *The Seasons* (ballet) and *Construction in Metal*. Cage has also written interestingly about his ideas.

Carissimi, Giacomo (*c*.1605–1674) A leading member of the second generation of Italian monodic composers, who developed recitative and brought greater instrumental variety to cantata and oratorio. Carissimi wrote five oratorios, of which *Jephtha* is still performed.

Cavalieri, Emilio de' (*c*.1550–1602) Italian composer, one of the group of early operatic experimenters, whose music drama *La rappresentazione dell'anima e del corpore* was performed in the Oratory of St Philip Neri, Rome, in 1600 and is therefore traditionally cited as the first oratorio. Cavalieri was also the first to use a figured bass.

Cavalli, Pietro Francesco (1602–76) A leading member of the second generation of Italian monodic composers, who wrote operas, cantatas and oratorios. Cavalli helped establish opera in France with a performance of his *Xerxes* for Louis XIV's marriage in 1660.

Cesti, Marcantonio (1623–69) A leading member of the second generation of Italian monodists, whose compositions included operas, cantatas and canzonets. Cesti's best-known work, *Il pomo d'oro*, began a new fashion in court opera.

Cherubini, Luigi (1760–1842) Prolific Italian composer of operas and church music. As director of the Paris Conservatoire, he was the *bête noire* of Berlioz, but was admired by Beethoven and Mendelssohn. Cherubini was a learned writer of and on counterpoint.

Chopin, Fryderyk, or **Frédéric** (1810–49) Polish piano virtuoso and

Bizet

Bliss

Bloch

Britten

Copland

Debussy

Delius

Elgar

composer, almost entirely for piano, Chopin was the archetypal romantic musician. Though he spent most of his adult life in Paris, Chopin's music was often inspired by patriotic feeling for Poland and he wrote many mazurkas and polonaises – national dances of his homeland. Besides these, his works include *études*, scherzos, preludes, nocturnes, waltzes, impromptus, sonatas and concertos.

Cimarosa, Domenico (1749–1801) Operatic composer, sometimes called "the Italian Mozart", who had a special talent for light-hearted comedy. Cimarosa wrote more than sixty operas, two of the most successful being *Il matrimonio segreto* and *Astuzie Feminile*.

Coleridge-Taylor, Samuel (1875–1912) British composer (of Anglo-African parentage), best known for his *Hiawatha* cantata trilogy. As a child he was a violinist and choirboy, and later studied at the Royal College of Music under Stanford. Before his early death Coleridge-Taylor established himself as a refreshingly original composer with a varied output including choral works, songs, orchestral works, chamber music and works for piano and violin.

Copland, Aaron (1900–) A leading twentieth-century American composer whose varied works include ballets, operas, and symphonies, and piano, chamber and film music. Born in Brooklyn, New York, he learned piano and became interested in composition as a teenager, later studying in Paris with Paul Vidal and Nadia Boulanger. Back in the USA, Copland gained public success and a Guggenheim scholarship for his organ concerto. After a period of austere, complex works in the early 1930s, Copland widened his appeal with music based on folk themes, such as *El Salón México*, for orchestra, and the ballet *Billy the Kid*. His ballet *Appalachian Spring* received the 1945 Pulitzer Prize and his third symphony was acclaimed as one of the finest works by an American composer. Copland is also a noted conductor, writer and lecturer on music.

Corelli, Arcangelo (1653–1713) Italian composer, among the greatest of the baroque period, whose outstanding talent as a violinist, violin teacher and composer for the violin hastened the obsolescence of the older viol and shaped later musical developments, particularly that of the concerto. Corelli wrote sixty sonatas and twelve *concerti grossi* for strings, in a style that sounds like a lighter, Italianate version of Bach (whom he considerably influenced).

Couperin, François (1668–1733) The best-known of a dynasty of French musicians (extending, like the German Bachs, over many generations), known as "the Great" to distinguish him from his relations. Couperin was organist for Louis XIV at Versailles and at St Gervais in Paris. He wrote organ music, choral works, chamber music and songs, but is particularly remembered for his fine harpsichord pieces, many of which are early examples of programmatic music.

Cui, César (1835–1918) Russian composer, one of the nationalist group called "The Five". Of French ancestry, Cui was a professional soldier and wrote music in his spare time. His works, some of them on a large scale, included operas, songs and piano music.

Debussy, Achille-Claude (1862–1918) French composer who was the founder of musical impressionism. His style, like that of the French impressionist painters and symbolist poets with whom he associated, had an atmospheric quality which in its understatement and avoidance of formalism was a reaction against both romanticism and classicism. Debussy's originality partly stemmed from his use of the whole-tone scale and chords based on the harmonic series. He entered the Paris Conservatoire as a piano student at twelve, winning the Prix de Rome at twenty-two. At thirty-two he achieved success with the orchestral tone-poem *Prèlude à l'après-midi d'un faune*, inspired by a poem of Mallarmé. Debussy's other works include the opera *Pelléas et Mélisande*, orchestral and incidental music, a string quartet and many piano pieces and songs.

Delibes, Léo (1836–91) French composer of successful ballets and operas, notable for the ease and grace of their melody, harmony and scoring. His best-known works include the ballets *Coppélia* and *Sylvia* and the operas *Lakmé* and *Roi l'a dit*.

Delius, Frederick (1862–1934) British-born composer of German parentage who wrote highly individual music in a romantic-impressionist vein. After growing oranges in Florida (where he was influenced by Negro songs) and teaching piano in Virginia, Delius studied at Leipzig, where in 1889 his music had its first public performance. He lived in France from his middle thirties, and though blind and crippled in later life he continued to compose with the help of his amanuensis Eric Fenby. Delius's large output included operas, orchestral works, concertos, choral works, chamber music and songs.

Després, Josquin (*c.*1450–1521) Flemish composer whose music linked the polyphonic style of the earlier and later Renaissance. A pupil of Ockeghem, he was a singer at the Papal chapel in Rome, and helped introduce the northern polyphonic style to Italy. His compositions, notable for their expressiveness, include masses, motets and other church music, and lively secular chansons.

Donizetti, Gaetano (1797–1848) Together with Rossini and Bellini, Donizetti was one of the great Italian opera composers of the earlier nineteenth century. His melodies were both attractive and technically demanding, giving singers ample opportunity to display tone and technique. Donizetti's best-known operas include *Don Pasquale*, *L'elisir d'amore* and *Lucia di Lammermoor*.

Dowland, John (1562–1626) Irish-born lutenist, the greatest of his day, and composer. His songs were mostly for singing in four parts (i.e. as madrigals) or as solos with lute accompaniment. Dowland was lutenist at the Danish and English courts.

Dufay, Guillaume (pre-1400–1474) The greatest Flemish composer of the fifteenth century. First a chorister at Cambrai cathedral, Dufay joined the papal choir in Rome, later studying in Paris and taking holy orders before returning to Cambrai where he spent his last thirty years. Dufay wrote polyphonic masses and motets, and also much lively secular music. His greatest mass, *Se la face ay pale* ("If my face is pale"), was based on his chanson of the same name, which was a popular tune of the times.

Dukas, Paul (1865–1935) French composer noted for his vivid, descriptive style in works such as his orchestral scherzo *The Sorcerer's Apprentice*, ballet *La Péri* and opera *Ariane et Barbe-bleue*. He studied at the Paris Conservatoire, where he later became professor of composition.

Dunstable, John (?–1453) One of the greatest English polyphonic composers, whose works included masses, motets and secular songs. Dunstable had an international reputation and his manuscripts circulated throughout the musical centres of Europe. He was also a mathematician and astrologer.

Dvořák, Antonín (1841–1904) Czech composer, together with Smetana the founder of the Czech nationalist school. The son of a village butcher and publican, Dvořák was born near Prague, where he went to study music at sixteen. His works began to be performed in the early 1870s, and he received a government stipend and encouragement from Brahms. He finally became professor of composition at the Prague Conservatory and from 1892–5 was in the USA as director of the National Conservatory in New York, where he wrote his best-known work, the symphony *From the New World*. His many works included nine symphonies, and choral works, operas, chamber music, songs and dances. Czech and other Slavic folk music inspired some of Dvořák's themes.

Elgar, Edward (1857–1934) British

composer, usually regarded as the greatest of his time, best-known for his *Enigma Variations*, a series of orchestral portraits of his friends. Among his other compositions are choral works, including the oratorio *The Dream of Gerontius*; three symphonies (one unfinished) and other orchestral works; a violin and a cello concerto and chamber music and songs. The son of an organist and bookseller, Elgar was born near Worcester and was self-taught in composition.

Falla, Manuel de (1876–1946) A leading Spanish nationalist composer, perhaps best-known for his popular ballet *The Three-Cornered Hat*. He spent several years in Paris, where he associated with Debussy and Ravel. Falla's compositions were much influenced by his keen interest in Spanish folk-music. They include operas, ballets, pieces for piano and orchestra, a harpsichord concerto, a guitar solo and some songs.

Farnaby, Giles (*c*.1560–1640) Long-lived English composer of Tudor and Stuart times, remembered for his fine madrigals and pioneering keyboard music. More than fifty of his pieces are in the *Fitzwilliam Virginal Book*.

Fauré, Gabriel Urbain (1845–1924) French composer whose many works, including songs, opera and chamber music, combined classical balance and romantic expression. A church musician for many years, Fauré became composition professor at the Paris Conservatoire (including among his pupils Ravel and Boulanger) and later its director. He is particularly remembered for his fine Requiem.

Franck, César Auguste (1822–90) Franco-Belgian composer, a prominent figure in French nineteenth-century romanticism. During his lifetime he was chiefly known as a church organist and teacher, becoming organ professor at the Paris Conservatoire at fifty. Franck's first major public success came shortly before his death with his string quartet, but he had a devoted circle of student-disciples, including D'Indy and Duparc. Among his works are a symphony and other orchestral music, two symphonic poems, the *Symphonic Variations* for piano and orchestra, a sonata for violin and piano and organ compositions.

Frescobaldi, Girolamo (1583–1643) Italian composer of the early baroque period and one of the greatest organists of his day. His works include organ and harpsichord music, motets and madrigals. Through pupils such as Froberger he strongly influenced German music.

Fux, Johann Joseph (1660–1741) Leading Austrian composer and theorist who was court composer and *Kapellmeister* to the imperial court at Vienna. He wrote many masses, operas and other music, and is particularly remembered for his counterpoint treatise *Gradus ad Parnassum* ("Steps to Parnassus").

Gabrieli, Andrea (*c*.1510–86) A leading Italian composer of the later Renaissance. He was a pupil of the Flemish master Adriaan Willaert, under whom he served as a singer at St Mark's, Venice, where he later became organist. Gabrieli's compositions include motets, madrigals and organ pieces, and ceremonial music for brass.

Gabrieli, Giovanni (1557–1612) Italian composer who succeeded his uncle, Andrea Gabrieli, as organist at St Mark's, Venice, and was equally noted. He wrote organ music and sacred and secular vocal music, and developed the role of the orchestra in accompaniment. The German composer Heinrich Schütz was his pupil.

Gershwin, George (1898–1937) American composer and pianist whose synthesis of American styles (jazz and blues) with impressionist harmony was a major influence on twentieth-century American music. Gershwin's greatest work, the Negro opera *Porgy and Bess*, is probably the best-known American opera. Among his other works are several compositions for piano and orchestra, including *Rhapsody in Blue* and the Piano Concerto in F, and the symphonic poem *An American in Paris*. Gershwin also wrote many musical comedies, including *Lady be Good* and *Of Thee I Sing*.

Gesualdo, Carlo (*c*.1560–1613) Prince of Venosa, Italy, and composer of madrigals and motets who "painted" the words of his texts with a daring and original chromaticism, heralding the break-up of the old modal system.

Gibbons, Orlando (1583–1625) Among the greatest English composers of the early seventeenth century and an important pioneer of keyboard composition, Gibbons was a boy chorister at King's College, Cambridge, and later became organist at the Chapel Royal and Westminster Abbey. He wrote church music, madrigals and music for viols and for virginals.

Glazunov, Alexander (1865–1936) Major Russian composer who, as a student of Rimsky-Korsakov, began as a nationalist but later adopted a more cosmopolitan style. He became director of the Leningrad Conservatory, but after the Russian Revolution emigrated to France. Glazunov's many works include eight symphonies, ballets and incidental music, and piano and violin concertos.

Glinka, Mikhail (1804–57) Russian opera composer, the father of the Russian national school. He was brought up on his father's estate, where he was in close contact with folk music, and in St Petersburg he had piano lessons. He went to Italy, where he heard Italian opera, and later studied in Berlin. The fruit of these experiences was his opera *A Life for the Tsar*, which, though Italianate, also had Russian and Polish folk influences in melody and rhythm. Glinka followed this with the opera *Russan and Ludmilla*, which laid the foundation of a truly national style. His other works include orchestral pieces, such as the Russian folk-fantasia *Kamarinskaya*, and two pieces inspired by Spanish folk music, *Jota Aragonese* and *Night in Madrid*.

Gluck, Christoph Willibald von (1714–87) German-born composer, of cosmopolitan career and style, who was one of the greatest eighteenth-century opera writers. Against the contemporary Italian style, with its emphasis on vocal virtuosity, Gluck championed a return to the dramatic ideals of early Italian opera. This dramatic emphasis made Gluck a hero of Berlioz and ranks him as a forerunner of Wagner. As well as his many operas (about forty-five, including *Orfeo*, *Alceste* and *Iphigénie en Aulide*) Gluck wrote four ballets, nine overtures (called "symphonies"), instrumental pieces and some vocal works.

Goehr, Alexander (1932–) A leading younger British contemporary composer, Goehr studied at the Paris Conservatoire with Messiaen. His has written orchestral, vocal and chamber music, much of it in contrapuntal style and using serial technique.

Gounod, Charles François (1818–1893) Popular nineteenth-century French composer of religious choral music, and operas. Among his works are fourteen operas, including *Faust*, *Sappho* and *Roméo et Juliette*; three symphonies, nine masses and several oratorios, and many songs.

Grainger, Percy Aldridge (1882–1961) Australian-born pianist and composer. He studied in Germany with Busoni and became a friend of Grieg and a leading interpreter of his piano music. Grainger took an interest in, and based some of his compositions on, British folk music. His compositions include choral works, song arrangements, a string quartet and orchestral pieces, such as his popular *Country Gardens*. Grainger lived in London from 1912–15, and afterwards in the USA, where he became naturalized.

Granados, Enrique (1867–1916) Leading Spanish nationalist composer of operas, piano and orchestral music and songs, also a noted pianist and conductor. Granados was a pupil of Felipe Pedrell, and was influenced by Albéniz. His seven operas include *Goyescas*, partly based on a set of piano pieces inspired by the art of the painter Goya.

Grieg, Edvard Hagerup (1843–1907) Norwegian composer who became a leading musical nationalist.

Franck

Gershwin

Glinka

Grieg

Holst

Honegger

Ives

Janáček

Encouraged by Ole Bull, he studied in Leipzig and Copenhagen. Grieg's music, strongly influenced by Norwegian folk music, combines an attractive simplicity with harmonic originality. His works include his ever-popular piano concerto, the *Peer Gynt* suite, choral works, two string quartets (one unfinished), violin sonatas, songs, piano pieces and folk-music arrangements. He wrote no symphonies or operas.

Halévy, Jacques François (1799–1862) French composer best-known for his operas, including the grand opera *La Juive* ("The Jewess") and the comic opera *L'Éclair*. A pupil of Cherubini at the Paris Conservatoire, Halévy was influenced by Meyerbeer. He wrote more than thirty operas, mostly in grand style, and ballets, cantatas and other compositions.

Handel, George Frideric (1685–1759) German-born composer who, with Bach, represents the culmination of the baroque period, but, unlike Bach, was a cosmopolitan musical businessman. Born in Saxony, Handel took up music against his father's wishes and became a violinist in the Hamburg opera. When in Italy (1706–10), he absorbed Italian influences and gained a reputation as an organist and harpsichordist. On his return he became *Kapellmeister* to the Elector of Hanover (later George I of England), but soon went to London. There he remained, becoming naturalized in 1727. From the age of sixty Handel gradually lost his sight and was completely blind for the last six years of his life. Handel reigned supreme in London, first with his Italian-style operas, including *Rinaldo*, *Berenice* and *Julius Caesar*, and then with his many English biblical oratorios, of which the *Messiah* is the greatest. Handel's other works include the *Water Music* and *Music for the Royal Fireworks* for orchestra, *concerti grossi* for strings and for strings and wind, organ concertos, harpsichord sonatas and cantatas.

Hauer, Josef Matthias (1883–1959) Austrian composer who developed a twelve-note technique independently of and possibly before Schoenberg, in which the twelve notes of the chromatic scale were grouped into patterns called "tropes". His works included concertos for piano and violin, chamber music, songs and the cantata *The Way of Humanity*.

Haydn, Franz Joseph (1732–1809) Prolific Austrian composer, the senior member of the Haydn-Mozart-Beethoven triumvirate of classical composers, whose development of C. P. E. Bach's sonata-symphony form and style earned him the title of "Father of the Symphony". The son of a village wheelwright, Haydn was born in Rohrau, Lower Austria, and was much influenced by the folk music of the local Croatian peasantry. At eight, he became a choirboy at St Steven's Cathedral in Vienna, where he later became a student of the Italian composer Porpora. After becoming musical director to the Esterházy household, Haydn achieved an international reputation, especially for his symphonies and string quartets (which form he also pioneered). He visited London twice, where he was highly popular, and wrote twelve *London* symphonies. Haydn's vast output includes 104 listed symphonies, eighty-four string quartets, 125 string trios and more than twenty operas, as well as oratorios, concertos, sonatas, keyboard works and songs.

Henze, Hans Werner (1926–) A leading contemporary German composer who studied with Leibowitz and Fortner, and has used the twelve-note system. Among his works are the operas *Boulevard Solitude*, *King Stag* and *The Bassarids*; ballets, including *The Idol* and *Ondine*; three symphonies; concertos for piano and violin; cantatas; and *Dance Marathon* for jazz band and symphony orchestra.

Hindemith, Paul (1895–1963) German composer, viola-player, teacher and theorist. His early works were marked by dissonant atonality, but he later reverted to an advanced tonal style based on his investigations of natural harmonics. For a time, Hindemith was also a leading exponent, under the inspiration of dramatist Bertholt Brecht, of a functional, educational style of *Gebrauchsmusik* ("music for use"). Born near Frankfurt, Hindemith became a composition teacher at the Berlin State Conservatory in the late 1920s, but left Germany after the Nazis banned him for "musical degeneracy", and eventually settled in the United States. His many and varied works include the operas *Mathis der Maler* and *The Harmony of the World* (on both of which he based symphonies); several ballets; a symphony in E-flat and many other orchestral works; string quartets, sonatas and songs.

Holst, Gustav Theodore (1874–1934) British composer (of part-Swedish descent), also pianist, trombonist, conductor and teacher. He was a pupil of Stanford, and developed a boldly experimental, austere style, using devices such as polytonality. His interest in oriental philosophy led him to make settings of the Hindu scriptures in his own translation, such as the one-act opera *Sāvitri*. Holst's compositions include orchestral pieces such as *The Planets* (his best-known work) and *Egdon Heath*, music for brass and military band, the choral *Hymn of Jesus*, and songs.

Honegger, Arthur (1892–1955) French-born Swiss composer. He studied with Widor and D'Indy and became one of the group known as "The Six". His works, often in declamatory, dissonant style, include several operas, five symphonies and other orchestral works, flute and piano music, and film music.

Hummel, Johann Nepomuk (1778–1837) German composer, taught by Haydn, and pianist, who was taught by Mozart and in turn taught Czerny. He wrote concertos and other piano works, and operas and church music.

Humperdinck, Engelbert (1854–1921) German composer best known for his children's opera *Hansel and Gretel*. He was Wagner's friend and assistant.

Ibert, Jacques (1890–1962) French composer who was a pupil of Fauré and became director of the French Academy in Rome. His works, often light in style, include several operas, a symphonic poem based on Oscar Wilde's *The Ballad of Reading Jail* and other orchestral music, the *Concertino da Camera* for saxophone, and piano pieces.

Indy, Vincent d' (1851–1931) French composer, a pupil and follower of César Franck, and Wagner enthusiast. He was a founder of the Paris Schola Cantorum and later taught at the Conservatoire. Among his compositions are six operas, including *Fervaal*; three symphonies including *Symphony on a French Mountaineer's Song*; a triple concerto (flute, cello, piano and orchestra); and songs, piano works and much chamber music.

Ireland, John (1879–1962) British composer, pianist and organist. Taught by Stanford, he destroyed his early works (up to 1908). His published works, in a personal though broadly romantic style, include a piano concerto and many other piano works, various orchestral works, a cantata and many songs. He wrote no symphonies, operas or ballet scores.

Ives, Charles (1874–1954) American composer whose work, the calibre of which has only recently been recognized, ranks him as one of his country's most original musical thinkers. He made use of polytonality, polyrhythms, quarter-tone intervals and musical "collages" with many simultaneous themes. He had a career in insurance, through which he supported his own musical activities as well as those of other composers, such as Carl Ruggles. Ives's compositions include his *Concord* piano sonata, five symphonies, *Three Places in New England* for orchestra, and songs.

Janáček, Leoš (1854–1928) Czech composer and choral conductor whose study of Czech folk music greatly influenced his nationalist style. Among his works are eleven operas including *Jenůfa* and *Katya Kabanová*, the *Glagolitic Mass* and many other choral works; the sinfonietta *Taras Bulba* and other orchestral works; and songs and folk-song arrangements.

Joachim, Joseph (1831–1907) Hungarian violinist, considered the greatest of his day, and composer. He lived mainly in Germany, and befriended and encouraged the young Brahms. His compositions include three violin concertos.

John of Fornsete (13th century) English monk of Reading Abbey, possibly the composer of "Sumer Is Icumin In", the oldest extant canon and six-part composition.

Kern, Jerome (1885–1945) American composer of markedly original popular songs, especially in musicals such as *Show Boat*. He also wrote some "serious" works, including *Portrait of Mark Twain* for orchestra.

Khatchaturian, Aram (1903–) Russian-Armenian composer whose works, many influenced by Armenian folk music, include a concerto each for piano, violin and cello; symphonies, ballets and choral and chamber music. He was twenty before he took up music, studying at the Moscow Conservatory with Miaskovsky and Gnessin. Though he became one of the leading Soviet composers he was rebuked for "formalism" in 1948, but has remained active.

Kodály, Zoltán (1882–1967) Leading Hungarian composer, whose strongly national idiom was influenced by the Hungarian folk songs he collected, partly with his friend Bartók. His best-known works include the opera *Háry János* and the orchestral suite based on this, and the *Psalmus Hungaricus* for tenor, chorus and orchestra. Among Kodály's other works are operas, orchestral and choral works, piano music, chamber music and songs. As a renowned teacher, Kodály was called upon to reform Hungary's school music curriculum, and his methods have led to a high level of musical literacy among Hungarian children.

Krenek, Ernst (1900–) Austrian-born composer (partly Czech) who emigrated to the USA in 1938. A pupil of Shreker, he used jazz influences in his successful opera *Johnny Spielt Aus* ("Johnny Strikes Up"), and later used the twelve-note technique, free atonality and electronic music. His works include symphonies, piano concertos, the *Symphonic Elegy* for strings (in memory of Webern) and the choral *Santa Fé Time-Table*.

Kreutzer, Rodolphe (1766–1831) French violinist and composer of many violin concertos, operas and other works. Beethoven dedicated the *Kreutzer* sonata to him.

Lambert, Constant (1905–51) British composer, arranger, conductor and critic. Among his works are the choral-orchestral *Rio Grande* and a piano concerto (both jazz-influenced), and several ballets, orchestral works, songs and film music.

Landini, Francesco (*c.*1325–1397) Italian composer of vocal music in the *Ars Nova* style. Blind from early childhood, he was a lutenist, organist and poet. In the "Landini sixth", a melodic cadence typical of much medieval music, the submediant is inserted between the leading-note and tonic.

Lassus, Roland de (*c.* 1530–1594) The greatest sixteenth-century Flemish composer, who with his contemporaries Palestrina, Byrd and Victoria represents the culmination of the later polyphonic era. Born at Mons, he travelled widely and spent some time in Rome before settling in Munich, where he spent over thirty years in the service of the Bavarian court. His vast output of more than 2,000 works included masses, psalms and other church music, and secular madrigals and chansons.

Leoncavallo, Ruggiero (1858–1919) Italian opera composer whose main success was *I pagliacci*. He also wrote his own version of *La Bohème*, which failed to compete with Puccini's.

Léonin (12th century) Medieval French musician of the "Notre Dame School" (at the church of Notre Dame in Paris); one of the first composers known by name. He composed in the organum style, from which polyphony evolved.

Liszt, Ferencz, or **Franz** (1811–86) Hungarian-born musician who as virtuoso pianist, composer, teacher and champion of new talent was one of the key figures of the romantic movement. First taught by his father, steward to the Esterházy family (Haydn's patrons), the boy Liszt studied piano with Czerny and composition with Salieri in Vienna, and as an eleven-year-old received public acclaim from Beethoven. As a youth he travelled to Paris and London, where he had a tumultuous reception. In Paris, he was much influenced by the painters and writers of the romantic school. As musical director at Weimar in the 1850s, Liszt encouraged many composers, including Wagner, Brahms and Grieg. He took holy orders in 1865, as the Abbé Liszt. As a piano teacher Liszt influenced nearly every brilliant young pianist of his time. His work consolidated and extended the virtuoso tradition of Mozart and Beethoven. Liszt wrote about 400 original compositions, including many piano works, and orchestral pieces and choral works. He developed the symphonic poem and the device of *metamorphosis of themes* (similar to Wagner's *Leitmotiv*). Although overshadowed by his playing, Liszt's compositions influenced many romantic and nationalist composers.

Lully, Jean-Baptiste (1632–87) Italian-born composer who, as court composer to Louis XIV of France, monopolized French opera. He blended Italian and French influences to create a fresh baroque style which was widely imitated, particularly in Germany; pioneered accompanied recitative in French opera, and introduced lively dances into his court ballets (some produced with Molière). As a personality Lully was unsavoury, participating to the full in the vices of the French court. He conducted by beating the floor with a long stick; while directing a *Te Deum* for Louis XIV's recovery from illness he hit his foot and later died from the abscess thus caused.

Macdowell, Edward (1861–1908) American composer and pianist, the first to gain an international reputation. Born in New York, he showed early talent and went to Europe as a teenager to study in Paris and Frankfurt. At twenty-one, Macdowell's first piano concerto was praised by Liszt. Returning to the USA, he settled in Boston and later became professor of music at Columbia University. His compositions are mainly in late German-romantic style, but in his *Indian Suite* for orchestra he used North American Indian material. Macdowell's other major works include a second piano concerto, four piano sonatas, short piano pieces and songs.

Mahler, Gustav (1860–1911) Bohemian-born composer noted for his symphonies, written in late German-romantic style. He studied in Vienna with Bruckner, who, with Wagner, was his chief influence. As a renowned conductor, Mahler had positions in Austria (Vienna State Opera), Germany and New York, and visited London. His works include nine numbered symphonies, some with voices, and a tenth unfinished symphony; the unnumbered symphony *The Song of the Earth*, with solo voices; and many songs.

Mascagni, Pietro (1863–1945) Italian opera composer best known for his popular one-act opera *Cavalleria rusticana* ("Rustic Chivalry"). His other operas, none of which were as successful, include *L'amico Fritz, Zanetto, Iris* and *Nero*.

Massenet, Jules (1842–1912) Prolific French composer, particularly known for his attractive, melodious operas. He studied at the Paris Conservatoire, where he won the Prix de Rome and eventually became a professor of composition. Some of the best-known of his many operas are *Manon, Thaïs* and *Sappho*. Massenet's other works include orchestral overtures and suites, cantatas and oratorios, incidental music and many songs.

Méhul, Étienne Nicolas (1763–1817) French composer remembered for his sacred opera *Joseph*.

Mendelssohn, Felix (1809–47)

Liszt

Mahler

Mendelssohn

Mozart

Offenbach

Paganini

Puccini

Rachmaninov

German composer of Jewish parentage who with Chopin and Schumann was one of the leaders of early nineteenth-century romanticism. From a wealthy and cultured background, he was precociously talented, writing many compositions before the age of fifteen (later discarded). In his early twenties he travelled widely, gaining a large English following, and later became the founder and director of the Leipzig Conservatory. His music, written for almost every form and instrumental combination, is notable for its polish and charm rather than its depth. He pioneered the concert overture (e.g. *The Hebrides*, or *Fingal's Cave*) and had a particular bent for scherzos. Mendelssohn had a major influence on German musical life, and did much to rescue J. S. Bach's music from neglect.

Messiaen, Olivier (1908–) A leading French composer, organist and composition teacher. He studied at the Paris Conservatoire under Dukas and Dupré, and later became a professor there. His uncompromising choral, orchestral and organ works, as well as his theories of composition, reflect a profound religious mysticism.

Meyerbeer, Giacomo (1791–1864) German-Jewish opera composer who had a cosmopolitan career in Italy, Paris and Berlin. A pupil of Weber, he had an early career as a pianist before turning to opera after meeting his pianistic match in Hummel. Though disliked by some of his fellow composers, Meyerbeer had great success with operas such as *Robert le diable*, *Les Huguenots*, *Le Prophète* and *Dinorah*, which displayed his individual and effective style.

Milhaud, Darius (1892–1974) A leading modernist French composer and member of "The Six". He studied at the Paris Conservatoire and later taught composition in the United States. Milhaud's wide and varied output, sometimes polytonal, includes symphonies, concertos, ballets, incidental music and chamber music.

Monteverdi, Claudio (1567–1643) Italian composer, one of the main figures in the transition from polyphony to homophony. His use of expressive chromaticism hastened the demise of the old modes, and he was a major pioneer of opera, enriching its orchestration and developing recitative in works such as *Orpheus* and *L'incoronazione di Poppaea*. Monteverdi was also an outstanding madrigalist, and wrote many masses and motets.

Mozart, Wolfgang Amadeus (1756–1791) Austrian composer who with Haydn and the early Beethoven makes up the triumvirate regarded as the archetypes of late eighteenth-century classical music. Despite his disciplined classical style, Mozart has a depth of feeling which is all the more effective for its elegant restraint. The son of Leopold Mozart, a gifted violinist, Mozart was born in Salzburg. As a child prodigy, he toured Europe giving piano recitals with his sister and father. He later became an employee of the Archbishop of Salzburg, with whom he was always at odds. Finally he settled in Vienna, where he married and achieved esteem (if not wealth) with his operas, especially *The Magic Flute*. In one year, 1788, he composed his three greatest symphonies, in E-flat, G minor and C (*Jupiter*). In later life Mozart was in constant financial difficulty, and he was buried in an unmarked pauper's grave. For speed and ease of composition Mozart was unrivalled, producing in his short life over 600 works, among them nearly fifty symphonies, nearly twenty operas and operettas, twenty-one piano concertos, twenty-nine string quartets, about forty violin sonatas, and much other music.

Mussorgsky, Modeste (1839–81) A leading Russian nationalist composer and member of "The Five". Much influenced by Russian folk music and stories heard in his childhood, his music is outstanding for its descriptive realism. He wrote seven operas, of which the most famous is *Boris Godunov*, based on the life of a seventeenth-century tsar. Other well-known works include his *Night on Bald Mountain* for orchestra and *Pictures at an Exhibition* for piano (orchestrated by Ravel and others). At first a soldier, then a civil servant, Mussorgsky had a drink problem which contributed to his early death.

Nicolai, Karl Otto (1810–49) German composer best known for his opera *The Merry Wives of Windsor* and for founding the Vienna Philharmonic Society. His career as an opera composer and conductor in Italy and Germany was cut short by apoplexy.

Nielsen, Carl August (1865–1931) Generally considered Denmark's greatest composer, he began as an army bugler and self-taught violinist, was taken up by Gade and then trained at the Copenhagen Conservatory. Among his many works are operas, including *Masquerade* and *Saul and David*; six symphonies, concertos, choral works, chamber music and piano music.

Ockeghem, Jean de (*c.*1430–*c.* 1495) Flemish composer, one of the leading fifteenth-century polyphonists and teacher of Josquin Després. His music, including masses, motets and chansons, combines expressiveness with technical ingenuity. A boy chorister at Antwerp, he later became composer and chaplain to Charles VII of France in Paris.

Offenbach, Jacques (1819–80) German-Jewish composer who lived most of his life in Paris; noted for his light, melodious operettas including *Orpheus in the Underworld* and *Tales of Hoffman*.

Pachelbel, Johann (1653–1706) German composer and organist, whose keyboard works had an important influence on J. S. Bach.

Paderewski, Ignacy Jan (1860–1941) Polish piano virtuoso, composer and statesman. He studied at Warsaw, Berlin and Vienna, and gained a reputation as one of the most outstanding pianists since Liszt. He wrote piano works, including a concerto, and an opera. A noted Polish patriot, he became independent Poland's first prime minister in 1919.

Paganini, Niccolò (1782–1840) Italian violin virtuoso, the greatest of his time. His remarkable technique did much to expand the scope of the violin, and brought him from humble beginnings to fame and riches – though there were rumours that he was supernaturally inspired. His violin compositions include eight concertos and other pieces; some of his themes were used by other composers such as Liszt, Brahms and Rachmaninov.

Palestrina, Giovanni Pierluigi (*c.* 1525–1594) Italian composer, the greatest of the polyphonic period. Responding to the influence of Flemish composers in Italy (e.g. Willaert, Lassus), he brought choral polyphony to its highest point, in which musical value and clarity of text were perfectly blended. For most of his life Palestrina was a church musician in Rome. He wrote many masses, motets and other church music, and about 140 madrigals. Despite the shift of style after his time, Palestrina's influence on later music was large; his methods were the basis of Fux's counterpoint text *Gradus ad Parnassum*, which was studied by the great composers of the classical period and after.

Parry, Hubert (1848–1918) British composer with a prolific output of choral and orchestral works (including five symphonies) and songs. He began composing at eight and took a music degree while still at school. After a short business career he became director of the Royal College of Music and later professor of music at Oxford. Parry was typically "English" in style; one of his best works is his choral setting of Milton's *Blest Pair of Sirens*.

Peri, Jacopo (1561–1633) Italian composer whose operas *La Dafne* (1597) and *Euridice* (1600) were probably the first ever staged. As one of the *camerata*, his experiments with accompanied musical declamation led him to pioneer recitative and thence opera.

Pérotin (*c.*1183–1236) Medieval French musician of the Notre Dame School (at the church of Notre Dame in Paris); one of the first composers known by name. Composed in the style later known as *Ars Antiqua*, which was organum-based polyphony.

Poulenc, Francis (1899–1963) "Anti-romantic" French composer and member of "The Six". He had little formal training but achieved early success with works such as *Le Gendarme incompris*, a *comédie bouffe*. His compositions include ballets, orchestral works, chamber music, piano music and songs.

Prokofiev, Serge (1891–1953) A leading Russian composer noted for his expressive modernist style. He studied at the Leningrad Conservatory under Rimsky-Korsakov and others, and gained an international reputation as a pianist, usually playing his own works. Among his compositions are ballets, including *Romeo and Juliet* and *Chout*; operas, such as *War and Peace* and *The Love of Three Oranges*; the popular children's piece for orchestra and narrator *Peter and the Wolf*; symphonies, concertos, chamber music, piano music and songs.

Puccini, Giacomo (1858–1924) Italian composer whose many operas, including *La Bohème*, *Tosca* and *Madam Butterfly*, achieved lasting success with their melodic fluency, dramatic effect and fine orchestration.

Purcell, Henry (1659–95) English composer, generally considered the greatest of all time. A boy singer at the Chapel Royal, he may have been taught by John Blow, whom he later succeeded as organist at Westminster Abbey. He marks a watershed in English music, some of his work being in the old English polyphonic style, and some of it in the lighter French baroque style pioneered by Lully. Despite his short career, his output was large and varied. He wrote much church and stage music, including the opera *Dido and Aeneas*, and instrumental music including harpsichord suites, string fantasies for viols and sonatas for violins, cello and harpsichord.

Rachmaninov, Serge (1873–1943) Russian composer, of cosmopolitan style and career. He trained at St Petersburg and Moscow, but left Russia in 1917, eventually settling in the USA, where he died. His compositions include operas, symphonies, piano concertos, solo piano pieces and songs. He was also a noted pianist and conductor.

Rameau, Jean Philippe (1683–1764) French composer and theorist. The son of a musician, he showed early talent, and after travelling in Italy and France he held several posts as a cathedral organist. In 1726 he published a treatise on harmony which was one of the first systematic attempts to link acoustics with musical theory and to develop the idea of inversions of chords. He later became famous for his operas, including *Hippolyte et Aricie*, and opera-ballets such as *Les Indes galantes*. He also wrote cantatas, chamber music and harpsichord pieces.

Ravel, Maurice (1865–1937) French composer who, with Debussy, was a leader of musical impressionism. More formal than Debussy in approach, his music is notable for its originality of melody, rhythm, harmony and orchestration. Ravel studied with Fauré at the Paris Conservatoire and was influenced by Chabrier and Satie as well as by the symbolist poets. His works include piano and orchestral music, operas, ballets, a string quartet and many songs.

Reger, Max (1873–1916) German late-romantic composer, and conductor, pianist and organist. He had a distinguished academic career, becoming professor of composition at the Leipzig Conservatory. His works include orchestral compositions, piano pieces, elaborate organ compositions, chamber music and songs.

Rimsky-Korsakov, Nikolai (1844–1908) Russian nationalist composer and member of "The Five". Much influenced by Russian folk music heard in his childhood, his compositions are notable for their dramatic impact, rhythmic force and orchestral colour. As a young naval officer, he wrote his, and Russia's, first symphony in his spare time. He later became professor of composition at the St Petersburg Conservatory, and wrote an important treatise on orchestration. A prolific composer, his works include fifteen operas, three symphonies, choral music and songs.

Rossini, Gioacchino Antonio (1792–1868) With Bellini and Donizetti, Rossini was one of the three greatest Italian opera composers of the earlier nineteenth century. After studying cello and composition at the Bologna Conservatory he quickly made a name with his operas, producing thirty-six of them in nineteen years, including *The Barber of Seville* and *William Tell*. Rossini's operas are notable for their melodic fluency, vocal appropriateness and effective orchestration.

Saint-Saëns, Camille (1835–1921) French composer, at first influenced by the romantics but later standing apart from them, also from the impressionists. He had a successful career as an organist, pianist, teacher and critic as well as composer. Among his best-known compositions are his symphonic poems (the first by a Frenchman), the popular children's piece *Carnival of the Animals*, for two pianos and orchestra, and the opera *Samson and Delilah*. He also wrote symphonies, choral music, concertos, chamber music, piano music and songs.

Satie, Erik (1866–1925) French composer and pianist. Though he had limited success, working mainly as a café pianist, his whimsical originality made him a cult figure among younger French composers and he was a friend of Ravel and Debussy. Satie wrote for the theatre and ballet, but only his piano pieces are much played. Some of these have amusing titles, such as *Pieces in the Shape of a Pear*.

Scarlatti, Alessandro (1660–1725) Italian composer, founder of the Neopolitan style of opera. His huge output included over 100 operas and 500 chamber cantatas, as well as masses and oratorios. His developments in harmony and form helped lay the foundations of the eighteenth-century classical style.

Scarlatti, Domenico (1685–1757) The son of Alessandro. Italian composer and keyboard virtuoso, almost an exact contemporary of Handel. When they were both twenty-three they competed on keyboard instruments (equal marks for harpsichord, a slight advantage gained by Handel on organ) and became lifelong friends. A major pioneer of keyboard technique and composition, Scarlatti wrote more than 500 harpsichord pieces.

Schoenberg, Arnold (1874–1951) Austrian-Jewish composer, whose development of the twelve-note system of atonal composition made him one of the most influential composers of the twentieth century. From earlier works in late-Wagnerian style, such as the string sextet *Verklärte Nacht*, Schoenberg's style evolved through a period of free atonality to a style of strict avoidance of key based on the twelve-note method. Born in Vienna, Schoenberg was mainly self-taught as a composer, but with Strauss's support he became a teacher at the Stern Conservatory in Berlin. He emigrated to the USA in 1934, where he became professor of music at the University of California. Schoenberg's many works include choral and orchestral compositions, suites, chamber music, operas, concertos and songs. He was also an expressionist painter and friend of Kandinsky.

Schubert, Franz Peter (1797–1828) Austrian composer who, with Beethoven, stands at the transition from the classical to romantic styles. In a career even shorter than Mozart's, Schubert achieved a large output ranging from symphonies and operas to chamber music and over 500 songs, all revealing his unique melodic purity. The son of a schoolmaster, he was born in Vienna and trained at the choir school of the royal chapel. After a short period as a teacher he became, like Beethoven, a musical freelance.

Schumann, Robert Alexander (1810–56) German composer, with Mendelssohn and Chopin one of the leading earlier romantics. The son of a publisher, he abandoned law for music, studying with the pianist Wieck, whose daughter Clara be-

Rossini

Schubert

Schumann

Smetana

J. Strauss II

Gilbert and Sullivan

R. Strauss

Tippett

came his wife. As a brilliant concert pianist, she was mainly responsible for popularizing Schumann's many piano compositions. Apart from these, he wrote four symphonies, choral music, chamber music and songs. As a critic and editor of his own journal, Schumann did much to encourage Chopin and other composers.

Schütz, Heinrich (1585–1672) German composer and organist who ranks as one of Bach's greatest precursors. He commuted between Italy, where he studied with G. Gabrieli, and Germany, where he became a court organist and *Kapellmeister*. His many works include *The Seven Last Words* and other passions and cantatas, madrigals, arias and the first German opera, *Dafne*.

Scriabin, Alexander (1872–1915) Russian composer and mystic, who experimented with colour and music combinations and devised his own "mystic" chord and scale. He studied at the Moscow Conservatory and became an internationally famous pianist, touring in Europe and the USA. In addition to piano music, Scriabin composed large-scale orchestral works including *The Divine Poem* and *Prometheus – the Poem of Fire*.

Shostakovich, Dmitri (1906–75) Prolific Russian composer known for his symphonies, operas, piano music and film scores. After studying at the Leningrad Conservatory, he became established as the leading Soviet composer, a position he maintained despite periods of official criticism.

Sibelius, Jean (1865–1957) Leading Finnish nationalist composer, many of whose works combine an uncompromising bleakness with a deep-seated romanticism, inspired by Finnish myth and landscape. He studied in Helsinki, Berlin and Vienna, later receiving a life pension to compose. His many compositions include symphonies, symphonic poems and other orchestral works, a violin concerto and over 100 songs.

Smetana, Bedřich (1824–84) Czech composer, with Dvořák, his junior, the founder of Czech musical nationalism. Born in Bohemia, he showed early talent as a violinist and pianist, studied and taught at Prague and later became conductor of the National Theatre. He is best known for his operas, particularly *The Bartered Bride*, and the series of symphonic poems *My Fatherland*. He also wrote a string quartet, choral music and piano music.

Spohr, Louis (1784–1859) German composer of the early romantic period, whom some musicians at one time ranked higher than Beethoven. He is mainly remembered for his oratorios *Calvary* and *The Last Judgement*.

Stanford, Charles Villiers (1852–1924) Irish-born composer, conductor and teacher who became a leading figure in British music. He studied at Cambridge and in Germany, and was much influenced by Brahms, whose friend he became. Later, as a teacher at the Royal College of Music, he trained many young British composers. His own compositions include operas, symphonies, church music, chamber music and songs.

Stockhausen, Karlheinz (1928–) A leading *avant-garde* German composer of twelve-note and electronic music. He studied with Milhaud and Messiaen. His compositions include *Play* for orchestra, *Counterpoint No. 1* and the "dramatic structure" *Kontakte*. Stockhausen is also noted as a lecturer on his ideas.

Strauss Family of Austrian musicians who were the main composers and popularizers of the Viennese waltz, also polkas. They include Johann Strauss the elder (1804–49), his sons Johann the younger (1825–99), composer of the operetta *Die Fledermaus* and known as "The Waltz King", Joseph (1827–70) and Eduard (1835–1916), and Eduard's son Johann (1866–1939).

Strauss, Richard (1864–1949) German neo-romantic composer, the leading successor to Wagner. His music is characterized by innovative harmony and masterly orchestration, and by its emotional intensity. With Hofmannsthal as librettist, he wrote many operas including *Der Rosenkavalier*, *Elektra* and *Ariadne auf Naxos*. His other compositions include symphonic poems, such as *Till Eulenspiegel* and *Don Juan*, and many songs. He was also an important opera conductor.

Stravinsky, Igor (1882–1971) Russian-born composer and one of the key figures of twentieth-century music. The son of an opera-singer, he turned from law to music after meeting Rimsky-Korsakov, with whom he studied. Working in Paris with the impressario Diaghilev, Stravinsky made his reputation with a series of remarkable ballets, including *The Firebird*, *Petrushka* and *The Rite of Spring* (the originality and "primitive" force of which caused a scandal at its première in 1913). From the early 1920s Stravinsky abandoned the broadly Russian nationalist style of his earlier works in favour of a more "absolute" or neo-classical style, as in his piano concerto and piano sonata. His later works, after settling in the USA in World War II, are highly modernistic, some of them based on twelve-note technique. Apart from his ballets, Stravinsky's works include symphonies, choral works, the opera *The Rake's Progress*, a violin concerto and the instrumental concerto *Dumbarton Oaks*.

Sullivan, Arthur (1842–1900) British composer, best known for his comic operas written to librettos by W. S. Gilbert, including *The Pirates of Penzance*, *Patience* and *The Mikado*, which are noted for their humorous melodic charm and skilful harmony and orchestration. Sullivan also wrote orchestral music, oratorios and songs.

Sweelinck, Jan (1562–1621) Dutch composer and organist who greatly influenced the baroque organ style of Northern Europe. His organ works include the first fully developed fugues, and he wrote much sacred and secular choral music.

Tallis, Thomas (*c.*1505–1585) English composer, with Byrd one of the greatest of the Tudor period. He harmonized the plainsong of the Anglican service and wrote much other church music, including the extraordinary forty-part motet *Spem in alium*, as well as string and keyboard music.

Taverner, John (*c.*1495–1545) English composer of the earlier Tudor period, who wrote much fine church music and pioneered the *In nomine* form of instrumental composition. His late *Ars Nova* style of polyphony combines technical ingenuity with personal expressiveness.

Tchaikovsky, Peter Ilyich (1840–93) Russian composer, the first to become widely popular outside his country. His work was notable for its melodic flair, emotional content and vivid orchestration. Abandoning the civil service for music, he studied at the St Petersburg Conservatory. Though influenced by Balakirev and Rimsky-Korsakov, he remained apart from the nationalist "Five". For many years he was supported by a rich widow, Nadezhda von Meck (without ever actually meeting her). Among Tchaikovsky's many works are ten operas, including *Eugene Onegin*; six symphonies and other orchestral works; three piano concertos and a violin concerto; ballets, including the ever-popular *Swan Lake*; chamber music, choral works, piano pieces and songs.

Telemann, Georg Philipp (1681–1767) German composer, one of the most famous of his time, with C. P. E. Bach and others an important pioneer of the *style galant* which led to eighteenth-century classicism. One of the most prolific composers ever, he turned out more than 600 overtures, twelve sets of cantatas, forty-four Passions and forty operas. His style, which was fluent and tuneful, was influenced by the French and Italian idioms.

Tippett, Michael (1905–) British composer, particularly noted for his oratorio *A Child Of Our Time* and opera *Midsummer Marriage*. He studied at the Royal College of Music and later taught composition. Among his other works, some of which employ rhythmic serialism, are symphonies, string quartets, and piano music, including two concertos and a sonata.

Torelli, Giuseppe (1658–1709) Italian violinist and composer of string music, considered to have been the first to have written a concerto for solo instrument and orchestra.

Turina, Joaquín (1882–1949) Spanish nationalist composer, pianist and conductor, particularly noted for his orchestral *Procesión del Rocio*. He studied in Spain, and later in Paris with D'Indy, where he also associated with Debussy and Ravel. His other works include stage music, chamber music and songs.

Varèse, Edgar (1885–1965) French-born composer, a leading modernist whose aim was a music of "pure sound", without any traditional associations. After studying in Paris, he settled in the USA in 1915. Among his works, some of them electronic music, are *Ionization* for percussion and sirens, *Intégrales* for orchestra, and *Déserts* for prepared tapes.

Vaughan Williams, Ralph (1872–1958) British composer, a leading figure in the twentieth-century revival of English music. After studying at Cambridge and the Royal College of Music, and then with Max Bruch and Ravel, he developed a personal and English idiom, strongly influenced by English folk music and music of the Tudor period. Among his main works are nine symphonies and other orchestral works including *Fantasia on a Theme of Tallis*; concertos for piano, violin and oboe; and operas, choral works, chamber music and songs.

Verdi, Giuseppe (1813–1901) Italian opera composer, generally considered the greatest of the nineteenth century. Refused a scholarship to the Milan Conservatory as lacking talent, he studied privately and had his first opera, *Oberto*, performed at twenty-five. Other operas from his tuneful and melodramatic early period include *Rigoletto*, *Il trovatore* and *La traviata*. His middle-period opera *Aïda*, written for the khedive of Egypt, is musically more developed, with richer orchestration. Verdi's remarkable later operas *Otello* and *Falstaff*, written in his seventies, show a symphonic style and Wagnerian influence. His other works include a string quartet and church music, such as his famous Requiem.

Victoria, Tomás Luis de (*c*.1549–1611) Spanish composer of polyphonic church music; possibly taught by Palestrina and with Byrd and Lassus one of his greatest contemporaries. His masses, motets and other choral works are notable for their passionate mysticism. He worked in Rome for about forty years.

Villa-Lobos, Heitor (1887–1959) Leading Brazilian composer, whose music combines Brazilian folk influences with modernist devices such as polytonality. His compositions include operas, an oratorio, symphonies, chamber music, piano music, guitar music and songs.

Vivaldi, Antonio (*c*.1685–1741) Italian composer and violinist who had some influence on his contemporary J. S. Bach. Vivaldi's many works include nearly 400 "concertos", mainly for strings but also for oboe, bassoon and flute; also operas and church music.

Wagner, Richard (1813–83) German operatic composer, one of the most influential of the nineteenth century, whose works achieved a new synthesis of music and drama, in which German romanticism found its fullest stage expression. He greatly increased the dramatic flexibility of opera music by breaking down the distinction between aria (for lyrical expression) and recitative (for direct statement) and through his use of *Leitmotiv*—melodic fragments associated with situations and characters—as a basis of development. Wagner was also revolutionary in harmony and orchestration. His expressive chromaticism stretched tonality to its limits, foreshadowing the atonality of Schoenberg, and he greatly increased the scope of the orchestra, even calling for some specially designed instruments to achieve new effects. Wagner also wrote his own librettos and stage directions. Born in Leipzig of a theatrical family, he had a number of positions in opera-houses before being banished from Germany for taking part in the 1848 revolution. While in exile in Switzerland he began writing his epic *Ring* cycle (*Der Ring des Nibelungen*) based on German myth. After Wagner's banishment was revoked, Ludwig II of Bavaria became his patron and Wagner founded the Wagner Festival Theatre (*Festspielhaus*) at Bayreuth. Among his operas are *Rienzi*, *The Flying Dutchman*, *Tannhäuser*, *Lohengrin*, *The Ring* (*The Rhinegold*, *The Valkyrie*, *Siegfried* and *Twilight of the Gods*); and *Tristan and Isolde*, *The Mastersingers of Nuremberg* and *Parsifal*.

Walton, William (1902–) British composer, mainly self-taught, whose music is notable for its rhythmic vitality and adroit orchestration. He first gained widespread attention with his *Façade*, instrumental music written to accompany Edith Sitwell's poetry. His other works include the *Sinfonietta Concertante* for piano and orchestra, the choral-orchestral *Belshazzar's Feast*, a symphony, violin and viola concerto, chamber and film music.

Weber, Carl Maria von (1786–1826) German composer who pioneered German nationalism and romanticism in opera and was an important influence on Wagner. His best-known operas include *Der Freischütz*, *Euryanthe* and *Oberon*. Weber's other compositions include concertos for piano, clarinet and bassoon, and piano pieces, choral music and songs.

Webern, Anton von (1883–1945) Austrian composer, a student and disciple of Schoenberg, whose music is mainly based on Schoenberg's twelve-note technique. Most of Webern's compositions are very concentrated and short, such as his *Five Pieces for Orchestra*, lasting nineteen seconds. Among his other works are two symphonies, an oratorio, string quartets and songs.

Weill, Kurt (1900–1950) German-born composer, best known for his operas including *The Threepenny Opera* and *Mahagonny*, written with Bertholt Brecht as librettist. Like Hindemith, Weill aspired to a functional, popularly-based style of *Gebrauchsmusik* ("music for use"). Among his other compositions are choral music, chamber music and a violin concerto. He left Germany in the early 1930s, settling in the USA.

Wilbye, John (1574–1638) English composer, widely considered the greatest writer of madrigals, English or continental. Some of his best-known madrigals are "Adieu, Sweet Amaryllis", "Flora, Give Me Fairest Flowers" and "Sweet Honey-sucking Bees". He also wrote some church music.

Willaert, Adriaan (*c*.1480–1562) Flemish composer, one of the greatest of the northern polyphonic school. After studying in Paris he travelled widely in Europe before becoming *maestro di cappella* at St Mark's, Venice, where he gained fame as a composer and teacher. He wrote many motets and masses, some for double choir, and contributed to the development of the madrigal.

Williamson, Malcolm (1931–) Australian composer. He studied at the Sydney Conservatory and in Paris with Boulez, and settled in Britain in 1953. His works include operas, notably *English Eccentrics* and *The Violins of St Jacques*; a symphony, concertos for violin and piano, a string quartet and keyboard works.

Wolf, Hugo (1860–1903) Austrian composer, considered one of the greatest writers of *Lieder*. Unjustly expelled from the Vienna Conservatory, he was poverty-stricken most of his life, working as a music teacher and critic. He died after six years in an asylum. His songs include many settings of Goethe, Mörike, Eichendorff and other leading German poets. Among his other works are a string quartet and the *Italian Serenade* for small orchestra.

Xenakis, Iannis (1922–) Romanian-born Greek composer and leading modernist, also an architect and engineer. He studied in Paris with Messiaen. His works, some based on mathematical formulae, include electronic music and music for conventional instruments. Among them are *Diamorphoses*, *Bohor*, *Achorripsis*, *Pithoprakta* and *Metastasis*.

Vaughan Williams

Verdi

Wagner

Weber

Glossary of Terms

Abbreviations in brackets denote linguistic origin: Eng., English; Fr., French; Ger., German; Gk., Greek; Hin., Hindi; It., Italian; L., Latin; Port., Portuguese; Sp., Spanish.

A Letter name of sixth note or submediant of C major scale. It is commonly used for instrumental tuning. *See also* CONCERT PITCH.
Absolute pitch Ability to sing a note asked for by name, or identify a note by name, without reference to any other note. *See also* RELATIVE PITCH.
Absolute or **abstract music** Music without descriptive or literary content or other external reference, and considered to exist purely for its own sake. J. S. Bach's *The Art of Fugue* is a prime example.
A cappella (It.) Vocal music without instrumental accompaniment. Much church music is sung in this way, hence literal meaning "in the church style".
Accelerando (It.) Getting gradually faster.
Accent Stress Regular emphasis which defines rhythm in metrical music; or specific emphasis on particular note(s), marked **>**.
Accidental Sign which modifies the pitch of a note when placed before it. A sharp (♯) raises a note one semitone; a flat (♭) lowers a note one semitone; a double sharp (𝄪) raises a note one whole tone; a double flat (♭♭) lowers a note one whole tone. A natural (♮) cancels a preceding accidental and restores the note to its original pitch.
Accompaniment Instrumental, choral or keyboard music supporting a solo voice or instrument(s).
Acoustics (1) Science of sound. (2) Architectural properties of a concert hall or room as they affect the sound of music played in it.
Adagio (It.) Slow tempo; a piece of music so performed.
Ad lib, ad libitum (L., "at pleasure") Tempo and expression to be decided by performer. Hence also, to improvise.
Aeolian mode *See* MODES.
Agnus Dei (L., "Lamb of God") concluding section of a musical setting of High Mass.
Air or **ayre** Simple tune for instrument or voice. *See also* ARIA.
Alberti bass Common form of left-hand accompaniment in eighteenth-century keyboard music, consisting of simple broken chords. Named after Italian composer Domenico Alberti (*c.*1710–40).
Aleatoric music Music in which random or chance elements are allowed to determine the course of the music.
Alla marcia (It.) In march style.
Allegretto (It.) Lively, fairly fast tempo, but slower than *allegro*.
Allegro (It.) Fast tempo.
Allemande (Fr., "German") Movement of a classical suite, in $\frac{4}{4}$ time and at moderate tempo, deriving from an old German dance.
Alto (It.) Lowest range of women's and boys' voices. **Male** – *See* COUNTER-TENOR. *See also* CONTRALTO; COUNTER-TENOR.
Ambrosian chant Early type of church plainsong introduced by Ambrose, Bishop of Milan, in the 4th century AD.
Andante (It., "walking") A medium tempo, slower than *allegro*, faster than *adagio*; walking pace.
Andantino (It.) Slowish tempo, but slightly faster than *andante*.
Animato (It.) Lively, animated.
Answer *See* FUGUE.
Anthem A choral composition, sometimes with soloists, sung at church services. Also, a national song.
Antiphony Music in "question-and-answer" form sung by two choirs or by the two sides of a divided choir.
Appoggiatura (It., "leaning") Strongly accented passing note.
Arabesque Highly ornamented passage or short piece, by analogy with Arabic or Islamic decorative design. Also, specific position in ballet.
Arco, con – (It., "bow", "with the bow") Direction to strings (violin, etc.) to play with the bow.
Aria (It., "air" or "song") Structured piece for solo voice with instrumental accompaniment, usually in opera or oratorio.
Arioso (It.) Melodious, in style of aria. Song-like recitative.
Arpeggio (It., "harp-like") Individual notes of a chord played in rapid succession, as on a harp, rather than at the same time.
Arrangement Adaptation of part or all of a composition for voices and/or instruments other than those for which it was first written.
Ars Antiqua (L., "old style") The earliest style of medieval polyphony, which developed in the thirteenth century.
Ars Nova (L., "new style") Often complex style of fourteenth-century polyphony which succeeded the *Ars Antiqua*.
Atonality Quality of having no definite key centre or tonality, as in twelve-tone or other serial music. *See* TONALITY (2).
Augmentation "Stretching" a melodic line or part by increasing the time values of its notes. Common device in counterpoint.
Augmented interval *See* INTERVAL.
Ave Maria (L., "Hail Mary") Latin prayer, the subject of many musical settings.
Ayre *See* AIR.

B Letter name for seventh or leading note of C major scale. In Germany, B signifies the note B♭, and H is used for B. Therefore Bach could base *The Art of Fugue* on the musical notes of his own name.
Bagatelle (Fr., "trifle") Short, light instrumental composition, often for piano.
Ballad A narrative song. Also, an eighteenth- or nineteenth-century drawing-room song.
Ballade (Fr., "ballad") Instrumental piece, usually for piano, in romantic style.
Ballad opera English dramatic form with spoken dialogue alternating with songs.
Ballet Spectacular dance form established in sixteenth-century French court which later became exclusive to the theatre. It is based on well-defined styles and techniques. *See pages 66–7.*
Ballett Polyphonic composition for voices, similar to MADRIGAL.
Bar, – line *See* METRE.
Barcarolle (It.) Venetian gondolier's song, or piece inspired by one.
Baritone Medium range of male voice, overlapping bass and tenor.
Baroque (from Port., "irregular pearl") In music, period from about 1600 to 1750, in which new styles of musical expression were developed. Vaguely analogous to extravagant architectural style of period. *See pages 30–33.*
Bass (1) Lowest male voice. (2) Lowest part in a musical composition. (3) Low-pitched member of an instrumental family. *See also* CLEF.
Basso continuo (It.) Thorough-bass. In seventeenth and eighteenth centuries, bass line for accompaniment by keyboard instrument, constructed from "shorthand" notation. *See also* FIGURED BASS.
Beat (1) Regular musical pulse, especially when "beaten out" rather than implied. (2) Indication of pulse by conductor. (3) In rock, jazz, etc., "beat" can mean a basic rhythm pattern. (4) Throbbing effect heard when two notes forming a dissonance are sounded together.
Bel canto (It., "beautiful singing") Lyrical style of singing, emphasizing beauty of tone, especially in seventeenth- and eighteenth-century Italian opera.
Benedictus (L., "blessed") Section of a musical setting of the High Mass; may be part of the Sanctus or, often, a separate section.
Binary form Simple musical form in two sections. The first moves from a home key to a related one. The second returns to the home key.
Bind *See* TIE.
Bitonality The use of two keys at once.
Blues Musical idiom developed by black Americans in the nineteenth and twentieth centuries. Characterized by fusion of African and European scales and "blue notes" (flattened third and seventh), and by a twelve-bar form using tonic, subdominant and dominant chords. A major influence on jazz, soul and rock. **– scale** Typical of blues, jazz and related styles, this is a combination of two five-note scales, the major and the minor, e.g. C-D-E-G-A (major) and C-E♭-F-G-B♭ (minor), and a "flattened fifth", F♯ (or G♭), giving a nine-note scale C-D-E♭-E-F-F♯-G-A-B♭. The E♭, F♯ and B♭ are expressively varied in pitch as "blue notes", producing a characteristic clash with the fixed pitch of the underlying harmony.
Bolero (Sp.) Spanish dance originally accompanied by singing and castanets.
Boogie-woogie Improvised piano style featuring repetitive left-hand patterns with rhythmically contrasting right-hand melodies, usually in twelve-bar blues form.
Bourrée French dance in duple time, sometimes included in classical suites.
Breve (from L., "short") In the Middle Ages, a note of half the length of a "long", which was the second longest time value after the "maximus" or "double long". The long dropped out of use, the breve became rare and today the longest note normally used is the semibreve or whole-note.

C Letter name of first note or tonic of C major scale.
Caccia (It., "chase", "hunt") Sixteenth-century two-part hunting-song, with second part (the hunter) taking up melody of first part (the quarry) in canon.
Cadence (from L. *cadere*, "to fall") or **close** Movement of two chords ending a piece of music, or phrase or section. There are four kinds of cadence, which can be thought of as musical "punctuation marks": (1) perfect cadence: dominant chord to tonic chord; (2) plagal cadence (or "Amen" cadence): subdominant chord to tonic chord; (3) imperfect cadence: tonic chord to dominant chord; (4) interrupted cadence: dominant chord to some chord other than the tonic. The first two cadences are also called "full closes". The second two are also called "half closes".
Cadenza (It., "cadence") Written or improvised passage in which the soloist's virtuosity is revealed.
Calando (It.) Becoming quieter and slower.
Canon Device in counterpoint in which a melody introduced by one part is, after a short time, exactly imitated by another part. The skill involved is in constructing a melody that will harmonize with itself. *See also* CANZICRANS.
Cantabile (It.) In a flowing, expressive, singing style.
Cantata (It., "sung") Vocal composition for solist(s) choir or chorus.
Canticle Sacred song, other than a psalm.
Cantilena (It., "small song") Smooth, melodious writing for voice or instruments.
Cantillation Unaccompanied chanting of a sacred text, usually in Jewish worship.

Cantor (L., "singer") Lead singer or precentor in Anglican and Catholic church service. In Jewish worship the cantor is called the *chazzan*.
Cantus firmus (L., "fixed song") In polyphony, a set melody around which other contrapuntal parts are woven.
Canzicrans or **crab canon** Type of canon in which second part consists of the notes of the first part in reverse order. Also called a canon by retrogression or retrograde inversion.
Canzona (It., "song", plural *canzone*) Originally type of troubadour poem, then applied to musical settings of such poems. In sixteenth and seventeenth centuries, short instrumental piece in fugal style. More recently, instrumental piece in song style.
Canzonet (Eng.), **canzonetta** (It., "little song") Term mainly applied to type of madrigal, e.g. by Thomas Morley. Later, a light solo song.
Capriccio (It., "caprice") Usually a fast piece in fantasia style. Later, a light solo song.
Carillon (Fr.) Set of bells, played manually or mechanically.
Carol Usually, a traditional Christmas song; there are also carols for other festivals, e.g. Easter.
Castrato (It.) In seventeenth and eighteenth centuries, adult male soprano or alto whose voice had been prevented from breaking by castration.
Catch Round or canon for three or four voices, the singers having to "catch" their parts at the right moment. Popular in England in seventeenth and eighteenth centuries.
Cavatina (It.) Short aria, or slow song-like instrumental movement.
Chaconne (Fr.) Slow vocal or instrumental piece, built on a ground bass and almost always in $\frac{3}{4}$ time. Originally a Spanish dance. A passacaglia is similar.
Chamber music Originally, any music intended to be played by a small group of musicians in a room (i.e. chamber). Today, strict meaning is music for two or more instruments played with one instrument to a part.
Change ringing Art of ringing a "peal" of bells (usually eight) through a series of permutations.
Chanson (Fr., "song") (1) Any simple French song. (2) Early French madrigal style, which developed from troubadour and trouvère songs.
Chant Style in which canticles and psalms are sung in church. The two main kinds are Gregorian and Anglican. *See also* AMBROSIAN CHANT; PLAINSONG.
Choir Body of singers.
Chorale German Lutheran hymn tune.
Chorale prelude Organ composition based on chorale melody. Developed mainly by German composers, but also (in late nineteenth and early twentieth centuries) by British composers.
Chord Effect produced by sounding two or more notes together. *See* HARMONY.
Chorus (1) Choir. (2) Composition or part of composition where each part is sung by several voices (3) Song refrain. (4) Second and usually most familiar part of American show-tune, preceded by the "verse". (5) Section of jazz solo, usually same length as initial theme.
Chromaticism (from Gk. "colour": the Greeks called small intervals "colourings") Style of composition based on the notes of the chromatic, as opposed to (for example) the diatonic, scale.
Chromatic scale Twelve-note scale of semitones. *See also* CHROMATICISM; DIATONIC-CHROMATIC SYSTEM.
Classicism In music, style in which form tends to take precedence over emotional expression. Usually applied to eighteenth-century music.
Clef Sign placed at beginning of stave which fixes the pitch of one line of stave and therefore the pitch of all the other lines and spaces. There are two fixed clefs, the G or treble clef and the F or bass clef; and one movable clef, the C clef, which is used as a soprano, alto or tenor clef.
Close *See* CADENCE.
Coda (It., "tail") Passage added to end of a piece of movement, e.g. in sonata form, to emphasize conclusion.
Coloratura (It., "colouring") Ornamental style in vocal music. A soprano whose voice is well adapted to this is a coloratura soprano.
Common time $\frac{4}{4}$ time, having four crotchets or quarter notes to the bar.
Compass Range of a voice or instrument.
Compound time Rhythm based on division of the pulse into three equal parts. The pulse is written as a dotted value, i.e. as one and a half pulses of simple time. *See* SIMPLE TIME.
Con brio (It.) With dash or speed.
Concertante *See* CONCERTO.
Concertato *See* CONCERTO.
Concerto (It., "together") Originally, composition for several contrasted instruments. Since classical period, a piece featuring a solo instrument together with an orchestra. Earlier forms were the *concerto grosso* and the *concertante*, in which a group of solo instruments (called the *concertante, concertato, soli* or *concertino*) was pitted against the orchestra (called the *ripieno*). *See page 36.*
Concerto grosso *See* CONCERTO.
Concert pitch Standard of pitch to which instruments are usually tuned. The note used for tuning is A above middle C, the frequency of which has been established internationally as 440 Hertz (cycles per second).
Concord *See* HARMONY.
Concrete music *See* MUSIQUE CONCRÈTE.
Conductor Director of an orchestra or choir. The job of the conductor is to ensure musical cohesion and to interpret the composer's intention.
Conductus Type of polyphonic church composition in Middle Ages, in which the cantus firmus was either a secular melody or original. Forerunner of the MOTET.
Consecutives Movements of two or more parts in parallel intervals. In classical harmony, consecutive unisons, octaves and fifths are avoided.
Conservatoire (Fr.), **conservatorio** (It.), **conservatory** (Eng.) An academy or school of music.
Consonance *See* HARMONY.
Consort In seventeenth-century English music, a group of instruments of the same family. A "broken consort" comprised instruments of various families.
Continuo *See* BASSO CONTINUO; FIGURED BASS.
Contralto Lowest female voice.
Counterpoint Art of weaving two or more melodic lines together so that they harmonize while each line moves independently. Developed with rise of vocal polyphony in Middle Ages and Renaissance. In baroque period, instrumental counterpoint became important. Counterpoint was less emphasized in later periods, but its study remained a vital part of a composer's apprenticeship.
The word came from the expression "point counter point", which referred to early practice of taking an existing melody and adding another part note-for-note.
Imitation, in which different parts enter with a melody similar to that of a previous part, is important in counterpoint. *See also* CANON; FUGUE.
Counter-tenor High male voice of similar range to female contralto. Another name for male alto.
Courante (Fr.) Movement of a classical suite in $\frac{3}{4}$ time. Originally an aristocratic (rather than folk) dance.
Credo (L., "I believe") Third section of a musical setting of High Mass.
Crescendo (It.) Gradually increasing in volume.
Crotchet, quarter-note British and American terms for a time value equal to a quarter of a semibreve or whole note. The length of one beat is often written as a crotchet.
Csárdás A national Hungarian dance, with slow and quick sections.
Cyclic or **cyclical form** Piece with movements connected by common musical ideas.

D Letter name of second note or supertonic of C major scale.
D.C. *See* DA CAPO.
Da capo (It., "from the head") Direction to repeat a piece from the beginning, or in operatic aria a piece so repeated. *D.C. al fine* means repeat from beginning to end. *D.C. al segno* means repeat from the beginning to the section marked with the sign.
Descant Decorative part, sometimes improvised, added above a melody.
Diapason (Gk., "through all") (1) Octave interval. (2) – **stops** *See* INSTRUMENT GLOSSARY.
Diatonic (from Gk., "through the notes") (1) – scale. Scale with seven different notes (the eighth note or octave being considered "the same" as the first), with five notes separated by tones and two by semitones. The various kinds of diatonic scale are named according to their order of tones and semitones. *See* INTERVAL; MAJOR SCALE; MINOR SCALE; MODES. (2) Melody or chords containing only notes belonging to diatonic scale of home key, i.e. with no chromatic notes. *See* CHROMATIC SCALE.
Diatonic-chromatic system System of twelve major and twelve minor keys. The old modal system was replaced in the seventeenth century by only three scale forms (one major and two minor) which could begin at different starting points or keys. When the octave was divided into twelve equal semitones, twelve keys became available. *See diagram on page 15;* KEY; MODULATION.
Dies irae (L., "day of wrath") Thirteenth-century plainsong hymn included in the requiem, or mass for the dead. The melody is sometimes used in choral and instrumental music.
Diminished interval *See* INTERVAL.
Diminuendo (It.) Gradually decreasing in volume.
Diminution Device, common in counterpoint, "shrinking" of a melodic line or part by decreasing the time values of its notes.
Discant Early form of polyphony in which a part was added above a melody. *See also* DESCANT.
Discord *See* HARMONY.
Dissonance *See* HARMONY.
Divertimento (It.), **divertissement** (Fr.) Light instrumental composition with several movements, like a suite, intended to entertain or "divert". A *divertissement* in ballet is a dance-interlude not organically connected to the main work.
Divisions Old term for varying a melody by dividing the time values of its notes. The long vocal phrases in much baroque music were called by this name.
Dodecaphonic music *See* TWELVE-NOTE COMPOSITION.
Dominant Fifth degree of the diatonic scale, the most important note after the TONIC.
Dorian mode *See* MODES.
Dot Over a note indicates STACCATO accent; after a note indicates that the time value is increased by half.
Double bar Two upright vertical lines on stave or score, marking the end of a piece or a section of it.
Down-beat (1) Lowering of hand or conductor's baton in beating time. (2) Accented beat of bar (indicated by down-beat movement).

Drone Sustained notes played by, for example, drone strings or the chanters on a bagpipe, which form a continuous accompaniment to the melody.
Duet Piece for two voices of instruments, or for two players on one keyboard instrument.
Dumka Ukrainian and Slavonic folk-ballad.
Duple time Metre in which every alternate beat is accented, i.e. two beats to the bar.
Dynamics Variation and contrast of intensity (loudness and softness) of musical sounds. Italian terms are used to indicate dynamic levels. The most common are *pianissimo* (*pp*), very soft; *piano* (*p*), soft; *mezzo-piano* (*mp*), fairly soft; *mezzo-forte* (*mf*), fairly loud; *forte* (*f*), loud; *fortissimo* (*ff*), very loud. *See also* CRESCENDO; DIMINUENDO.

E Letter name for third note or mediant of C major scale.
Ecossaise Eighteenth-century French dance in Scottish style.
Eighth-note *See* QUAVER.
Electronic music Music composed with electronically generated or processed sound, usually produced in a sound laboratory using tape, electronic oscillators, etc.
Encore (Fr., "again") Request by enthusiastic audience for more music at the end of a concert or opera; and piece played in response.
Enharmonic interval Very small interval between the sharp of a note and the flat of the note a tone above, e.g. F♯ and G♭. On modern keyboard instruments this difference is eliminated, but it can be achieved by strings and voices.
Ensemble (Fr., "together") (1) Any group of two or more musicians, but usually limited to groups with one player or singer to a part, as in chamber music. (2) In opera, set piece for group of soloists. (3) **"Good –"**: good musical teamwork.
Episode (1) In sonata form, a secondary theme occurring between two statements of the main theme. (2) In fugue, section in which modulation occurs. *See also* RONDO.
Equal temperament System of tuning by which the octave is divided into a CHROMATIC SCALE of twelve equal semitones. *See diagram on page 13.*
Exposition (1) In sonata form, first part of a movement, in which main themes are stated. (2) In fugue, section in which all the voices make their first entries.
Expression marks Signs which guide a player's interpretation of a work. They cover most aspects of musical performance that cannot be exactly notated, e.g. tempo, phrasing, accent, dynamics.

F Letter name of fourth note or subdominant of C major scale.
False relation In harmony, effect of two notes with same letter-name but different pitches (e.g. A and A♭) heard in succession or at the same time, in different parts. Common in polyphonic music.
Falsetto Highest register of the voice, often used by male altos.
Fanfare Flourish played by brass instruments.
Fermata (It., "held") Pause sign 𝄐 placed above a note to prolong its length.
Fifth *See* INTERVAL.
Figured bass Shorthand notation for keyboard accompaniments used in seventeenth and eighteenth centuries. The notes of the bass line are shown together with figures (i.e. numbers) indicating the basic chords to be used.
Fingering (1) Use of fingers to play instrument. (2) Indication above notes to show which fingers are to be used.
First-movement form *See* SONATA FORM.
Flamenco Spanish style of folk song and dance, also style of guitar playing associated with it.
Flat *See* ACCIDENTAL.
Florid Decorative, ornamental (applied to musical passage work).
Folk music, folk-song Traditional music of a particular people, culture or nation, passed down by aural tradition. *See pages 68–71.*
Form Design or ground-plan of a piece of music. *See* BINARY FORM; CANON; CHORUS; CONCERTO; CYCLIC FORM; FANTASIA; FUGUE; MADRIGAL; MOTET; ORGANUM; OPERA; QUODLIBET; RONDO; SONATA FORM; SUITE; SYMPHONY; SYMPHONIC POEM; TERNARY FORM: THEME-AND-VARIATION FORM.
Forte *See* DYNAMICS.
Fourth *See* INTERVAL.
Frottola Fifteenth- and early sixteenth-century song style, preceding the madrigal.
Fugue (Fr., "flight") Highly developed contrapuntal form. Starts with *exposition*, in which each part enters in turn with short melody or *subject*; followed by *episodes* where the music changes key, and *stretti*, where the time between entries is "squeezed together". **Double –** A fugue founded upon two subjects.

G Letter name of fifth note or dominant in C major scale.
Galant *See* STYLE GALANT.
Galliard (from It. *gagliarda*) Lively sixteenth-century dance in triple time. Originally Italian, became popular in England.
Gavotte Optional movement of a classical suite, in duple or quadruple time. Originally a French dance.
Gebrauchsmusik (Ger., "music for use") Music by some earlier twentieth-century composers, especially Paul Hindemith and Kurt Weill, based on popular idioms and intended to be easily understood by the masses. Inspiration came from the poet-dramatist Bertholt Brecht.
Gigue (Fr., "jig") Generally the last movement of a classical suite, in binary form and lively triplet rhythm (compound duple or quadruple time). Originally an English dance. *See* JIG.
Glee Short, typically English piece for unaccompanied voices, moving in block chords.
Glissando (It., from Fr., "gliding") (1) On keyboard, rapid scale passage played by sliding back of thumb or fingers along keys. (2) Similar effect produced by "sweeping" harp strings. (3) Continuously falling or rising sound on instruments without fixed notes, e.g. violin.
Gloria (L., "glory") Second section of musical setting of mass.
Grave (It., Fr.) (1) Low in pitch. (2) Slow, solemn tempo.
Grazioso (It.) Gracefully.
Gregorian chant Ancient style of plainsong as revised by Pope Gregory in 6th century AD. Since then the standard chant of Roman Catholic Church.
Ground bass Bass figure constantly repeated with changing upper parts. *See* CHACONNE; PASSACAGLIA; OSTINATO.
Guidonian hand Mnemonic for notes of scale, introduced by Guido d'Arezzo in eleventh century, which allotted different notes to the tips and joints of fingers and thumb. *See page 58, also* GUIDONIAN SYLLABLES; HEXACHORD.
Guidonian syllables Syllabic names (UT queant laxis/REsonare fibris/MIra gestorum/FAmuli tuorum/SOLve polluti/LAbii reatum) for the six notes of the HEXACHORD, devised by Guido d'Arezzo in eleventh century. Tonic sol-fa is an updated version of the same idea. *See* HEXACHORD; TONIC SOL-FA.

H In Germany, letter name for seventh or leading note of C major scale. *See also* B.
Half-note *See* MINIM.
Harmonics Higher notes (also called partials or overtones) produced by vibrating string or air column in addition to basic note or fundamental. *See page 13, also* HARMONY.
Harmony (from Gk., *harmonia*) Art of combining notes so as to make *chords* – simultaneous combinations of two or more notes. Any chord consists of a series of intervals, and its effect depends on whether its intervals are consonant or dissonant. A concord, e.g. C-E-G, has only consonant intervals (C-E, C-G, E-G). A discord, e.g. C-D-E, has one or more dissonant intervals (C-D, D-E). The distinction between consonance and dissonance is one of proportion, because simple proportions of string lengths produce consonances and complicated ones produce dissonances (*see page 13*).
Western harmony began to develop in the Middle Ages when composers began to systematize the combinations of notes that arose in polyphony. The basic harmonies were consonant *triads* – chords built up in intervals of thirds (e.g. C-E-G). The texture was varied by dissonances which were *prepared* and *resolved*, i.e. preceded and followed by consonant harmonies. At first, harmony was chiefly *diatonic*, with the choice of notes restricted to the scale or mode of the music. *Chromatic harmony*, using notes not restricted to the key, developed from the early seventeenth century.
Head voice Higher register of the voice produced by using the nasal cavities.
Hemidemisemiquaver, sixty-fourth-note British and American terms for time value of half a demisemiquaver (thirty-second-note): a sixty-fourth of a semibreve or whole note.
Hexachord Group of six consecutive notes of diatonic scale, taken as a unit for learning sight-singing in Middle Ages. Introduced by Guido d'Arezzo in eleventh century. *See also* GUIDONIAN SYLLABLES.
Hill-billy music White American folk music originally from Appalachians.
Homophony (from Gk., "same voice") (1) Music in unison as opposed to in harmony. (2) Style of music in which one part has the lead, the other parts being subsidiary and generally moving in step with the lead. Opposite of POLYPHONY.
Hornpipe Lively old English dance originally in triple and later in duple time.
Hymn Song of praise for congregational singing.

Impromptu (1) Improvised piece of music. (2) Written composition with improvised character.
Improvisation Art of spontaneous music-making, i.e. ability to conceive and play music without writing it down beforehand. Basis of jazz, and formerly very important in classical music.
In alt (It.) Pitch range of notes G to F above treble stave.
Incidental music Music composed to supplement and point up stage drama.
In nomine (L., "in the name of") Type of sixteenth- and seventeenth-century English contrapuntal composition based on a plain-song theme, usually for viols.
Instrumentation Selection of instruments for which a particular piece is written. *See also* ORCHESTRATION.
Interlude (1) Short piece inserted between two sections of an entertainment, e.g. play or opera. (2) Instrumental passage between verses of a hymn or lines of a verse.
Intermezzo (It., "in the middle") (1) Operatic or dramatic interlude. (2) Movement in sonata, symphony, etc.

(3) Name sometimes used for short, independent pieces.
Interval Difference in pitch between two notes. In Western music, intervals are named by the number of scale notes which they span. Using C major scale as an example, number names of intervals are: second (C-D); third (C-E); fourth (C-F); fifth (G-G); sixth (C-A); seventh (C-B); eighth or octave (C-C′). These are *simple* intervals, of an octave or less. Intervals larger than an octave are called *compound*, and can be regarded as an octave plus a simple interval.

There are two sizes of second interval between scale steps. The larger ones are called *major* seconds, or tones (C-D, D-E, F-G, G-A, A-B); the smaller ones are *minor* seconds, or semitones (E-F, B-C). Other intervals (except the octave) can also have the same number name but be larger or smaller. Thirds, sixths and sevenths of different sizes are distinguished as major and minor, e.g. C-E, major third (spanning two tones); E-G, minor third (tone and semitone). A perfect fifth (C-G) spans three tones and a semitone, and a perfect fourth (C-F) two tones and a semitone. Major or perfect intervals increased by a semitone are called *augmented*, and minor or perfect intervals reduced by a semitone are called *diminished*. An interval spanning three tones (the *tritone*) is called a diminished fifth (e.g. B-F) or an augmented fourth (e.g. F-B), depending on context.

By moving the lower note up an octave, any interval can be *inverted* to make another interval. Each interval in the following pairs is the inversion of the other in its pair: second/seventh; third/sixth; fourth/fifth. When inverted, major intervals become minor and vice versa, but perfect intervals remain perfect.

In melody and harmony the main distinction between intervals is whether they are consonant or dissonant. Octaves, fifths and fourths are perfect consonances; thirds and sixths are imperfect consonances; and seconds and sevenths are dissonances. *See pages 12–13, also* HARMONY; SCALE.
Intonation (1) Production of note by voice or instrument. (2) Chanting of words *"Gloria in excelsis Deo"* and *"Credo in unum Deum"* in the mass.
"Good –" Playing or singing in tune.
Just – *See page 13.*
Invention Name given by J. S. Bach to his two-part contrapuntal compositions for keyboard.
Inversion (1) Changing relative position of the two notes of an interval. *See* INTERVAL. (2) A chord is inverted if a note other than the root is in the bass. (3) A melody is inverted when it is turned upside down so that upward movements become equivalent downward movements and vice versa. **Retrograde** – A melody played backwards.

Ionian mode *See* MODE.
Isorhythm (from Gk., "equal rhythm") Repetition of a rhythm with variations of notes. A device of medieval polyphony.

Janissary music Style of percussive military music popular in eighteenth-century Europe and influenced by Turkish music (janissaries were the sultan's bodyguard).
Jazz Afro-American musical idiom which developed in United States from early twentieth century, drawing on spirituals, blues, ragtime, etc. *See pages 72–4.*
Jig Lively old folk dance of British Isles. *See also* GIGUE.
Jongleur Travelling musician and entertainer in medieval France. *See page 24.*

K *See* KÖCHEL NUMBER.
Kapellmeister (Ger., "chapel master") Director of music at a German or Austrian church or court. Today, any musical director.
Key (1) When a scale starts at a specified pitch, it is said to be in the *key* of the starting note. A piece in the key of C major is therefore based on a major scale whose starting note is C. *See* DIATONIC-CHROMATIC SYSTEM; SCALE. (2) Lever depressed by the finger to actuate mechanism of piano, organ, etc.
Köchel number Standard numbering of Mozart's compositions, undertaken by Ludwig von Köchel (1800–77). Usually abbreviated to "K.", as in Sonata in A, K.331.
Kyrie eleison (Gk., "Lord, have mercy") First section of musical setting of High Mass.

Ländler South German folk dance in triple time. Forerunner of WALTZ, but slower.
Largamente (It.) Broadly, largely.
Largo (It., "broad") Very slow, stately tempo.
Laudi spirituali Popular Italian devotional songs of Middle Ages and Renaissance, the style of which foreran that of ORATORIO.
Leader (1) Conductor or musical director. (2) Principal first violinist of an orchestra. (3) First violinist in a string quartet.
Leading-note Seventh degree of diatonic scale, so-called because it "leads" up to tonic.
Ledger or **leger lines** Short additional lines above or below stave, for notes beyond range of stave.
Legato (It., "bound") Playing so that notes are smoothly connected; opposite of STACCATO.
Leitmotiv (Ger., "leading motif") Melodic figure used to characterize situation or person. Much used by Wagner in his music-dramas.
Lento (It.) Slow, but not as slow as *largo.*
Libretto Text of an opera.
Lied (Ger., "song", plural *Lieder*) Used by English-speaking world to mean nineteenth-century German art songs, e.g. those by Schubert.

Madrigal Polyphonic composition for voices, in use in Italy in fourteenth and sixteenth centuries.
Maestoso (It.) Majestic, stately.
Maestro di cappella (It., "chapel master") Director of music.
Major "Larger". *See* INTERVAL; SCALE.
Marcato (It.) Marked, accented.
March Military music to accompany marching, or other music in similar style. Usually in $\frac{4}{4}$ time, with strongly marked rhythm.
Masque Sixteenth- and seventeenth-century English dramatic entertainment, with vocal and instrumental accompaniment.
Mass Musical setting of the service of the celebration of the Eucharist in the Roman Catholic Church. The passages normally set to music for choir, or choir and soloists, are the Kyrie, Gloria, Credo, Sanctus, Benedictus and Agnus Dei.
Mazurka National dance of Poland, in triple time.
Mediant Third degree of the diatonic scale.
Meistersinger (Ger., "mastersingers") German singers, traders and craftsmen, who flourished in guilds from fourteenth to sixteenth centuries; the successors of the noble MINNESÄNGER. *See page 24.*
Melisma (Gk., "song") Musical phrase of several notes sung to one syllable.
Melodrama In specific musical sense, use of spoken voice against musical background.
Menuet (Fr.), **Menuett** (Ger.) Minuet.
Metre In rhythm, regular grouping of beats in measures or bars. In written music, metre is shown by a time signature and by vertical barlines. *See page 14.*
Mezzo, mezza (It.) Half, medium.
Mezzo-forte *See* DYNAMICS.
Mezzo-piano *See* DYNAMICS.
Mezzo-soprano Medium range of female voice, overlapping soprano and contralto.
Mezza voce Half the power of voice(s) or instrument(s).

Microtone Any interval smaller than a semitone, e.g. a quarter-tone.
Microtonic scale Scale comprised of notes less than a semitone apart; e.g. the Hindu scale has twenty-two notes to the octave; as many as sixty notes to the octave have been distinguished (i.e. five divisions of each semitone).
Minim, half-note British and American terms for time value of half the length of a semibreve or whole note.
Minnesänger (Ger., "love-singers") German singers, aristocrats, who flourished in guilds in the twelfth and thirteenth centuries; the forerunners of the merchant-class MEISTERSINGER. *See page 24.*
Minor "Smaller". *See* INTERVAL; SCALE.
Minstrel Musical entertainer in Middle Ages and after.
Minuet (Eng.), **minuetto** (It.) Movement of a classical suite, in slow triple time and ternary (three-part) form. Usually played twice, with a second minuet (the "trio") inserted in between. Originally a French dance.
Modes In the key system which developed in the seventeenth century, tonal variety is achieved mainly by changing key, i.e. reproducing the same scale structure at a different pitch. In earlier European music, this concept was relatively unimportant. Tonal variety was achieved by using "modes", or different octave segments, of the same diatonic scale, which can be thought of as the "white-note" scale on the piano. The mode starting and ending on C is only one of seven possible modes (i.e. "manners" of looking at this basic series of intervals). Each of the modes formed by starting on different notes of the scale has its own name, and each has a different melodic flavour because its semitones occur at different distances from the starting note (*see diagram*).
Modulation Change of key.
Moderato (It.) Moderate tempo.
Molto (It.) Much or very, as in *allegro molto* (very fast).
Monody (from Gk., "singing alone") Style of composition in which interest

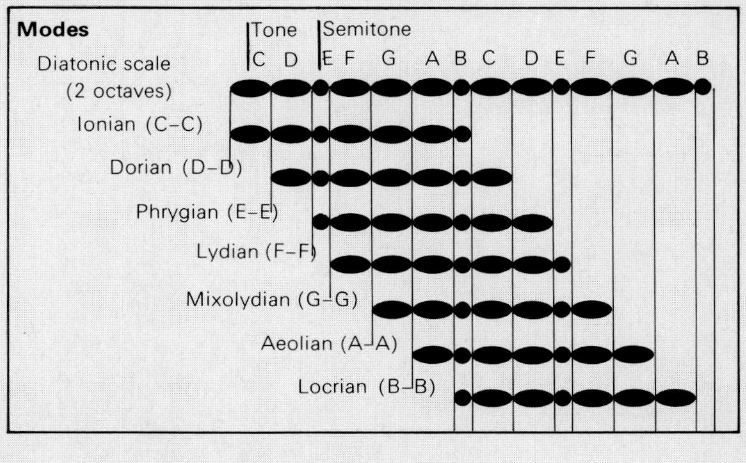

is focused in one part, the others forming an accompaniment.
Monothematic composition Work in which only one theme is developed.
Morris dance Lively English folk dance, usually in duple or quadruple time.
Motet Form of polyphonic composition which superseded the CONDUCTUS from the thirteenth century, set to words not forming part of the mass.
Motif (Fr.), **Motiv** (Ger.), **motive** (Eng.) The nucleus, or smallest unit, of a melody. *See also* LEITMOTIV.
Motto theme Melodic device similar to LEITMOTIV.
Movement Distinct section of a composition in cyclic form, e.g. sonata, symphony, etc.
Musica ficta (L., "feigned music") Use of chromatic alterations to certain notes in the old modes, to avoid awkward intervals.
Music-drama Large-scale operatic form developed by Richard Wagner.
Musique concrète (Fr., "concrete music") Music built from random sounds, which are then arranged and varied electronically. The music therefore exists only in recorded form.

Nationalism In music, a form of patriotic expression which developed in nineteenth-century Europe, incorporating ethnic tunes and rhythms and/or inspired by some event of national importance.
Natural (of a note or key) Not sharp or flat. *See* ACCIDENTAL.
Neoclassicism Musical movement of earlier twentieth century, led by Stravinsky and Bartók, which rejected the excesses of romanticism and sought inspiration in the formal balance of eighteenth-century classicism.
Neume Individual sign in the notation used for Eastern chant and Western plainsong.
Ninth (1) Interval spanning nine notes (an octave plus a tone). (2) Chord formed by adding to a seventh chord the ninth note above its root.
Nocturne (Fr.) Dreamy, romantic piece evocative of night.
Nonet Composition for nine voices or instruments.
Notation System of writing music.
Note (1) Single sound of specific duration and pitch. (2) Symbol representing this. **– -row** In twelve-note and other serial music, a basic pattern comprising the twelve notes of the chromatic scale on which such a composition is built up.

Obbligato (It., "obligatory") Instrumental accompaniment to song, etc., having musical importance of its own.
Octave Interval formed by two notes, of which the upper has twice the frequency of the lower. So called because the upper note forms the eighth note of a diatonic scale commencing on the lower note. *See* INTERVAL; *pages 12–13.*
Opera (It., "works") Musical stage drama originating in Italy in about 1600. *See pages 60–63 for types of opera.*
Operetta (1) Short opera. (2) Light opera.
Opus (L., "work") Piece(s) of music. **– number** Number given to works in order of composition or publication. An opus may contain more than one work, in which case it is identified by an additional number, e.g. op. 1, no. 1.
Oratorio Extended setting of religious text for chorus, solo singers and orchestra.
Orchestra Large group of instrumentalists.
Orchestration Branch of composition concerned with making effective use of the sound combinations offered by orchestral instruments.
Organum Earliest form of polyphony, in which the different parts moved in parallel intervals of octaves, fifths and fourths.
Ornament Melodic decoration.
Ostinato (It., "obstinate") Repeated musical figure, as in *basso ostinato* or GROUND BASS.
Overtone *See* HARMONICS.
Overture (from Fr. *ouverture*, "opening") (1) Orchestral introduction to opera or other vocal work. (2) A concert overture is an independent piece for concert performance.

Part One performer's music in an ensemble; a single line in a musical score.
Partita (It.) (1) A variation. (2) Set of pieces; similar to classical SUITE but not restricted to dance forms.
Part-song Vocal composition for two or more vocal parts.
Passacaglia (It.) *See* CHACONNE.
Passage work Rapid scale or arpeggio passages.
Passepied (Fr., "pass-foot") Optional movement of classical suite, in triple time, with contrasting sections in major and minor keys. Originally a French folk dance.
Passing note Note in melody or part which does not belong to prevailing chord, coming between two notes forming part of the chord and approached and quit by step. Passing notes usually occur on unaccented beats or parts of beats.
Passion Musical setting of biblical description of Christ's crucifixion, according to one of the Gospels.
Pastoral (Eng.), **pastorale** (It., Fr.) (1) In fifteenth to eighteenth centuries, musical stage work with rural and mythological theme. (2) Instrumental piece evoking country-side.
Pause 𝄐 Prolongation of a note, chord or rest. *See* FERMATA.
Pavan (Eng.), **pavana** (It.), **pavane** (Fr.) Stately sixteenth-century dance in quadruple or duple time. Originally Italian, popular in Spain and England.
Pedal (1) Sustained bass-note over changing harmonies. (2) *See instrument glossary.*
Pentatonic scale Five-note scale, as formed by piano's "black notes", with intervals of tones and minor thirds. Widespread in e.g. Chinese, African and Celtic music.
Pesante (It.) Heavy, heavily.
Phrase Unit of a melodic line or part; shorter than a musical "sentence", but longer than a MOTIF.
Phrygian mode *See* MODES.
Pianissimo *See* DYNAMICS.
Piano *See* DYNAMICS.
Picardie third *See* TIERCE DE PICARDIE.
Pitch "Height" or "depth" of a note as defined by the frequency of its vibrations. *See* ABSOLUTE PITCH; CONCERT PITCH; RELATIVE PITCH.
Pizzicato, pizz. (It.) Direction that strings (violin, etc.) should be plucked rather than bowed (*arco*).
Plainchant, plainsong The most ancient style of Christian church music, sung in unison and in free rhythm determined by metrical accent of words. *See* AMBROSIAN CHANT; GREGORIAN CHANT.
Polka Bohemian dance. *See page 65.*
Polonaise (Fr., "Polish") National dance of Poland in triple time. Occasionally included in classical suite; highly developed by Chopin.
Polyphony (from Gk., "many voices") Music having several independently moving parts; particularly applied to vocal music of the Middle Ages and Renaissance. Opposite of HOMOPHONY. *See also* COUNTERPOINT.
Polyrhythm Simultaneous use of several rhythms.
Polytonality Simultaneous use of several keys.
Portamento (It.) (1) Same as GLISSANDO. (2) On piano, "half-staccato".
Postlude Closing piece (opposite of PRELUDE).
Prelude Introductory piece (opposite of POSTLUDE).
Prestissimo (It.) Very fast indeed.
Presto (It.) Very fast.
Process music Music in which short phrases are repeated many times in accordance with a set of instructions (the process) producing complex rhythmical combinations. *See page 54.*
Programme music Music intended to evoke extra-musical emotions and visual images. Opposite of ABSOLUTE MUSIC.
Progression (1) Melodic progression: movement from one note to the next. (2) Harmonic or chord progression: movement from one chord to the next.
Pulse Beat. Periodic stress in metrical music.

Quartal harmony Harmony built up in intervals of fourths.
Quarter-note *See* CROTCHET.
Quarter tone Interval of half a semitone.
Quartet Ensemble of, or sonata-like composition for, four voices or instruments.
Quaver, eighth-note British and American terms for time value of one-eighth of a semibreve or whole note.
Quintet Ensemble of, or sonata-like composition for, five voices or instruments.
Quodlibet (L., "what pleases") (1) Medley of popular tunes. (2) Simultaneous combination of two or more popular tunes.

Raga (Hin., "colour" or "feeling") One of the many possible selections of notes on which a performance of Indian music is based. *See pages 84–5.*
Ragtime Early twentieth-century style of black American piano music, so-called from "ragged" i.e. syncopated rhythm.
Rallentando (It.) Becoming slower.
Recapitulation *See* SONATA FORM.
Recitative (Eng.), **recitativo** (It.) In opera, style of musical declamation falling between speech and song. *See pages 31 and 60.*
Register Particular section of range of voice or instrument.
Related or **relative keys** Keys having several notes or tones in common. (1) Relative minor and major keys (e.g. C major and A minor) have the same key signature. (2) The related keys of a major key are the major keys of the dominant and subdominant, and the relative minors of all three. (3) The related keys of a minor key are the minor keys of the dominant and subdominant and their relative majors.
Relative pitch Ability to sing or identify a particular note after hearing a named note. *See also* ABSOLUTE PITCH.
Répétiteur (Fr., "repeater") The chorus-master of an opera-house who rehearses (repeats) the chorus.
Reprise (Fr.) (1) A repeat of a section of music. (2) Recapitulation section in sonata form.
Requiem Musical setting of the mass for the dead.
Rest In musical notation a sign indicating a silence of a definite length. *See page 14.*
Retrograde inversion *See* INVERSION.
Rhapsody Usually, a free-ranging fantasia on folk-melodies or similar.
Rhythm The organization of music in *time*, as opposed to its organization in *pitch* (tonality). Establishment of relative durations and time-positions of notes. *See page 14.* **"A –"** A repeated rhythmic pattern.
Ricercare (It., "seek out") (1) Fugal composition of sixteenth and seventeenth centuries in which composer "seeks out" elaborate devices of counterpoint. (2) Toccata or fantasia.
Ritardando (It.) Getting gradually slower.
Ritornello (It.) (1) Refrain in earlier

Italian madrigal. (2) Instrumental passage in accompanied vocal music. (3) Orchestral TUTTI in classical concerto. (4) Any musical repeat.
Rococo (from Fr. *rocaille*, a type of fancy rock-work) Eighteenth-century "galant" style, by analogy with architecture of the period. *See* CLASSICISM; STYLE GALANT.
Romanticism In music, style in which emotional content tends to take precedence over formal balance. Usually applied to nineteenth-century music. *See pages 39–47*.
Rondo Form in which a principal theme alternates with contrasting themes or episodes.
Root The lowest note of a chord in uninverted form (i.e. – position).
Round Simple canon for two or more voices.
Rubato, tempo – ("robbed", "robbed time") Style of playing in which a steady over-all tempo is maintained while some notes are speeded up and others slowed down, for expressive purposes.

Sanctus (L., "holy") Fourth section of a musical setting of the High Mass.
Saraband (Eng.), **sarabande** (Fr.) Movement of a classical suite, in binary (two-part) form and triple time. Derived from ancient dance, possibly of Spanish or Moorish origin.
Scale (from It. *scala*, "ladder") Series of notes arranged in pitch order (ascending or descending) and forming the "set" from which notes of melodies and chords are selected. A scale spans the entire pitch, with its particular pattern of intervals repeated in each octave. For study purposes scales are taken as starting and ending on two notes an octave apart (the finishing note being also the starting note for continuing the scale in the next octave). Different kinds of scales are classified (i) by the number of notes contained in an octave and (ii) by the size and order of intervals between their notes.
The Western diatonic scale has seven different notes (the eighth note being the "same" as the first, an octave higher), spaced by tone and semitone intervals. One "major" and two "minor" forms of this scale exist. The major scale has the notes C D E F G A B C, and is so named because its first and third notes are a major third apart. The first and third notes of both forms of minor scale are a minor third apart. The "melodic" minor scale has different ascending and descending forms: C D E♭ F G A B C (upwards) and C B♭ A♭ G F E♭ D C (downwards). The "harmonic" minor scale is the same both ways, with the sixth and seventh notes separated by an "augmented second": C D E♭ F G A♭ B C. *See also pages 12 and 15*; CHROMATIC SCALE; DIATONIC; DIATONIC-CHROMATIC SYSTEM; INTERVAL.
Scherzo (It., "joke") Instrumental piece of sometimes humorous character. Can be a single piece or a movement of a longer composition, e.g. a sonata or symphony.
Score Written or printed music with all the parts of a composition set out one above the other on the page.
Scoring Instrumentation, orchestration.
Scotch snap Rhythmic figure of a short on-the-beat note, followed by a longer one; found in some Scottish folk music.
Second *See* INTERVAL.
Semibreve, whole-note British and American terms for the longest time value in common use, equivalent to two minims or four crotchets. *See* BREVE.
Semiquaver, sixteenth-note British and American terms for time value of a sixteenth of a semibreve or whole-note.
Semitone *See* INTERVAL.
Septet Ensemble of, or composition for, seven voices or instruments.
Sequence (1) Repetition of a melodic phrase, or harmonic movement, at successively higher or lower pitches. (2) Chord sequence: movement of chords, harmonic progression.
Serenade (1) Properly, music composed to be sung or played at night; often, a light vocal or instrumental piece. (2) In classical period, a sort of sonata for an instrumental ensemble.
Serial technique Method of composition in which every aspect of the music, including pitch, rhythm and volume, is worked out according to a predetermined plan or series. The series can be repeated, inverted, reversed, augmented or diminished, etc., as long as mathematical relationships are preserved. The NOTE-ROW is one type of series.
Seventh (1) Interval spanning seven notes. (2) Chord formed by adding to a triad the seventh note above its root.
Sextet Ensemble of, or composition for, six voices or instruments.
Sforzando, sf., sfz. (It., "forcing") Direction for note or chord to be strongly accented. Sudden force.
Shake *See* TRILL.
Sharp *See* ACCIDENTAL.
Siciliano (It.) Old dance, possibly Sicilian, in swaying triplet rhythm ($\frac{6}{8}$ or $\frac{12}{8}$). Eighteenth-century composers used it as slow movement in suites and sonatas.
Simple time Rhythm based on dividing pulse into two or four equal parts.
Sinfonietta (It.) Small-scale symphony.
Singspiel (Ger., "sing-play") Musical stage drama with spoken dialogue and interpolated songs.
Sixth *See* INTERVAL.
Sol-fa *See* TONIC SOL-FA.
Solfeggio (It.), **solfège** (Fr.) System of sight-reading and ear-training which uses sol-fa syllables.
Solmization Sight-singing from sol-fa syllables according to any of the various systems in use.
Solo (It., "alone") Piece or part of a piece for performance by an individual singer or instrumentalist.
Sonata (It., "sounded") Originally, a piece to be "sounded" rather than "sung" (*cantata*), i.e. instrumental as opposed to vocal music. From eighteenth century, composition for one or two instruments in two to four contrasted movements, e.g. (1) allegro; (2) slow movement; (3) scherzo, of minuet and trio; (4) allegro. *See pages 33 and 36*.
Sonata form Ground-plan commonly (but not always) used for first movements of classical sonatas. Based on two themes or subjects, it is divided into three main sections: (1) *exposition*: first theme stated in home key, second theme commencing in different key; (2) *development*: both themes freely developed in fantasia style; (3) *recapitulation*: restatement of original themes, both in home key. Sonata form is binary in the sense of being built from two themes, ternary in sense of having three main sections; therefore it is sometimes called "compound binary form". Also known as "first-movement form". *See page 36*.
Song Musical setting of poem or piece of prose.
Soprano (1) The highest range of female voice. (2) High, or highest-pitched, member of a family of instruments.
Sostenuto (It.) Sustained.
Sotto voce (It., "under the voice") Barely audible.
Spiccato (It., "articulated") In string- (violin, etc.) playing, staccato effect achieved by loose bow movement.
Sprechstimme (Ger., "speech-song") A way of using the voice that is half-way between speaking and singing. Invented by Schoenberg and used in his *Gurrelieder*.
Staccato (It., "detached") Direction for notes to be played in detached, separated manner. Indicated by dot above (or below) the note.
Staff, stave Horizontal five-line grid on the lines and spaces of which musical notes are written to indicate their pitch. *See page 15, also* CLEF; KEY SIGNATURE; TIME SIGNATURE.
Study Composition written mainly to develop or display instrumental technique.
Style galant (Fr., "gallant style") Light, elegant style of later eighteenth-century composers such as Haydn and Mozart. Nearly synonymous with "classical" style in strict sense. *See also* ROCOCO.
Subdominant Fourth degree of the diatonic scale.
Subject Main or other theme of a composition, e.g. fugue, sonata, symphony, etc.
Submediant Sixth degree of diatonic scale (i.e. third degree below tonic, as mediant is third degree above tonic).
Suite (Fr., "following") The classical suite was an instrumental composition consisting of a set of movements in various dance forms, such as allemande, courante, sarabande, gigue, bourrée, gavotte and minuet. *See page 33*. Modern suites often consist of movements not in dance form, or of sections from larger works, e.g. ballet.
Supertonic ("above the tonic") Second degree of diatonic scale.
Suspension In harmony, dissonance produced by holding over a note of a chord until another chord, to which the held note does not belong, has sounded. In classical harmony, suspensions are treated in three stages: (1) *preparation*: appearance of note in first chord; (2) *suspension*: prolongation of note as dissonance in second chord; (3) *resolution*: movement of suspended note by step to a consonant note in second chord.
Symphonic poem (sometimes **tone poem**) Extended orchestral descriptive composition, not divided into separate movements.
Symphony Orchestral work, usually in four movements; the characteristic extended form of later eighteenth- and nineteenth-century music. Term originally implied SONATA for orchestra. *See page 36*.
Syncopation Stressing or accenting a beat, or subdivision of a beat, which is not the main accented beat of the measure or bar.

Tablature Simple method of musical notation for guitar, etc., using diagrams to show position of player's fingers.
Tacet (L., "is silent") Direction that a part so marked is not to be played (or sung), e.g. during the first rendition of a repeated section.
Tala (Hin.) A measure or rhythm cycle in Indian music. *See page 85*.
Tarantella (1) Lively Italian dance in $\frac{6}{8}$ time. (2) Brilliant instrumental piece inspired by same.
Temperament Any system of adjusting (i.e. "tempering") the tuning of intervals of the "natural scale" so that music played in different keys sounds equally "in tune". In mean temperature tuning, used in the seventeenth and eighteenth centuries, some keys sounded in tune and others very much out of tune. This system was gradually replaced by the equal temperament tuning generally used today. *See page 13*.
Tempo (It., "time", plural *tempi*) Speed of pulse or beat in music. *See* ADAGIO; ALLEGRETTO; ALLEGRO; ANDANTE; ANDANTINO; LARGO; LENTO; MODERATO; PRESTO; PRESTISSIMO; VIVACE. *See also* ACCELERANDO; RALLENTANDO.
Tenor Highest natural (i.e. not falsetto) range of male voice. Also applied to instruments of similar range, e.g. tenor horn, tenor saxophone.
Ternary form Musical form in three

sections, the third being a repetition of the first.
Tessitura (It., "texture") Comfortable range of a voice or instrument.
Tetrachord (from Gk. *tettares*, "four") Scale of four notes, with lower and upper notes a perfect fourth apart (e.g. C D E F). Originally the tuning of the strings of ancient Greek lyre. The diatonic scale was derived from two tetrachords, separated by a tone: C D E F, and G A B C.
Theme "Subject matter" of a composition, i.e. the main musical idea or melody from which a piece is developed. *See also* SUBJECT.
Theme-and-variation form Musical structure in which a theme or tune is presented and then repeated several or many times in varied but still recognizable shape.
Third *See* INTERVAL.
Thorough-bass *See* BASSO CONTINUO.
Tie or **bind** Curved line connecting two or more notes of the same pitch, showing that they are to be played as a continuous note.
Tierce de Picardie (Fr., "Picardy third") Major chord used to end a piece in a minor key.
Timbre (Fr.) Tone quality or colour, i.e. characteristic sound of a particular instrument.
Time signature Numerals at beginning of stave to show number of beats to the bar or measure and the time value of each beat. *See page 14.* The time signature $\frac{4}{4}$ is called "common time" and can be shown as **C**. **₵** means two minims or half notes to the bar (*"alla breve"* time).
Time value Time length of a musical note. *See page 14.*
Toccata Keyboard composition in fast-moving fantasia style; usually a vehicle for virtuoso technique.
Tonality (1) General aspect of music concerned with pitch relationships of notes, i.e. melody, harmony, scales, etc., as opposed to rhythm, dynamics and timbre. (2) More specifically, music having tonality is organized around a "central" note or tonic, and has a sense of being in a particular scale or key. ATONALITY is the opposite of this.
Tone (1) Same as TIMBRE. (2) Interval of a major second (*see* INTERVAL).
Tone poem *See* SYMPHONIC POEM.
Tonic First degree, or key-note, of the diatonic scale.
Tonic sol-fa System of sight-singing developed in 1840s by John Curwen, using a syllable name for each degree of the scale and a rhythm notation based on punctuation marks. Tonic sol-fa uses a "movable doh", i.e. the first note of a scale is "doh" in any key. Continental sol-fa systems (i.e. *solfège, solfeggio*) use a "fixed doh", i.e. "doh" is always C.
Transcription Arrangement of a composition for instrument(s) other than that for which it was originally written.
Transition Passage that joins one theme to another in a composition.
Transposition "Translation" of a composition into a key other than that in which it was originally written.
Treble (1) High voice, usually of children ("boy soprano"). (2) Highest part in a musical composition. (3) High-pitched member of an instrumental family. *See also* CLEF.
Tremolo (It., "trembling") (1) On strings (violin, etc.), effect produced by rapid up-and-down movement of bow on strings. (2) Rapid alternation of notes on keyboard. (3) Rapid vocal VIBRATO.
Triad *See* HARMONY.
Trill The most important musical ornament, formed by regular, rapid alternation between a note and the note above it. Also called SHAKE.
Trio (1) Ensemble of, or sonata-like composition for, three voices or instruments. (2) *See* MINUET.
Triplet Rhythmic group of three evenly spaced notes played in the time of one or two beats, shown by a "3" under or over the notes.
Tritone *See* INTERVAL.
Troppo (It.) Too much; e.g. *Adagio ma non troppo* = slow but not too slow.
Troubadour Medieval poet-musician of southern France in eleventh to thirteenth centuries. *See pages 24 and 56.*
Trouvère (Fr., "finder") Medieval poet-musician of northern France in eleventh to thirteenth centuries. *See pages 24 and 56.*
Tutti (It., "all") (1) Direction for all performers to play. (2) Orchestral passage played by all musicians.
Twelve-note or **dodecaphonic composition** Technique based on a tonal theme or NOTE-ROW which consists of the twelve notes of the chromatic scale. Developed by Schoenberg in early twentieth century.

Unison Relationship between two notes of the same pitch played (or sung) together.
Up-beat (1) Raising of hand or conductor's baton in beating time. (2) Unaccented beat of bar (indicated by up-beat movement).

Variation *See* THEME-AND-VARIATION FORM.
Vibrato Rapid upwards and downwards deviation from pitch of note, achievable on bowed and fretted stringed instruments, wind instruments and voices.
Villanella Fifteenth- and sixteenth-century Italian part-song.
Virtuoso Instrumentalist or singer of outstanding technique.
Vivace (It., "lively", "brisk") Tempo equal to *allegro*, or faster.
Voice (1) For various ranges, *see* SOPRANO; TREBLE; MEZZO-SOPRANO; CONTRALTO; ALTO; TENOR; BASS; COUNTER-TENOR. *See also* TESSITURA; HEAD VOICE. (2) An instrumental part or line, as in a fugue.
Voluntary Organ solo played as PRELUDE or POSTLUDE to, or during, a church service.

Waltz Dance in triple time, which developed from South German *Ländler*.
Whole-note *See* SEMIBREVE.
Whole-tone scale Six-note scale which progresses by intervals of tones only.

Yodelling Singing style featuring alternation between natural and falsetto voice.

Glossary of Instruments

Abbreviations in brackets denote linguistic origin: Eng., English; Fr., French; Ger., German; Gk., Greek; It., Italian; L., Latin; Nor., Norwegian.

Accordion Portable, box-shaped instrument operated on a bellows principle. The wind created by contracting the bellows causes free metal reeds to vibrate. Notes are selected by depressing studs with the fingers. **Piano** – Similar to accordion, but with studs for left hand only, a keyboard for the right.
Adenkum Ghanaian stamping stick, consisting of a gourd.
Aeolian harp Wire- or gut-strung sound-box, the strings of which are vibrated by wind. (Aeolus was the Greek god of the winds.)
Aerophone Any instrument sounded by the vibration of air.
Alboka Basque hornpipe with two cane pipes, a horn at each end and a handle.
Alghaita Nigerian folk shawm with a metal mouthpiece and a leather-covered body.
Alpenhorn Alpine trumpet made of wood, once used for signalling and about three metres long.
Alto (Fr.) Viola.
Altohorn Nineteenth-century instrument consisting of seven separate horns joined by a single mouthpiece and six valves.
American organ Harmonium-like free-reed organ with reeds vibrated by suction bellows.
Angle harp Ancient harp with two-sided, almost right-angled frame.
Anklung Japanese bamboo rattle.
Apache fiddle Apache Indian one- or two-stringed fiddle made from a hollowed-out cactus.
Appalachian dulcimer Fretted zither with melody and drone strings. The strings are stopped by the player's spare hand, possibly using a quill or stick for the purpose. Because the strings are plucked, rather than struck with hammers, this is not a true dulcimer.
Arched harp *See* BOW HARP.
Archlute Generic term for large two-headed lute with one peg-box surmounting the other.
Arghul (1) Ancient Egyptian multiple clarinet. (2) Arab bagpipe.
Armonica Glass friction instrument devised by Benjamin Franklin in the 1760s. Consisting of different-sized glass bowls fitted on a rod suspended over a trough of water. Sounded by holding the fingers against the rims of the bowls while they are rotated mechanically.
Arpa (It.) Harp.
Arpanetta (It.) (Ger. *Spitzharfe*) Domestic table harp popular from 1650 to 1750.
Arpeggione Viennese bowed stringed instrument with metal frets, of the size and pitch of the cello, invented in the 1820s.
Atumpan Wooden Ghanaian kettle-drum.
Aulos (plural *auloi*) Ancient Greek shawm.
Autoharp Fretless zither with felted levers which when pressed on to the strings damp all the strings not needed to make a particular chord.

Bagana Ethiopian lyre used by noble and priestly classes.
Bagpipe Folk reed-pipe instrument. Air is stored in an animal bladder which is filled either by the player's breath or by a bellows held under his arm.
Balalaika Russian three-stringed guitar-like instrument with four movable frets and a triangular body.
Banana drum Congolese wooden drum.
Bandora or **pandora** (1) Sixteenth-/seventeenth-century plucked stringed instrument of lute type; a bass cittern. (2) Ancient long-necked, small-bodied lute which has survived in various forms in the Middle East.
Banjo Plucked guitar-like instrument. The gut strings, of which there are five or more, are stretched across a round parchment belly and a fretted finger-board.
Banjolele Small banjo with four gut strings, like a ukulele.
Baritone (1) Brass instrument of bugle family, with pitch between flugelhorn and tuba. (2) Abbreviated name for baritone SAXHORN, used in brass bands.
Barrel drum Single- or double-headed drum in the shape of a barrel.
Barrel organ Mechanical organ controlled by a barrel fitted with pins and bridges and rotated by hand, clockwork, steam or electricity.
Baryton(e) Seventeenth-century bass viol with six bowed strings and up to forty sympathetic strings.
Bassanello Renaissance deep-pitched shawm blown through a crook.
Bass drum Large double-headed orchestral and band drum of indefinite pitch.
Basset horn Tenor instrument of the clarinet family, now usually replaced by the alto clarinet.
Bassgeige (Ger.) Cello.
Basson (Fr.) Bassoon.
Bassonore Wide-bore bassoon for military band use.
Bassoon Jointed double-reed instrument derived from the CURTAL. Bass member of the oboe family.
Bata Wooden conical drum from Cuba.
Battery Collective term for untuned orchestral percussion instruments.
Becken (Ger.) Cymbals.
Bell Metal percussion instrument which when struck vibrates, most strongly at its rim.
Bhaya Indian kettledrum. The left-hand drum of the TABLA.
Bible regal Portable book-shaped folding reed-organ.
Bird-scarer Simple clappers, often of wood, used for sounding a rhythm.
Biwa Japanese flat-backed lute.
Bladder-pipe Simple medieval bagpipe.
Board zither Rectangular or trapezoid zither. Its strings are stretched across a board which forms the top of a box resonator.
Bodhran Irish frame drum.
Bombard(e) (1) General term in fifteenth to seventeenth century for bass and tenor shawms. (2) Breton folk shawm. (3) Bass (sixteen-foot) reed-organ stop.
Bombardon Alternative name for the bass tuba.
Bonang Indonesian gamelan chime of bossed gongs.
Bongo drum Small Cuban drum struck with flattened fingers. Usually played in pairs.
Bourdon (1) Low-pitched organ stop. (2) Bass strings of plucked instruments. (3) Early term for drone pipes of the bagpipes.
Bouzouki A long-necked Greek folk lute.
Bow (1) Hunting bow used for musical purposes: primitive single-stringed instrument played by plucking or by vibrating the string with a stick or second bow. The end may be held in the player's mouth, which then acts as a resonator. (2) More elaborate instrument with its own resonator attached and perhaps comprising a number of bows set in parallel, each producing a note of different pitch. (3) An implement used for vibrating the strings of certain stringed instruments, usually consisting of a wooden stick with a ribbon of animal hair stretched from end to end.
Bow or **arched harp** Folk harp with strings attached to a bowed frame.
Bowl lyre Lyre with a bowl-shaped sound-box.
Box lyre Lyre with a box-shaped sound-box.
Brass Generic name for all instruments made of metal and blown with some sort of cup- or cone-shaped mouthpiece.
Bratsche (Ger.) Viola.
Buccina (L.) Ancient Roman animal-horn trumpet.
Bugle (1) Wide-bore conical valveless horn. (2) Family of brass instruments with wide conical bore and varying registers, including flugelhorns (highest), tenor horns and baritones, tenor tubas or euphoniums, bass tubas or bombardons, and contrabass tubas (lowest).
Buisine Medieval long straight trumpet, in several joined sections with ornamental bosses.
Bull-roarer or **thunder stick** Primitive instrument usually consisting of a shaped piece of wood attached to a string. When the player whirls it round his head, a roaring sound is produced, considered to be like that of thunder or the wind.
Bumbass Monochord-type instrument, like a musical bow with a resonator inserted between string and wood.
Buzz-disc Primitive instrument consisting of a disc through two holes in which a string is threaded, then tied at the ends. The string is twisted and, when pulled taut, the disc rotates creating sound.

Cabaza Simple percussion instrument consisting of a gourd covered in strings of beads. The player slaps the gourd while it rotates.
Calliope Mechanical organ with whistles operated by steam from a boiler.
Carillon (1) Set of tuned bells which are sounded by hammers operated from a keyboard. (2) Bell-like organ stops.
Carynx First-century Celtic bronze trumpet, usually with a bell in the form of an open-mouthed animal.
Castanets Pair of shell-shaped wooden clappers manipulated by the fingers or, in orchestras, mounted on a stick.
Celesta (Eng., It.), **céleste** (Fr.) Keyboard instrument incorporating tuned metal bars struck by hammers.
Cello, violoncello Large bass member of the violin family. Played resting between the knees until the 1850s, when the retractable spike which allows the instrument to rest on the floor was added.
Cembalo (It.) Literally, dulcimer. Generally, any *keyboard* instrument, but especially the harpsichord.
Chakay Long tube zither from Thailand in crocodile form.
Chalumeau (1) Single-reed folk instrument which was the forerunner of the clarinet. (2) Now, lowest register of the clarinet.
Chamber organ Non-portable flue-pipe organ for domestic or church use, a later form of positive organ.
Chanter Melody pipe of the bagpipe which is fingered by the player.
Chelys Small ancient Greek lyre.
Chime Set of tuned bells or gongs.
Chime bar Simple metallophone consisting of tuned metal bars which are struck by hand-held hammers.
Ch'in Classical long unfretted zither of China.
Chinese wood block Wooden block which is tapped with a beater to give a loud penetrating sound.
Chitarra battente Seventeenth-/eighteenth-century five-stringed Italian guitar.
Chitarrone Long-necked Renaissance archlute.
Chocallo Simple shaken percussion instrument consisting of a hollow cylinder containing dried seeds.
Chordophone Any instrument sounded by the vibration of strings.
Cimbalom Hungarian dulcimer.
Citole Forerunner of the CITTERN.
Cittern Metal-stringed, pear-shaped plucked instrument with a flat back, fretted finger-board and a variable number of strings.
Clappers Percussion instrument consisting of two hinged arms with wooden shells or metal cymbals at

their extremities which clash together when shaken.
Clarinet (Eng.), **clarinette** (Fr.), **clarinetto** (It.) Single-reed woodwind instrument with a cylindrical bore.
Clarinetto d'amore (It.) Obsolete bass clarinet.
Clavecin (Fr.) Harpsichord.
Claves Wooden percussion sticks used to mark rhythm in Latin-American music.
Clavicembalo (It.) Harpsichord.
Clavichord Keyboard instrument in use from the fifteenth to the late eighteenth century, with wire strings, running the length of a horizontal soundboard, which are struck by small metal tangents. The player can achieve a range of dynamics by varying his touch.
Clavicor Brass-band horn with valves.
Clavier (Ger.) *See* KLAVIER.
Clavicytherium Early upright harpsichord.
Claviorgan Instrument combining features of both organ and harpsichord, with a single keyboard, two sets of strings and three ranks of lever-controlled pipes.
Cog rattle Percussion instrument, similar to a football rattle, sounded by a flat piece of wood on a handle round a notched cog wheel.
Colascione Long-necked Italian three-stringed lute popular in the sixteenth and seventeenth centuries.
Concertina Portable hexagonal free-reed instrument operated on a bellows principle with a stud "keyboard". *See* ACCORDION.
Conical drum Drum of varying diameter. Shapes vary from a flattish bowl to a long tapering cone.
Contrabass (Ger.), **contrebasse** (Fr.), **contrabasso, contrabbasso** (It.) Double-bass.
Contrabassoon or **double-bassoon** Wind instrument with a range an octave lower than a bassoon.
Contrafagotto (It.) Double-bassoon.
Contre-basson (Fr.) Double-bassoon.
Cor anglais (Fr., "English horn") Alto oboe.
Cornemuse (1) French bagpipe. (2) (or **cornamuse**) Renaissance double-reed instrument.
Cornet Brass instrument with three valves, descended from the post-horn and shaped like a squat trumpet.
Cornett Soprano wind instrument of the sixteenth and seventeenth centuries made of wood (or ivory) bound in leather, with finger-holes and a cup-shaped mouthpiece.
Corno (It.) Horn.
Corno inglese (It., "English horn") Cor anglais.
Cornu (L.) Ancient Roman semicircular horn.
Courtaut Renaissance double-reed instrument.
Crécelle (Fr.) Cog rattle.
Crook Detachable section of tubing fitted to some brass instruments (horns, trumpets etc.) in accordance with the key of the piece to be played. Each crook produces a harmonic series for the key concerned. From the 1850s valves were fitted to instruments instead.
Crook horn Brass horn with a selection of crooks for changing key.
Crotal Ancient metal clapper, like tongs with cymbal-like ends.
Crowd *See* CRWTH.
Crumhorn Double-reed instrument used from the fifteenth to the seventeenth century.
Crwth, crowd Celtic bowed lyre with four melody strings over a finger-board and two drone strings, in use from the Middle Ages to the early 1800s. Survived longest in Wales, hence its more common Welsh name.
Curtal Renaissance double-reed one-piece instrument, the predecessor of the bassoon.
Cylindrical drum Drum of constant diameter.
Cymbal (Eng.), **cymbale** (Fr.) Untuned metal dish. Pairs are clashed together to mark an accent, single instruments struck with a stick.

Deutsche Schalmei Renaissance double-reed instrument with a single key.
Diapason stops The main stops on an organ.
Diatonic harp Italian harp which could play in one key only. Popular in the seventeenth and eighteenth centuries, before the problems of producing chromatic models were solved.
Didgeridoo Aboriginal large cylindrical wooden trumpet.
Double-bass Deepest member of the violin family, usually about two metres high.
Double-bassoon Contrabassoon.
Double-reed instrument One in which sound is produced by the vibration of two blades of dried cane when air is blown between them.
Drum One of the two types of membranophone (the other being the mirliton). Percussion instrument consisting of skin stretched over one or both ends of a hollow sound-box
Dudelsack Old German bagpipe.
Duff Arabic tambourine.
Dulcimer Zither-like stringed instrument consisting of a flat trapezoid sound-box over which are stretched metal strings with movable bridges. Played with hand-held hammers or "beaters".
Dulzian (Ger.) CURTAL.
Dvojachka Slovakian double flute.
Dvonice Folk instrument of Yugoslavia in the form of a double flute.

Earth zither Primitive instrument consisting of a string stretched between posts set in the ground and positioned over a bark-covered pit which acts as resonator.
Electric guitar Solid-bodied, metal-stringed instrument with a metal pick-up (instead of a sound-box) enabling the string vibrations to be converted into sound electronically by an amplifier and speaker. Played with a plectrum.
Electric organ Organ that produces sound from signals produced by oscillating electronic circuits.
Electric piano Stringless keyboard instrument with piano-like tone in which sound is produced electronically.
Electric violin Modified violin with an internal pick-up.
End-blown flute Reedless woodwind instrument played by blowing against the sharp rim of its open end.
English horn (Eng.), **Englisches Horn** (Ger.) *See* COR ANGLAIS.
Enharmonic harpsichord Renaissance instrument capable of playing a number of microtonic intervals.
Eunuch or **onion flute** Mock shawm of the seventeenth and eighteenth centuries for humming tunes into. A membrane such as an onion skin lends a buzzing quality to the sound.
Euphonium Tenor tuba.

Fagott (Ger.), **fagotto** (It.) Bassoon.
Fandur Caucasian bottle-shaped folk fiddle.
Fanfare trumpet Valveless trumpet used on ceremonial occasions.
Fiddle (1) Early bowed stringed instrument. (2) Colloquial or "folk" name for violin.
Fidel Early fiddle.
Fidla Icelandic board zither which is played with a bow.
Fife (1) Small, soprano transverse flute intended for playing with the drum (tabor). (2) General name in the sixteenth century for any kind of pipe, including the shawm.
Fipple or **whistle flute** End-blown flute in which air is directed against the sharp edge of a hole cut just below the mouthpiece.
Fithele Early fiddle.
Flageolet Fipple flute with six finger-holes and a narrow tapering bore. Precursor of the recorder.
Flauto (It.) Flute.
Flauto piccolo (It.) Piccolo.
Flexatone Percussion instrument consisting of a metal sheet which is tensed by the player's thumb (to give different notes) then shaken to make it vibrate.
Flöte (Ger.) Flute.
Flügel (Ger., "wing") Grand piano.
Flugelhorn Valved brass instrument with wide conical bore of same pitch as trumpet but with mellower tone.
Flute (Eng.), **flûte** (Fr.) Reedless woodwind instrument, now sometimes made of metal, with no mouthpiece. A jet of air blown from the side into a mouth-hole hits a sharp edge inside the instrument. This sets up a vibration, the pitch of which is controlled by stopping and unstopping the finger-holes.
Footed drum Single-headed wooden drum with legs.
Fortepiano (It., "loud-soft") Early name for piano.
Frame drum Percussion instrument with one or two membranes stretched over a simple frame.
Frame harp Harp with a complete three-sided frame, like the medieval and the modern orchestral models.
Free-reed instrument Wind instrument with separately vibrating reeds, e.g. accordion, concertina, harmonica.
French horn Valved oiled brass double horn; the standard orchestral horn.
Friction drum Drum whose membrane is made to vibrate by friction.
Friction instrument One sounded by rubbing two surfaces together.
Fujara Large wooden Slovakian fipple flute.
Fuye Japanese bamboo side-blown flute.

Gamelan Indonesian orchestra essentially composed of tuned percussion instruments, but with the addition of stringed and wind instruments in larger ensembles; also, music played by such ensembles.
Gansa Balinese metallophone.
Geige (Ger.) Violin.
Gemshorn Early fipple flute made from the horn of a goat.
Gender Type of marimba used in Indonesian *gamelans*.
Glass harmonica *See* ARMONICA.
Glockenspiel Percussion instrument consisting pf a row of metal bars of graded lengths and pitches, struck with hard wooden hammers or, alternatively, with a keyboard mechanism.
Goblet drum A small VESSEL DRUM, single-headed and with a foot of smaller diameter than that of its head.
Gong Percussion instrument consisting of a metal disc, often with a central boss, which is struck with a stick. Vibrations are strongest at the centre of the disc.
Gong chime Percussion instrument consisting of a series of tuned gongs.
Gong drum Modern orchestral drum with a single head.
Gran cassa (It.) Bass drum.
Grand piano Piano with horizontal soundboard. Sizes include "baby", "boudoir" and "concert".
Grosse Bassgeige (Ger.) Double-bass.
Grosse caisse (Fr.) Bass drum.
Grosse Trommel (Ger.) Bass drum.
Ground zither *See* EARTH ZITHER.
Gunbri Lute-like instrument of Morocco and Egypt with two strings and a wooden or shell sound-box.
Gusle Yugoslav folk fiddle with a single string.

Hackbrett (Ger., "butcher's block") Dulcimer.
Hammond organ Patented name for an American electronic organ.

Hammerklavier (Ger.) Piano.
Hand bell Hand-held bell whose pitch depends on its size.
Hand horn *See* HUNTING HORN.
Hardanger fiddle (Nor.: *Hardangerfele*) Norwegian folk fiddle with sympathetic strings.
Harfe (Ger.) Harp.
Harmonica or **mouth-organ** Mouth-blown instrument with free reeds.
Harmonium Keyboard instrument with free reeds which are vibrated by air from a bellows.
Harp (Eng.), **harpe** (Fr.) Plucked stringed instrument consisting of a frame to which are attached strings of different lengths. Pitch can be chromatically altered on the modern or double-action pedal harp, which is tuned to the scale of C♭, by adjusting one of the seven foot-pedals.
Harpsichord Keyboard instrument of great importance from the sixteenth to the eighteenth century, with wire strings, plucked by plectra, stretched over a horizontal soundboard. No variation in dynamics can be achieved by varying the touch.
Hautbois (Fr.) Oboe.
Hawaiian guitar Electric guitar with metal strings and no frets, played flat on the lap with "thimbles" on the fingers.
Hazozra Ancient Hebrew straight trumpet.
Heckelclarina Clarinet-like single-reed instrument invented for Wagner's *Tristan and Isolde*. (Cor anglais is usually substituted today.)
Heckelphone Baritone oboe with a wider bore than the oboe and globular bell.
Hi-hat Pair of cymbals on a stand which are played by means of a foot-pedal.
Hoboe (Ger.) Oboe.
Horn Curved, conical instrument (originally an animal's horn) which is sounded by the player's vibrating lips. The term is generally used for the valved orchestral coiled brass instrument, or French horn.
Horn-pipe Single-reed instrument (a sort of folk clarinet) consisting of a piece of cane fitted into a cowhorn.
Hunting or **hand horn** Simple valveless horn capable of playing only the notes of the harmonic series, though pitch can be altered if required by inserting the hand into the bell.
Hurdy-gurdy Portable mechanical viol with strings that are vibrated by the rotation of a wheel turned by one hand and stopped with the other hand by means of a tiny keyboard.
Hydraulis (from Gk. for "water" and "pipe") Ancient (perhaps the earliest) organ, for which water was used to maintain air pressure.

Idiophone Any instrument made of naturally sonorous material.

Jank Arab harp.
Jew's harp Primitive instrument consisting of an open metal or bamboo frame with a flexible tongue which is plucked while the player holds the frame in his mouth. The mouth acts as a resonator.
Jingle Small rattling object or bell, such as those attached to tambourines, or mounted to form a separate instrument, e.g. sleigh bells.
Jingling johnny Old military-band instrument consisting of a stick hung with little bells.

Kachapi Long zither of Java.
Kakko Japanese barrel drum with two deerskin heads.
Kalungu African TALKING DRUM.
Kantele Finnish board zither.
Kazoo Simple toy mirliton.
Kemange Three-stringed Persian spike fiddle.
Kerar Ethiopian folk lyre.
Kettledrum Tuned percussion instrument with a single membrane stretched over a pot or vessel body. In the orchestra, kettledrums are often known as timpani.
Kielflügel (Ger.) Harpsichord.
Kinnor Small ancient Hebrew lyre.
Kissar Sudanese lyre.
Kit or **pocket violin** (Fr. **poche** or **pochette**) High-pitched, pocket-sized violin used by dancing masters in eighteenth and nineteenth centuries.
Kithara Ancient Greek lyre with a box-shaped sound-box, the strings of which are plucked with the fingers.
Kitharis Large ancient Greek lyre, forerunner of the KITHARA.
Klarinette (Ger.) Clarinet.
Klavier, Clavier (Ger.) Keyboard; hence any stringed keyboard instrument.
Kleine Trommel (Ger.) Side drum.
Koboro Ethiopian conical drum.
Ko-kiu Japanese fiddle.
Komungo Six-stringed long zither of Korea.
Koto Japanese long zither, with thirteen silk strings passing over movable bridges.

Lira da braccio (It., "arm lyre") Fifteenth-/sixteenth-century bowed stringed instrument with a wide finger-board, five strings, and two sympathetic strings.
Lira da gamba (It., "leg lyre") or **lirone** Bass version of the lira da braccio with from nine to fifteen strings and two sympathetic strings.
Lirone *See* LIRA DA GAMBA.
Lithophone Simple percussion instrument consisting of a set of sonorous stones, sometimes in xylophone formation.
Log drum *See* SLIT DRUM.
Lute Plucked stringed instrument with a deep pear-shaped body, a fretted finger-board on a short neck and a long peg-box turned back at an angle to the neck. The strings are usually tuned in pairs (courses) in unison or octaves. The number of strings varies considerably.
Lyra (1) Ancient Greek lyre, a simpler version of the KITHARA, but with strings plucked with a plectum. (2) *See* LYRE.
Lyra viol or **viola bastarda** Stringed instrument of the viol family, between the tenor and bass viols in size.
Lyre Ancient plucked stringed instrument with a four-sided frame consisting of a resonator, two arms and a crossbar. The strings are stretched between the crossbar and a bridge on the resonator. The strings of the ancient Greek lyre were plucked with a plectrum. *See also* LYRA.

Mandola Small lute with a sickle-shaped peg box.
Mandoline Plucked stringed instrument of the lute family with a fretted finger-board, four pairs of wire strings and a deeply arched back. A treble MANDORA.
Mandora Type of lute. Its best-known representative is the MANDOLINE.
Maraca South American rattle consisting of a dried hollow gourd containing hard dried seeds. Usually played in pairs.
Marimba Xylophone with resonators placed beneath each bar. Played by beating with sticks. Also an orchestral instrument which is a deeper version of the xylophone.
Marine trumpet *See* TROMBA MARINA.
Mayuri South Indian sitar.
Mbira *See* SANSA.
Mellophone Type of horn, of similar shape to the orchestral horn but easier to play. Also known as the "tenor cor".
Melodeon Portable free-reed instrument operated by wind from bellows.
Melodica Mouth-organ with a keyboard.
Membranophone Any instrument sounded by the vibration of a stretched membrane.
Mirliton One of the two types of membranophone (the other being the drum). The player makes the membrane vibrate by humming, singing or speaking, and the vibration of the membrane modifies the sound.
Mizraf (1) Arab lyre. (2) Wire plectrum used for playing the SITAR.
Mokugyo Japanese fish-shaped slit drum.
Monochord Teaching device used for demonstrating musical intervals. It consists of a single string stretched over a movable bridge between two nuts fixed to a rectangular soundbox. The latter bears a calibrated rule. The TROMBA MARINA is a musical instrument based on the same principle.
Mouth bow Musical bow in which the mouth is used as a resonator, much as it is for the JEW'S HARP.
Mouth-organ *See* HARMONICA.
Mridanga South Indian barrel drum.
Musette (1) Double-reed instrument developed from the bagpipe chanter. (2) Old French bagpipe.
Musical bow *See* BOW.

Nakers Very small medieval kettledrums brought to Western Europe by the Crusaders. Relatives of the NUQAYRAT.
Naqara, naqqara *See* NUQAYRAT.
Natural horn Valveless and keyless brass instrument with a narrow conical bore and a wide bell, current in eighteenth century. Capable of playing only the notes of the harmonic series.
Natural trumpet Valveless and keyless trumpet with a high pitch, used in the later baroque period.
Nose flute Primitive flute, usually side-blown, sounded by wind from the nostrils instead of the mouth.
Ntenga Ugandan double-headed conical drum usually found in pairs of different sizes.
Nuqayrat Pair of very small Arab kettledrums usually played with cloth-covered sticks. Predecessors of modern kettledrum.
Nyckelharpa Swedish folk instrument with four (manually) bowed strings which are stopped mechanically.

Oboe Double-reed woodwind instrument with a conical bore, successor of the shawm.
Oboe da caccia (It., "hunting oboe") Eighteenth-century predecessor of the cor anglais, occasionally used by Bach.
Oboe d'amore (It., "love oboe") Eighteenth-century woodwind instrument pitched a minor third below the oboe.
Ocarina Small vessel flute with carrot-shaped body, usually of pottery.
Octobass Huge nineteenth-century stringed instrument pitched an octave below the double-bass and with levers to stop the strings.
Okedo Japanese cylindrical drum.
Oktave-Flöte (Ger.) Piccolo.
Oliphant Medieval ceremonial horn, made of elephant's tusk or of gold; a symbol of rank.
Ombgwe South African vessel flute.
Ondes-martenot Electronic instrument invented in the 1920s by Maurice Martenot. Controlled by a keyboard, it produces one note at a time.
Ophicleide Obsolete large keyed bugle, superseded by the tuba in the 1850s.
Orchestrion Nineteenth-century mechanical instrument governed by perforated rolls or a music-box cylinder, designed to imitate orchestral instruments.
Organ Keyboard instrument sounded by wind blown by bellows through single-pitched pipes. Tone is governed by the use of stops. There is usually one pedal-keyboard, operated by the feet, and up to five manual keyboards. Modern organs are usually powered by electricity.
Organistrum (L.) Medieval name for the hurdy-gurdy.
Orpharion Cittern-type stringed in-

strument with slanting string holder and frets.
Ottavino (It.) Piccolo.

Pa'amon Jingles worn by ancient Hebrew priests.
Pandora, pandore *See* BANDORA.
Pan-pipes Set of graduated flutes bound together in a bunch and end-blown.
Papago Wooden scraper of North American Indians.
Pauke (Ger.) Kettledrum.
Pedal Foot-operated level. **–keyboard** One played with the feet.
Pellet bell Enclosed bell sounded by a free pellet inside it.
Penny whistle. *See* TIN WHISTLE.
Percussion Generic name for instruments, tuned or untuned, which sound when struck.
Petite-flûte (Fr.) Piccolo.
Pianino Electrical roll-operated mechanical piano operated on the coin-in-the-slot principle, made by Wurlitzer.
Piano, pianoforte (It., "soft loud") Stringed keyboard instrument in which felt-covered hammers vibrate metal strings. Varying degrees of volume can be produced according to the speed at which the key is depressed.
Piano player Roll-operated mechanical device in which hammers projecting from a cabinet depress the keys of a piano.
Piatti (It.) Cymbals.
Pibcorn Obsolete Welsh single-reed horn-pipe.
Piccolo (It., "small") Small flute pitched an octave higher than the orchestral flute.
Piccolo cello Small eighteenth-century version of the standard cello.
Piccolo trumpet Military-band instrument which plays higher notes than the standard trumpet.
Pien ch'ing Chinese lithophone with L-shaped stones hung in a frame.
P'i p'a Chinese short-necked lute.
Pipe (1) Long fipple flute. (2) General name for any hollow cylinder in which air vibrates, e.g. any woodwind instrument, or an organ-pipe.
Player piano (sometimes known by trade-names, e.g. "Pianola") One fitted with a mechanism controlled either electrically or by air jets passing through a perforated paper roll which depresses the keys.
Poche, pochette (Fr., "pocket") *See* KIT.
Portative organ Small portable organs with flue-pipes, made from *c.*1100–1650.
Posaune (Ger.) Trombone, also sackbut.
Positive organ Small non-portable organ with flue-pipes for domestic or church use.
Post-horn Predecessor of the cornet, used for signalling by coachmen.
Psaltery Ancient and medieval zither plucked by fingers or plectra, of similar shape to the lyre but with a soundboard behind the strings. A development of the Middle Eastern QANUN.
Putorino Maori one-piece wooden trumpet.

Qanun Middle Eastern board zither, the ancestor of most European zithers, brought to Europe by the Crusaders.
Quena South American end-blown flute.
Quinton Eighteenth-century five-stringed violin.
Qussaba Arab vertical flute.

Rabab *See* REBAB.
Rackett or **sausage bassoon** Medieval double-reed bass instrument, the tube of which is doubled up on itself many times.
Ranasringa Asian copper horn with two bells.
Rattle (1) Hollow vessel (usually a pot or gourd) containing dried seeds, played by shaking. (2) Football-type rattle, incorporating a ratchet, e.g. COG RATTLE.
Rauschpfeife (Ger., "swelling pipe") Medieval double-reed instrument with a reed-cap.
Rebab Short-necked Arab folk fiddle with two strings. Ancestor of all Western bowed stringed instruments.
Rebec Medieval and Renaissance fiddle with three or four strings and a narrow pear-shaped body made from a single piece of wood. Derived from Arabian REBAB.
Recorder Wooden fipple flute. Important in Renaissance and baroque music.
Reed-organ Keyboard instrument with a free-beating reed for each note and no pipes.
Regal(s) Portable reed-organ used from fifteenth to seventeenth century. The reeds had either very small pipe resonators or none at all.
Reproducing piano Sophisticated type of player piano which can reproduce performances – including dynamic nuances – from piano rolls.
Reshoto Russian frame drum fitted with metal jingles.

Sackbut Early trombone with narrower bore than the modern instrument.
Samisen Three-stringed, flat-backed Japanese long lute.
Sansa, mbira or **thumb piano** African plucked instrument consisting of metal or cane flexible tongues attached to the bridge of a board or box resonator.
Santoor Indian dulcimer.
Santouri Greek dulcimer.
Santur Arab dulcimer.
Sarangi North Indian fiddle.
Sarod North Indian stringed instrument which can either be plucked or played with a bow.
Saron, –demong Javanese metallophone.
Sausage bassoon *See* RACKETT.
Saw Carpenter's hand-saw played with a bow. The pitch of the note is altered by bending the saw with the left hand.
Saw-thai Spike fiddle from Thailand.
Saxhorn Valved bugle invented by Adolphe Sax in 1845.
Saxophone Single-reed conical-bore brass wind instrument invented by Adolphe Sax in about 1840.
Saz Long-necked Turkish lute.
Scabellum Ancient percussion instrument consisting of a flapping hinged board.
Schellentrommel (Ger.) Tambourine.
Scraper Notched or ridged object (such as piece of wood) sounded by running a stick over its surface.
Sehem Egyptian equivalent of the SISTRUM.
Serpent Bass wind instrument consisting of an S-shaped wooden (occasionally metal) tube of wide bore with finger-holes and sometimes keys. Became obsolete in about 1850.
Setar Iranian equivalent of SITAR.
Shaker *See* RATTLE.
Shakuhachi Japanese end-blown flute.
Shawm Old double-reed wind instrument with conical bore, superseded by the oboe in seventeenth-century art music but still widespread as a folk instrument.
Sheng Chinese free-reed mouth-organ.
Shô Japanese free-reed mouth-organ derived from the Chinese SHENG.
Shofar Ancient Hebrew cult horn, made from a ram's horn, which produces only two notes.
Side-blown flute Reedless woodwind instrument with a mouth-hole pierced in its side, the pipe being stopped at the end nearest the mouth-hole.
Side drum Small double-headed orchestral drum of indefinite pitch fitted with detachable snares (lengths of gut or wire which give a rattling sound) and played with wooden sticks. *See* SNARE DRUM.
Single-reed instrument One in which sound is produced by blowing a single beating reed or tongue attached to, or cut out of, a cylindrical tube.
Sistrum Ancient wooden rattle with jingling metal discs on metal cross-bars.
Sitar Long-necked fretted Indian lute with sympathetic strings and a gourd-shaped body.
Sleigh bells Hand-held jingling bells mounted on a piece of wood for orchestral use.
Slit or **log drum** Hollowed-out tree-trunk or length of bamboo with a slit in one side, the lips of which are beaten.
Snare drum Side drum, so called when forming part of a drum-kit.
Sordine Seventeenth-century Italian boat-shaped KIT.
Sordone Large Renaissance double-reed instrument blown through a crook.
Sousaphone Large bass tuba which encircles player's body and has a huge forward-facing bell. Played in bands conducted by John Philip Sousa (1854–1933), the famous American march-composer.
Spike fiddle Primitive stringed instrument whose neck pierces the body, emerging as a spike at the base.
Spinet Small wing-shaped harpsichord.
Spitzharfe (Ger.) *See* ARPANETTA.
Spoons Domestic metal spoons used as clapping instrument, mainly by buskers.
Square piano Obsolete early piano with a box-shaped body.
Steel drum Caribbean tuned percussion instrument made from an empty oil-drum.
Stick zither Simple zither consisting of a stick, with a single string attached at either end, mounted on a resonator such as a gourd.
Strumento di porco (It., "pig instrument") Medieval psaltery.
Surnay Arab shawm.
Swannee whistle American fipple flute with a plunger for varying the pitch.
Switch Percussion instrument of split cane struck against the hand.
Sympathetic strings Unplayed strings which pass through holes in or over the bridge of a stringed instrument and vibrate "in sympathy" when the instrument is played.
Synthesizer Instrument invented in the 1940s which produces music by means of electronic impulses. It may or may not have a keyboard.
Syrinx Ancient Greek pastoral panpipe.

Tabl Arab drum. *See* TABLA.
Tabla Pair of Indian hand drums, of different pitches. One is cylindrical, the other conical.
Table piano Nineteenth-century rectangular piano which with lid closed provided a table top.
Tabor Medieval military drum, usually worn by the player by means of a strap. Often played with the fife or pipe.
Tabret *See* TOF.
Talking drum African double-headed drum, the pitch of which is varied by adjusting the lacing which is threaded through both upper and lower membranes. Skilled players can thereby produce sounds resembling native speech.
Tam âm la Vietnamese gong chime.
Tambour (militaire) (Fr.) Side drum.
Tambourin (Ger.) Tambourine.
Tambourin basque (Fr.) Tambourine.
Tambourin de Béarn French zither with gut strings which are beaten with a stick.
Tambourin de Provence Modern orchestral version of the TABOR.
Tambourine Frame drum with metal

jingling discs attached to the rim.
Tambura *See* TANPURA.
Tamburino (It.) Tambourine.
Tamburo (militare) (It.) Side drum.
Tampura *See* TANPURA.
Tam-tam Orchestral gong of indefinite pitch suspended in a frame.
Tanbur Persian TANPURA.
Tanpura, tambura, tampura Long-necked fretted lute, used in India as drone instrument. *See* TANBUR; TUNBUR.
Tar (1) Turkish frame drum with jingling discs. (2) Long-necked lute.
Tarogato (1) Single-reed instrument invented for Wagner's *Tristan*
Tenor cor *See* MELLOPHONE.
Tenor drum Orchestral and military drum.
Theorbized cittern Cittern with two peg-boxes.
Theorbo Bass archlute with two peg-boxes developed in the sixteenth century.
Theremin Early electronic instrument, invented in Russia in the 1920s by L. Theremin. Its sound is governed by the proximity of the players' hands to a loop and rod.
Thumb piano *See* SANSA.
Thunder stick *See* BULL-ROARER.
Tibia Roman shawm.
Timbale (1) (Fr.) Kettledrum. (2) One of a pair of drums of different pitch, mounted on a stand and played, with sticks, in Latin-American dance-bands.
Timpano (It., plural **timpani**) Modern orchestral kettledrum(s).
Tin or **penny whistle** Simple inexpensive fipple flute usually sold as a toy.
Ti-tzu Chinese bamboo side-blown flute.
Tof or **tabret** Ancient Middle Eastern frame drum.
Tom-tom Red Indian double-headed barrel drum.
Transposing instrument One producing a sound at a definite interval above or below the written note, a stratagem which saves the player of a family of instruments having to learn new fingerings for each.
Triangel (Ger.) Triangle.
Triangle Metal percussion instrument consistently of a rod bent into the shape of an open triangle, played by striking with a metal stick.
Triangolo (It.) Triangle.
Tromba (It.) Trumpet.
Tromba marina (It., "marine trumpet") Neither a trumpet nor connected with the sea, but a large monochord, played with a bow, which depends on harmonics for the production of its sound.
Trombone Brass instrument of cylindrical bore and flaring bell with simple slide mechanism for obtaining notes outside the harmonic series.
Trompete (Ger.) Trumpet.
Trompette (Fr.) Trumpet.
Trumpet Brass wind instrument of cylindrical bore. Modern instruments are valved to enable them to reach notes outside the harmonic series. *See* NATURAL TRUMPET.
Tsambal Romanian dulcimer.
Tsuri daiko Japanese barrel drum.
Tuba (1) Bass brass instrument of bugle family with wide conical bore, flaring bell and cup mouthpiece. Tenor tubas or euphoniums, bass tubas or bombardons, and contrabass tubas (bombardons in B♭) are, in descending order of pitch, the commonest types. (2) Ancient Roman long straight wooden trumpet, covered with bronze or leather.
Tube zither Zither with tube resonator.
Tubular bells Series of metal tubes of varying lengths hanging in a frame. Played by striking near the top with small wooden mallets.
Tunbur Arab TANPURA.

'Ud Middle Eastern short-necked double-strung and unfretted lute.
'Ugab Ancient Hebrew name for wind instruments other than horns (e.g. flutes).
Ukulele Small guitar-like plucked instrument with four gut strings and a round wooden body.
Upright piano Vertically-strung piano.

Veena Classical Indian stringed instrument with two gourd resonators.
Vessel drum Single-headed drum with a vessel-shaped body, e.g. kettledrum.
Vessel flute Flute with globular, rather than tubular, body shape, often containing a pellet or water.
Vibra-marimba Hybrid instrument combining features of vibraphone and marimba.
Vibraphone Xylophone with a vibrato sound produced by electric fans at the top of each resonator tube.
Vielle (Fr.) General medieval term whose meaning ranges from medieval fiddle to hurdy-gurdy.
Vihuela Renaissance plucked stringed instrument of Spanish origin, a predecessor of the guitar.
Vina *See* VEENA.
Viol Fifteenth-/seventeenth-century bowed stringed instrument with a flat back and a fretted finger-board.
Viola Alto member of the violin family, slightly larger than the violin.
Viola bastarda *See* LYRA VIOL.
Viola da gamba (It., "leg viol") General name for all viols, sometimes specifically applied to the bass viol.
Viola d'amore (It., "love viol") Popular eighteenth-century bowed stringed instrument, held under the chin, with sympathetic strings.
Viola pomposa (It., "pompous viol") Large eighteenth-century viola with five strings.
Violetta Alto viola d'amore with two sets of sympathetic strings.
Violin Bowed stringed instrument, held under the chin, with an arched back, four strings, a waisted body, shaped sound-holes and a sound-post to amplify the sound within the body. It superseded the viol in the mid-seventeenth century.
Violine (Ger.) Violin.
Violino (It.) Violin.
Violon (Fr.) Violin.
Violoncelle (Fr.) Cello.
Violoncello (It.) *See* CELLO.
Violone Double-bass member of the viol family.
Virginal(s) Small harpsichord common during the sixteenth and seventeenth centuries.

Wagner tuba Bass brass instrument devised for Wagner's *Ring* tetralogy.
Waisted drum Any drum with heads of approximately the same size and a middle of smaller circumference.
Washboard Domestic washboard scraped with a metal rod, played in "skiffle" groups in the 1950s.
Water drum African drum consisting of two half gourds, one floating open-side-down in water contained by the other.
Whistle flute *See* FIPPLE FLUTE.
Whistling pot Type of vessel flute, possibly water-filled.
Woodwind Generic name for all wind instruments which were originally made of wood.

Xylophone Percussion instrument consisting of a row of tuned wooden blocks on a frame, struck with hard wooden sticks.

Zil Small copper cymbals of Islamic origin attached to finger and thumb.
Zither Instrument consisting of a flat sound-box placed flat on a table for playing. Unlike the DULCIMER, it has a fretted finger-board over which some or all of the strings run. The finger-board strings, played with the thumb and forefinger of the right hand, provide the melody, the other fingers playing an accompaniment on the free strings beyond. The player usually wears small plectra on his fingers.
Zummara Tunisian double clarinet.
Zurna Middle Eastern shawm. Turkish equivalent of the SURNAY.

Acknowledgements

The publishers wish to thank the following for their advice and cooperation:

Boosey and Hawkes, London, for lending the musical instruments used in photographs throughout the book;
British Piano Museum, Brentford;
John Broadwood and Sons, London;
Diagram Group, London;
EMI Records, London;
Horniman Museum, London;
London Library;
Piano Manufacturers Association;
Victoria and Albert Museum, London;
Westminster Central Music Library.

Thanks are also due to the following instrument manufacturers:

W. T. Armstrong and Co., USA;
Vincent Bach/Bueschner, USA;
Blüthner, East Germany;
Chappell, UK;
Clavitune, UK;
Deg Music Products, USA;
Arnold Dolmetsch, UK;
Getzen, USA;
Gretsch, USA;
Harmony, USA;
Harwood and Isaacs, UK;
Hoffman, West Germany;
Leblanc, France;
Marshall and Rose, UK;
Mirafone, USA;
Moeck, USA;
Robert Morley & Co., UK;
Neve, UK;
Noblet, France;
Norlin, USA;
F. E. Olds, USA;
Pearl, Japan;
Premier, UK;
Reynolds, USA;
Selmer, USA;
Slingerland, USA;
Sonor, West Germany;
Whelpdale Maxwell and Codd, UK;
Yamaha, Japan.

Photographs by courtesy of:

ADAGP, p 53;
Archiv für Kunst und Geschichte, Berlin, pp 46–7;
Clive Barda/CBS, p 132 (b);
British Library, pp 22, 23;
British Museum, p 146 (r);
British Museum/Fotomas, pp 141, 149, 150 (l), 151, 152, 153;
British Tourist Authority, p 115;
CBS Records, p 78;
Dobson Books, p 124;
EMI Ltd., 132 (t);
Werner Forman Archive, pp 19, 84, 86–7, 146 (l), 147;
Fotomas Index, pp 18, 149, 155;
The Gallery Upstairs Press, Buffalo, New York, USA, pp 54–5;
Ronald Grant/MGM, p 65;
Sonia Halliday, pp 2, 16–17, 24;
Alan Hutchison, p 83;
International Festival of Youth Orchestras, p 143 (top);
Juilliard School of Music, p 143;
Koninklijk Museum, Antwerp, pp 26–7;
Lords Gallery, p 156;
Macdonald Educational, pp 37, 58, 59;
Mansell Collection, pp 43, 45, 116, 154;
Margaret Murray, p 143 (centre);
Musées Nationaux, France, pp 30–31;
Museum of Modern Art, New York/Cooper;
Bridgeman, p 51;
National Gallery, London, p 148;
Novosti, p 143 (bottom l);
Mike Peters, p 79;
Picturepoint, p 82;
Popperfoto, p 142;
Radio Times Hulton Picture Library, p 150 (r);
Schools Music Association, p 141;
SEF, p 20;
Snark International, p 63;
SPADEM, pp 52, 53;
Tate Gallery/John Webb, p 37;
Theatrical Museum, Munich, pp 34–5;
John Topham, pp 140, 143 (bottom r);
Universal Edition (Alfred A. Kalmus Ltd.), p 52;
University Library, Heidelberg, p 25;
Reg Wilson, p 67;
ZEFA, pp 42, 102, 126;

Index

Entries in bold type denote illustrations or caption references.